Environmental Regulation in the New Global Economy

The Impact on Industry and Competitiveness

Rhys Jenkins

Professor of Economics, School of Development Studies, University of East Anglia, Norwich, UK

Jonathan Barton

Lecturer in Environmental Policy, School of Development Studies, University of East Anglia, Norwich, UK

Anthony Bartzokas

Senior Research Fellow, United Nations University, Institute of New Technologies, Maastricht, The Netherlands

Jan Hesselberg

Professor, Department of Human Geography, University of Oslo, Norway

Hege Merete Knutsen

Senior Lecturer, Department of Human Geography, University of Oslo, Norway

Edward Elgar

Cheltenham, UK • Northampton, MA, USA

Published by
Edward Elgar Publishing Limited
Glensanda House
Montpellier Parade
Cheltenham
Glos GL50 1UA
UK

Edward Elgar Publishing, Inc.
136 West Street
Suite 202
Northampton
Massachusetts 01060
USA

A catalogue record for this book
is available from the British Library

Library of Congress Cataloguing in Publication Data

Environmental regulation in the new global economy.
    p. cm.
    Papers resulting from a conference held in 1999 at the University of
    East Anglia.
    ISBN 1-84064-540-7
    1. Environmental policy—Economic aspects—Europe—Congresses.
  2. Environmental policy—Economic aspects—Developing countries—Congresses.
  3. Environmental law—Compliance costs—Europe—Congresses.
  4. Environmental law—Compliance costs—Developing countries—Congresses.
  5. Factory and trade waste—Environmental aspects—Europe—Congresses.
  6. Factory and trade waste—Environmental aspects—Developing countries
  —Congresses. 7. Globalization—Environmental aspects—Europe—Congresses.
  8. Globalization—Environmental aspects—Developing countries—Congresses.
  9. Competition, International—Congresses.
  HC240.9.E5 E632 2002
  333.7—dc21

2002020239

ISBN 1 84064 540 7 (cased)

Printed and bound in Great Britain by MPG Books Ltd, Bodmin, Cornwall

Environmental Regulation in the
New Global Economy

Contents

v

Figures

Tables

Preface

This book is the result of a collaborative effort between researchers at three institutions in three different European countries: the School of Development Studies, University of East Anglia in the UK, the Department of Human Geography of the University of Oslo in Norway, and the United Nations University, Institute of New Technologies located in Maastricht in the Netherlands. It represents both an international and an interdisciplinary effort since it brought together researchers from different disciplinary backgrounds, particularly geography and economics.

The starting point of the research was a common interest in the impact which environmental regulation is having on the competitiveness and the location of industry in the context of an increasingly integrated global economy. The Department of Human Geography at the University of Oslo had initiated a programme of research on 'Location of Pollution-Intensive Industry in a North/South Perspective' in 1989. Researchers at the School of Development Studies had worked on various aspects of globalization for a number of years, while INTECH specialized in technology issues and organized a 'Workshop on Transfer of Environmentally Sound Technology' in the mid-1990s. All three groups of researchers had a particular interest in North–South relations.

The specific research on which this book is based commenced in 1996 and was funded under the European Union's Fourth Framework Programme on Environment and Climate. Over the course of three years, participants in the programme met at regular intervals to discuss the methodology and research findings. In July 1999 a conference was held at the University of East Anglia on Environmental Regulations, Globalization of Production and Technological Change. The authors presented the findings of the research to a selected audience of some 40 specialists in issues of environmental regulation and international competitiveness, drawn from academia, government, business and non-governmental organizations. This provided a stimulating atmosphere for discussion and generated valuable feedback.

Acknowledgements

The research on which this book is based would not have been possible without the funding provided by the European Commission (contract number ENV4-CT96-0235), which funded research assistance, fieldwork and the meetings and workshops for the participants. We would like to acknowledge this support.

In addition to the authors, a number of others contributed directly to the research project and their inputs are reflected in the final product. The team at the University of Oslo, working on the leather industry, consisted of Jan Hesselberg, Hege Merete Knutsen, Anne Gjerdåker, Jan Thomas Odegard and Karin Wiik. The bulk of the fieldwork was carried out by Gjerdåker and Odegard. In addition, the team benefited from the assistance of Mr C.G. Pandya, who collected field data in India. We would also like to thank Sylvi Endresen and Britha Bergstø for their contributions to the early discussions of the project.

At the United Nations University, Institute of New Technologies in Maastricht, the team working on the fertilizer industry consisted of Anthony Bartzokas, Ivo Demandt and Yarime Masaru. In addition case studies were contributed by Dr Dilek Cetindamar of Sabanci University, Turkey, and Tom HuTao of the Policy Research Center for Environment and Economy, SEPA in China. We would like to thank all of these.

Research of this kind depends heavily on the collaboration of firms, industry associations and government regulators for access to the kind of detailed industrial information which is required. We would like to thank all those who gave their time for interviews and plant visits. For reasons of confidentiality, most of them are not specifically mentioned by name. However, we would like to give particular thanks to Mr Graham Funnell (UK Steel Association), Dr B.W. Lee (POSRI, Korea), Mr S. Chehebe (IBS, Brazil) and Mr R. Talarek (Metallurgical Chamber of Industry and Commerce, Poland).

List of abbreviations

APIC	Associação Portuguesa dos Indústrias de Cortumes (the Portuguese leather tanning association)
BAT	Best available techniques
BATNEEC	Best available techniques not entailing excessive cost
BOD	Biological oxygen demand
BOF	Blast oxygen furnace
CEPT	Common effluent treatment plant
CICUR	Cámara de la Indústria de Curtidura del Estado de Guanajuato (the association of the leather industry in Guanajuato)
CO	Carbon monoxide
COD	Chemical oxygen demand
COMECON	Council for Mutual Economic Aid
COREX	Direct reduction system
DM	Deutsche Mark
DRI	Direct reduction iron
EAF	Electric arc furnace
EC	European Commission
ECSC	European Coal and Steel Community
ECU	European Currency Unit
ELV	Emission limit value
EMAS	European Community Eco-management and Audit Scheme
EMS	Environmental management system
EU	European Union
FAO	Food and Agriculture Organization of the United Nations
FINEX	The use of non-coking coal and iron ore without pretreatment (unlike the traditional method of making molten iron in a blast furnace)
GDP	Gross domestic product
IBS	Brazilian Steel Institute
IFA	International Fertilizer Industry Association
IISI	International Iron and Steel Institute
IPC	Integrated pollution control
IPPC	Integrated pollution prevention and control
LCA	Life cycle analysis
NAFTA	North American Free Trade Area

NO_x	Nitrogen oxides
OHF	Open hearth furnace
PAC	Pollution abatement cost
PCI	Pulverized carbon injection
PCP	Pentachlorophenol
PM10	Particles with diameter less than $10\mu m$
ppm	part per million
PPM	Process and production method
SO_2	Sulphur dioxide
TRT	Top recovery turbine
TSP	Total suspended particles
VDL	Verband der Deutschen Lederindustrie
VOC	Volatile organic compound
WTO	World Trade Organization

PART I

An overview

Rhys Jenkins

1. Introduction

Two significant trends characterize the recent evolution of the world economy. The first of these is the increased globalization of economic activity. The second is growing concern, particularly in the advanced industrialized countries, over the environment. This latter trend has led to a tightening of environmental regulation within the OECD countries and international efforts to resolve global environmental problems. This book explores the implications of these two trends and the potential conflicts to which they give rise, with a particular focus on the North–South dimensions.

The concept of globalization itself is much debated. The sense in which it is used here follows the definition of *economic globalization* used by the OECD, which sees it as 'a *process* in which the structures of *economic markets*, *technologies*, and *communication patterns* become progressively more international over time' (OECD, 1997, p. 7). A corollary of this is that competition becomes increasingly based on the world market rather than on the markets of individual nation states.

Despite the fact that there is considerable debate over both the extent of globalization and its consequences, the growth of international trade, the expansion of transnational corporations and the increased interconnections of financial markets are all indicative of a *process* which has significant implications for national economies and global change (cf. Rodrik, 1997; Sachs, 1998).

Associated with globalization has been a significant shift in the proportion of world industrial production which is accounted for by the countries of the South. Although the bulk of the world's industrial production continues to be located in the advanced industrialized countries, since the early 1970s the share of developing countries in world manufacturing value added has increased three-fold from around 7 percent to 21 percent, and their share of manufactured exports has increased even more (Jenkins, 1984, Table 3, and Table 1.1).

Although some writers are prone to exaggerate the extent to which industrial production has become internationally dispersed and mobile, it is undoubtedly the case that the locational options which are available to firms seeking to establish new plants, and the number of countries competing in international markets for industrial products, has increased noticeably over the past three decades.

In the present context this assumes importance because, despite the existence

of a number of international environmental agreements, environmental regulation continues to be predominantly nationally based and major differences exist
in the strictness of environmental regulation between countries. Casual
observation suggests that the degree of regulation tends to be positively
correlated with a country's income level and this is supported by some
empirical evidence (Dasgupta *et al.*, 1995). Particularly when account is taken
of the level of monitoring and enforcement of environmental standards, it is
clear that major differences exist between the advanced industrial countries and
the developing and transition economies. EU countries such as Germany, the
Netherlands and Denmark have some of the strictest environmental standards
in the world, and although other EU countries lag behind the leaders, they still
have higher standards and more stringent enforcement than apply in the South.

Table 1.1   *Share of LDCs in world manufacturing value added in ten*
           pollution-intensive industries, 1980, 1985, 1990, 1996

	1980	1985	1990	1996
Leather	23.3	24.8	26.0	29.9
Paper	9.4	9.7	10.5	11.8
Industrial chemicals	11.4	13.4	14.8	17.9
Other chemicals	14.7	14.1	14.4	15.8
Petroleum refineries	30.0	36.0	39.3	43.2
Rubber products	15.4	16.1	18.5	21.5
Other non-metallic products	15.0	16.8	17.8	23.1
Iron and steel	12.1	14.3	17.0	23.3
Non-ferrous metals	15.4	16.5	17.0	20.3
Metal products	8.2	9.0	9.5	11.0
Manufacturing value added	14.4	15.3	16.8	21.7

Source: UNIDO (1999, tables 1.1 and 1.5).

It is these differences that give rise to much of the concern about the
interaction between globalization and increased environmental regulation in
the countries of the North. These are focused on the links between environmental regulation and competitiveness and fears over 'industrial flight',
'pollution havens' and 'eco-dumping'.

BACKGROUND TO THE RESEARCH

Two features of the current debate on globalization and the environment prompted the research on which this book is based. First of all, there seemed to be a sharp contrast between the heat with which the issues are debated in the political arena and the existing empirical evidence on the impact of environmental regulation on competitiveness and industrial location. The very terms which are used in the discussion – 'flight', 'pollution haven', 'dirty industries' – are themselves illustrative of the emotion with which the political debate has been suffused. The debate around the environmental effects of the North American Free Trade Agreement (NAFTA) provides striking examples of this, with even environmental groups divided. Thus anti-NAFTA environmental groups accused pro-NAFTA groups of 'selling off the North American environment' while the head of the National Wildlife Federation accused the anti-NAFTA groups of 'putting their protectionist polemics ahead of concern for the environment' (quoted in Esty, 1994, p. 28).

At the same time the empirical evidence regarding the impact of environmental regulation on competitiveness and the effects on investment is far from clear-cut. Indeed many economists argue that environmental factors do not play a significant role in international trade and investment, while others go even further, arguing that environmental regulation tends to increase competitiveness. The literature on these issues is reviewed in the next chapter.

A second factor which prompted this research was the realization that the overwhelming bulk of previous work on these issues was focused on the United States. This is not surprising since the US has been active in environmental protection for a number of years, and it has the best sources of data on which to base such studies. It has also had the most active public debate around these issues; this reached new heights in the early 1990s in connection with the negotiation of the NAFTA agreement with Mexico.

However, particularly in the 1990s, the implications of environmental regulation for competitiveness in the countries of the European Union has also moved up the political agenda. The Maastricht Treaty of 1991 made the environment one of the major concerns of the European Union and called for the integration of environmental objectives into other EU policy matters. The EU's Fifth Environmental Action Programme, *Towards Sustainable Development 1993–2000*, emphasised the precautionary principle and encouraged the introduction and adoption of cleaner production processes (Bartzokas *et al.*, 1997). In 1992 the European Commission committed itself to 'turning environmental concern into competitive advantage' (EC, 1992, p. 31).

There are grounds for thinking that these issues are as important, if not more important, for Europe as they are for the United States. There has been a significant increase in environmental measures both at the European level and within member states during the 1990s, and some EU members have amongst the highest environmental standards and strictest enforcement in the world.

Compared to the United States, European economies are relatively open in terms of the significance of trade, and are therefore likely to be, if anything, more subject to international competitive pressures than the US. Moreover, many traditional European industries have suffered from a loss of competitiveness in recent years. Thus the impact of environmental regulation on investment and industrial location is just as much of an issue in Europe as it is in North America. This makes the relative lack of research on these issues in a European context all the more striking. It is this gap that the present study seeks to fill.

GLOBALIZATION AND THE ENVIRONMENT

Globalization and environmental issues are interrelated in a variety of ways and there is a growing literature on these relationships.[1] This literature can be subdivided into five main areas, although, as will be seen, there are a number of fields in which they overlap. These are:

- governance;
- competitiveness;
- environmental quality;
- North–South issues;
- corporate strategy.

The first set of issues relates to *governance* both within the global economy and at a national level. Increased awareness of global environmental problems such as climate change and the depletion of the ozone layer have led to the negotiation of international environmental agreements, while economic globalization has given an increasingly significant role to international bodies such as the World Trade Organization (WTO). Thus there has been a growing literature on multilateral environmental agreements (Porter and Brown, 1991) and on the relationship between international trading rules and the need to prevent environmental degradation (Esty, 1994).

In addition to the literature on the global aspects of environmental and economic governance, there is also an extensive discussion of the implications of globalization for environmental regulation at the national level. The debate here has focused on whether globalization tends to lead to a 'race-to-the-bottom' in terms of environmental standards or to a convergence of standards at a higher level. A related suggestion is that environmental regulation tends to become 'stuck-in-the-mud' as globalization makes it more difficult for countries to raise their environmental standards unilaterally (Zarsky, 1997).

A second area of concern is the issue of *competitiveness* (OECD, 1993;

Jaffe *et al.*, 1995). The corollary of the fear that globalization will tend to reduce environmental standards is the concern that, in a globalized economy, increased environmental regulation will place a country at a competitive disadvantage because of the costs of internalizing environmental externalities. A different view of the environmental regulation–competitiveness linkage, however, sees the possibility that firms may gain competitive advantage from stricter regulation which will give rise to 'innovation offsets' (Porter and van der Linde, 1995). As will be seen in the next chapter, there is considerable debate in the literature concerning the likely impact of environmental policy on competitiveness.

Another body of literature deals with the impact of globalization on *environmental quality*. Often the effect of globalization is decomposed in terms of its impact on the scale of economic activity, its composition, and technology (Grossman and Krueger, 1991). This literature draws on the discussion of the links between growth and environment which has in recent years focused on the environmental Kuznets curve.[2] A major area of both theoretical and empirical study has been the impact of trade liberalization on the environment (see Beghin and Potier, 1997; Nordström and Vaughan, 1999). Another rather less well researched area is the growth of transport and its environmental effects, although this is clearly also an important consequence of globalization (Anderson *et al.*, 1995, box 2).

There is considerable debate over the implications of globalization for relations between developed and developing countries (*North–South Issues*). Within this debate the implications for the location of pollution-intensive industries is an important environmental aspect. Since environmental regulation is less stringent in the South, some critics fear that globalization will lead to 'industrial flight' from the North and the growth of 'pollution havens' in the South. On the other hand, a more positive view is that it increases the prospects for diffusion of cleaner technologies and improved environmental management standards in developing countries. These have been referred to as 'pollution haloes' (Mabey and McNally, 1999).

Finally, there is a considerable literature on the links between business and the environment which focuses on *corporate strategy*. In the context of globalization, the environmental performance and responses of transnational corporations (TNCs) is of particular interest. Issues of transboundary environmental management and the corporate standards applied by TNCs in their subsidiaries have been a focus for study, as have the negative environmental impacts of some major corporations (Pearson, 1987; UNCTAD, 1999, ch. x).

Although many of the issues dealt with in the different bodies of literature discussed above are interrelated, it is not the intention of this book to cover all of them. The main focus is on two of the areas identified, namely the effects on competitiveness and on the North–South location of pollution-intensive industries. These have implications for environmental quality in developed and developing countries, so the book also provides some insights into these issues. Moreover, since the research on which the book is based involved interviewing managers at the firm level, it also relates to the literature on corporate strategy, although the industries studied in depth were not characterized by a dominant role for TNCs, with the partial exception of fertilizers. Governance issues are only touched on in passing, since there was no systematic attempt made to evaluate how globalization affected environmental policy at the national level.

TRENDS IN THE GLOBAL DISTRIBUTION OF MANUFACTURING ACTIVITY

As was mentioned earlier, the past two decades have seen an increasing share of world manufacturing being located in developing countries. Although the bulk of manufacturing value added continues to take place in the North, the share of the South has increased significantly to between a fifth and a quarter by the end of the twentieth century (see Table 1.1). It is true that much of this expansion in the South's share of manufacturing has been concentrated in a relatively few countries in South and East Asia, and that Africa's share of world manufacturing value added has remained at less than 1 per cent of the total; nevertheless these changes in the distribution of production have important environmental implications. For instance, in terms of global environmental problems such as greenhouse gas emissions, it becomes less feasible to find solutions without the involvement of the major industrial producing countries of the South.

It is sometimes thought that industrialization in the developing world has mainly taken the form of the growth of light industries such as garments and electronic assembly in export processing zones, and that therefore the environmental implications of industrial growth are relatively limited.[3] However, as Table 1.1 shows, the increase in the South's share of world manufacturing value added has also occurred in those industries which are identified as the most pollution-intensive sectors internationally.[4]

The increasing share of less developed countries in the production from pollution-intensive industries is not simply a reflection of the general growth in their share of world manufacturing. In fact the share of such industries in total manufacturing value added in the South has increased since 1980, while their share in the North has fallen (see Table 1.2).

The table also shows that, contrary to popular perceptions, the most polluting industries account for a greater share of manufacturing in the less developed

*Table 1.2 Share of ten pollution-intensive industries in manufacturing
value added, 1980, 1985, 1990, 1996 (%)*

	LDCs	Developed countries
1980	36.6	33.5
1985	37.0	31.8
1990	37.8	31.3
1996	39.0	31.3

Source: Author's elaboration from UNIDO (1999, table 1.8).

countries and that the gap between the share of such industries in North and
South has been widening over time.

The implication of this increased share of polluting industries within the
manufacturing sector in the South is that pollution loads are likely to increase,
and the need to find ways of mitigating industrial pollution will become more
urgent. The current state of environmental regulation in most developing
countries is not adequate to cope with increasing pollution trends, particularly
in terms of enforcement.

One relatively benign interpretation of the trends in terms of the global
distribution of pollution-intensive industries observed above is in terms of the
environmental Kuznets curve (EKC). This predicts that as incomes rise in a
country from low levels, pollution will at first increase. However, after a
certain level of income has been achieved, the level of pollution will begin to
fall. Plotting pollution levels against per capita income levels will therefore
give an inverted-U shaped curve. This pattern is explained in terms of changes
in the structure of the economy and the fact that, as countries become richer,
the resources available to reduce pollution increase, and the demand for a
cleaner environment also increases. Although the empirical evidence to
support the EKC is very mixed, and different patterns have been found for
different pollutants, it remains quite a widely held view.

The trends observed in Table 1.2 above are consistent with the EKC
hypothesis in so far as it could be argued that the less developed countries
were located on the rising portion of the curve during the period 1980–96, with
an increasing proportion of output coming from pollution-intensive industries,
while the developed countries were on the downward sloping portion. If this
were indeed the case, the present trend of an increasing share of pollution-
intensive industries in developing countries and a falling share in developed
countries would eventually be replaced by a falling share in both North and
South, once less developed country income levels had passed the turning
point.

The EKC approach implicitly assumes that the trends in the North and the South are independent of each other and that the countries of the South will follow the same path over time as those of the North. However, globalization means increased international interdependence and it is unrealistic to regard trends in the composition of industry in the North and South as totally independent of each other. Most studies of the EKC have concentrated on local pollution effects and have identified emissions with local production. However Rothman (1998, p. 177) has suggested that if a consumption-based approach is adopted, then 'what appear to be improvements in environmental quality [in developed countries] may in reality be indicators of increased ability of consumers in wealthy nations to distance themselves from the environmental degradation associated with their consumption'.

Such an approach implies that the opposite trends in the share of pollution-intensive industries in developed and less developed countries are linked to each other. Thus an alternative to the EKC interpretation could be one where industrial relocation occurs from countries with more stringent environmental regulation in the North to less regulated environments in the South. An important aim of this book is to document the shifts in location which are taking place in a number of industries and to analyse the role played by environmental and other factors in these changes.

THE RATIONALE FOR INDUSTRY STUDIES

A major feature of this book is the focus on in-depth study of three industries – iron and steel, leather and fertilizers. This contrasts both with those studies which tend to concentrate on the national level and with those based on the experience of individual firms. There are a number of reasons why the specific focus chosen for the research was at the level of the industry.

First of all, the dynamic of competition takes place within an industry. The behaviour of an individual firm, its competitive strategies, investment decisions and locational choices need to be understood in the context of the competition which it faces. Thus the structure of an industry and the nature of competition within it are key factors determining its evolution. The responses of firms to environmental regulation are critically dependent on the competitive characteristics of the industries within which they operate.

Second, technological developments and production processes are industry specific. The environmental impact of an industry and the way in which it changes over time depend on the technological trajectory of the industry. Moreover, to understand how environmental regulation leads to changes in technology and how these affect competitiveness, it is also necessary to look at specific industries.

Third, as will be seen in greater detail in the next chapter, more macro studies in the past have failed to come to very clear conclusions concerning the impact of environmental regulation on competitiveness, technological change and industrial location. On the other hand, examples of specific firms which have relocated production or gained competitive advantages as a result of environmental regulation can be dismissed as 'anecdotal'. Firm level case studies, therefore, are never likely to produce conclusive evidence on either the negative impact or the advantages of environmental regulation.[5] An industry study cannot be dismissed so easily as being anecdotal, and at the same time offers more specific insights than can be obtained from often quite aggregate macro studies.

Furthermore, the approach adopted in this book rejects monocausal explanations of competitiveness and industrial location. It is therefore necessary to take account of the interaction of environmental regulation with other factors which influence corporate decisions. More macro approaches find it difficult to incorporate these considerations since these other factors are often industry specific.

Finally, it is important to look at linkages between different stages in the production process, because often these have very different implications in terms of pollution generated and value added created. In order to look at the international distribution of environmental stress, it is necessary to consider not only how different products are produced in different regions, but also how different stages of the production process are distributed internationally. This again leads to an industry focus and can be usefully explored through a commodity chain approach.

DEFINITIONS AND TERMINOLOGY

Two phrases recur during the course of this book and it is necessary to clarify at the outset the sense in which they are used and the way in which they have been defined. These are *pollution-intensive industry* and *environmental regulation*.

The industries on which we wish to focus in this book are those:

1. that cause considerable environmental degradation, and
2. where the costs of reducing pollution are substantial.

It is in these industries that the impact of environmental regulation on investment decisions and competitiveness are likely to be marked. It is also these industries which are most likely to have substantial environmental impacts on the areas where they are sited and therefore where location decisions are likely to be most critical. Generally throughout the book, we use the term *pollution-intensive industries* to describe these industries. Some authors prefer to use the terms 'environmentally sensitive' rather than 'pollution-intensive'. The latter term is preferred here since it captures certain parallels between the debates on environmental regulation and trade, and other areas of trade theory where industries are classified as capital-intensive, labour-intensive or skill-intensive.

There are two ways in which industries have been identified as pollution-intensive in the literature on trade, competitiveness and environment. The most common approach identifies those industries which have a relatively high share of pollution abatement costs in total costs, or relative to their turnover, as pollution-intensive.[6] The second approach considers the volume of pollution generated by an industry per dollar of output or value added, or per person employed.[7] Usually this approach relies on one indicator of pollution, often some weighted value of toxic releases.

Conceptually these two approaches could lead to the identification of very different industries as pollution-intensive. If, in the absence of any expenditure on pollution abatement, all industries generated the same volume of pollution relative to say output, and the marginal cost of pollution abatement were the same in each industry, then those industries with the highest pollution abatement costs would tend to rank lowest in terms of pollution per unit of output, while those with no expenditure on pollution abatement would rank highest in terms of emissions. Thus the choice of indicator would lead to totally different industries being identified as pollution-intensive.

In practice this is not generally the case since the assumptions which were made are patently not valid. Industries differ substantially in the amount of pollution which they generate per dollar of output, and the costs of abatement also differ considerably between industries. Thus whether pollution abatement costs or emission-based indicators are used to identify industries as pollution-intensive, the same group of sectors tend to emerge as the most problematic. As a result there is a strong correlation between the ranking of industries by share of pollution abatement costs and by measures of toxic pollution intensity (Lucas *et al.*, 1992, table A.1; Eskeland and Harrison, 1997, table 2).[8]

A second potential problem in identifying pollution-intensive industries would arise if the ranking of industries differed significantly from country to country. Again, however, this is a theoretical problem rather than a practical one. Although the levels of both pollution per dollar of output and the share of pollution abatement costs may differ absolutely between countries as a result of differences in environmental regulation, the ranking of industries is broadly similar (Lucas *et al.*, 1992, appendix).

Because of the far greater availability of data for the United States, virtually all empirical studies use US data as the basis for classifying industries and this study is no exception. Industries were considered as pollution-intensive if they were ranked in the leading ten industries in terms of emissions per dollar of output for at least two key pollutants in the US in 1987, or if they were amongst the ten top industries in terms of pollution abatement costs as a share of output.[9] These are therefore the industries which are environmentally most problematic in Northern countries and where tighter environmental regulation is most likely to affect investment, location of production and technology.

Although it is generally the case that pollution-intensive industries tend to have both high emissions levels and high abatement costs, there may be firms within such industries which have relatively low levels of emissions and effluents as a result of significant investments in pollution control. Within industries, at the firm level, the assumptions set out above are more likely to apply than between industries. In other words, where basic processes are similar, firms with high abatement costs will tend to have lower emissions per unit of output and firms which do not invest in pollution abatement will tend to have high emissions, so that the inverse relation between the two criteria will hold. In practice, again the picture is complicated by the fact that firms in the same industry will operate with different vintages of capital and that older equipment may involve both higher pollution abatement costs and higher emissions than more modern plant. There may also be differences where firms specialize in different stages of the production processes, so that a situation similar to that described across industries can arise.

The second term running through the book is *environmental regulation*. The point that needs to be emphasized is that this is used in a broad sense. In other words, it refers not only to the legal and institutional framework of environmental norms and standards, but also to other environmental policies which can influence a firm's costs or the incentives that it faces. That is to say, regulation is not applied just to 'command and control' type environmental measures but also includes market-based instruments.

The second way in which environmental regulation is broadly defined is that it includes not only the legal framework but also its implementation on the ground. This is particularly important to bear in mind when considering the impact in transition and newly industrializing economies. Environmental standards often appear to be quite high on paper, but the key issue is the degree of enforcement. This study found numerous examples of regulators who, because of lack of resources and/or lack of political will and the priority given to other considerations such as employment and exports, were unable to enforce effectively the standards which were legally required. Thus when referring to environmental regulation this should be taken to encompass enforcement aspects.

STRUCTURE OF THE BOOK

The main body of this book consists of in-depth studies of three pollution-intensive industries, iron and steel, leather tanning and fertilizers. Before entering into the case studies, however, we begin with a review of the literature on environmental regulation and international competitiveness. As has already been mentioned, this literature is largely based on the US experience and relatively little research has been done on the European Union. Chapter 3 therefore provides an overview of the significance of pollution-intensive industries within the EU manufacturing sector. It also develops a framework for analysing the relationship between environmental regulation and competitiveness at the sectoral level.

Each of the three industry studies is based on fieldwork carried out in a number of European countries and in several industrializing and transition economies where it was anticipated that environmental regulation would be much less stringent than within the EU. Both within and outside Europe, interviews were carried out with environmental and/or plant managers in a number of firms and with national and European trade associations, technical experts and regulators. In each industry, the aim was to understand the environmental problems of the industry, the impact of regulation and the evolving competitive position of the sector. This involved establishing where the critical environmental pressures were within each industry and understanding the corporate strategies which have been adopted.

While by no means attempting to cover the whole range of pollution-intensive industries, the selection of one chemical, one metallurgical and one agriculturally based industry, means that the three industries are drawn from the broad groups which account for the bulk of industrial pollution. In the last chapter of the book, an attempt is made to answer some of the broader issues raised in Chapter 2, on the basis of the evidence from the three case studies.

NOTES

1. For a brief overview of the issues, see OECD (1997).
2. The environmental Kuznets curve (EKC) refers to a predicted relationship whereby environmental quality first deteriorates and then improves as per capita income levels rise. See Elkins (1997) and Stern (1998) for reviews of the literature on the EKC.
3. In fact, of course, the electronic industry itself has important environmental impacts, for example, through the use of toxic materials and solvents.
4. These are identified as the ten most pollution-intensive industries overall among ISIC 3-digit industries by Mani and Wheeler (1999, table 8.1).
5. For example, Levenstein and Eller (1985) in a piece entitled 'Exporting hazardous industries: "for example" is not proof' criticize the work of Barry Castleman, which had claimed that there would soon be a wholesale exodus of polluting industries from the United States. Similarly Palmer *et al.* (1995) in their critique of Porter and van der Linde point out that with

hundreds of thousands of firms subject to environmental regulation, it would be hard not to find some cases where regulation benefited the firm, but that this does not establish a general presumption in favour of such an outcome.

6. Studies which classify industries on the basis of pollution abatement costs include Low and Yeats (1992), Sorsa (1994), Xu (1999).

7. Studies which classify industries on the basis of emissions data include Mani and Wheeler (1999) and Ferrantino and Linkins (1999).

8. Eskeland and Harrison (1997), however, find that there is no correlation between pollution abatement costs and either suspended particulate or BOD emission intensity.

9. For further details, see Chapter 3.

2. Environmental regulation, international competitiveness and the location of industry

INTRODUCTION

The impact of environmental regulation on competitiveness and the location of industry is the central theme of this book. It is a major issue of concern to policy makers and to industry. It has also been the subject of considerable academic debate in the last few years between those who see an inherent conflict between the protection of the environment and international competitiveness, and those who believe that environmental regulation can in fact improve economic performance.

The conventional economic approach assumes that there is a trade-off between environmental regulation and competitiveness. Regulation is a means whereby environmental costs are partly or wholly internalized. Firms that undertake additional expenditures in order to abate pollution and reduce environmental damage will therefore tend to have higher costs than those that do not. At the international level this implies that producers in countries with more stringent environmental controls will be less competitive than those in countries which take a laxer approach towards protection of the environment.[1] This takes a North–South dimension in so far as it is usually assumed that developing countries tend to have lower environmental standards or to enforce their standards less strictly than the advanced industrial countries.

While this approach assumes an inherent conflict between environmental regulation and competitiveness, the reverse hypothesis, that regulation can promote competitiveness, has gained currency in recent years. This derives from a more dynamic view of competitiveness which gives a central role to technological change (EC, 1992). This 'win–win' view has been espoused not only by the European Commission, but also by former US Vice President Al Gore (1992) and the World Bank (1992). A corollary of this perspective for developing countries is that a high standard of environmental protection will be a source of competitive advantage in the future (West and Senez, 1992, pp. 69–70).

16

The purpose of this chapter is to clarify some of the different meanings which have been given to the term 'competitiveness' and to review the existing empirical literature on the relationship between environmental regulation and competitiveness. There are three different levels at which the concept of competitiveness is commonly used and often the differences between these are not given sufficient emphasis.[2] They are the firm level, the industry level and the national level. These differences are important, both for conceptual clarity and in order to develop appropriate measures of competitiveness.

COMPETITIVENESS AT THE FIRM LEVEL

The most obvious level at which the notion of competitiveness can be applied is that of the firm. It is, after all, firms which compete with one another in the market place. Management textbooks focus on competitive strategy and ways in which firms can increase their competitiveness. 'Bench marking' against competitors has become an important tool for improving business performance.

The meaning of competitiveness at the firm level is fairly clear. In the US the President's Commission on Industrial Competitiveness defined it in the following terms:

> A firm is competitive if it can produce products or services of superior quality or lower costs than its domestic and international competitors. Competitiveness is then synonymous with a firm's long-run profit performance and its ability to compensate its employees and provide superior returns to its owners. (Quoted in Francis, 1989, pp. 15–16)

Environmental Regulation and Firm Competitiveness

A major consequence of globalization is that competition is no longer primarily confined within national boundaries. Firms compete on a world scale for global markets. Where competition is nationally based, firms tend to be subject to the same environmental regulations.[3] However, there are substantial differences between countries, in terms not only of environmental standards but also in monitoring and enforcement. Thus firms operating in different jurisdictions are subject to different levels of environmental stringency. This is the basis of the frequently voiced call from the corporate sector for a 'level playing field'.

The concern about a level playing field becomes particularly acute where competition involves firms located in countries with widely differing levels of environmental regulation. Amongst developed countries, it has been found that differences in environmental compliance costs are relatively small (Atkinson, 1996). However, developing countries tend to have much less stringent regulation than developed countries, especially when enforcement is taken into account, so this issue gives rise to particular concern in a North-South context.

It is possible to identify three broad positions regarding the impact of environmental regulation on firm competitiveness. First, there are the *pessimists* who see a conflict between efforts to protect the environment and economic performance. At the other extreme there are the *optimists* who see win-win outcomes in terms of the environment and competitiveness. Finally, there are *sceptics* who reject both these positions and see no clear relationship between environmental and economic performance.

The view that strict environmental regulation places firms at a competitive disadvantage is essentially *cost based*. This follows from the way in which environmental economists conceive of pollution as an externality. Environmental regulation (or a pollution tax) is a means whereby such externalities are partly or wholly internalized. Firms undertaking additional expenditures in order to abate pollution and reduce environmental damage will tend to face increased costs which will, other things being equal, reduce profits. Regulation also diverts capital resources away from other potential projects in favour of investment to reduce pollution, and will therefore tend to reduce productivity growth. Finally, compliance with strict environmental regulation, as well as absorbing financial resources, may take up a significant proportion of management's time, reducing its availability for other tasks (cf. Walley and Whitehead, 1996). This view coincides with the perception of many firms, leading them to lobby against stricter regulation.

This view has been criticized as being very static and it has been argued that, taking a more dynamic approach which gives a central role to technological change, environmental expenditures can be a source of competitive advantage for a firm. This *innovation based* approach has been expressed most forcefully by Michael Porter and his associates (Porter, 1991; Porter and van der Linde, 1995, 1996).

In contrast to the static nature of the *cost based* approach, it is argued that innovation to reduce environmental damage often leads to reduced costs and increased competitiveness. These 'innovation offsets' can arise in a number of ways. From a physical point of view, pollution is simply a form of waste generated in the production process. Environmental regulation which leads the firm to seek ways of increasing resource productivity in order to reduce such waste will also reduce the costs of inputs. Alternatively regulation may lead the firm to find ways of converting the waste into saleable products which provide additional revenues (Porter and van der Linde, 1996). Reducing waste or converting it into saleable products also saves on the costs of waste treatment and disposal. Legal expenses and pollution-related fines might also decline as a result of adopting cleaner technologies (Reinhardt, 2000, ch. 4). Thus environmental regulation can either reduce costs or increase revenues and hence improve competitiveness.

Central to the *optimists'* case is the belief that environmental regulation promotes innovation at the firm level. This may lead to changes in production which reduce costs by using cheaper materials or adopting different processes. Moreover, the firm which leads in introducing more environmentally friendly technology may enjoy a 'first mover advantage' *vis-à-vis* laggards who continue to use traditional production methods.

A further way in which competitiveness may be increased is where a firm is able to obtain a niche market by producing a 'greener' product. This can be seen as a form of product differentiation which enables the company to charge premium prices for its product, compared to less environmentally friendly products (Reinhardt, 2000, ch. 2). Some firms have indeed established their market position on the basis of their environmental image (the Body Shop is a case in point).[4] Increased environmental awareness amongst consumers and the growth of eco-labelling may increase the importance of such considerations in the future.

A third group rejects both the *pessimist* and the *optimist* positions. These *sceptics* argue that pollution control costs are relatively low and that other factors are far more important as determinants of cost competitiveness (Dean, 1992; Jaffe *et al.*, 1995). Moreover, costs are only one determinant of a firm's competitiveness, which depends also on product and process innovation, marketing and brand image, after-sales service and a host of other non-price factors. However, although they recognize the importance of innovation, they do not share Porter's optimism. It is perfectly possible to hold that technological change is crucial for competitiveness without also accepting that innovation will simultaneously improve environmental performance and reduce costs. One area of disagreement is over the prevalence of 'innovation offsets'. Porter and van der Linde (1995, p. 98) claim that: 'Innovation offsets will be common because reducing pollution is often coincident with improving the productivity with which resources are used', and later that 'the opportunity to reduce cost by diminishing pollution should thus be the rule, not the exception' (p. 106).

In contrast Palmer *et al.* (1995, p. 120), while acknowledging 'that regulations have sometimes led to the discovery of cost-saving or quality-improving innovations', question the pervasiveness of such effects. There may be some 'low hanging fruit' (that is, low-cost opportunities for improving environmental performance) but the costs of pollution abatement tend to rise sharply as pollution is reduced, so that negative effects on competitiveness would soon be felt.

Even if it is shown that innovation promoted by environmental regulation reduces costs, there is an opportunity cost in terms of the potentially more productive investments or avenues for innovation forgone (Jaffe *et al.*, 1993, p. 32; Palmer *et al.*, 1995; Walley and Whitehead, 1996). There is also the question of the time horizon over which innovation offsets are realized. Porter claims that environmental improvements have very short pay-back periods. Others are more cautious however. Bruce Smart comments that: 'Pollution prevention does pay a prompt return on investment – in some cases' (Various Authors, 1996, p. 52). There is a question, therefore, not only of how general are the situations which give rise to cost reductions in response to environmental regulation, but also of how long it takes for the dynamic benefits to offset the static losses where both occur.

So far the implications of different levels of environmental regulation on firms has been stressed, but it is also important to note that a particular level of environmental regulation may affect different firms differently and hence impact on competitiveness. One key factor is likely to be the size of firm. Particular pollution abatement technologies, such as wastewater treatment, may be subject to economies of scale, so stricter regulation which requires firms to undertake such treatment may have a negative effect on the competitiveness of smaller firms whose costs increase disproportionately compared to larger competitors. A further factor is that all the firms within an industry do not operate with identical equipment and the costs of retro-fitting old plant may be high, putting firms with older vintages at a disadvantage. Firms may also operate different technologies, using different inputs and giving rise to different waste streams, so this too may lead to differential effects on their competitiveness.

Taking a longer-term view, even if the effects of regulation on costs in the short term are identical as between firms, the competitive effects may differ since different firms have different resources and capabilities which create path dependencies that condition a firm's response to environmental regulation (Rugman and Verbeke, 1998). There is some evidence that environmental improvements result from broader corporate efforts to innovate and implement improved, more efficient manufacturing systems. Thus responses to environmental regulation cannot be divorced from the firm's overall technology strategy. A firm with a strong brand name or operating in a niche market may be in a better position to absorb cost increases than a firm which produces for a standardized segment of the market. This is supported by research from the United States, cited by Rugman and Verbecke, which shows that firms with greater spending on advertising and those undertaking more R&D were likely to commit more resources to environmental performance.

This leads to a consideration of the ways in which firms respond to environmental regulation in terms of their competitive and technological strategies. Faced with a potential loss of competitiveness as a result of tighter environmental regulation firms can adopt a wide variety of strategies to maintain their competitive position. It is common for firms to exaggerate the potential negative impacts of a new regulation when it is being discussed, whereas after the event it turns out that the impact is much less than predicted. A study of the pulp and paper industry in Canada found that compliance costs were between $4 and $5.50 a ton whereas the industry had estimated them at three or four times that level. Similarly the costs of complying with a 1990 US regulation on sulphur dioxide proved to be half what analysts had originally estimated (Porter and van der Linde, 1996). Another example is the significant overestimation *ex ante* of the costs of reducing CFC emissions (Pickman, 1998).

An important reason for this overestimation of compliance costs is the tendency for firms to assume 'business as usual' in calculating these costs, whereas in practice they adjust their strategies to the new circumstances. Firms may adopt a number of different strategies, either singly or in combination. Changes in either the quantity or type of inputs used can reduce the volume of waste generated or the pollution problem created. Process innovations involving 'cleaner' technology can also reduce the volume of pollution and hence the costs of end-of-pipe treatment. The firm may also change its product range, substituting alternative products whose production creates less environmental damage. Changes in corporate strategy can also help reduce the impact of additional environmental costs. Thus a firm may target less price sensitive segments of the market, in order to be able to pass on the additional costs of pollution abatement. Another possibility is to outsource particularly polluting parts of the production process, thus externalizing the pollution.

This suggests that, although the short-term impact of stricter environmental regulation is to increase costs, the impact on firm competitiveness is not clear cut. The outcome, at the level of the individual firm, will depend on how well it is able to respond to changing conditions and develop strategies to adjust to the new conditions. It is also likely to affect different firms in different ways, so that some may gain a competitive advantage, while others will lose out.

Empirical Studies

The discussion of the previous section indicates that the impact of environmental regulation on competitiveness at the firm level is largely an empirical question. First there is the question of how far environmental regulation leads to innovation. There is evidence both from cross-section studies (Pickman, 1998) and case studies of individual companies (Wubben, 1999) of a positive response to environmental regulation. If, therefore, there is a positive impact on innovation, does it lead to innovation offsets which in the longer term reduce costs or increase revenues to the firm? If there are such offsets, then how quickly can they be realized and how does the rate of return compare with that to be obtained through alternative uses of resources?

One way of addressing these questions is to look at the experience of specific companies and to see whether meeting higher environmental standards has also led to economic gains. This involves looking at the environmental programmes adopted by particular firms and estimating the economic returns associated with such programmes. Another approach is to compare conventional production processes with alternative 'cleaner' technologies in terms of investment and operating costs.

The main alternative to the case study approach is to look at a cross-section of firms or plants producing the same product but with different levels of emissions or discharges or environmental expenditures. This does not directly test the impact of environmental regulation, since different levels of emissions or expenditures may not be the result of differences in regulatory stringency, but it does test the hypothesis that there is a conflict, at the firm level, between environmental and economic performance. A variety of techniques can be applied, including comparison of 'matched pairs' of firms and more conventional multiple regression. Different variables can also be used to measure firm economic performance. Direct cost comparison is one approach, although the limitation of this is that it concentrates on only one aspect of a firm's competitive performance. Another approach is to compare a firm's environmental performance with various measures of profitability (return on sales; return on assets; return on equity). Alternatively, since measures of profitability may be affected by other factors such as market power, some measure of productivity (total or single factor productivity) may be used as a proxy for competitiveness on the assumption that a firm with a high level or growth rate of productivity is likely to be in a favourable competitive position.

Case studies

The case study approach usually involves documenting examples of specific environmental initiatives which firms have adopted and which have resulted in increased profitability, or examples of specific environmentally friendly technologies which also reduce costs. The business and environment literature quotes a number of corporate examples of green success stories, including 3M Company's Pollution Prevention Pays (PPP), Dow Chemical's Waste Reduction Always Pays (WRAP) programme, Texaco's Wipe Out Waste (WOW) programme and Chevron's Save Money and Reduce Toxics (SMART) programme (Cairncross, 1995; Schmidheiny, 1992; Reinhardt, 2000; Shrivastava and Hart, 1994 quoted in Rugman and Verbeke, 1998; Shrivastava, 1995). What is striking about these examples, apart from the snappy acronyms by which they seem to be invariably known, is how often different authors cite the same companies.

More specific examples have been drawn from a range of industries where innovations have improved environmental performance and reduced costs. Porter and van der Linde (1996) quote examples from the pulp and paper, paint, electronics, refrigerator, dry cell battery and printing ink industries where reductions in emissions have either reduced costs or enabled firms to obtain a price premium. Similarly Park and Labys (1998, ch. 5) provide case studies of cleaner production processes which are also cost-reducing in electroplating, printed-circuit board manufacturing and photographic processes. Such savings arise not only in the advanced industrial countries but can also be achieved in a developing country context, as is illustrated by some of the case studies quoted by UNIDO (1995, annex 1).

These examples provide convincing evidence that environmental improvements can also generate economic benefits to the firms that introduce them, and that process changes (as opposed to end-of-pipe measures) to reduce pollution do not *necessarily* increase costs. However, as evidence that there is no conflict between improving environmental performance and achieving competitiveness, the studies suffer from two major limitations. First, they cannot, by its very nature, throw any light on the pervasiveness of such technologies which is the crucial point at issue. A series of case studies simply indicates that a positive outcome can obtain under certain circumstances, but does not indicate how general such outcomes are. Indeed, the frequency with which different authors quote the same examples seems to suggest that major green success stories are not all that common.

The second limitation of many of these studies is a lack of clarity concerning the baseline which is being used as the point of reference in calculating the rate of return to environmental investments or the costs of different production processes. Spectacular returns are often quoted by the companies themselves. For instance, Dow's WRAP programme was reported to be earning a 55 percent return on investment seven years after it began (Reinhardt, 2000, p. 86). However, as Reinhardt points out, because environmental regulations were becoming more stringent, it is not clear whether these returns are calculated on the basis of existing regulatory requirements or future ones.

A similar problem arises with the case studies which compare the costs of different technologies. These studies often compare the cost of using new technologies with the cost of meeting the same environmental standards with conventional technologies, or the cost of disposing waste under the same regulations. For example, a cleaner technology which reduces waste can lead to considerable savings in the cost of waste disposal where landfill charges are high. However, if the relevant comparison is with a situation where waste is unregulated or where charges for disposal are much lower, the cost advantage of the cleaner technology may disappear. Many examples of profitable 'cleaner' technologies are in fact only commercially attractive *because of regulation.*[5]

Case studies do provide convincing evidence that some firms have obtained economic benefits from improving their environmental performance. However, since the comparisons usually assume a particular regulatory environment, this evidence does not answer the question that is central to this book. Because of the way in which the evidence is often presented in these studies, it is by no means clear that increased environmental expenditures can actually increase competitiveness *vis-à-vis* firms operating in countries with much lower standards. If, as suggested above, it is often regulation that makes it attractive to introduce cleaner technologies, then competition from firms in less regulated jurisdictions will at the very least reduce the return to environmental expenditures and lengthen the time horizon over which they generate a return.[6]

Cross-section studies

The second type of empirical study relevant to competitiveness at the firm level looks at whether firms which perform well in environmental terms tend also to have a better economic performance. Given the limited availability of data on environmental performance at the firm level, there are relatively few empirical studies which have addressed the issues at this level. Most of those that do exist have concentrated on a relatively small number of industries and are predominantly US based.

One group of studies has focused on the link between environmental performance and profitability.[7] In the United States some early studies were undertaken in the 1970s using a Council of Economic Priorities database of firms in oil refining, steel, pulp and paper and electricity. These found that there was a positive correlation between pollution control and profitability; however, it has been noted that the database used referred to 1972, before a major tightening of environmental regulation in the US (Jaggi and Freedman, 1992). Although the existence of such a correlation is consistent with the view that reducing pollution increases profitability, it may be the case that the causation runs the other way, with the more profitable firms being better able to spend on pollution abatement; or there may be a third factor such as firm size which is correlated with both profitability and pollution control.

Jaggi and Freedman's (1992) own study of the pulp and paper industry found a weak negative relationship between some economic performance indicators and water pollution at the firm level. However, for the key indicators of return on equity and return on assets the correlation is never significant, and for some periods it is positive rather than negative. Similarly, a study of a sample of transnational corporations found that firms with larger reductions in toxic emissions tended to have a worse financial performance, although again the relationship was not statistically significant (Levy, 1995).

A bigger study of 127 large US firms came to the opposite conclusion finding that there was a positive relationship between reductions in emissions and subsequent profitability, and that this relationship was particularly marked for the firms with the highest level of pollution (Hart and Ahuja, 1996). Again the question of possible reverse causality arises and the authors indicate that this will need to be addressed in future work. Another study of large US firms came to similar conclusions, again without ruling out the possibility of reverse causality (Russo and Fouts, 1994 quoted in Levy, 1995).

The most comprehensive study so far of the profitability–environmental performance relationship was based on data for almost 2000 plants in the United States (Repetto, 1995). This found that there was very little relationship between pollution levels (in terms of toxic releases, water discharges or air particulate emissions) and either returns on capital or sales. At the industry level, correlations were as likely to be negative (supporting the Porter hypothesis) as positive, but in most cases were not statistically significant. There are several limitations to this study, particularly the fact that it is based on data for a single year, the adequacy of the profitability measures, and the issue of causality.

All the studies referred to so far have been of the United States. A methodologically rather less sophisticated study in the UK compared the financial performance of 51 'green companies', from the Jupiter Environmental Research Unit Approved List for their Ecology Fund, with that of other companies from the same sectors listed on the London Stock Exchange (Edwards, 1998). This concluded that good environmental performers do not perform less well in terms of profitability and in many cases perform better than their non-green comparators.

As far as the link between profitability and environmental performance is concerned, there is so far insufficient evidence to assess the validity of the contending views. This is obviously an area that requires more research. The recent studies by Hart and Ahuja (1996) and Repetto (1995) point the way for further empirical work.

This is even more true in the case of the relationship between pollution and productivity at the firm level, where there have been even fewer empirical studies. Two papers by Gray and Shadbegian (1993, 1995) of plant-level productivity in the pulp and paper, oil refining and steel industries found a negative relationship between environmental compliance costs and the level of productivity. However, when they looked at the relationship between compliance costs and productivity *growth*, this was much weaker than for productivity levels, and was not statistically significant. A study of oil refineries in Los Angeles found that despite high costs associated with environmental regulations, productivity rose rapidly in the late 1980s and early 1990s while refinery productivity in other regions was falling (Berman and Bui, 1998).

The only study carried out in Europe, by Hitchens *et al.* (1998), used the 'matched pairs' approach to examine the impact of environmental regulation on competitiveness in the meat and dairy industries in Germany, Ireland and Italy. The study used a number of indicators of labour productivity and comparisons were made both across countries and within countries. No clear relationship was found between productivity performance and environmental compliance costs. German firms, which had relatively high environmental compliance costs, were still competitive, so the view that lax environmental regulation was a prerequisite for competitiveness was rejected.

Overall, looking at both the studies which use profit indicators and those based on productivity, there is no clear evidence to support the view that environmental regulation has a negative impact on competitiveness. Nor, however, do the studies provide clear empirical evidence of the prevalence of innovation offsets, which mean that higher environmental expenditure leads to improved economic performance. The picture that emerges is a very mixed one that suggests that some firms, at least, are able to maintain their competitive position despite facing increased environmental costs.

A limitation of most of these cross-section studies is that they are usually single-country (US) studies, with the exception of Hitchens *et al.* (1998) which covered three EU countries. What is of interest in the context of this book is competition between firms with plants located in different countries. It is not valid to transfer conclusions drawn from studies of firms with different levels of environmental costs within one country to comparisons between firms located in different countries with different levels of environmental regulation. For example, within a country an older plant may have both a higher level of compliance costs, because of the relatively high cost of abating pollution to the necessary standard, and lower productivity, because of the age of equipment. However, this negative correlation does not necessarily imply that firms located in a country with more stringent environmental regulations would have lower productivity than one in a less regulated country.

Thus the studies of firm competitiveness do not provide very much insight into the main question with which we are concerned in this volume, namely the impact of differences in the stringency of environmental regulation in different countries on competitiveness. However, taking the case study approach and the cross-section approach together, it can be concluded that:

- there may be opportunities for firms to improve their environmental performance without losing competitiveness;
- these opportunities are not universal, and often environmental compliance imposes costs at the firm level.

An implication of these conclusions is that it is important to try to understand what kinds of firms are best placed to maintain their competitive position, and the strategies which they are able to use to do so. This finding is relevant to the international context where firms in Europe and North America compete against firms from less regulated jurisdictions and need to find ways to adjust to such competition.

COMPETITIVENESS AT THE INDUSTRY LEVEL

Although the concept of competitiveness is clearest when applied to the individual firm, this may not provide a good indicator of the overall impact of environmental regulation on competitiveness. Firms compete against each other and some of the competitive gains which a firm may make through becoming more environmentally sound may be at the expense of other firms. Not all firms can benefit from being first movers or from exploiting niche markets.

Furthermore, a particular interest of this book is the change that is taking place in the location of industrial production. Although this is a result of decisions taken at the firm level, it is manifested at the level of the industry. This makes it particularly important to examine what constitutes competitiveness at the industry level in the global economy.

Since Ricardo in the early nineteenth century, economists have explained international patterns of specialization in terms of the theory of *comparative advantage*. As its name suggests, this stresses the *relative* performance of different industries within a country as a determinant of what gets produced where. A key assumption of this theory is that factors of production are immobile between countries, but mobile within countries. Thus a move from autarchy to free trade leads to a flow of resources from the industries in which the country is relatively disadvantaged (usually because of its factor endowments) to those industries where it enjoys a comparative advantage. In this context, industry competitiveness might be regarded as the ability to attract resources from other industries within the same country.

However, in a global economy, with a high degree of capital mobility, a different interpretation is required. As a number of authors, especially Marxists such as Shaikh (1979) and environmentalists such as Daly and Cobb (1989, ch. 11), have argued, in the global economy, trade is governed by *absolute* and not *comparative advantage*. A theory of absolute advantage leads to a rather different view of competitiveness at the industry level, in that it suggests comparison between the same industry in different countries, rather than different industries in the same country. Put another way, the question of competitiveness relates to the relative attractiveness of different locations for a particular industry, as countries compete to attract internationally mobile capital.

Environmental Regulation and Industry Competitiveness

While at the firm level *pessimists* are concerned that differences in environmental regulation between countries leads to an uneven playing field, at the industry level the concern is that it will lead to the relocation of large parts of more pollution-intensive industries to countries which have less stringent regulation. This is reflected in the fear that environmental regulation will lead to *industrial flight*: in other words, that environmental regulation will be a push factor leading to migration of industry.[8] This is paralleled by a concern that developing countries will become *pollution havens*, deliberately using lax environmental regulation as a way to attract more polluting industries.

There is an extensive theoretical literature which examines the links between environmental regulation and international trade.[9] Two related issues are of relevance here. First, there is the effect of measures to combat environmental damage taken in one country on that country's trade flows, assuming that its trading partners do not introduce similar measures. Second, there is the impact of trade liberalization between countries with widely different levels of environmental protection. Although a significant part of the literature in this area discusses the welfare effects of such changes, our main concern here is with their implications for trade flows and the location of industry.

The effects of environmental regulation on trade can be analysed using a conventional model of comparative advantage in which capital is immobile internationally and markets are perfectly competitive. Since stricter environmental regulation is seen as internalizing environmental externalities, the effect on the home country will be to reduce exports of pollution-intensive goods and increase imports of such goods (Rauscher, 1997, ch. 5). In a North–South context, where it is assumed that environmental standards have been increased more in the North, the result will be a shift of more polluting industries to the South.

The outcome of trade liberalization between countries with different levels of environmental standards is more ambiguous. If the South has a comparative advantage in the more polluting industries, then liberalization too will lead to a shift of such industries to the South (Copeland and Taylor, 1994). If, however, other considerations such as labour costs are a more important determinant of competitiveness, then the effects of liberalization may not be so apparent. Indeed, if the South has a comparative advantage in labour-intensive industries and these tend to be less pollution-intensive, as some writers suggest, trade liberalization leads to an increase in polluting industries in the North (Antweiler *et al.*, 1998).

Although theoretically an increase in the stringency of environmental regulation should lead to a country specializing more in cleaner industries, the degree to which this occurs will depend on the extent to which environmental regulation raises costs. If there are large differences in pollution control costs between different industries, then there would be a significant change in comparative advantage and thus in trade flows. If, however, inter-industry differences are relatively small, changes in trade patterns are also likely to be small.

Sceptics point out that environmental costs are only a small proportion of total costs for most industries (Dean, 1992; Jaffe *et al.*, 1995). In the US in the late 1980s, pollution abatement operating costs for the industrial sector averaged only just over 0.5 percent of the value of output, and the highest level in any industry was only 3.2 percent, in cement (Low, 1992, annex table A). Thus within the conventional trade model, comparative advantage is not likely to be much affected by differences in environmental costs.

However, this model makes two extremely unrealistic assumptions. First, as has already been pointed out, it assumes that capital is internationally immobile. With capital mobility, then, the impact of environmental regulation on competitiveness and location is likely to be much more marked (Rauscher, 1997, ch. 3). If trade is determined by absolute rather than comparative advantage, what is relevant is the differences in the environmental costs facing an industry in different countries and the effects which these have on profitability. The possibility of capital flowing out of the country with the strict regulation, as well as being reallocated to other sectors within the country, means that the impact on location of production is likely to be much greater.

The second unrealistic assumption is that markets are perfectly competitive. In fact, many of the most polluting industries such as chemicals, iron and steel, and non-ferrous metals are highly concentrated, so that perfectly competitive models are not well suited to analyse the impacts which environmental regulation will have on them. The problem is that, whereas competitive models are fairly simple, models of oligopoly are much more complex and there is no single model that commands universal acceptance.[10] The existence of economies of scale and oligopolistic interactions, however, generally undermine the assumption that changes in location will be marginal and it is a distinct possibility that at a particular point relatively small changes in costs may have large effects on competitiveness.

In marked contrast, *optimists* believe that environmental regulation can have positive effects on competitiveness at the industry level. One way in which this can occur is through the development of a new industry producing pollution monitoring and control equipment (Sorsa, 1994; OECD, 1996a). A country which is in the forefront of environmental regulation is likely to give its environmental equipment industry a first-mover advantage in international markets. In the case of the European Union, Germany provides a good example of this, with its leading position in advanced technologies for reducing airborne pollutants (Sprenger, 1998). These 'environmental industries' have become a significant sector within a number of developed countries and grew rapidly in the 1990s (Barton, 1998).

They also believe that international flows of capital and technology will help improve environmental performance. It is often claimed that TNCs adhere to their own corporate environmental standards which are higher than those of the developing countries in which they operate (Gladwin, 1987). Thus increased inflows of foreign capital tend to bring with them higher environmental standards. Even when multinational companies do not have explicit corporate environmental policies, their tendency to use parent company technology, which has been developed to meet the stricter regulatory requirements of their home countries, will lead to them having less polluting production than local firms in developing countries (Ferrantino, 1995). On this view, globalization, far from leading to a loss of competitiveness for producers in countries with strict environmental regulation, is a means by which higher environmental standards are diffused internationally.

Empirical Studies

A number of surveys published in the mid-1990s concluded that there is little evidence to support either the *pessimists'* or the *optimists'* view concerning the impact of environmental regulation on competitiveness and industrial location (Jaffe *et al.*, 1995; Levinson, 1996; Adams, 1997). In the light of this broad consensus, is there any purpose in re-examining these issues and any justification for further research in this area?

There are four main reasons for looking at the empirical evidence once more. First, as was indicated in the previous section, there are strong theoretical reasons for predicting that, particularly when capital is mobile and markets are imperfectly competitive, differences in environmental regulation can have a significant impact on competitiveness and industrial location.

Second, these debates continue to have a major impact at the policy level. Corporate interests in pollution-intensive industries argue that increased environmental regulation in developed countries puts them at a competitive disadvantage and lobby governments for exemptions and seek to block environmental measures. Environmentalists believe just as strongly that global competition and trade liberalization are threats to environmental standards because of their impact on the competitiveness of industry in countries with high environmental standards. Neither side of the debate has been convinced by economic studies that claim to show that the effects of environmental regulation on competitiveness are negligible.

A third reason for revisiting the issue is that circumstances are changing. Many of the studies reviewed in the surveys mentioned above covered mainly the 1970s and 1980s. Although globalization as a process has been underway for some time, there is little doubt that it advanced considerably during the 1990s. As a result global competition has intensified, so that differences in regulation between countries are likely to become an increasingly important factor in competitiveness. This is particularly true as far as competition with developing and newly industrializing countries is concerned as their economies were liberalized and became much more integrated into world markets from the mid-1980s onwards. The second major change has been the increased level of environmental awareness in the industrialized countries and the more stringent nature of environmental regulation. One of the main explanations given for the lack of impact of environmental regulation on competitiveness and location in the past was the relatively low level of pollution abatement costs. However, environmental costs for firms in the most hazardous industries have increased significantly since the mid-1980s. It has also been suggested that the ban on exporting hazardous wastes from OECD countries, agreed by the Conference of Parties to the Basel Convention in 1994, could increase the pressures for the relocation of entire hazardous industries to developing countries (Clapp, 1998).

The final reason for re-examining the links between environmental regulation and competitiveness once more is in order to refer to several new studies which have been published since the earlier reviews.

There are two sets of issues which will be discussed in this section. The first is whether differences in environmental regulation between developed and developing countries have had an impact on competitiveness and the global distribution of industrial activity. The second, more specific issue, is that of *industrial flight* in the sense that firms' decisions about location of production are responsive to differences in environmental regulation. This can be examined by looking at data on foreign investment flows and the motives for investing abroad.[11]

Production and trade studies

One of the concerns of the *pessimists* is that the gap in environmental regulation between North and South will lead to an increasing share of production by the most polluting industries being located in developing countries. Earlier studies have mainly used trade data to look at the impact of regulation on competitiveness (cf. Low and Yeats, 1992; Sorsa, 1994; UNCTAD, 1994). However, a recent study by Mani and Wheeler (1999) looked at the share of pollution-intensive industries in industrial production in different regions.[12] They found that this has declined in the major developed regions between the 1960s and the 1990s, while the same industries have increased their share of production in both Latin America and Asia. Since the overall share of world industrial production accounted for by developing countries has increased significantly over the same period, then clearly the share of pollution-intensive manufacturing in such countries must also have increased.

While this is consistent with the relocation of polluting production to the South, it could also simply reflect changing demand patterns as incomes increase, which are followed by shifts in production, without necessarily being caused by changes in competitiveness. Mani and Wheeler also look at trends in net exports and find that for North America and Japan these are consistent with the view that there has been a net displacement of polluting production to trading partners, although this was not evident for Western Europe.

Another recent study which provides some evidence to support the view that environmental regulation has an impact on trade flows used a gravity flow model of international trade (van Beers and van den Bergh, 1997). They found that, although in aggregate environmental stringency had no effect on exports of 'dirty' industries, this could be explained by the fact that such industries are often resource based and therefore not 'footloose'. A significant negative effect on exports of non-resource based dirty industries was found. Unfortunately this study only covered developed OECD countries and hence excluded those countries with the laxest regulation; it might have given rise to an even clearer impact had they been included.

In contrast two other recent empirical studies have concluded that there is no *general* trend for competitiveness to decline in pollution-intensive industries in developed countries or for production to be relocated to less regulated countries. A study of 11 basic industries by Jänicke *et al.* (1997) found a mixed pattern, with some industries showing increased net exports from developed countries and others showing a decline. They conclude that there was no general tendency for these industries to relocate to developing countries.

Similarly, Xu (1999) found that the export performance of environmentally sensitive goods remained unchanged for most countries between the mid-1960s and the mid-1990s despite the introduction of more stringent environmental standards in most developed countries. Nevertheless he does find that both Japan and the United States lost competitiveness in environmentally sensitive goods, at least up to the end of the 1980s (ibid., fig. 2). There is also evidence that some developing countries, including Brazil, Indonesia, Korea, Taiwan and Venezuela, are gaining competitiveness in pollution-intensive industries (ibid., table 2).

In another study, which looked at trade within the APEC region, Xu and Song (2000) found evidence of a cascading pattern in trade between Japan and East Asia which supports the view that pollution-intensive industries have migrated from Japan to less regulated countries in the region. However, no such pattern was found in trade between North America (US and Canada) and the two Latin American members of APEC, Mexico and Chile.

Studies of foreign direct investment

Unfortunately, data on foreign investment is never available with anything like the kind of disaggregation which is obtained in trade statistics. As a result attempts to analyse empirically the relationship between environmental regulation and international capital flows are bound to be relatively crude.

Two types of study have a bearing on the issue of competitiveness. One looks at the pattern of foreign investment in pollution-intensive industries to see whether there has been a shift in investment away from countries with strict environmental regulation towards less regulated jurisdictions. The other type of study focuses on the determinants of investment decisions through either surveys or econometric studies.

Looking at the overall pattern of direct foreign investment, there is little evidence that investment has grown particularly rapidly in the most polluting industries. During the late 1970s and the 1980s the share of the main polluting industries (chemicals, pulp and paper, petroleum and coal products, and metals) in total outward investment showed no consistent pattern amongst the major developed countries (UN, 1992, table IX.3). The same is true in the 1990s with an increased share of the stock of FDI in manufacturing in pollution-intensive industries in France, the United Kingdom and the United States and a declining share in Germany and Japan (UNCTAD, 1999, table X.2). These data refer to total outward investment in manufacturing, a large part of which goes to other developed countries, so that it provides little basis for analysing the impact of differences in environmental regulation.

The most detailed analysis of trends in foreign investment has been carried out by Leonard (1984, 1988) on US investment. The conclusion of his studies is that environmental regulation has had little impact on competitiveness overall, although in certain specific cases it may have been an important factor. Ferrantino (1995) has updated this analysis to the early 1990s and again found no shift in US investment in pollution-intensive industries towards developing countries. A more recent study, which looked at both the pattern of foreign investment in four developing countries (Ivory Coast, Morocco, Venezuela and Mexico) and outward investment from the US, concluded that there was no evidence to support the pollution haven hypothesis, although a simple correlation between foreign investment and pollution abatement costs in the US did exist[13] (Eskeland and Harrison, 1997).

The other type of evidence concerning the possible impact of environmental regulation on competitiveness comes from the analysis of firm foreign investment decisions. If indeed environmental regulation were an important determinant of competitiveness, then it would have an influence on investment decisions. Econometric studies of the determinants of investment do not generally include an environmental variable, reflecting the difficulty of finding a suitable proxy.[14] Some surveys have included questions on the significance of either stringent environmental regulation at home or laxer regulation overseas as a factor in investment decisions. These have generally found that other factors are far more important determinants of investment (Knodgen, 1988; Blazejczak, 1993; Sprenger, 1997).

Although the consensus from most empirical studies of the impact of environmental regulation on foreign investment is that *industrial flight* has not been significant overall, a number of caveats are in order. First of all, there are a number of methodological weaknesses in these studies (Knutsen, 1995). Those based on foreign investment flows are generally at much too high a level of aggregation, both in terms of the sectors analysed and in terms of the countries considered. On the other hand, surveys of investment decisions may not be very revealing since managers are likely to be unwilling to reveal that avoiding environmental regulation is an important factor, even where this is the case.

Another problem with focusing exclusively on flows of foreign direct investment is that firms in developed countries may respond to environmental regulation through externalizing the pollution costs to subcontractors overseas (Bergstø *et al.*, 1998). Since this does not involve any investment by the foreign company, such a phenomenon would not be reflected in foreign capital flows.

Despite the scepticism concerning the significance of industrial relocation as a result of environmental regulation that is found in most of the studies discussed in this section, there are a number of examples of industries where this has occurred. Leonard (1984) identifies a number of industries, such as asbestos, dye-stuffs, pesticides, non-ferrous metals and some intermediate organic chemicals, where there was evidence that new investment had been pushed overseas. Some furniture manufacturers in the Los Angeles area were reported to have relocated to Mexico as a result of more stringent regulation of volatile organic compound (VOC) emissions in the late 1980s (US GAO, 1991). Jha (2000) cites some examples of environmentally damaging technologies being relocated to India, including a chlorine process which could no longer be used in Norway. As was noted in discussing case studies at the firm level, however, such evidence can never indicate the pervasiveness of the phenomenon concerned, only that it can arise under certain circumstances.

Despite the apparent consensus in earlier surveys that environmental regulation has not had a major impact on competitiveness, the recent literature shows that the debate is by no means over. There is some evidence from production and trade data that developed countries are losing competitiveness in pollution-intensive industries while less regulated developing countries are becoming more competitive in these industries and increasing their share of world production. What these studies have not established is whether there is a causal link running from stricter environmental controls to declining competitiveness and industrial relocation. The studies which focus on direct foreign investment are much less detailed than those based on trade flows and have so far produced little evidence to indicate that industrial flight is a generalized phenomenon in pollution-intensive industries. However, there is evidence that under some circumstances firms have relocated production for environmental reasons (see, for example, Knutsen, 1996).

COMPETITIVENESS AT THE NATIONAL LEVEL

Although this book is primarily concerned with competitiveness at the industry level, by its very nature such a concept of competitiveness is a partial one and this is an important limitation. There is therefore an argument for saying that the impact of regulation on competitiveness should be considered at the level of the economy as a whole.

The notion of competitiveness at the national level has come into increasing use. International Management Development and World Economic Forum publishes an annual *World Competitiveness Yearbook* which ranks the leading economies in terms of indicators of national competitiveness (IMD/WEF, 1996). Numerous official reports have addressed the problem of competitiveness of particular countries (for example, US President's Commission, 1985; House of Lords, 1985). Moreover, governments frequently remind their populations of the need to be internationally competitive, often in order to justify unpalatable measures such as wage restraint or cuts in public expenditure.

Despite frequent usage, the definition of competitiveness at the national level is much less clear than at firm or industry level. Some economists even deny that national competitiveness has any meaning (Krugman, 1994, 1996). Those authors who explicitly use the concept of national competitiveness see it as the basis of economic performance. Thus the *World Competitiveness*

Yearbook uses more than 200 criteria grouped under eight headings which include unit labour cost, R&D spending, inward and outward investment, growth rates, education levels, and infrastructure. These are essentially indicators of, and factors which contribute to, a 'good climate for investment'.

Other writers on national competitiveness prefer to define it in terms of economic performance. They reject definitions based solely on trade performance, tending to focus on overall performance indicators such as productivity or economic growth. Porter (1990, p. 6), for instance, argues that:

> The only meaningful concept of competitiveness at the national level is national productivity. A rising standard of living depends on the capacity of a nation's firms to achieve high levels of productivity and to increase productivity over time.

Environmental Regulation and National Competitiveness

The links between environmental regulation and competitiveness at the national level depend on how one perceives competitiveness. If competitiveness is viewed in terms of the climate for investment in a country, then essentially the question is whether stricter environmental regulation makes for a less or a more attractive climate. Generally most forms of regulation are seen by those who focus on these issues as obstacles which restrict the free flow of resources and thus have an adverse effect on competitiveness. *Pessimists* would extend this view to environmental regulation.

On the other hand, *optimists* argue that attempts by governments to compete for foreign investment by having lax environmental standards are likely to be counterproductive. In developing countries the social stress and health problems caused by the neglect of environmental protection can lead to lower productivity, enhanced uncertainty for investment and increased social instability from acute air and water problems. Low environmental standards can be a disincentive to investment. A highly polluted environment is not attractive for managers who have to live in the affected areas. There are also fears concerning future liabilities or adverse publicity in countries where environmental protection is inadequate. Governments should therefore enforce domestic environmental standards and seek to encourage the transfer of 'clean technologies' (West and Senez, 1992, pp. 69–70).

When competitiveness is defined in terms of economic performance, *pessimists* emphasize the diversion of resources to meet environmental goals and the increased bureaucracy associated with regulation. This leads to fewer resources being available for productive investment, obstacles to innovation and delays in setting up new plants, all of which lowers the level of productivity in the economy and the rate of growth.

Sceptics, on the other hand, point out that losses in some industries as a result of environmental regulation can be offset by gains in other sectors.

Where regulation internalizes an environmental externality in one industry, this may mean an increase in the competitiveness of another industry whose costs were previously higher because of the negative effects of the non-regulated industry on the environment. An example would be an industry which had to treat the water it used in its production process because of upstream contamination by another industry. Although the upstream industry might become less competitive as a result of regulation that forced it to treat its waste water, the downstream industry would be able to reduce treatment costs and thus become more competitive. In looking at the total effects of regulation on competitiveness, both these impacts need to be considered.

The more general point is that, irrespective of production externalities which affect other firms, there are general equilibrium effects which should be considered in looking at national competitiveness. Thus, although regulation may lead to slower growth in a pollution-intensive industry, this may be compensated by more rapid growth in other industries which are less polluting. Looking at particular industries will not take into account such general equilibrium effects. Since there are both costs and benefits from environmental regulation, the aim should be to design policies which obtain environmental benefits with the minimum cost in terms of competitiveness.

Optimists are critical of the view that measures environmental expenditures as a cost but does not count environmental gains as a benefit. They point out that with conventional methods of measuring economic growth, such as gross domestic product, environmental damage can contribute to income (for example, because of clean-up costs) whereas environmental improvements (for example, through increased energy efficiency) may appear as a reduction in income. It is concerns such as these which have led to a move to develop 'green' national accounts and estimates of 'sustainable' national income.

Empirical Evidence

The World Economic Forum (2000) has recently developed a Pilot Environmental Sustainability Index which attempts to measure the ability of economies to achieve environmentally sustainable development. While, as its name indicates, this is still at the pilot stage, it provides a preliminary indicator which can be linked to the WEF's Competitiveness Index in order to see whether there is any relationship between environmental performance and competitiveness at the national level.

The WEF finds that there is no relationship between the Environmental Index and GDP growth rates, but at first sight there appears to be a strong positive correlation between it and the Competitiveness Index. On closer inspection it was found that when the countries were divided into developed and less developed countries, there was only a weak correlation within each group, so the strong overall correlation was mainly accounted for by the fact that developed countries tended to have high values on each index and less developed countries had low values. However, the study did show that there was no evidence of a negative correlation between competitiveness and environmental sustainability, which suggests that a greater emphasis on the environment did not adversely affect competitiveness. However, at this stage, too much weight should not be given to this study, in view of its preliminary nature.

Looking more specifically at the effects on growth, there have been numerous macroeconomic studies of the impact of environmental regulation; however, since these are less relevant to the questions which we wish to address here, they will not be discussed in detail. A study by the OECD (1985) of six member countries (Austria, Finland, France, Netherlands, Norway and the United States) concluded that the impact of environmental regulation on economic growth was relatively small and could in some cases be positive. Similar conclusions were arrived at by Portney (1981) in reviewing US studies of the macroeconomic impacts of regulation. In another survey, which covers the more recent literature modelling the impact of environmental taxes, Ekins and Speck (1998) conclude that at the macro level there is very little effect on economic growth and competitiveness, although particular sectors will be affected.

As was pointed out above, the problem with such studies is that they included the cost of environmental regulation without including the benefits. A similar point can be made in relation to studies of environmental regulation and productivity at the national level. A number of studies in the United States have claimed that environmental regulation has been a factor contributing to the productivity slowdown of the 1970s and 1980s. At the level of the manufacturing sector as a whole, estimates of the contribution of environmental regulation to the overall reduction in productivity growth range from 8 percent to 16 percent (Jaffe et al., 1995, p. 151). Repetto et al. (1996) argue that conventional measures of productivity used in such studies are biased against environmental protection since they do not incorporate the environmental damage avoided as a result of stricter environmental regulation. He shows empirically how this leads to significant changes in measured productivity performance in certain US industries.

These studies at the national level serve to remind us of two points. First, in purely economic terms the loss of competitiveness in those industries which are negatively affected by environmental regulation may be offset by gains in other industries where competitiveness is increased, so that the net effect on competitiveness for the economy as a whole may be relatively small (Ekins and Speck, 1998). Second, although there may be a loss in competitiveness as conventionally measured, in welfare terms these need to be set against the gains from reduced environmental damage which results from stricter regulation, which is not captured in conventional economic indicators.

CONCLUSION

This chapter has identified three main positions regarding the relationship between competitiveness and environmental regulation. *Pessimists* believe that there is a trade-off between environmental protection and competitiveness. *Optimists,* in contrast, see improvements in environmental performance and competitiveness going hand in hand. Finally, the *sceptics* see environmental and economic performance as separable so that there is no fixed relationship between the two.

This review of the theoretical and empirical literature on the interface between environmental regulation and competitiveness has shown a very mixed picture. Looking at the firm level, it has proved very difficult to establish causal links between environmental and economic performance. What is clear, however, is that some firms have been able to combine a good environmental record with successful economic performance. The interesting question here for further analysis is what strategies such firms have used to achieve this combination. This is an issue which will be addressed in the case studies of the iron and steel, fertilizer and tanning industries later in this volume.

At the industry level, there is evidence of a shift of pollution-intensive industries to less regulated countries in the South. There is also evidence that competitiveness has increased in a number of these industries in developing countries while it has declined in the advanced industrialized countries. However, as with firm level studies, it has been difficult to establish causal linkages. It is also the case that there has not been a generalized shift of all pollution-intensive industries to the South. Developed countries continue to be competitive in a number of pollution-intensive industries. This raises the question of what kinds of industries have been able to maintain their competitive position in the North, despite more stringent environmental regulation. This is considered in more detail in the next chapter.

Studies of national competitiveness are useful in highlighting two broader considerations. The first is the importance of taking into account general equilibrium effects in arriving at any overall evaluation of the impact of environmental regulation. Although this is not the focus of this study, it is important to bear in mind that a negative impact on competitiveness in a specific industry does not necessarily reduce overall economic performance. Second, it is important to remember that if competitiveness is defined in terms of an economy's success in delivering a rising standard of living, this should include those improvements in the environment which result from regulation, which contribute to the population's overall welfare.

A major conclusion to be drawn from this review of the literature is that the relationship between environmental regulation and competitiveness is a complex one. Monocausal explanations, which attribute changes in competitiveness solely to differences in environmental regulation, do not adequately capture this. They cannot explain why relocation occurs in some pollution-intensive industries and not in others, or why some countries with relatively strict environmental regulation have been able to maintain their competitiveness in such industries. What is required is a framework which allows the impact of changes in regulation to be analysed in the context of other factors affecting competitiveness and the structural features of the industry concerned. In the next chapter such a framework is developed and applied to pollution-intensive industries in the European Union.

NOTES

1. Jaffe *et al.* (1993) present a simple analytical model to illustrate this point.
2. An exception is Adams (1997) which makes a similar classification to the one employed here. Ekins and Speck (1998) also identify three levels of competitiveness (the firm, business sector and national economy) but focus their attention on the first and last of these.
3. This is an oversimplification, particularly in the case of federal systems where differences do exist between states within the same country. These tend, however, to have national minimum standards which all states have to comply with, but which they can exceed through local regulations.
4. It may also be possible for a company to create a 'green' image through its marketing efforts without a significant change in its product.
5. Irwin and Hooper (1992) give specific examples drawn from a UK Department of Environment booklet designed to publicize clean technology. In the majority of the cases which they examined regulation played a critical role in making these technologies profitable.
6. The corollary of this is that in developing countries, where environmental regulation is weak, high cost has been a major obstacle to the transfer of clean technologies (Jha and Teixeira, 1994).
7. There is also a literature which links stock market performance to corporate environmental behaviour but this will not be discussed here since the main focus is on whether or not capital markets create incentives for firms to adopt environmental measures, rather than the impact of environmental regulation on competitiveness. For reviews of this literature, see Lanoie *et al.* (1998) and Cordeiro and Sarkis (1997). For a study of developing countries, see Dasgupta *et al.* (1999).
8. This is also referred to as the 'exodus hypothesis' (see Knutsen, 1994).
9. For recent reviews of this literature, see Nordström and Vaughan (1999), Jayadevappa and Chhatre (2000), Rauscher (1997).
10. See Rauscher (1997, ch. 6) and Ulph (1997) for reviews of the literature on oligopolistic models which relate trade and environment.
11. There are several studies for the United States which look at the impact of differences in environmental stringency between states on plant location. These will not be discussed here since we are interested in international competitiveness and in particular the impact of differences in regulation between developed and newly industrializing and transition

economies, which are likely to be far greater than exist between US states. For a survey of these studies, see Levinson (1996).

12. The industries identified by Mani and Wheeler as pollution-intensive were iron and steel, non-ferrous metals, industrial chemical, pulp and paper and non-metallic minerals.

13. This became insignificant when other explanatory variables were included in the model.

14. One exception is a preliminary study by Kolstad and Xing (1994) (quoted in Jaffe *et al.*, 1995, p. 147). This found a positive relation between inward investment in the chemical industry and sulphur dioxide emissions per dollar of GDP, which was used as a proxy for environmental laxity.

3. Environmental regulation and competitiveness in the European Union

INTRODUCTION

One of the striking features of the empirical literature reviewed in the previous chapter is the predominance of North American studies and the relative lack of studies on Europe. This is somewhat surprising given the commitment of the European Union to combining competitiveness with protection of the environment. Despite the growing role played by the EU in relation to the environment and the attention which policy makers give to improving European competitiveness, there has been nothing like the amount of empirical research looking at the impact of environmental regulation on competitiveness in Europe that there has been in the US.

It is true that there tends to be far more detailed data available on the environmental impact of industry in the US, where the Environmental Protection Agency has been extremely active and freedom of information ensures public access. However, this does not explain the relative lack of studies of this issue in Europe. In most cases studies of competitiveness, at least those at the industry level, do not require extensive data on actual emissions and environmental performance, but rather trade and production data which is readily available at a European level.

By focusing on the countries of the EU, this book fills the gap that has existed up to now in the environmental regulation and competitiveness debate. The bulk of the book involves case studies of three industries, iron and steel, fertilizers and leather tanning, and the way in which regulation has affected competitiveness, particularly *vis-à-vis* producers in newly industrializing and transition economies. Before looking in detail at these industries, this chapter considers the trends in competitiveness in European industry and more specifically the pattern which emerges in a group of industries which are identified as particularly environmentally sensitive.

ENVIRONMENTAL REGULATION IN THE EU

The Treaty of Rome, which created the European Economic Community (EEC) in 1957, did not include any legal provision for environmental regulation and pollution control and it was only in the early 1970s that the EEC began to pay attention to environmental issues. The First Environmental Action Programme started in 1973, the year after the first United Nations conference on the environment was held in Stockholm, and the European Commission (EC) began to enact directives aimed at improving the quality of air and water, controlling waste disposal, monitoring industrial risk and protecting the environment. The number of items of EC environmental legislation enacted each year increased to an average of around ten in the latter half of the 1970s and early 1980s, and then to over 20 in the second half of the 1980s (Haigh and Lanigan, 1995, fig. 3.1).

Until the mid-1980s the EC paid relatively little attention to the implementation of environmental legislation but this changed when some drums of hazardous waste from Seveso went missing and the European Parliament censured the Commission for failing to take the necessary measures to ensure implementation of its Directives. In 1987 the adoption of the Single European Act, which included an environmental chapter, provided a clear legal basis for EU environmental policy for the first time. This was further strengthened with the adoption of the Maastricht Treaty in 1991 which made environmental policy one of the major concerns of the EU. Thus at the European level there was an increase in the stringency of environmental regulation from the mid-1980s onwards.

The EU seeks to achieve harmonization of environmental regulation in order to eliminate any trade distorting effects. In some cases, however, member states may be allowed to maintain standards which are more stringent than those approved at EU level. There are also differences between member states in terms of implementation. Member states are formally obliged to implement EU regulations and directives into their national legislation. However, not all countries meet the deadlines which are set in the directives. Even where these have been incorporated into national laws, it is the national governments which are responsible for seeing that these are enforced and there are considerable differences in the levels of enforcement between different member states. It is generally considered that enforcement is more effective in the Northern European countries than in Southern Europe. In the case of directives relating to air pollution, for instance, Greece, Spain and Portugal lagged behind in terms both of formal compliance and of implementation of the directives (Bennett, 1991, ch. 7).

POLLUTION-INTENSIVE INDUSTRIES IN THE EUROPEAN UNION

In order to examine the impact of environmental regulation on competitiveness it was necessary first of all to identify the industries which were prone to environmental problems and hence likely to be most affected by such regulations. Thus a first step in the analysis was to establish criteria for defining industries as pollution-intensive.

As was indicated in Chapter 1, there are two approaches to identifying industries as pollution-intensive. One approach is to consider the level of emissions of particular pollutants relative to some other indicator such as the value of sales, value added or employment. This gives an indication of how much actual pollution a given level of economic activity causes in different industries.

The other approach is to use the level of pollution abatement expenditure in an industry as a share of total sales, cost or value added. Where the focus is on the impact of environmental regulation on competitiveness and location, such an approach, which attempts to measure the cost of compliance with such regulation, might seem to be more appropriate. After all, an industry which is highly polluting in terms of emissions, but does not internalize the costs and so has low pollution abatement costs, will not find its competitiveness adversely affected.

Despite our interest in competitiveness issues, there are several reasons why it was decided not to rely solely on abatement cost as an indicator of pollution-intensity. First of all, measured pollution control costs are relatively low, as was mentioned in the last chapter, and therefore differences between industries are not particularly marked. A number of writers argue that such figures underestimate the true cost of environmental regulation to the firm. There is, for example, an element of risk involved in terms of future liabilities for environmental damage which is not accounted for in current costs, but may affect decisions about location of production.

Although measures based on emissions may be a better indicator of potential costs of environmental regulation, it would also be a mistake to rely solely on such measures. To do so might lead to the paradox that an industry which had achieved low levels of emissions as a result of substantial expenditure on pollution abatement would not be considered a pollution-intensive industry. However, the competitiveness of such an industry is particularly likely to be affected by environmental regulation, so that it would make no sense to omit it from those considered environmentally sensitive.[1]

Both types of measures have been used in previous studies which have identified a group of pollution intensive industries. This has often been done at a fairly high level of aggregation and the industries considered 'dirty' are commonly iron and steel, non-ferrous metals, industrial chemicals, pulp and paper and non-metallic minerals (cf. Tobey, 1990; Mani and Wheeler, 1999). For the present study it was decided to use a more disaggregated classification based on the EU's NACE classification of economic activities at the three-digit level.

Because of the lack of detailed European data, it was necessary to use US figures in order to identify those industries which could be regarded as pollution-intensive. First of all the top ten four-digit ISIC industries were identified in terms of emissions per dollar of output for a number of pollutants. This was based on data from the World Bank's Industrial Pollution Projection System (Hettige *et al.*, 1995). This system ranks ISIC four-digit industries according to a number of key pollutants (toxic releases, SO_2, NO_2, CO, VOC, particulates, PM10, BOD, TSS). Similarly the top ten industries in terms of pollution abatement costs per dollar of output were also identified. Industries were classified as 'dirty' if they were in the top ten in terms of pollution-intensity for at least two pollutants or in terms of abatement costs. Twenty ISIC sectors were identified in this way, and these were correlated with 30 NACE sectors. Because of uncertainties over the comparability of residual categories of industries under the two classifications, it was decided to drop three NACE sectors[2] and textile finishing (437) was dropped because of lack of information. The NACE industries classified as highly polluting are listed in the appendix to this chapter.

TRENDS IN POLLUTION-INTENSIVE INDUSTRIES IN THE EUROPEAN UNION

A relatively highly aggregated study by Mani and Wheeler (1997, fig. 14) which traced the share of polluting industries in manufacturing production in Europe found evidence of a decline, particularly from around the mid-1970s to the early 1990s. A more disaggregated analysis for the 12 EU members using the classification of dirty industries adopted above was undertaken for the present study for the period from 1980 to 1994. The share of pollution-intensive industries fluctuated between 22 percent and 24 percent of manufacturing value added from 1980 to 1988, but after 1988 the share of such industries dropped by some two percentage points from 23.6 percent to 21.6 percent (see Figure 3.1).

There are considerable differences between the member countries of the EU in terms of the share of manufacturing value added accounted for by pollution-intensive industries (see Table 3.1). The three Southern European countries identified as having the least stringent environmental regulations (Greece, Portugal and Spain) are all among those countries with the highest share of polluting industries. On the other hand, the smaller Northern European countries (Netherlands, Denmark and Ireland) have a low participation from such industries. The Netherlands and Denmark are generally considered to have relatively strong environmental regulation.

Although the remainder of this chapter will concentrate on the European

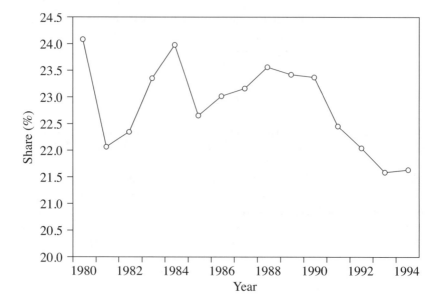

Figure 3.1   Share of pollution-intensive industries in manufacturing value
              added

Union as a whole, it is important to bear in mind that significant differences
do exist between the member countries. Thus, although a major issue for the
study as a whole is the impact of environmental regulation on the
competitiveness of European industry *vis-à-vis* other countries with less
stringent environmental regulations, and the impact which this has on
industrial location, it is also possible that differences in regulation between the
member countries may have an impact on location within the EU. This aspect
is picked up again in some of the sectoral case studies later in this volume.

For the same group of industries, an analysis was undertaken of the overall
trade balance as a share of manufacturing value added in these industries, for
the 12 EU countries between 1980 and 1994 (see Figure 3.2). The first point
to be noted was that throughout the period the EU was a net importer in these
industries, apart from a very small surplus in 1993. Generally the trade deficit
for the industries fluctuated between 0.5 percent and 3 percent of total
manufacturing value added. It is difficult to detect any marked trend in the
trade balance, although the deficit did decline in the early 1990s.

Thus in common with many other authors who have studied the aggregate
performance of polluting industries, it is difficult to sustain any generalized
thesis about the relocation of such industries away from the advanced
industrialized countries or that competitiveness has declined in a significant

Table 3.1   Share of pollution-intensive industries in manufacturing value added, 1994 (%)

France	16.9
Belgium/Luxembourg	22.7
Netherlands	9.4
Germany	20.0
Italy	21.1
UK	20.2
Ireland	4.6
Denmark	12.2
Greece	30.2
Portugal	21.3
Spain	23.0

Source: EUROSTAT.

way *vis-à-vis* pollution havens which have less stringent environmental regulation. However, there is good reason to believe that the impact of environmental regulation may differ from industry to industry and that a better picture can be obtained from a more disaggregated analysis.

A DISAGGREGATED ANALYSIS OF COMPETITIVENESS IN POLLUTING INDUSTRIES IN THE EU

In the previous chapter, a distinction was drawn between comparative and absolute advantage when discussing competitiveness at the industry level. Whereas the Ricardian notion of comparative advantage refers to the relative position of different industries within a country, absolute advantage, which is more akin to Porter's concept of competitive advantage, refers to the relative position of different countries within a particular industry.

The most common measures used in empirical studies of trade are various indicators of revealed comparative advantage (Ballance, 1998; Greenaway and Milner, 1993, ch. 10). A number of different measures have been proposed, some of which are based entirely on trade data and others which combine trade and production data. Some of the indicators use gross exports while others use net exports (exports minus imports).

A limitation of these indicators, in the context of the present study, is that they generally rank industries within a country in terms of their trade performance. They are therefore, as their name implies, indicators of *comparative* advantage. Such indicators have occasionally been used to rank

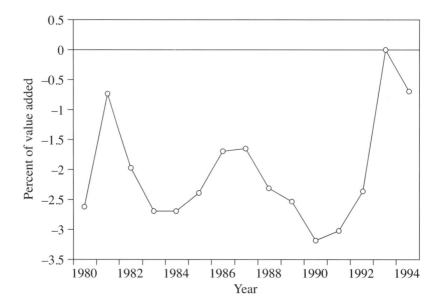

Figure 3.2   Trade balance of pollution-intensive industries as a share of manufacturing value added

the comparative advantage of different countries within an industry. However it has been shown that the two types of rankings are not necessarily consistent (Yeats, 1985).

Unfortunately, the data available for EU industry do not permit comparison with other countries and therefore it is only possible to look at the performance of an industry relative to other EU industries.[3] The possibility that an industry which appears to perform well relative to other EU industries may not in fact be doing so relative to the same industry in other countries needs therefore to be borne in mind.

Most studies of comparative advantage look at the position of different industries at a point in time. However, our interest here is in seeing how competitiveness has changed as a result of environmental regulation and it is therefore necessary to look at changes over time. In order to do this, a sectoral indicator was required which could be used to compare trends over time in different industries. A number of alternative indicators were considered, based on net exports as either a proportion of total trade (exports plus imports) or as a proportion of gross production, and the cover ratio (exports divided by imports). The measure finally selected for analysis was the relative cover ratio, that is, the ratio of exports to imports of the sector divided by the ratio of exports to imports for the manufacturing sector as a whole.

A number of factors contributed to the choice of this indicator. First, it was available for a greater number of industries than some of the alternative indicators. Second, normalization by the cover ratio for manufacturing as a whole meant that factors which might have affected manufacturing competitiveness across the board such as exchange rate changes were factored out of the index. Third, the cover ratio always takes positive values, making it possible to calculate exponential as well as linear trends for the index, which is not the case with measures based on net exports. Thus of the various trade based measures of competitiveness it was felt that it was the most useful indicator of relative trends in the international competitive position of different industries in the EU.[4]

Data from the Eurostat Competitiveness Database were used to calculate the competitiveness index. The database covers the period from 1980 to 1994. This is an appropriate period to take since, as was indicated above, EU environmental regulation became more stringent from the mid-1980s.[5] The index was calculated for each year of the period for each three-digit industry (classified by the NACE) and both a linear and an exponential time trend fitted.

A total of 101 industries were identified, of which 26 were classified as dirty industries for the purposes of the current project. Of the 101 industries, 42 showed an improvement in competitive performance relative to manufacturing as a whole, and 59 showed a decline in competitiveness. Interestingly, when the industries are separated into two groups, 34 of the cleaner industries showed a better performance than manufacturing as a whole, while 41 did worse. In contrast, amongst the dirty industries, only eight performed better than manufacturing while 18 did worse.

Since the index for manufacturing as a whole shows that EU industry lost competitiveness over the period, this result suggests that there were additional factors at play in some dirty industries which led to an even greater decline in competitiveness. Although this is by no means conclusive evidence that environmental regulation has contributed to loss of competitiveness, it is consistent with this hypothesis. Clearly, however, not all of the industries identified as highly polluting experienced a loss of competitiveness and it is therefore important to consider some of the factors which might have contributed to inter-industry differences in performance.

DETERMINANTS OF ENVIRONMENT – COMPETITIVENESS LINKAGES AT THE INDUSTRY LEVEL

The discussion in the last chapter indicated how difficult it is to find universally valid hypotheses concerning the impact of environmental regulation on competitiveness. A more useful way forward is to consider the reasons why the impact of environmental regulation on competitiveness may differ according to particular circumstances. In what follows we consider particularly the reasons why different industries may show different interactions between regulation and competitiveness. It is also likely that the nature of regulation will have different implications for competitiveness, reflecting the relative efficiency of different instruments and the effectiveness of different institutional arrangements (cf. Murphy and Gouldson, n.d.). Although this is an important issue, it is not our principal concern in what follows.

The first factor determining the differential impact is the extent to which industries create environmental damage. The environmental impact of industries clearly differs considerably from branch to branch. For example, in the US, toxic releases per $1,000 of shipments (weighted by risk to humans) were almost 500 times greater in the most toxic industry, fertilizers and pesticides, as it was in the last industry, soft drinks (Hettige *et al.*, 1995, table 4.1). Similar massive inter-industry differences also occur for atmospheric emissions and water discharges.

Differences in pollution-intensity will tend to give rise to differences in abatement costs between industries. For instance, in the United States the ratio of pollution abatement operating cost to value of output varies from 3.17 percent in the cement industry to 0.01 percent in printing and publishing. These differences depend not only on the environmental damage associated with different industries, but also on the cost of the different technologies available to reduce or treat emissions, discharges and waste, and the strictness of environmental regulation and implementation affecting different industries.

Although figures on the share of pollution abatement in operating cost are relatively low, the proportion of investment devoted to pollution control is usually much higher. In the late 1980s and early 1990s pollution control accounted for 3.5 percent of capital expenditure in Japan, 4.5 percent in the Netherlands and 5.5 percent in the US (UNCTAD, 1994, p. 10). These averages hide much higher figures, well into double figures, for the most polluting industries such as chemicals, oil refining, basic metals, pulp and paper, and leather (Atkinson, 1996, table 2).

The impact of investment in pollution control equipment on competitiveness depends not only on the operating costs of available technologies but will also be influenced by the importance of sunk costs in the industry, which makes it necessary for existing assets to be written off. For individual firms it will also depend on the point in the firm's investment cycle at which it has to undertake new environmental investments (Stevens, 1993, p. 11). Capital-intensive industries such as pulp and paper, oil refining and basic chemicals are likely to find competitiveness affected much more than light industries such as food processing or footwear.

Another factor which determines the extent to which environmental regulation leads to cost increases is the extent of innovation within the firm or industry. The argument that regulation leads to 'innovation offsets' is more likely to apply where there is substantial innovatory activity. Bearing in mind that cost reductions are far more likely to occur where new clean technologies are developed than in industries which adopt end-of-pipe solutions, the level of R&D is likely to be a factor in determining the impact on competitiveness.

For any given level of cost increase, a further important factor is the ability to absorb costs. Profit margins are an important indicator of the ability of an industry or firm to absorb cost increases (Alanen, 1996, p. 20). The size of firm, which affects the financial and technical resources available to cope with regulatory requirements, is also a factor in determining the impact on competitiveness (Stevens, 1993, p. 11).

The impact of increased costs on competitiveness also depends on the ability to pass on those costs to consumers in the form of higher prices. One determinant of this is market power, so firms in highly concentrated industries are more likely to be able to pass on cost increases than those in atomistic industries. The availability of close substitutes is another factor which influences the elasticity of demand and hence the ability of firms to increase prices without losing sales. A third factor is the market which is supplied (Alanen, 1996, pp. 20–21). Where this is a protected local market the firm is more likely to be able to pass on cost increases than where it has to compete in global markets against firms which do not have to meet the same regulatory requirements (Leveque, 1993, p. 81).

So far we have only considered the impact of environmental factors on the cost side of the competitiveness equation. However, at the firm level particularly, competitiveness depends not only on costs but also on price. If better environmental standards permit firms to obtain higher prices (through marketing 'greener' products) independently of cost increases, then there may be further competitive advantages to be gained (Sprenger, 1998, box 2). For firms to be able to do this, it is necessary first of all that they produce differentiated products rather than homogeneous bulk products where competition is based largely on price.

Not all differentiated products necessarily lend themselves to differentiation according to their environmental characteristics however, and some sectors seem to be much more susceptible to environmental attention than others. For example customers worry about the environmental impacts of forest products, but not so much about those of mineral products (Alanen, 1996, p. 22). It is probable that consumer goods are more likely to be subject to environmental pressures than industrial goods, although these pressures may focus more on the impact of their use (for example, energy efficiency) or disposal (for example, recyclability) than their production (Leveque, 1993, p. 80). However, particularly with the growth of eco-labelling and life-cycle analysis, the possibilities of obtaining premium prices or market niches through the production of environmentally friendly products are likely to increase.

This discussion provides the elements for analysing the differential impacts of environmental regulation on competitiveness at the industry or firm level. It suggests that even within the group of industries which have been identified as pollution-intensive, environmental regulation will have a greater impact on competitiveness in some industries than in others, and on some firms. In the next section this framework will be applied in an analysis of competitiveness in EU industry since the early 1980s.

EU COMPETITIVENESS AT THE INDUSTRY LEVEL

The starting point for this analysis is the environment–competitiveness matrix developed by Alanen (1996).[6] On the cost side we identify two factors which determine the extent to which environmental regulation affects competitiveness. The first is the importance of pollution abatement costs (PAC) relative to output. In the absence of disaggregated data for EU countries we have used US data as a proxy to divide industries into those which have above and below average PACs.

The second factor which we have used is the degree of concentration in the industry. This is taken as an indicator of the ability of firms to pass on or to absorb cost increases: the more concentrated the industry the greater the ability to pass on cost increases to customers. A recent study has estimated European-wide concentration ratios for three-digit NACE industries for the first time and we use these data to classify industries into those with above and below average five-firm concentration ratios (Davies and Lyons, 1996, appendix 2).[7] Using these two variables, a 2×2 matrix reflecting cost conditions can be constructed, with the least favourable situation arising in the cell where PACs are high and concentration low, and the most favourable situation where PACs are low and concentration high. It is assumed that the other two cells represent intermediate combinations.

The industries identified as being pollution-intensive were classified into two groups according to whether they maintained their competitiveness relative to manufacturing as a whole (including those which increased their competitiveness) or lost competitiveness relative to manufacturing.[8] Industries were then distributed into four cells according to the likely impact of environmental factors on competitiveness (Table 3.2). Not surprisingly, since all the industries included were classified as 'dirty' industries on the basis of their emissions and discharges, the majority of them had high pollution abatement costs, although, for several, costs were below average. The industries included were almost equally divided between high and low concentration industries.

Table 3.2   Cost factors and environment–competitiveness interactions

	Concentration	
PAC	High	Low
High	*Maintained competitiveness*	*Maintained competitiveness*
	1. Non-ferrous metals	1. Asbestos
	2. Abrasive products	2. Leather
	3. Basic chemicals	3. Pulp and paper
	4. Ind. and agri. chemicals	
	5. Oil refineries	*Lost competitiveness*
		1. Clay products
	Lost competitiveness	2. Stone and non-metallic
	1. Iron and steel	mineral products
	2. Steel tubes	3. Foundries
	3. First processing of steel	4. Forgings
	4. Cement	5. Wood building components
	5. Synthetic fibres	6. Coke ovens
Low	*Maintained competitiveness*	*Maintained competitiveness*
	1. Oils and fats	1. Sawmills and processing
	2. Alcohol and spirits	2. Wood board
	Lost competitiveness	*Lost competitiveness*
	1. Sugar	1. Concrete
		2. Plastic products

The north-east quadrant of the matrix includes those industries in which environmental factors are likely to have the greatest negative impact since it includes those industries which have the highest PACs and are least able to absorb them or pass them on to consumers because of low levels of concentration. The south-west quadrant, on the other hand, is the most favourable since PACs are below average and concentration is high. The remaining two quadrants represent intermediate positions.

A similar matrix can be constructed on the marketing side, again using two variables. First, the extent to which competition is based on price or on non-price factors, particularly advertising or innovation, affects the competitive implications of environmental regulation. Where price competition dominates, negative effects on competitiveness are more likely; where there is considerable innovation or product differentiation, innovation offsets are more likely. Again we follow Davies and Lyons' (1996) classification of industries in distinguishing between the two types.[9]

The second variable on the marketing side recognizes that some industries have been subject to environmental concerns more than others, and that in these industries it may be possible for firms to position themselves in the market by emphasizing the environment-friendly nature of their activities. Over time the range of industries which have been in the public eye for environmental reasons has broadened. In the 1970s and 1980s the main areas of concern were chemicals (including detergents, fertilizers, pesticides and herbicides, and paints), pulp and paper mills, tropical hardwoods, and asbestos (Pollack, 1995, figure 2.2). Other industries such as metals and non-metallic minerals (apart from asbestos) have not been the subject of such close consumer and public concern. Thus the first group of industries are classified as being of high environmental concern, while other industries rate as low. Again a 2×2 matrix is constructed (Table 3.3) with the least favourable quadrant being characterized by undifferentiated products of low environmental concern produced in industries with little R&D, while the most favourable situation in terms of being able to reconcile environmental protection with competitiveness comes in those industries which are highly differentiated or R&D-intensive and have been subject to public concern.

Table 3.3 shows that the majority of the industries classified as pollution-intensive produce undifferentiated products and are characterized by low R&D-intensity. Over half the industries fall into the south-west quadrant, which in this case includes the industries which have least possibilities of turning a positive environmental performance into a competitive advantage on the marketing side. Conversely, the north-east quadrant includes those industries where environmental factors can most easily be positive because they are industries where there is public concern over environmental performance and in which competition is not based primarily on price considerations. As in the previous table, the other two quadrants represent intermediate situations.

The two 2×2 matrices can now be combined into a 3×3 matrix in which the two axes represent the likely impact of environmental factors on the cost and the market side respectively. These are derived as high, medium and low (negative impacts) from the two previous matrices. In each case where both factors on the cost side are favourable in terms of the environment–competitiveness interaction (high concentration/low pollution abatement costs) the industry is classified in the low row. Where one of the factors is favourable and one is unfavourable, it is classified as medium, and where both are unfavourable it is classified in the high row. A similar procedure was

Table 3.3   Market factors and environment-competitiveness interactions

	Environmental sensitivity	
Differentiation	Low	High
High	*Maintained competitiveness* 1. Oils and fats 2. Alcohol and spirits *Lost competitiveness* 1. Synthetic fibres	*Maintained competitiveness* 1. Basic industrial chemicals 2. Ind. and agri. chemicals 3. Oil refining
Low	*Maintained competitiveness* 1. Leather 2. Non-ferrous metals 3. Abrasive products *Lost competitiveness* 1. Iron and steel 2. Steel tubes 3. First processing of steel 4. Clay 5. Stone and non-metallic mineral products 6. Cement 7. Concrete 8. Foundries 9. Forgings 10. Sugar 11. Plastic products 12. Coke ovens	*Maintained competitiveness* 1. Sawmills and processing 2. Wood board 3. Pulp and paper 4. Asbestos *Lost competitiveness* 1. Wood building components

applied on the market side to classify industries by column.[10] For ease of presentation two 3 × 3 matrices are constructed, one for those industries which were able to maintain their competitiveness and the other for those industries where competitiveness declined relative to manufacturing as a whole.

Table 3.4 presents the situation in the industries where competitiveness has declined even more than manufacturing as a whole. According to the previous argument, these industries should tend to be characterized by an unfavourable constellation of cost and market factors and therefore would be concentrated in the north-east corner of the matrix. This is indeed the case, and all the industries with declining competitiveness, apart from synthetic fibres, are located above the diagonal. In other words those dirty industries which have performed worst in terms of competitiveness have tended to be badly placed within the competitiveness-environment matrix.

Table 3.4   Environment–competitiveness interactions in industries where competitiveness has deteriorated

Cost	Market factors		
	Low	Medium	High
High		Wood building components	Clay Stone Foundries Forgings Coke ovens
Medium		Synthetic fibres	Iron and steel Steel tubes First processing of steel Cement Concrete Sugar Plastic products
Low			

Table 3.5 depicts the situation in those industries which showed a competitive performance at least as good as the manufacturing average. If better competitive performance in these industries reflected a positive interaction between environmental factors and competitiveness, then there would be a tendency for successful industries to be concentrated towards the south-west corner of the table. This is not however the case since the industries are distributed symmetrically throughout the table. The most surprising aspect of this table is the case of leather, which, despite being classified as an industry subject to high negative effects on both the cost and marketing side, has outperformed manufacturing in terms of competitiveness.

Thus there are clearly some industries which have been able to maintain or improve their competitive position despite apparently being in a situation where cost and market factors would tend to lead to environmental regulation having a deleterious effect. In order to understand the underlying factors which account for relatively successful performance in such industries, it is necessary to undertake more in-depth study of the industries concerned.

A further qualification to this analysis can be introduced by considering the

Table 3.5   Environment–competitiveness interaction in industries where competitiveness did not deteriorate

	Market factors		
Cost	Low	Medium	High
High		Pulp and paper Asbestos	Leather
Medium	Basic chemicals Ind. and agri. chemicals Oil refining	Wood board Sawmills	Non-ferrous metals Abrasive products
Low		Oils and fats Alcohol and spirits	

sources of competition for EU production in different industries. The argument that industries which are unfavourably placed in the competitiveness–environment matrix will tend to lose competitiveness applies strictly speaking to competitiveness *vis-à-vis* other countries that have less stringent environmental regulation. The indicators which have been used in the above analysis are global indices of competitiveness reflecting the EU's trade *vis-à-vis* the rest of the world. It is possible therefore that in some industries competitiveness has declined *vis-à-vis* other developed countries which have equally stringent environmental regulation.

When the source of competition is identified, the picture is modified somewhat. Two of the 13 industries where competitiveness declined faced insignificant competition from developing countries (synthetic fibres and steel tubes). Thus it is unlikely that the decline in competitiveness of the EU synthetic fibres industry had anything to do with environmental regulation. Three of the industries where competitive performance did not deteriorate (industrial and agricultural chemicals, pulp and paper, and abrasive products) also faced insignificant competition from developing and transition economies. This leaves only three industries (leather, asbestos and non-ferrous metals) in the anomalous position of having apparently improved their competitiveness, despite unfavourable conditions.

The case of leather, which is discussed at length later in this book, gives further pause for thought. In terms of the indicator of competitiveness used in this chapter, the trend is clearly positive with the EU moving from being a net importer of leather in the early 1980s to being a net exporter in the mid-1990s. However, the use of data on EU exports and imports obscures the fact that, in terms of both world production and world exports, the tanning industry in Europe has been losing ground, and that overall production and employment has been declining. One way of interpreting this is that, although perhaps in terms of its position relative to other industries in Europe (that is, comparative advantage), tanning has done relatively well, in terms of its position relative to other countries (that is, absolute advantage) the European tanning industry has been losing ground.

The asbestos industry is possibly a similar case. Despite apparently gaining competitiveness according to the indicator used here, the industry in fact experienced the largest decline in output of any EU industry between the mid-1980s and the mid-1990s (Panorama, 1997). Although the industry was probably in worldwide decline as a result of the concerns about the health hazards associated with asbestos, it is unlikely that there was any real gain in international competitiveness on the part of the European industry. Again the anomaly appears to be a result of the imperfect measure of competitiveness used in the analysis, rather than being truly a reflection of an unexpectedly strong performance by a highly polluting industry.

CONCLUSION

In common with many other studies of the environment–competitiveness relationship, the empirical evidence in this chapter provides little support for the view that environmental regulation leads to an across-the-board loss of competitiveness in pollution-intensive industries. Despite a slight fall in the share of these industries in total manufacturing value added and a generally negative balance of trade, trends are not sufficiently marked to draw strong conclusions.

At a more disaggregated level, however, it was found that competitiveness declined in the majority of pollution-intensive industries, although a minority held their own and a small number showed a competitive improvement. This led to consideration of the factors which might lead to differences in the impact of environmental regulation at the industry level. Factors considered included certain structural and market characteristics which would lead to some industries approximating the cost-based view of the environment–competitiveness interaction, while others were more likely to fit the innovation based approach.

The efforts to clarify the linkages between environmental regulation and competitiveness are still rudimentary, and it has not been possible to determine conclusively which are the main variables that intervene in the relationship. The evidence presented in this chapter can only be illustrative rather than definitive. Moreover, environmental regulation is only one of a number of factors which may have an impact on competitiveness and a full analysis would require a much more detailed consideration of the impact of other factors.

Such a detailed analysis can best be carried out at the industry level, which is where the dynamic of competition is played out. For this reason the next three parts of this book consist of case studies of three pollution-intensive industries and the way in which environmental regulation has affected production within the European Union and a number of developing and transition economies.

Iron and steel has been a key industry for the European Union since its origins in the 1950s with the creation of the European Coal and Steel Community in 1951. It is also an industry which, because of its size and pollution-intensity, has historically had major environmental impacts in the countries where it is located. Iron and steel has undergone considerable restructuring in recent years and, as was seen above, the competitiveness of the industry in the EU has declined. It has faced considerable competition both domestically and in third markets from new producers in East Asia and Latin America and, since the fall of the Berlin Wall, from Eastern Europe and the former Soviet Union. In Part II the impact of environmental regulation on the steel industry in a number of EU countries and in Brazil, South Korea, Poland and the Czech Republic will be analysed.

As was pointed out in the last section, the leather industry is a particularly interesting case. It would appear to be an industry in which differences in the stringency of environmental regulation could have an important impact on the location of industry and EU competitiveness. However, the indicator of competitiveness used here shows that in terms of its trade performance the European leather industry has performed relatively well, although other indicators suggest that internationally it has lost ground in terms of its share of world production and exports. Part III considers recent developments in the tanning industry in a number of Western European countries, as well as in Eastern Europe, Brazil, Mexico and India.

Part IV considers the case of the fertilizer industry. This is an industry where, in overall terms, the European Union has done relatively well competitively. In terms of the analysis of this chapter, this is not entirely surprising since, although it is a pollution-intensive industry, market structure and other characteristics are such that the competitive position of the industry is less likely to be negatively affected than is the case of many other such industries. By considering the different strategies applied by fertilizer producers, Part IV illustrates how firms have responded to competitive pressures. As well as looking at developments in Europe, the case study also considers the experience of the fertilizer industry in China, Turkey and Morocco.

APPENDIX: 26 INDUSTRIES CLASSIFIED AS HIGHLY POLLUTING (NACE THREE DIGITS)

120 Coke ovens
140 Mineral oil refining
221 Iron and steel industry
222 Manufacture of steel tubes
223 Drawing, cold rolling and cold folding of steel (first processing of steel)
224 Production and preliminary processing of non-ferrous metals
241 Manufacture of clay products for constructional purposes
242 Manufacture of cement, lime and plaster
243 Manufacture of concrete cement or plaster products for constructional purposes
244 Manufacture of articles of asbestos
245 Working of stone and non-metallic mineral products
246 Production of grindstones and other abrasive products
251 Manufacture of basic industrial chemicals
256 Manufacture of other chemical products, mainly for industrial and agricultural purposes
260 Man-made fibres industry
311 Foundries
312 Forging; drop forging, closed-die forging, pressing and stamping
411 Manufacture of vegetable and animal oils and fats
420 Sugar manufacturing and refining
424 Distilling of ethyl alcohol from fermented materials; spirit distilling and compounding
441 Tanning and dressing of leather
461 Sawing and processing of wood
462 Manufacture of semi-finished wood products
463 Manufacture of carpentry and joinery components and parquet flooring
471 Manufacture of pulp, paper and board
483 Processing of plastics

NOTES

1. As was pointed out in Chapter 1, this problem is not so serious in practice since industries which are highly polluting in terms of emissions also tend to have a high level of pollution control expenditure.
2. These were Other Chemical Products for Household and Office use (NACE 259), Miscellaneous Textile Industries (439) and Other Wood Manufactures (465).
3. The Eurostat Competitiveness Database does provide data from other OECD countries but since the focus here is on competitiveness relative to countries with less stringent environmental regulation which are generally not members of the OECD, comparisons with

OECD countries would not be particularly useful.

4. The EU here is defined as the 12 members prior to the accession of Sweden, Finland and Austria.

5. Unfortunately it was not possible to extend the period beyond 1994 because the more recent version of the Competitiveness Database provides indicators for the current 15 European Union members and uses the revised version of the NACE classification, so that comparable data are not available.

6. As is clear from this section and the previous one, the empirical analysis of competitiveness presented in this chapter has been largely inspired by Alanen's approach.

7. The Davies and Lyons study did not include two of the pollution-intensive industries covered in this study, Coke Ovens (NACE 120) and Mineral Oil Refining (NACE 140). On the basis of other information Coke Ovens has been classified as having low concentration and Oil Refining as having a high concentration level.

8. Industries were regarded as having lost competitiveness when the relative cover ratio fell by over 1 per cent per annum.

9. In addition Coke Ovens were classified as having low levels of differentiation, while in view of the importance of brand names in the sale of petroleum products, the oil industry was classified as highly differentiated.

10. This is admittedly a crude way of establishing a typology and implicitly gives equal weight to each of the factors identified as affecting environment–competitiveness interactions while ignoring others. It does however provide a starting point for trying to specify the situations in which conflicts between competitiveness and environmental protection may arise.

PART II

Environmental regulations, globalization of production and technological change: the iron and steel sector*

Jonathan Barton

* The research on the steel industry was carried out between 1996 and 1998. Some firms have changed in terms of ownership and activities since that time and these details have been updated where possible. Citation of individual interviewees or comments made in meetings with groups of representatives is made only with respect to specific points regarding a firm or regulatory experience; the comments should not be taken to represent the views of the organization itself. The opinions expressed throughout are those of the author alone.

4. The industry and its environmental impacts

ISSUES AND DEBATES

Since the late 1970s, the international iron and steel industry has been transformed. From an industry characterized by a number of mostly state-owned firms, it is now globalized and in the process has undergone massive restructuring, privatization, increases in capital intensity, product specialization and increased levels of trading. During this time, and with gradually increasing intensity, there has also been a greater focus on the environmental impacts of the industry, with consequent adoption of environmental technologies, cleaner process technologies and environmental management strategies. This case study of the steel sector documents these developments and argues that environmental responses by firms have not led to 'pollution haven' investments or vast increases in production by 'dirty' producers in developing and transitional economies. Rather than explaining sectoral change in terms of environmental regulations and firm responses, it is more important to place environmental issues within the context of a complex global restructuring of the sector, in terms of factors of production, output and trade.

A snapshot of the sector after two decades of environmental awareness reveals wide variations across firms, with different strategies having been adopted. Many of these strategies are linked to international business innovations such as the ISO 9.000 and ISO 14.000 series for quality and environmental management, national and regional economic development policies, and global patterns of steel trading. Other strategies are highly localized, having been adopted in response to environmental regulations at regional and municipal levels or from pressures emanating from civil society and other stakeholder groups.

It is evident that iron and steel firms around the world have responded to demands for environmental protection and control but that the responses are highly varied and do not necessarily correspond to simple firm type and geographical categorizations. Regulatory flexibility, effective enforcement, technological innovations, and firm and sectoral commitments to environmental management procedures and policies have all emerged as important contributory factors in firm responses, but to different extents around the world and with different outcomes.

There are two principal debates that have emerged with respect to industry and environment themes, which can be discussed with reference to the increasingly globalized iron and steel sector. The first is the 'industrial flight' hypothesis which asserts that stricter environmental regulations in one location will lead to displacement of activities. This can be extended to include the 'pollution haven' scenario whereby lax regulatory environments are offered by countries in order to attract firms, and also the 'hide and source' methods of outsourcing or subcontracting processes in order to avoid regulatory pressures. There are analyses and arguments to suggest that there is no international movement of firms to avoid, specifically, environmental regulations. This is mainly because locational decision-making by firm executives involves a range of other factor and market variables (see Leonard, 1984; Low and Yeats, 1992; Birdsall and Wheeler, 1992). In the case of the iron and steel sector, it would appear that firms are relatively flexible in their operations in terms of input strategies and that environmental regulations *per se* do not displace firms.

The second debate that has flourished in the industry, trade and environment literature is the so-called 'win–win' scenario of Porter and van der Linde (1995, 1996). Their argument is that regulations lead (or at least should lead) to positive environmental outcomes and that businesses can gain from these regulations and treat their responses to them as a long-term benefit rather than as a long-term cost. They argue that regulations lead to innovation and adaptation in order to deal with the cost implications of the regulations. Managers become aware of the need to recognize efficiencies in production and sales and they introduce more dynamic managerial practices and new technologies. While this may be costly in the initial stages, the argument is that these firms become increasingly well situated in the global market place as regulations become stricter elsewhere and firms are forced to follow suit. In this way, firms may become 'first movers' and enjoy a competitive advantage from having implemented environmental procedures and technologies at an early stage. Evidence of such a process can be found in firms producing environmental technologies for other firms in the sector or across sectors (see Jaggi and Freedman, 1992; Hart and Ahuja, 1996; Barton, 1998).

The counter-argument to Porter and van der Linde is offered by Palmer *et al*. (1995) who suggest that innovation is not necessarily an outcome of tighter regulations since some firms may be unable to compete within the new framework. It is not logical therefore to state that innovation will be a response throughout the industrial sector under regulation. It is likely that some firms will innovate in response to regulation and others will lose competitiveness. Unlike Porter and van der Linde, the counter-argument assumes more of a zero-sum game within which not all firms can gain but firms will gain at others' expense. We return to these two debates – 'industrial flight' and the 'win–win' scenario – in the conclusions.

What this sectoral case study does is present aspects of sectoral trends, firm experiences of regulation and environmental management, and introduce the role of other factors in terms of environmental change. In bringing together sector-wide issues, individual firm and regulatory authority detail and international comparisons, the research is able to reflect on the industry and environment issues in the iron and steel sector and to consider the most influential aspects.

PRODUCTION PROCESSES AND STAGES

The conversion of iron ore and coking coal into pig iron in a blast furnace and the transformation of this iron into steel by reducing the carbon content from 4 percent to 1 percent in a basic oxygen furnace remain the two stages for making virgin steel by the integrated (ironmaking and steelmaking) route (see Figure 4.1). The process is energy intensive due to the high temperatures required, but the energy input per tonne (metric ton) of output has been reduced considerably since the 1970s when energy price rises prompted innovations.

The integrated route is not the only steelmaking activity however. Since the 1950s, the electric arc furnace (EAF) route of steel production has been developed to complement the integrated production route. This process converts steel from used products into new steel products, acting as an extensive recycling system for ferrous materials. Although the EAF route is considerably cleaner, it is dependent on virgin steel since scrap availability and conversion value do not meet steel demand. Therefore, the two processes will continue side by side for the foreseeable future, and any analysis of steel and environmental impacts should be wary of focusing on EAF as a way forward on its own (see Crandall, 1996). For example, Reppelin-Hill's (1999) analysis of open trade policies and EAF diffusion as a measure of environmental protection fails to consider the global picture of virgin steel production and scrap availability, quality and cost. The current trend for developing countries with no tradition of steel production to move towards EAF production is possible only within a context of virgin steel production elsewhere. An important consideration, for example, is that emissions from EAF plants will be largely determined by the quality of the scrap used. Despite these caveats, however, the growth of EAF plants has provided a cleaner option for some steelmaking activities and will continue to grow, especially in developing economies with limitations in the areas of domestic demand, energy and raw materials.

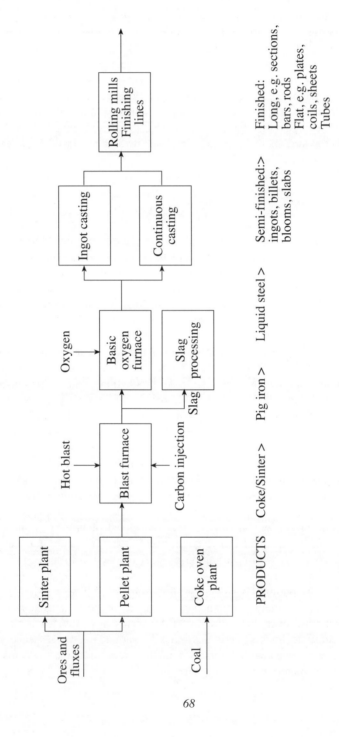

Figure 4.1   The primary iron and steel production process

Within the integrated steelmaking route, the process technologies that show least variation between firms are in ironmaking and primary steelmaking, where pollution risk and control is greatest. In ironmaking, alternatives have been sought in the pollution-intensive sintering and cokemaking processes. Direct reduction iron (DRI) and smelting reduction processes are now available but their take-up has been slow since commercial viability at high volumes is largely unproven except under particular circumstances, such as low-price coal or natural gas, and also because the intermediate product (sponge iron) demand has been affected by the development of the international scrap trade. A successful example of DRI take-up is in South Africa, where steam coal is widely available and scrap is scarce, resulting in the COREX process being a highly effective, locally appropriate technology (IISI/UNEP, 1997). In terms of the steelmaking process, the most important transformation has been the shift from open hearth furnaces (OHF) to basic oxygen furnaces (BOF) which are cleaner and more efficient. Only in the former Soviet Union, Central and Eastern European countries and China do OHF technologies continue, suggesting weaknesses in both environmental control and technology upgrading (see Table 4.1).

The downstream processes of the industry have benefited from more technological changes. The most important of these is continuous casting.

Table 4.1   Crude steel production by process, 1987 and 1997 (%)

	1987			1997		
	BOF[a]	EAF[b]	OHF[c]	BOF	EAF	OHF
EU 12/15	71.1	28.9	—	63.1	36.9	—
USA	58.9	38.1	3.0	56.2	43.8	—
Japan	70.2	29.8	—	67.2	32.8	—
USSR/former USSR	33.7	13.4	52.9	51.9	11.8	36.2
China	n.a.	n.a.	n.a.	58.3	17.6	8.9
E. Europe/Turkey	43.3	24.9	31.6	74.7	19.1	6.2
Latin America	51.4	39.8	8.8	50.0	49.3	—
World Total[d]	55.9	26.4	17.7	58.3	33.8	5.7

Notes:
[a] BOF: basic oxygen furnace.
[b] EAF: electric arc furnace.
[c] OHF: open hearth furnace.
[d] Incomplete totals are due to the inclusion of other processes.

Source: IISI (various).

Continuous casting enables producers to cast directly, rather than cooling molten steel in moulds as billets and ingots and reheating them to be rolled into products. This development has enabled producers to reduce their energy use and also increase production. The original driver for the shift to continuous casting came from the desire to improve yield and product quality but the environmental impacts have been extensive. Continuous casting not only reduces the energy requirements in the process, by removing a cooling and reheating phase between casting and rolling, but it also enables greater control over fugitive atmospheric emissions at this stage which are controlled via refractories which shroud the steel. The estimated saving in energy is between 0.5–0.8 GJ/t, and the savings in casting area emissions management are also significant (UNEP/IISI, 1997).

Due to the shift in the industry away from bulk steels towards the inclusion of stainless and speciality steels, the processes of steel production following the EAF or BOF stage have multiplied. Traditionally, steel firms produced simple forms and low quality products but this picture of the sector has changed with the movement towards client needs and a wide array of steels of differing qualities, strengths and application possibilities. With a wider range of products emerging from a single plant, with closer relations with clients and often interlinked R&D projects, and within a competitive market place where niche markets are offering alternatives to high-volume, low-quality bulk steel markets, steel firms have become more flexible and more complex organizations. In developed economies, these changes have come as responses to declining construction and industrial demands for steels, with different steel products of varying qualities increasing for specialized uses in white goods, vehicle parts and furniture. Steel beverage cans, lightweight car bodies and steel frame houses are three opportunities that are currently being exploited in different regions of the world to compete with other materials, particularly plastics and aluminum.

TECHNOLOGIES AND ENVIRONMENTAL PROBLEMS

The evolution of the climate change debate from the early 1980s, and discussions of European carbon taxation in particular, has highlighted the need to manage atmospheric emissions more effectively. While the oil price hikes of the 1970s prompted rapid responses from firms in terms of energy reductions, inter-governmental commitments to atmospheric emissions reductions have created similar pressures for a review of plant level energy use. In the UK, the spectre of an energy tax has already challenged firms, especially in the energy-intensive sectors such as iron and steel, to take a further look at ways in which energy use can be reduced, more energy can be recycled around the plant, and energy that is used can be applied more effectively. Nevertheless, the industrial associations are fighting hard against environmental taxes. For example, the European Round Table of industrial interests adopts arguments of scientific uncertainty and possible pollution displacement via industrial relocation in its opposition to EU carbon taxation (ERT, 1997). The International Iron and Steel Institute's (IISI) policy statement regarding climate change and the carbon tax is clear on this (IISI, *Policy Statement*, n.d.):

> Measures that involve the introduction of taxes on carbon dioxide emissions from the steel industry would not result in any significant reduction in such emissions but in draining the financial resources of the sector they would impact negatively on the industry's investment programme and research and development. These represent the best way for the industry to meet the challenge of sustainable development in the longer term.

Wider environmental debates, also discussed internationally and legislated for nationally, around water quality, land remediation, raw materials exploitation and recyclability of products and by-products have all put further demands on firms to seek 'off-the-shelf' or innovative solutions to their particular environmental weaknesses. In most cases, it is the application of end-of-pipe or cleaner technologies that is the common response; however, there is also a growing focus on better management of systems, attention to maintenance and housekeeping generally, and training to support these developments.

Despite extensive emissions reductions across all media since the 1970s, resulting from technological change and better management, the iron and steel sector remains an energy-intensive sector with high total emissions loads and large volumes of solid by-products to manage. Alongside the chemicals industry, pulp and paper, and mineral processing, it is still recognized as one of the leading 'pollution intensive' activities; this can be confirmed by looking at its total pollution load per unit of output (see Tables 4.2 and 4.3). To maintain the downward trajectory in emissions to date requires ever greater attention to detail to combat the diminishing returns on pollution abatement investment (unit of emission reduction/capital investment), increased awareness of environmental management issues across the board, and innovative approaches to bypassing or controlling the most polluting processes.

Within the steel process, it is the ironmaking phases that are the most problematic in terms of environmental protection. The sinter and cokemaking plants and the blast furnaces are major sources of atmospheric emissions, and they also give rise to specific wastewater and solid waste problems. Although the EAF route leads to considerably less emissions per tonne of liquid steel

Table 4.2 Integrated plant: energy and emissions balance

Process stage	Inputs	Air	Water	Solid
Sinter 1 tonne screened sinter	950 kg iron ore 35 kg coke dust 30 l water 150 kg flux 250 kg returned fines	20 kg CO 1.5 kg SO_2 0.6 kg NO_x 150 kg CO_2 0.2 kg particulate	—	0.5 kg ESP dust 250 kg returned fines
Coke 1 tonne coke	1250 kg coal	1 kg CO 400 g SO_2 0.3 kg NO_x 500 kg CO_2 550 g particulate 300 g hydrocarbons	0.6 m³ wastewater (ss, oil, NH_3) 20 g suspended solids 0.2 kg BETP sludge	90 g sulphur 85 kg tar, benzene, pitch, etc.
Blast furnace 1 tonne hot metal	415 kg coke 60 kg coal 150 kg lump ore 1500 kg pellet/ sinter/limestone	1 kg CO 140 g SO_2 90 g NO_x 300 kg CO_2 85 g particulate 75 g PAH	0.2m³ wastewater (ss, oil, NH_3) 10 g suspended solids 20 g oil 1 g cyanide 2 g metals	324 kg slag 0.4 kg cast house dust, other solid waste 19 kg sludge (gas cleaning)
Blast oxygen furnace 1 tonne cast product	850 kg hot metal 212 kg scrap 3 kg iron ore 22 kg lime 5 kg dolomite	1 kg CO 140 g SO_2 90 g NO_x 30 kg CO_2 85 g particulate 75 g PAH	0.1 m³ wastewater (ss, oil, NH_3) 5 g oil 4 g suspended solids 1.4 g metals	131 kg slag 25 kg sludge 4 kg grit 4 kg refractory 14 kg millscale 65 g waste oil

Total				
1 tonne crude steel	1500 kg iron ore	28 kg CO	3 m³ wastewater (ss,	455 kg slag
	610 kg coking coal	2.2 kg SO₂	oil, NH₃)	56 kg dust/sludges
	60 kg mineral coal	2.3 kg NOₓ	1.6 kg suspended solids	16 kg millscale
	150 kg lump ore	2.3 t CO₂	150 g oil	4 kg refractory
	200 kg flux	0.3 kg VOC	110 g ammoniacal	0.8 kg oil
	175 kg scrap	1.1 kg particulate	nitrogen	54 kg other
	5 m³ water	65 g other (metals, H₂S)	8 g (phenols, meths, cyanides)	

Notes: Input energy breakdown: 19.2 GJ coal; 5.2 GJ steam; 3.5 GJ electrical (364 kWh); 0.3 GJ oxygen; 0.04 GJ natural gas. Output energy breakdown: 5.2 GJ steam; 3.4 GJ electrical (359 kWh); 0.9 GJ coal tar; 0.3 GJ benzene.

Source: IISI/UNEP (1997).

Table 4.3   EAF plant: energy and emissions balance

Process stage	Inputs	Air	Water	Solid
Total				
1 tonne crude steel	1130 kg scrap/DRI/	2.5 kg CO	2 m³ wastewater (ss,	146 kg slag
	hot/cold iron	60 kg SO₂	oil, NH₃)	19 kg furnace dust
	10 kg alloying	0.5 kg NOₓ		16 kg millscale
	elements	120 kg CO₂		2.5 kg sludge
	40 kg flux	165 g particulate		17 kg refractories
				0.8 kg oil
				3 kg other

Note: Input energy breakdown: 5.5 GJ electrical (572 kWh); 1.3 GJ natural gas (40 m³); 450 MJ coal/coke (15 kg); 205 MJ oxygen (30 m³); 120 MJ electrode consumption (3.5 kg).

Source: IISI/UNEP (1997).

(see Tables 4.2 and 4.3), there is an ongoing demand for virgin steel from integrated plants, therefore attention to these processes in terms of technologies and management is highlighted within iron and steel management circles. Much of the late twentieth century research into process developments and environmental protection in the steel industry has focused on ways of reducing the dependence on sinter and coke plants, such as the introduction of direct reduction iron technologies. However, until these are proven under a wide range of conditions it is unlikely that the ironmaking processes will be phased out, which means further investment in end-of-pipe measures and onerous maintenance work (for coke oven plants in particular). A comparison of integrated and EAF plants in terms of atmospheric emissions reveals the environmental concerns linked to the sinter plant, and the clear advantages of the EAF if compared directly rather than as related processes (see Table 4.4).

In the case of cokemaking, the lack of suitable technologies to reduce the considerable problems with fugitive emissions from its various stages (charging, coking, firing, pushing and quenching), also the toxicity of

Table 4.4   *Integrated and EAF plants: principal emissions (%) –*
            contributions by processes (excl. coke plant)

| Emission | Total g/t | Integrated | | | |
		Sinter plant	Blast furnace	BOF and CC	Rolling
Dust	640	69.5	13.3	7.0	10.1
CO	27 280	92.7	1.3	5.9	—
SO_2	1 830	66.9	7.9	—	25.1
NO_x	1 050	60.0	8.5	0.9	30.5
Landfill	51 kg/t	—	9.8	81.4	8.8

Emission	Total g/t	EAF	EAF and CC	Rolling
DUST	165		60.6	39.4
CO	2 500		100.0	—
SO_2	60		83.4	16.6
NO_x	500		50.0	50.0
Landfill	205.5 kg/t		97.3	2.7

Source: EC (1996).

water discharges and solid byproducts make the search for alternative processes more urgent. While most processes can be improved upon with end-of-pipe and cleaner technologies, the example of cokemaking reveals that certain processes need to be phased out and replaced with considerably cleaner alternatives. An important development in this area is the option of pulverized carbon injection (PCI) directly into the blast furnace. It will be many years before cokemaking will be replaced in the integrated process, but it is unlikely that it will continue in its present form for long due to the environmental management challenges and costs that it creates. Until that time, good housekeeping and technologies such as coke dry quenching and desulphurization of coke oven gas are encouraged as ways of reducing the emissions burden from this phase of the production process.

Despite the slow introduction of replacements for traditional ironmaking, the sector has achieved considerable emissions reductions since the 1970s when regulations became more widespread and better enforced, in developed economies in particular. In the US, 14.5 percent of capital spending between 1971 and 1978 was for pollution abatement (Hirschhorn, 1981), while the UK steel industry now uses 40 percent less energy to produce a tonne of steel compared with the 1970s, effectively halving CO_2 emissions (UK Steel Association, pers. comm.). Beyond emissions and energy reductions, there have also been projects to improve plant landscapes, to reduce noise and to remediate past damage dating back to this period (Shikimura and Miyawaki, 1974; Hirai, 1974).

Atmospheric emissions continue to be the key pollution medium of concern since firms have to meet regulatory standards across a wide range of pollutants, from SO_2, CO, NO_x and VOCs to zinc, molybdenum and cadmium. The principal strategy utilized against atmospheric emissions continues to be end-of-pipe capture and collection. While attention to the quality of raw materials and better use of those materials increases, thus ensuring more efficient transformation and reduced byproduct emissions, air emissions still account for the largest investment in environmental control. In terms of production, the factors of equipment, scale, age, raw materials inputs, and process and control systems all play a role in determining emissions levels; site location is also highly influential in terms of impacts and regulatory constraints.

For EAF firms, dust emissions are currently the principal cause for concern. Dust collection systems are present on all sites but these dusts require reprocessing in order to separate metals that can be reused. With high maintenance costs for bag filters and increasing landfill costs for byproduct disposal, firms are innovating in this area. Examples of this include the partnership of Co-Steel (UK) and Britannia Zinc for recycling zinc, and dust recycling through the furnace in the cases of Krupp

Edelstahlprofile (Germany) and DDS (Denmark). In Spain, many EAF plants have their own landfill sites, making landfill deposits rather than treatment and recycling the more practicable option and reducing the need for innovative alternatives.

The division of emissions into primary and secondary ('fugitive') categories is an important one since it is difficult to measure secondary emissions which evade the principal collection technologies. It is estimated that plants underestimate these latter emissions and that, compared with plants which capture these emissions, the underestimation can be as much as two orders of magnitude (EC, 1996). Since the technologies to combat primary emissions are highly effective when well managed, and are widely applied, it is these secondary emissions which require increased attention. Much of the management of these fugitive contaminants involves effective maintenance, such as in the coke oven batteries, and the channelling of emissions into capture systems within enclosed production areas. Continued investment in gases and particulate control, collection and recycling will be required for some time in order for firms to meet continuing reductions in emissions limits, to deal with contaminants previously weakly regulated (such as dioxins and furans), and to combat pressures for new economic instruments such as carbon and energy taxes.

Water pollution control in the industry is well advanced around the world. As chemical and biological waste water treatment technologies improve, water contamination will continue to diminish. Apart from specific incidents (in response to production problems) and specific locational problems, technological efforts and new circulation and treatment systems have largely resolved previous problems. The outcome is that few firms have problems meeting environmental compliance for water discharges. Beyond improved treatment, firms have also sought to recycle water more effectively, in closed or semi-closed circuits within the whole plant, cascading from one piece of equipment to the next, or independent systems for each major operation in the production process.

Water preservation with the use of circuits can result in zero discharge although a normal target figure would be 95 percent recirculation; loss may be derived from evaporation such as slag cooling although this does not qualify as discharge (EC, 1995, 1996). On-site purification plants ensure that water discharges meet the standards required prior to discharge. Each plant has its own particular water issues, ranging from brackish water availability which impacts upon equipment efficiency (Sidmar in Belgium), to the case of a Belgian firm (ALZ) which changed its use of acids for the pickling process in order to reduce high nitrogen emissions in its low flow water discharge stream. The latter is an example of regulations leading to innovative responses within the production process rather than weaker end-of-pipe responses.

Despite major advances, the range of potential pollutants and indicators such as BOD, COD and temperature mean that water monitoring and control remains a critical activity for environmental management teams. As wastewater treatment systems improve, so do the demands of the regulatory standards. Beyond standards that are similar across the world (often based on US Environmental Protection Agency regulations), specific standards are also implemented to cater for local conditions, water supply and quality (surface and groundwater), for example, low ammonia limits in the case of Brazil. It is these local quality demands that lead to wide variations between countries and individual firms, making comparative analysis difficult. As with dioxins in the case of atmospheric emissions, discharges of specific contaminants such as phenols and cyanide, which may threaten waterways and drinking water supplies, are being more strictly controlled.

In the area of solid waste, rising landfill costs have provoked innovative responses from firms. Most firms now aim to reuse, sell or recycle over 90 percent of their products and byproducts. The intention is to move beyond the current situation whereby 11 Mt of integrated plant slag and 5.7 Mt of EAF slag are landfilled each year around the world (IISI, 1994). Landfill charging and the recognition that recycling and reuse of byproducts can reduce waste volumes and raw materials costs have had strong impacts across the sector. Responses have varied since there are national policy variations for the use of byproducts, particularly for blast furnace slag and steelmaking slag. In many countries they can be used in cement production, construction and agricultural use; however, there are restrictions in other countries that lead to additional disposal costs.

Without doubt, the rise in landfill charging has provided an important incentive in encouraging higher levels of reuse and recycling of solid byproducts, to the extent that the term 'byproduct' has superseded the term 'waste' within the industry. Where landfill regulations and charges are having a powerful impact on strategy, there are cases of firms reassessing existing landfills, for example, extracting ferrous materials previously landfilled, increasing on-site recycling, and firms and associations bringing pressure to bear on relevant authorities involved in categorizing byproducts for further use in order to open up downstream opportunities for sale or transfer. An important caveat to this development, however, relates to those firms that own their own landfill sites, therefore pay little or no landfill charge and that, as a result, have few incentives to reconsider their solid waste management strategies.

Other areas of concern include demolition of redundant plant and subsequent land remediation. Increasingly remediation costs are being considered by firms which are coming under regulatory pressure for past environmental degradation and clean-up costs. Noise pollution is a further consideration for urban-based firms since noise complaints are the most common form of plant criticism. For older firms, separation between the site and residential areas is often limited, whilst newer firms have experienced the encroachment of residential areas on to the limits of industrial spaces. Noise has always been a concern of firms but traditionally local residents were steel workers or linked to the mill in some way (multiplier activities, services, and so on), but this situation has changed in recent decades, leading to less tolerance and rising complaints.

With energy costs accounting for up to 20 percent of production costs (IISI, 1998), the desire to improve energy efficiency has been a significant driver in environmental performance improvements. When viewed in terms of life cycle analysis, these energy concerns and responses are also very influential in relation to energy production and environmental contamination from the power sector. There is no doubt that energy savings have had a positive effect on the overall environmental impact of each firm. One only has to assess the decline in CO_2 emissions from plants since the 1970s and equate this decline with energy price rises during this period, that is, 1973 and 1979, to note the energy–environment synergy. A concern in terms of energy is that major reductions were achieved during the 1970s and 1980s but that the rate of energy consumption reduction has moderated significantly and it will be difficult to maintain previous downward trends.

There is a wide range of pollution media and contaminants involved in contemporary iron and steel production. The task facing environmental regulators and environmental management teams is to reduce emissions and discharges without transferring the pollution burden to other media, and without negatively affecting production and productivity. As regulations are tightened for particular contaminants and are introduced for others, the complexity of the task increases. It is clear that end-of-pipe strategies are reaching their limits, that the steel industry continues to be a significant contributor to national aggregate pollution, and that individual firms are leading polluters in numerous local contexts. For these reasons, the environmental factor in iron and steel production will increase rather than decrease in terms of short- and medium-term planning.

International changes in steel production, ownership and orientation have occurred alongside an increased awareness of industry–environment challenges, with consequent responses in terms of environmental management strategies and investments in environmental technologies. Pressures from government and stakeholders (that is, shareholders, workers and neighbours) have led to increased regulatory compliance, greater environmental transparency (for example, environmental reporting), and increased responsiveness to environmental protection in the larger firms in particular. New process technologies have improved not only environmental performance but have also contributed to greater efficiency and rising total factor productivity. In management terms, environment departments and environmental responsibilities across production departments have led to increased environmental awareness of workers and neighbouring communities (via training and outreach programmes), improved monitoring and procedures, and better communication of environmental change within the firm and beyond. Despite these positive notes, however, many challenges remain. Variations between large and small firms, plants of different vintages, technologies and products, plants in urban and rural areas, and plants operating under different regulatory constraints all lead to diverse pressures and responses on a firm-by-firm, plant-by-plant basis. Some of these variations are highlighted within the country case studies.

GLOBAL TRENDS

The iron and steel industry of the 1970s has been revolutionized by the processes of liberalization and privatization during the 1980s and 1990s. The sector is now highly globalized, with increased levels of trade and significantly different geographical patterns of supply and demand. The world trade in finished steel as a percentage of world steel production increased from 23.2 percent in 1975 to 43.3 percent in 1997 (IISI, various), revealing the shift away from domestic steel production for domestic consumption towards a more internationalized picture of production, trade and consumption. There have been important regional dimensions to the globalization process, with firms and national sectors focusing on different types of products depending on specific client linkages, such as British Steel (UK) (now Corus), or broader national economic demands, such as POSCO (Republic of Korea).

In terms of environmental management issues, it is significant to reflect on the location and trade of products such as coke, sinter and semi-finished products which bear most of the environmental load of the production process, and the high value-added long and flat products which generate greater revenues from each unit of crude steel. Those firms or countries which retain high coke and sinter inputs per unit of production and produce semi-finished products for export would appear to be internalizing more of the environmental costs involved in iron and steel production, and performing less well than firms which have moved towards alternative ironmaking technologies and high value-added products.

The most rapid increase in this process took place during the 1990s, following the extensive rationalization and privatization of developed world iron and steel production in the 1980s. In Western Europe, excess capacity, competitive international prices and the end of government subsidies were all factors contributing to this process and leading to plant closures, labour contraction, increased capital intensity, and the reorientation of production towards new products and markets (see Bain, 1992; Hudson, 1994). Changes in ownership have been critical to the restructuring and reorientation processes as the traditional links between the state, powerful trades unions and nationalized steel plants have been replaced.

Globalization of trade has been accompanied by the globalization of investment characterized by joint ventures, takeovers and new branch plants, for example, the formation of Thyssen-Krupp and the merger of British Steel and Hoogovens to form the Corus group. Joint ventures may range from technical training and assistance agreements (low integration) to full equity joint ventures (high integration) but the notion of integrating activities and capacities rather than acting in isolation has become a characteristic of the global sector, being particularly strong in the case of Asian firm arrangements with US firms operating plants in the US (Kim, 1997). These new organizations are leaner than their predecessors, having shed the previous state social functions associated with regional development and high levels of employment which gave the steel sector such a strategic importance within national and regional economies. Apart from labour contraction, productivity increases are another indicator of how different firms and national iron and steel sectors have adapted, rationalized and refocused their activities via new technologies (such as continuous casting), products and markets. The rise in environmental pressures, from regulations and public awareness, has accompanied these changes and created a new area of attention for plant level management (pollution abatement) and also for strategic management (for example, public relations issues, producer–client linkages).

While in some countries the process was achieved dramatically during the early and mid-1980s, other countries are still in the process of change. This trend is similar in other developed economy contexts while the changes in industrializing and transitional economies have been more varied, such as domestic demand increases in Brazil and heavy recent rationalization in the transitional economies of Eastern and Central Europe.

Although steel production growth rates have declined considerably since the 1970s, global steel output still increases decade by decade. The key difference is that the increases are taking place in industrializing economies, thus changing the traditionally high contribution of developed economy steel sectors to global steel production year on year. Figures 4.2 and 4.3, and Table 4.5 reveal these changes in terms of national and regional production and shares. Of greatest interest is the collapse of former Soviet Union production and the steady rise of Chinese production. In contrast to the wider EU situation of very slow growth and large-scale capacity reductions, the industrializing

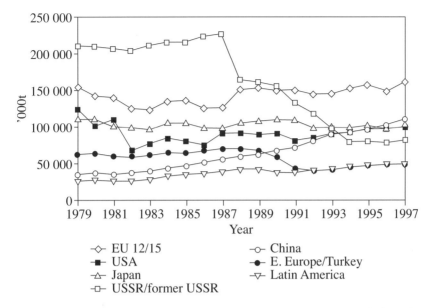

Notes: EU 12/15: figures from 1988 include EU 15 calculations. Eastern Europe includes the following countries: Bulgaria, Czechoslovakia, German Democratic Republic (to 1990), Hungary, Poland, Romania. Latin America includes Argentina, Brazil, Chile, Mexico, Venezuela.

Source: IISI (various).

Figure 4.2   Crude steel production, 1979–97

economies have revealed a quite different pattern over the period. In particular one can focus on Korea and Brazil, which contribute the lion's share of Asian (excluding Japan and China) and Latin American production respectively (see Table 4.5).

Trends in terms of products and technologies are also different from those of the early 1980s. In many developing and transitional economies, there is still a tendency towards high volumes of bulk steel products of lower qualities produced at low prices. In many cases domestic demand assists in the high production volumes achieved and this feeds into exports and competitive export prices. Against this industrializing economy perspective on steel production, many developed economies have taken a different approach to the global steel market. New technologies and demands for specialized, higher quality steels and steel tailored for clients' needs have created a lower volume, higher quality market. With added value on their products, many developed economy producers have revealed a clear strategic approach to the changing

1979 Crude steel production (%)

1988 Crude steel production (%)

1997 Crude steel production (%)

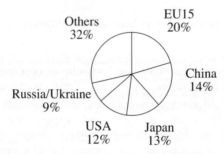

Source: IISI (various).

Figure 4.3   Share in steel production, 1979, 1988, 1997

Table 4.5   Leading steel producing countries, 1979 and 1997: international ranking by output (million tonnes)

1979				1997			
Developed		Developing and communist bloc		Developed		Developing and transitional	
USA	123.7	Soviet Union	149.1	Japan	104.5	China	107.6
Japan	111.7	China	34.5	USA	97.5	Russia	46.4
W. Germany	46.0	Brazil	13.9	Germany	45.0	Rep. Korea	42.6
Italy	24.2	Poland	19.2	Italy	25.8	Ukraine	24.7
France	23.4	Czechoslovakia	14.8	France	19.8	Brazil	26.2
UK	21.5	Romania	12.9	UK	18.5	India	23.7
Canada	16.0	India	10.1	Canada	15.6	Taiwan	16.0
Belgium	13.5	Rep. Korea	7.6	Spain	13.7	Mexico	14.3

Source: IISI (various).

global steel market; the US and Japan are particularly successful in this respect (see Figure 4.4).

An overview of production by quality (1996) reveals that 14.3 percent of EU 15 production is alloy steel (as opposed to carbon steel), of which 4.1 percent is stainless steel. Comparisons are as follows: Brazil 5.1 percent (0.9 percent); Korea 10.2 percent (2.1 percent); and Czech Republic 6.9 percent (0.4 percent) (IISI, various). Whilst a division of global production into these two camps (bulk, low price and specialized, high price) is oversimplified, most firms have had to pursue one of these strategic avenues. A complication of this situation is the orientation of the firm between domestic and international markets, also the production process involved and the particular demands created in terms of flexibility and product composition and quality. Generally speaking, EU firms have moved towards production and international trade in value-added flat products, as has Korea, while Central and Eastern European countries continue to produce and trade lower value bulk steel, such as ingots and semis.

A further indicator of the quality of the product and the degree of sophistication of the process is the division between crude steel ingot production and the production of continuously cast steel. Continuous casting is both a more efficient means of producing steel (in terms of productivity and quality), as well as being more environmentally friendly, therefore, high levels of continuously cast steel are regarded as state-of-the-art in terms of technology adoption and a process-based measure of environmental protection (see Figure 4.5). In this area, the EU reveals its technological intensity

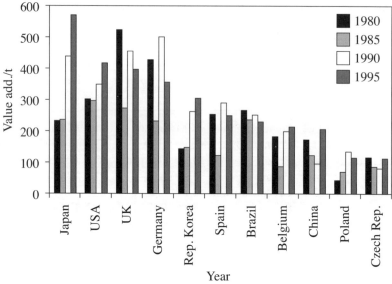

Sources: UNIDO (1997); IISI (various).

Figure 4.4   Manufacturing value added per unit of crude steel production (ISIC 371: iron and steel, US$/tonne)

although it is surpassed by Korea which has the highest level of continuously cast steel of any of the leading steel producing economies (98.7 percent in 1997). An explanation for this phenomenon is the relatively recent construction of the leading Korean steel plants, in which continuous casting technologies have been employed from the outset.

In terms of environmental protection, more important than the product range is the production of sinter and coke. Since these are the two most potentially polluting processes within the steel plant (although considerably controlled by end-of-pipe equipment in most cases), to reduce production of these materials will inevitably lead to environmental performance improvements. In the case of the developed economies there is a clear trend of reduced production, whereas China has accelerated its production in this area, led by the large and expanding firms such as Shoungang and Baoshan; the Taiwanese firms China Steel and Mieh Loong Co. have also increased capacity (Moody's Investors Service, 1995; see also Figures 4.6 and 4.7).

Although some developed economy firms may well have decreased their demand for coke through technologies such as pulverised carbon injection (PCI), the trade balance of coke for different regions and countries reveals that there was a shift in global coke production and consumption during the early

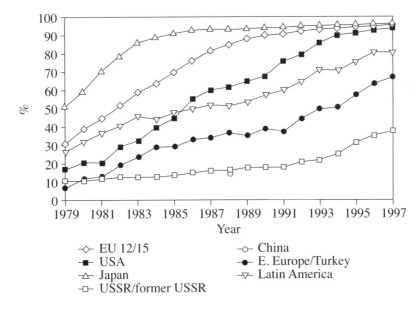

Source: IISI (various).

Figure 4.5   Production of continuously-cast steel, 1979–97

1990s (see Table 5.1 in following chapter). This trend can be linked to the regulatory pressures on coke production controls in developed countries in particular, and the difficulties in 'cleaning up' this process.

The major transformation to take place in the next decade will be in the supply of steel to meet increased domestic demand in the industrializing economies. The question is the extent to which this can be met by domestic production and how developed economy producers can enter these markets, through either exports or production *in situ*. Since it is unlikely that exports of anything but high quality, high value steels would be price competitive within such economies, the choice of market entry via production activity has become important for many leading companies. This globalization of ownership and location of production will require not only major restructuring in terms of firm organization but also in terms of sensitivity to the specifics of each country, such as industrial and trade policies and trends in steel demand.

At the national level, there is a wide range of steel production strategies. One can contrast the situations in China and India, for example, which have a large number of plants for regional development and national scale reasons, with the cases of Korea, the UK, France and Luxembourg, which have large single firms that contribute the bulk of national production. In many cases the

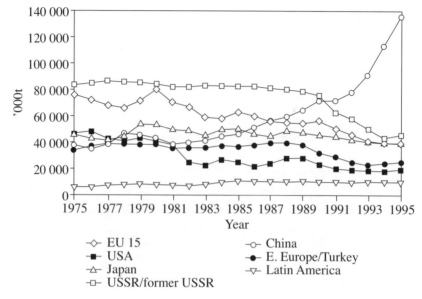

Source: IISI (various).

Figure 4.6   Production of coke, 1975–95

leading firms have become involved in group activities, buying up other steel
plants and forming joint ventures. Their production is therefore based on
production at more than one site. It is these strategic activities which
characterized the globalization of the iron and steel sector during the 1990s.

It is still the case that firm production is predominantly based in one
country; however, there is a slow movement towards an increased contribution
from fully or partly owned plants around the world. For example, the Korean
firm POSCO is developing production activities in East and South East Asia,
while Corus has a plant in the southern US. In Europe, sectoral restructuring
has led to a significant increase in non-national ownership of plants, for
example, Cockerill Sambre's purchase of the East German company Ekostahl;
also the grouping of firms, as in Spain where two major groups of EAF firms
developed during the 1990s, one of which is the Marcial Ucin Group of four
previously independent companies. A further example of the globalization of
the industry is the strategy of the Ispat International group which owns a large
number of mini-mills (EAF plants) in countries as disparate as Iran and
Trinidad. Despite noting these recent and growing trends, however, it is still
the case that most companies remain nationally owned and are not reorienting
themselves quickly towards global production and commercial networks. It is
principally the leading international firms which are engaged most actively in

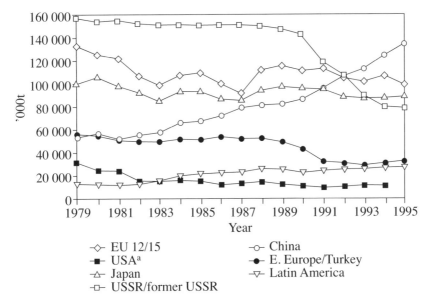

Note: [a] USA figures are for sinter consumption rather than production.

Source: IISI (various).

Figure 4.7 Production of sinter, 1979–95

this process. Most smaller firms, especially those producing for domestic regional markets, are either unable to adopt similar strategies for financial and scale reasons, or are uninterested in doing so since they have sufficient local demand at current production levels.

INITIAL OBSERVATIONS

In terms of the iron and steel industry and its impact on the environment, a separation must be made between the two principal routes of steelmaking: EAF and integrated. The argument that EAF is a cleaner route must be balanced by the fact that there will always be a demand for virgin steel in order to maintain the levels of scrap with which the EAF operates. In each route there are different environmental considerations. For EAF, there is the concern of dust capture efficiency, landfilling and zinc recovery, also that of the negative effects of impurities in scrap metal (which increase with each scrap-steel conversion). Integrated plants have the considerations of remedying the emissions-intensive technologies of the ironmaking phase, and of dealing with large volumes of byproducts. For both routes there continues to be the need for better monitoring and measuring of equipment and procedures, also the need to improve energy efficiency and reduce atmospheric emissions by improving capture systems and reducing fugitive releases. In order to assess improvements that are being made in these areas, there must be more sampling and analysis standardization. Currently this does not exist and comparative work is therefore complicated for regulators and research organizations; the EU's own research in this area in 1996 raised this as a principal obstacle to further investigation into the steel industry and its environmental impacts.

Despite concerns regarding data comparisons, the arguments of producers that they have achieved considerable emissions reductions since the 1970s and that they now face higher environmental investments with less environmental performance improvements (a case of diminishing returns) is a valid one. However, the suggestion is that the current approach to environmental performance, of end-of-pipe systems and very high levels of recycling, is reaching its limits. The next step is one of significant process change that current technology developments have yet to meet. Best available techniques (BAT) will assist in this process, but this approach is not in itself a solution since it remains voluntary and a distinction has to be made between technologies and their use since the same technology will have differing emissions impacts according to how it is installed and operated, and the local conditions that prevail (EC, 1996). Although firms and trade associations are aware of the need to move forward on environmental performance issues, such as IISI and individual firm support for the Business Charter for Sustainable Development, the achievement of sustainable steel production will require an intensification of efforts at the firm and sectoral level, not only in technology, but also in management and communication.

5. The European Union iron and steel sector

SECTORAL DEVELOPMENT AND COMPETITIVENESS

The European Union iron and steel sector has been influential in the international production and consumption of steel products for over a century, yet the changes that have taken place since the late 1970s in terms of national restructuring and international patterns of demand and product diversification have been the most significant in its history. The principal characteristics of the sector following the most intensive phase of restructuring are its continuing domination by German output, followed by Italy, France and the UK, with a Northern European focus on integrated production and a Southern European shift towards EAF technologies. While European firms were closely tied to national clients until the 1980s, they are now operating in a highly competitive global market and exports as a percentage of EU production have increased from 31.4 percent (1980) to 61.7 percent (1997), although in spite of this increase the region has experienced a declining share of worldwide steel exports (see Table 5.3).

In response to the falling apparent consumption per capita of steel in the EU, the regions of rising consumption, particularly Asia, have been targeted for exports, joint ventures and foreign direct investment. The product range has also changed, with a movement towards higher value-added production and a specialization in particular products tailored to client needs, especially for the motor industry. This specialization in steel products can be seen in the rise in non-alloy carbon steel production by only 8 percent (1990–7) whereas higher value alloy steels (45 percent) and stainless steels (57 percent) have grown rapidly during the same period (IISI, various).

In trade terms, the picture is one of a successful concentration on flat and long products, and a tendency towards importing ingots and semi-finished steel for finishing. Since the environmental impacts of the sector are concentrated in the phases of crude steel production, there are environmental benefits that accrue from adding value to the product rather than producing it in its crudest form for sale to other steel firms for finishing or processing. It is clear that the EU steel sector has been effective in focusing on value-added

strategies by generating large trade surpluses of flat and long products, against
a more variable performance for ingots and semi-finished products (see Figure
5.1). The rising relative contribution of EAF production (29.3 percent in 1988
to 36.9 percent in 1997; IISI, 1998) against integrated production is also a
positive step in terms of the EU sector's total emissions load due to the lower
per unit emissions of this route. However, the true environmental cost should
also take into account the environmental impacts from the initial virgin steel
which later becomes scrap for use in the EAF.

   The massive restructuring during the 1980s and 1990s has heavily influenced
these production trends and the overall competitiveness of the EU sector in the
globalized iron and steel industry. This restructuring came as a response to the
long-term protection of the industry by the European Coal and Steel
Community (ECSC) and member states. High levels of output and declining
demand in Western Europe triggered a crisis which was recognized as early as
1974. Two influential processes were already emerging (see Howell *et al.*,
1988; Carruth, 1989; Bain, 1992; Hogan, 1994): the shift in production and
consumption to developing economies which affected growth rates in
developed economy production; and a slowdown in international consumption.
With declining rates of domestic consumption in many developed economies,
the trade in steel products became more important and more competitive.

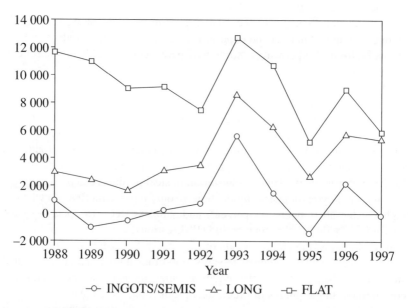

Source: IISI (1998).

Figure 5.1   EU 15: trade balance by major product group ('000 tonnes)

Some EU countries, such as the UK, began restructuring early in the 1980s; in other countries the restructuring has been more recent, as in Spain where restructuring took place following entry into the EC in 1986. In all cases, there have been significant changes in ownership, processes and production levels, driven by privatization, takeovers, grouping and strategic alliances (Eurofer, personal communication; Hudson, 1994). Different timings of transformation have led to continuing criticisms of subsidy and state intervention in the sector; for example, in 1996 the British Iron and Steel Producers Association (BISPA, now the UK Steel Association) successfully filed a case against the EC's decision to authorize the Luxembourg government to pay environmental aid to the company Arbed. The European Steel Aid Code established in 1991 allows state aid to companies to bring existing plants into compliance with new environmental standards but Arbed sought aid for a new EAF construction. Examples of projects that have been approved under the Steel Aid Code include adaptation of a desulphurization installation for coke gas (Sidmar) and insulation of an EAF to reduce noise emissions (ALZ). Both of these cases were in order to comply with the Flemish environmental legislation (Vlarem II of August 1995) and were approved in 1996 (BISPA, 1996; EC, 1997a).

The different timescales of restructuring and support reveal the highly heterogeneous nature of the sector across the EU. Differences are evident in terms of integrated versus EAF plants and also in terms of product ranges. The bulk of EU steel is produced in Northern Europe by German, French and UK integrated firms, and in Southern Europe by Italian and Spanish EAF firms. Integrated production is also evident in other countries but in only a few locations and at lower production levels. In contrast, EAF production sites are numerous and scattered widely across the region, being particularly important within Italy and Spain. In terms of products, the large integrated firms concentrate on the automotive and construction sectors while the smaller EAF plants focus on niche products, such as seamless tubes and specialist steels, particularly stainless.

Trade is also variable across the region. There is considerable trade within the EU for reasons of product availability and also the advantage of lower transport costs compared with American, African or Asian sources. Prior to integration with the EU, Scandinavian and Austrian steel accounted for most imported steel by value. Currently, Russia and Central and Eastern European countries are also important exporters to the EU, alongside sources further afield, particularly Brazil, South Africa and the US. In the case of South Africa, stainless steel forms a large share by value whereas other sources provide more standard flat, long or semi-finished products.

Steelmaking costs across Western Europe and the world underline the differences in production costs that have been effectively created by the market interventions of various states and commissions. Although steel prices are the key to the success of steel industries around the world, in recent decades the impact of non-price competition, marketing and distribution have gained ground and affected competitiveness. Also, product innovations such as coated steels and near net shape casting have headed the new process technologies which have also altered the wider picture of steel pricing. Despite these factors, however, the overcapacity in international production of steel continues to put pressure on the sector, especially within developed economies where domestic growth in demand remains low.

Following the major restructuring of the 1980s, the 1990s were characterized by highly competitive steel prices on international markets and increasing relative output from newly industrializing and transitional economies. The EU sector has been transformed from the heavy industrial sector of the 1960s and 1970s with the rise of EAF production and the push towards more specialized, client-oriented rather than bulk steels. To remain competitive, the pursuit of ever-increasing productivity levels, improved management and marketing techniques and niche market domination are likely to dominate the EU steel agenda. Environmental protection and control is also on this agenda (see Barton, 1999).

All these developments have led to competitiveness impacts. The competitiveness issue has grown as the EU sector has been forced into increased trading levels and a more 'global approach' to business. With the EU market now significantly less subsidized and less restrictive than previously, there is more intense competition between EU and non-EU producers. For example, while the volume of EU steel exports increased by 27 percent (1988–97), imports increased by 43 percent (IISI, various). The basic argument behind competitiveness within the EU sector is that of a lack of a level playing field, due to subsidies and other support mechanisms. The response from non-traditional producers to increased competition within the global economy has been to develop in terms of technologies and products. The head of the ECSC Steel Division makes the point that it is the 'intelligence' of the material, in terms of market suitability, which will determine EU competitiveness in the near future in the face of low-added-value products from low production cost locations (Zegers, 1997).

The role of environmental factors in competitiveness is as yet not fully understood, principally due to poor data. However, as profit margins have diminished, the impacts of environmental pressures have risen and a host of managerial responses have been generated, from raw material selection and energy use through to marketing and sales strategies influenced by 'green' consumer demands downstream of the steelmaking process. This is especially the case in relation to the motor industry, which has been moving towards lighter cars and higher recyclability in response to government and consumer pressures for cleaner, more efficient transport options. Although there are market drivers which are influencing sectoral responses to environmental issues, it is state regulation that remains as the principal driver of environmental protection measures.

REGULATORY REGIMES AND IMPACTS

Although the EU environmental directives and regulations encourage minimum standards in terms of emissions, discharges and byproduct controls, it is the role of member states to enforce these standards via their relevant authorities. Stricter standards may be applied beyond these minimum criteria, but the goal of a level playing field is central to the notion of European regulations and their enforcement. In the case of iron and steel, a division between Northern and Southern European producers has often been drawn. The implication is that Southern European producers produce under relaxed regulatory conditions, while Northern European producers struggle to comply with stricter regimes. Under the microscope, the variations across the EU are considerable, not only in monitoring and inspection norms, but in terms of emissions levels (beyond the minimum), and the legal process for dealing with infringements.

At a 1993 UNECE seminar on 'Metallurgy and Ecology', the theme of environmental impact and economic performance was addressed. Three important aspects were raised:

- uniformity of standards alongside the need for flexibility based on scientific values, clarity, adaptability, and effective application;
- the 'polluter pays' principle and the need to identify who is the polluter: the steelmaker, the user of the scrap, or the consumer;
- the legal definitions of waste and the balance between recycling and dumping. (*Steel Times*, July 1993, 308–10)

These are the same issues that regulators have to engage with since it is not only the issue of emissions control that they must confront, but also the economic performance of the firm relative to other producers, and the firm's ability to develop an environmental strategy. This has been recognized by the UK Environment Agency within its 3Es approach which incorporates Emissions, Efficiency, and Economics in an assessment.

Regulatory bodies across the EU are at varying levels of institutional development and change. In the UK, for example, the precursors to the EU IPPC (Integrated Pollution Prevention and Control) directive are already in place. The IPC strategy is currently in operation and the voluntary BS7750

Environmental Management Standard was introduced in 1992 to prepare for the EC's EMAS scheme. The variations are important since different bodies have different institutional strategies, leading to varying levels of compliance. The greater differences between member states derive from regional and local variations on requirements above and beyond minimum levels. The factors that stimulate firms are highly variable, therefore it is difficult to state that one approach or another should be universally applied. Different firms have different environmental weaknesses, according to process, raw materials quality, geographical location, and other variables. The difficulty for regulators is to be sensitive to these specificities but also to implement the law. The issues most often repeated by regulators in terms of difficulties with firms (rather than non-compliance) are those of diversion of resources and lack of suitable environmental technologies (in terms of process and production methods – PPMs). It is apparent that there are competitive implications in the diversion of investment capital into environmental technologies and strategies in order to meet new directives and regulations.

At the level of environmental law, the EC has been very active since 1992 through IMPEL (European Union Network for the Implementation and Enforcement of Environmental Law). IMPEL promotes legislation and programme development, compliance procedures, and enforcement strategies. The Network attempts to move towards greater uniformity across member states in terms of regulatory systems for environmental protection (EC DGXI, personal communication; IMPEL, 1996). It is clear that the relationship between regulators and producers continues to vary considerably according to region, country and to cases in particular. For example, the Flemish regulatory authority AMINAL (Environment, Nature, Land and Water Administration) is an institution which has adopted strict German air emissions legislation, the 'TA Luftnorm', within its VLAREM regulations, and is constrained in its options of flexibility and collaboration with firms by a legal code which requires infringements to be followed up through the judicial process (AMINAL, personal communication; AMINAL, 1996). Within the Flemish regulatory system established for 1997–2001 (MINA 2) there are three pivots: the environmental report which is drawn up every two years; the environmental policy, every five years; and the annual environment plan. These pivots aim to establish five defined principles (AMINAL, 1996): the prevention principle or the principle of preventative action; the precaution principle; the preference for measures aimed at the source; the stand-still principle; and 'polluter pays'. The pivots and principles are well developed but their execution is hampered by the lack of judicial cooperation.

The Flemish experience can be compared with a highly collaborative and localized system of regulation employed in the Basque Country, where the autonomous regional government is the authority responsible for the environment but where local municipalities also have competencies. The outcome is a flexible system organized as locally as possible (Basque Government Environment Division, personal communication). While the Flemish system is strict and can enforce compliance with regulations through the courts, the Basque system is cooperative and achieves environmental objectives via firm collaboration as far as possible. The recognition that regulators can achieve environmental performance improvements via encouragement and assistance rather than a 'big stick' approach appears to be generally accepted. For this reason, prescriptive legislation and single protocol regulations are not helpful to regulators who require flexibility in their operations (Spanish Ministry of Environment, personal communication). The issue relating to the latter, however, is to what extent should flexibility allow set, legal emissions standards to be exceeded. The regulatory agency has to tread the fine line between an environmental police force and an environmental performance facilitator, and this stance is likely to vary in terms of relations with different firms.

Ultimately, compliance with directives and regulations depends on a variety of factors. Within the EU, the question of member state enforcement and the establishment of a level playing field is a principal concern (EC DGXI, personal communication; Eurofer, personal communication). Not until there is a greater balance across member states along the regulatory path, from regulatory development, monitoring and enforcement to penalties, can issues of competitiveness and the environmental impacts of the industries in different countries become clearer. It will be the role of the EC then to encourage compliance by eliminating some of the elements that impede the translation of European level agreements into active legislation at the member state level (Carruth, 1989).

The system that is currently in place is based on limits in terms of quality and quantities of particular pollutants, that is, maximum levels and maximum volumes. These limits vary according to particular technologies and are organized on a local basis via authorizations whereby the regulator stipulates the conditions applicable to a specific firm. Although there are EU and nationally agreed limits in place for certain contaminants, the limits stipulated within authorizations will differ widely across firms due to production levels, installed equipment and local conditions (that is, topography, residential proximity). It is the responsibility of the firm to provide emissions data to the regulatory authority and it is on these data that penalties are imposed. The extent of these data and requirements of periodic independent verification varies across authorities. It is the highly variable character of these regulatory limits and their monitoring that has prompted the more technological control approach of IPPC. Although the same technology may vary significantly in terms of performance according to maintenance and plant specifics (for example, in connection with other equipment, production levels, raw materials used), it is likely that this type of approach will be easier to monitor, provide greater security of improved environmental performance and less regional and national variations than are currently experienced across the EU.

The EU iron and steel industry is currently undergoing transition in terms of regulatory pressures. In September 1996, the EC Council adopted the IPPC directive, following the integrated pollution control regime implemented in the UK in 1992. Under the IPPC, the concept of best available techniques (BAT) has been established which will impact on producers in terms of operating permits and associated emission limit values (ELVs) (Eurofer, 1996). The specifications for IPPC have been set for targeted sectors and the necessary equipment should be installed by October 2007. Indicators of BAT for the steel sector can be found in a pre-emptive report by the Ministry of Housing, Spatial Planning and Environment (the Netherlands) (1997) in association with Hoogovens (now part of the Corus group).

Despite extensive technological innovation and investment (particularly in capture systems) that have reduced byproduct emissions and discharges substantially since the 1970s, the volumes, range and impacts of contaminants demand a continuous process of reduction. A significant hurdle for the industry and regulators is information regarding the extent of emissions and the ability to compare firms. This was a conclusion of a 1996 EC report on steel and environment based on questionnaire responses from Western European firms. Although emissions measurement methodologies are not always comparable (in terms of sampling methods, analysis methods, time intervals, computation methods, and reference conditions), environment managers are clear about which areas of production require attention: air emissions precede water discharges and solid waste issues, followed by noise and soil remediation issues.

The extent to which the different regulatory regimes impact on firm competitiveness in different countries is not an easy calculation. Clearly there are differential effects from the varying regulatory regimes across the EU, therefore there will be different costs associated with the regime due to the purchase of pollution abatement equipment, the creation of environmental management systems or the payment of penalties. In this respect it is difficult to measure sectoral pollution abatement cost within a specific country since different firms of different ages and technological specifications will lead to different licensing arrangements. For this reason, there is no uniform pollution abatement cost across steel firms in each country.

Rather than identify national variations in regulatory regimes and their impacts in order to establish competitiveness impacts relating to the environment, it is more appropriate to distinguish whether these environmental regulation regimes have a significant impact on competitiveness more generally. In few cases do firms find environmental regulations to be a significant component of their competitive position. When measured against other factors such as raw materials, energy prices and labour, the environmental cost dimension plays a diminished role and it is only when there is a significant and specific requirement for technological changes that these regulations become more influential in competitive considerations.

The introduction of IPPC and a set of technological benchmarks will alter the situation somewhat. Although the IPPC requirements specify a range of technological options and management practices, it will be necessary for some firms to upgrade old equipment or install new equipment. This may lead to high technology expenditure over a limited number of years for these firms but such technologies should also bring benefits in terms of production and energy efficiencies and fewer pressures from regulators. It is unlikely that such firms will be disadvantaged over the longer term by such measures but in view of the highly competitive situation of the international steel market at present there is a question mark as to whether it is possible for some firms to pursue further investment. Despite possible problems, however, the specifications of IPPC have been drawn up with some care by the EU and the sectoral associations. For this reason most of the requirements are already widespread across the steel sector within the EU, and there will be negative repercussions for only a very small number of firms which are unable to respond by 2007.

TECHNOLOGICAL CHANGE

Technological developments with environmental performance aims in the iron and steel industry fall principally into the category of end-of-pipe technologies. These technologies, alongside environmental management procedures and strategies, provide the backbone of environmental responses within the industry. Other technologies of importance are those involved in recycling. The end-of-pipe technologies employed in plants are relatively similar throughout the EU. A common end-of-pipe abatement system is that which deals with dust collection, filtration and purification technologies, trapping and separating a range of byproducts. In most cases, end-of-pipe systems are for capture and landfill or reuse rather than metals recovery for sale; nevertheless, the direction of technological development is towards viewing end-of-pipe systems as ways of making materials and energy savings as well as meeting emissions targets. The need to reduce byproduct disposal (therefore waste) because of cost and competition is a driving factor in this development (Gustave Boël, personal communication; FAFER, personal communication).

Behind the technological innovation and installation issue is the question of finance. Investment decisions at the corporate level have tended to prioritize capital projects with healthier returns rather than environmental technologies. There is also the issue that a global approach to technological change – that any installation not giving satisfactory results should be replaced by a new installation meeting relevant standards – overestimates necessary investment since better process and maintenance procedures may lead to standards achievement (EC, 1996). The member states of the EU have the capacity to assist firms in their environmental technology investments, but the take-up of this programme is varied. Under EU regulations, the government may provide up to 15 percent of the cost of environmental technology investment; however, only in Spain is this extensively employed, via the Industrial and Technological Environmental Programme (PITMA) established in 1990 with the aim of protecting the environment by modernizing industrial apparatus.

With most firms estimating that 5–10 percent of their investment and operating costs are devoted to environmental measures, the issue of how new finance is raised for environmental investments and what types of investment should be postponed to respond to environmental needs (from regulators, clients and civil society pressures) have become a rising concern for executive management rather than just the concern of environmental managers. Although it may be possible to introduce relatively low-cost technologies and methods of managing different types of emissions, such as spraying raw material stockpiles and site roads to reduce dust levels, it is more often the case that significant investment decisions have to be taken on technologies that are similar in scale and cost to many production technologies themselves. This is particularly the case for large atmospheric emissions control technologies such as electrostatic precipitators, or for large, integrated water circulation and treatment systems.

Most decisions regarding the environment focus on the investment issues of control and prevention technologies, yet there are significant environmental issues relating to changes in production technologies such as continuous casting. Continuous casting is important both for productivity and quality outcomes, and also environmental benefits from reduced energy requirements and more manageable emissions from the process *vis-à-vis* traditional casting methods. The same is true for pulverized carbon injection (PCI) which reduces dependence on environmentally problematic cokemaking technologies and also has positive impacts for blast furnace management. Since it is in the EU, Japan and the US that many of the most significant new technological innovations have been adopted most swiftly during the 1980s and 1990s, it is fair to say that there have been significant steps made in the area of environmental protection that have been classified by firms as largely production area investments. For this reason there is an undervaluation of environmental investment more generally since almost all new technologies are more energy efficient and are installed with more efficient emissions control technologies in place.

Pollution abatement costs as understood in terms of environmentally specific emissions control technologies fail to capture the total investment in environmental protection. Rather than taking crude figures based on end-of-pipe environmental technology expenditure, which give a low valuation of environmental investment at 5–10 percent of the total, a figure which allows for the positive environmental outcomes from production technology innovations during the 1980s and 1990s in the EU would register a figure in excess of 10 percent, especially if the energy factor is also calculated as an environmental issue rather than as a separate factor which makes no allowances for environmental impacts from upstream processes. It may well be the case that the narrow firm vision of what constitutes the environment leads to a significant under-representation of the importance, in terms of investment and operation, of environment-related costs.

There are several areas in which firms can improve their performance. For example, it is possible to identify cleaner technologies according to scale: large-scale changes and incremental small-scale changes. The large-scale changes fall into the areas of steel process change (BOF to EAF), iron production process change, and continuous casting. The small-scale changes fall into motor development, burner modifications and other incremental process developments. The ironmaking part of the steel process is highlighted by integrated plant managers as needing attention for its environmental impacts. Due to the environmental impacts to air from these stages of the process, much research and development work on the environment has taken place. These processes have traditionally been suppressed by end-of-pipe abatement systems, principally fabric filters, electrostatic precipitators, wet scrubbers and dry cyclones (IISI/UNEP, 1997).

The bag filter is the most common apparatus for dust removal, with electrostatic precipitators providing the main collection mechanism from the sinter plant, which generates most atmospheric emissions; the electrostatic precipitator is efficient in removing 99.9 percent of dust from flue gases (IISI, 1993; British Steel, personal communication). The problem that now faces managers is the separation of finer particles and trace organics (PCBs and dioxins) and radioactive isotopes since these are expected to be targeted by regulatory authorities in the medium term as other emissions levels are progressively attained. For instance, a large percentage of British Steel's R&D budget has gone into setting-up a Trace Organics Laboratory to focus on how dioxins are created, the extent of their dispersal and their cumulative effects.

Rather than capture systems, it is in the area of technological innovation that environmental protection in the steel sector will be improved. To take the case of cokemaking, for instance, it is only in alternatives to cokemaking rather than cokemaking capture technologies that emissions levels can be managed more effectively. Cokemaking is regarded by most environmental managers of integrated plants as the most problematic production area due to the factors of fugitive emissions from coke oven doors during heating and on filling and discharging the coke ovens also. The range of toxic wastewater effluents also poses significant problems for managers.

In the EU there has been a concerted effort to seek alternatives to cokemaking, especially in Germany for instance where high atmospheric emissions standards make compliance difficult. To date, the opportunities from direct iron reduction as opposed to conventional ironmaking with coke are not suitable to the production conditions in the EU due to high energy costs and current production levels in northern Europe where most integrated steel production takes place. Somewhat more successful has been the use of pulverized carbon injection (PCI) directly into the blast furnace, thus eliminating some of the coke demand. Although new technologies such as PCI are responsible for a general fall in coke production in the EU, which is a very positive sign for local environmental quality, it is also clear that there has been a surge in coke imports into the EU during the 1990s (Figure 5.2). The source of most of these imports is countries which are regarded as having high levels of industrial contamination, such as Poland and China, therefore there would appear to be a process of stricter atmospheric emissions standards and insufficient technological options leading to an outsourcing of coke from outside the EU. The trade balance in the EU, the rest of Europe which is mainly derived from former Central and Eastern Europe, and China can be seen in Table 5.1. The most striking figures are those for Germany which accounts for approximately 40 percent of the EU's coke imports; this would appear to be a clear case of pollution displacement.

The case of cokemaking is the most environmentally significant case of technological change being unable to meet increasingly stringent environmental regulations within the EU steel sector. In most areas there are production and capture technologies that can be installed to facilitate compliance. The reasons why further upgrading of existing technologies or the

Table 5.1   Trade balance: coke, 1990–5 ('000 tonnes)

	1990	1991	1992	1993	1994	1995
EU 15	−495	−1 600	−1 775	−2 572	−2 735	−5 531
Rest of Europe	455	2 648	2 223	1 112	2 211	2 367
China	1 120	1 038	1 571	2 600	3 860	8 860

Source: IISI (1998).

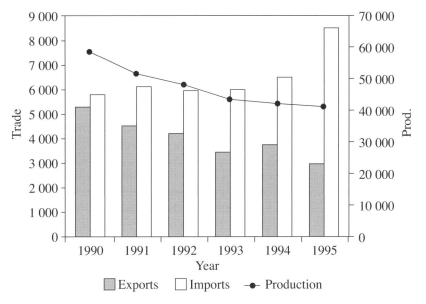

Source: IISI (1998).

Figure 5.2   EU coke production and trade ('000 tonnes)

installation of new technologies do not take place, leading to weaker environmental performance of firms *vis-à-vis* other similar firms (that is, integrated or EAF), are often related to investment strategies and perceived competitiveness issues. Nevertheless, the most important influence over these decision-making processes remains the role of the regulator and other external influences such as clients or community pressures, rather than internal management influences. In most cases, it is possible for firms in the EU to act more proactively in terms of environmental decision-making and investment. However, there are certain areas where technological initiatives remain unsuitable for widespread commercial use, such as direct reduction iron and equipment for EAF dust emissions reductions. In these cases, firms are concerned about future regulatory strengthening and their ability to respond in a cost-effective manner.

ENVIRONMENTAL MANAGEMENT

Management practices are increasingly important in developing successful strategies for environmental protection (see Morris, 1993; von Moltke, 1993; Panorama of EU Industry, 1996). Since the mid-1980s, environmental regulations have become more influential in driving business strategies, with positive environmental performance outcomes as well as energy savings. Costs of infringements, with the ultimate sanction of plant closure, the increasing costs of environmental responses due to competitive steel prices and impending customer demands for environmental accreditation have been behind these responses.

Environment departments vary considerably in terms of staffing levels, centralization or decentralization of activities, and where they fit within the firm structure. Most larger firms established their departments during the early to mid-1980s to respond to the demands and the rising costs in this area. Prior to this, environmental issues were dealt with within utilities, energy or health and safety units. The proximity of these departments and sections remains evident today. For smaller firms, the scale of operation and type of process often means that there is no dedicated environmental department. In the cases of FAFER (Belgium) and Marcial Ucin SA (Spain), environmental functions are included within the remit of a production manager. This can be compared with the large integrated plants such as Sidmar where there are 15 dedicated environmental personnel, and British Steel which has group level environmental personnel and also plant level teams. The principal difference in terms of this range is the ability to respond to the increases in regulatory demands from national and EU regulations, and to innovate and think proactively about ways in which environmental protection can best be achieved in the longer term. Where environmental personnel are few, the likelihood that compliance will be almost the sole objective is considerably higher. For group level environment departments, environmental R&D and environment management for market and public relations ends can also be developed, above and beyond the compliance function.

It is apparent from company publicity and environmental statements, where they exist, that environmental issues are firmly on the corporate agenda although the extent to which this is the case throughout the sector and the degree to which these policies are carried through are more debatable. With most companies investing an average of 5–10 percent of total investment each year in environmental projects, increased awareness of the environment has followed. Most companies do not hold with Porter and van der Linde's 'win–win' approach to environmental investments, however, apart from those that have moved into the environmental technology market specifically. There is little evidence to suggest that there are major cost reductions or profit generating 'win–win' scenarios beyond the environment industry opportunity. For the vast majority of firms, compliance is the driver, rather than a perception of 'green' commercial gain. 'First mover' tactics in environmental technologies and management are not clearly apparent (bar an elite handful), although a broader separation can be made between large groups of companies

– such as Usinor-Sacilor in France and British Steel in the UK – which are advanced in environmental management strategies and environment research and development, and smaller lone companies which struggle to resource environmental needs, from personnel to investments, such as Gustave Boël and FAFER.

It is clear from the larger companies that the forthcoming demands for life cycle analysis (LCA) and EMAS are being tackled vigorously in preparation for future developments in the market and from regulators. For smaller companies operating within a group, such as the Marcial Ucin Group in Spain, these developments are taking place at a group rather than plant level. This environmental pressure from the market place, moving upstream from consumers of steel-based final products through manufacturers to the steel producers themselves, has been an important development since the 1980s. It is no longer solely the regulator bringing pressure to bear on firms but also steel consumers and public pressure at large on environmental issues. In this last regard, many companies have improved their communication with the local community and local government in recent years. In Belgium, Cockerill Sambre maintains communications within the locality as one of the key pivots of its environmental strategy, dedicating a member of staff to this work. Other firms are also working in this direction.

A problem for many companies in terms of the environment is the paucity of data they have regarding the actual costs of environmental strategies. The European Commission is currently working with EUROSTAT in order to develop, with member states, an effective environmental accounting strategy that will allow comparative study. Until that time, firms will remain unsure of their actual environmental costs. The development of EMAS (operationalized voluntarily since 1995) in some larger groups will require that they confront this issue, but the comparability of these data from firm to firm and country to country may be questionable. Despite the lack of strong accounting for environmental costs, environment managers maintain that costs are significant and increasing. The underlying factor of their importance is that environmental investments and operating costs for the maintenance of environmental technologies and systems (which are themselves significant energy users) are a capital diversion.

Besides EMAS, the more globally widespread innovation of the ISO 14.000 series has received little attention from the EU steel sector. Only the largest firms appear to have an interest in certification and this appears to be for public relations and market purposes rather than for environmental performance objectives. Since 14.001 take-up around the world from its beginnings in 1995 is mostly based on market access motivations, fearing indirect environmental protectionism in developed economy markets, the logic for EU firms to be certified clearly has to be different. Most firms are uninterested in the ISO norms since the introduction of IPPC/BAT will dictate how they act and invest for environmental protection in the near future.

Alongside its competitor products (aluminium and plastics), the recyclability of steel and its byproducts gives steel an advantage as LCA, recyclability and sustainability strategies gather pace. The steel industry recycles 425 million tonnes of steel each year and the EU iron and steel industry has a self-appointed target of recycling 60 per cent of household steel waste by 2005 (IISI, 1993; Cockerill Sambre, 1996). In 1998 a long-term study on the steel life cycle was published. Rather than a 'cradle to grave' approach, it focused on a 'cradle to factory gate' level. This was for reasons of complexity of the iron and steel process itself and the sheer variety of products. A number of firms participated throughout the world and particular products were selected. Rather than an LCA, the intention was to produce a life cycle inventory (IISI, n.d.). It will enable steel producers to make environmental strategy links with their suppliers and their customers, and also to respond to the growing public awareness of making environmental connections in their consumption choices; the rise in eco-labelling is one example that is likely to filter down to the white goods and automobile industries in the medium term and this will in turn impact on steel producers (ISSI, personal communication; British Steel, personal communication; Nakajima, 1995).

ENVIRONMENTAL REGULATIONS AND SECTORAL CHANGE

The EU steel sector underwent extensive restructuring during the 1980s and this continued into the 1990s with further mergers, takeovers and closures. The increase in environmental concerns within the industry from the mid-1980s have led to significant changes, reacting on the whole to the regulatory developments at the EU and national levels. Whilst it is end-of-pipe technologies that still provide the primary response to emissions control, there are a growing number of process and production developments that are leading to reduced emissions and efficiency gains. Future developments in process research may well lead to significant changes in the production system in the early part of this century as producers attempt to find a way around the emissions from coke and sinter plants; however, existing techniques are not currently viable at high production levels and under certain circumstances, such as high energy costs.

What is important in terms of EU steel production and the environment is the issue of competitiveness and non-EU production. EU producers make environmental investments to comply with regulations, but they are competing in global markets with major producers such as China, India, Republic of

Korea and Brazil who are producing under different environmental frameworks. With steel prices highly competitive, environmental costs contribute greatly to the product price margins, especially since these investments are not oriented towards the product directly (in terms of energy or quality for instance). While there is no evidence of industrial flight by EU iron and steel producers due to environmental regulations – although there is a clear movement to locate in areas of increasing demand such as Asia, particularly in joint ventures – the regulatory burden must be contextualized alongside competitiveness issues in other factors of production.

There is a need for effective employment of international environmental agreements and regulatory systems in non-EU producing nations if the global market is to be environmentally 'levelled'. Although the level playing field is an unattainable goal, its pursuit is a worthwhile one in terms of global environmental sustainability since 'dirty' producers should not establish competitive advantages from the environmental degradation that results from low pollution abatement investment. To provide competitive advantages to 'dirty' producers is not a movement in this direction. The European environmental regulatory systems must work in collaboration with producers to reduce emissions, and also to promote efficiency and respect economic imperatives. The responsibility of the producers must be to comply with existing regulations, innovate to maintain positive environmental performance trends, and promote cooperation with regulatory agencies and other stake-holders to make awareness of their environmental impacts more transparent and to improve communication with affected third parties. The assessment of such developments, and the creation of suitable systems to undertake this, are critical to the success of these innovations.

COMPARATIVE EXPERIENCES IN THE GLOBALIZING IRON AND STEEL SECTOR

There is a clear separation in the global iron and steel industry between the more mature firms of the developed world, characterized by the EU, and the more recent entrants of the industrializing economies during the second half of the twentieth century. The firms of the former communist bloc countries have characteristics of both in that they are mature in terms of longevity but developing in terms of competitiveness. From Tables 5.2 and 5.3 it can be seen that, in both production and export terms, the contribution of developed countries (such as those in the EU) to the world total has declined over the 1979–97 period while that of less developed countries has increased. The Central and Eastern Europe transition economies have reduced their production volumes but increased their export shares.

The most striking figures are those for Korea as it has expanded its production intensively during the 1980s and 1990s. The Brazilian sector has altered in terms of composition during the post-privatization years of the 1990s and has focused on increasing the value of its production and the domestic demand for steel, in the automotive sector in particular. Where Brazilian steel remains strong in terms of exports is in low-cost semi-finished steels. For Poland and the Czech Republic, the 1990s was a decade of extensive restructuring that led to a collapse in domestic demand, capacity reductions and a severe rationalization of remaining capacity.

Table 5.2   Steel production, 1979, 1988, 1997

Countries	'000 metric tonnes			%		
	1979	1988	1997	1979	1988	1997
Developed	427 725	369 982	389 381	57.3	47.4	48.7
Less developed	105 878	181 244	294 076	14.2	23.2	36.8
C/E. Europe	212 979	228 896	115 513	28.5	29.3	14.5
World	746 582	780 122	798 970	100.0	100.0	100.0
EU (15)	166 110	149 982	159 834	22.2	19.2	20.0
Brazil	13 891	24 657	26 153	1.9	3.2	3.3
Rep. of Korea	7 610	19 118	42 554	1.0	2.5	5.3
Czechoslovakia[a]	14 817	15 380	10 585	2.0	2.0	1.3
Poland	19 218	16 873	11 591	2.6	2.2	1.5

Note: [a] The 1997 figure is for the Czech Republic.

Source: IISI (various).

The overall picture remains one of a shift from developed economy dominance of world steel production and trade to that of an increasing contribution from developing economies, with transition economies exporting a considerably higher proportion of their production than previously. If these percentage shares are accepted as reasonable indicators of trade competitiveness, it is clear that the EU steel sector is becoming progressively less competitive in volume production and trade terms.

To assess whether environmental regulations in the developed world have negatively affected the competitiveness of developed economy firms, it is necessary to look at comparative experiences. The EU experience of regulations and competitiveness will be compared with experiences in two industrializing economies – Brazil and the Republic of Korea – and two

Table 5.3   Exports of semi-finished and finished steel products, 1979, 1988, 1997

Countries	'000 metric tonnes			%		
	1979	1988	1997	1979	1988	1997
World	143 215	171 113	265 657	100.0	100.0	100.0
EU (15)	72 998	77 661	98 712	51.0	45.4	37.2
Brazil	1 478	10 916	9 163	1.0	6.4	3.4
Rep. of Korea	3 117	7 196	11 739	2.2	4.2	4.4
Czechoslovakia[a]	3 527	4 027	6 838	2.5	2.4	2.6
Poland	1 988	2 348	4 176	1.4	1.4	1.6

Note: [a] The 1997 figure is for the Czech Republic.

Source: IISI (various).

transition economies with mature iron and steel sectors – the Czech Republic and Poland. These countries were selected based on an examination of the EU's trade in iron and steel products and their contribution to EU imports in this sector (see Tables 5.4 and 5.5).

Although the Republic of Korea does not figure in Table 5.5, the Korean firm POSCO is the leading producer in the world (by volume, 1999) and is

Table 5.4   Imports of iron and steel into Western Europe, 1990 and 1999

	Value (US$ billion)		% share in Western Europe's imports	
	1990	1999	1990	1999
World	56.02	54.27	100.0	100.0
Latin America	1.17	0.97	2.1	1.8
C./E. Europe/Baltic/CIS	3.07	4.49	5.5	8.3
Africa	0.77	1.05	1.4	1.9
Middle East	0.01	1.35	0.0	0.2
Asia	0.57	2.32	1.0	4.3
of which: China	0.05	0.25	0.1	0.5

Note: Shares include intra-Western Europe trade. Data are affected by changes in collection from 1993.

Source: WTO (1997, 2000).

influential in the Asian region, where demand has risen rapidly during the 1980s and 1990s. In global terms, POSCO is an example of a firm which will compete with EU firms in international markets rather than within the markets of the EU which is the case for products from the Czech Republic and Poland.

Table 5.5   EU 15 iron and steel imports by percentage share (SITC 67)

	1990		1993		1996		1999	
	Share	Rank	Share	Rank	Share	Rank	Share	Rank
Russia	—	—	9.2	3	9.5	1	8.3	1
Norway	8.3	2	10.8	2	9.2	2	7.5	2
Switzerland	10.1	1	11.8	1	6.9	3	6.7	3
South Africa	5.5	5	5.3	6	6.4	5	6.1	4
Czech Republic	—	—	7.3	4	6.1	6	6.0	5
Turkey	4.4	8	—	—	2.8	9	5.8	6
USA	5.9	4	6.0	5	6.7	4	5.2	7
Poland	4.9	7	5.2	7	5.2	7	5.1	8
Brazil	7.5	3	4.6	8	4.9	8	4.7	9
Extra EU15 (value, mill. ecu)	5 525		4 879		8 333		10 159	

Note: Shares exclude intra-EU trade.

Source: Eurostat (1997, 2000).

Unfortunately it is not possible to generate sufficient comparative data across firms and regulatory bodies to assess pollution per unit of steel output, mainly as a result of firm data collection methods, the complexities of firm operations which make comparisons difficult (for example, different technologies, different energy mixes, different recycling ratios, different steel qualities and products, and so on), and a high degree of confidentiality between regulators and the regulated about the conditions of licensing and data exchanged between the two institutions.

The following comparative national experiences are examined in light of these wide-ranging firm differences and experiences. Despite these restrictions, it is still possible to establish some general trends of firm behaviour *vis-à-vis* their regulatory environments, and to assess the extent to which it is environmental circumstances (natural and regulatory) which positively or negatively affect their competitiveness. The material presented is based on published quantitative data and interviews with a range of key respondents, including firm managers, regulators, and trade association and government representatives (see Table 5.6).

Table 5.6   Research selection rationale and information sources

Country	Factors in selection	Firms	Regulatory agencies
Spain	Large EAF sector; low industrial concentration; niche products	Productos Tubulares Marcial Ucin SA Esteban Orbegozo SA Rico & Echeverria AZMA SL	Basque Government Environment Section (Vitoria); Ministry of the Environment (Madrid)
UK	Large integrated sector; industrially concentrated	British Steel – Llanwern Co-Steel UK	UK Environment Agency (West Ridings)
Belgium	Large integrated sector, low domestic demand; two regulatory authorities	ALZ NV Usines Gustave Boël Sidmar NV Cockerill-Sambre Fabrique de Fer	AMINAL (Brussels); Dept for Clean Technologies (Namur)
Rep. of Korea	Sector dominated by modern, innovative, high production firm; region of rising demand	POSCO – Pohang POSCO – Kwangyang Inchon Iron and Steel Co. Dong Kuk	Ministry of the Environment (Seoul; Pohang)
Brazil	Rising domestic demand; capacity increases; important exporter to EU	COSIPA USIMINAS CNT CSN	CETESB (São Paulo); FEEMA (Rio de Janeiro); FEAM (Minas Gerais)

Table 5.6 (continued)

Country	Factors in selection	Firms	Regulatory agencies
		Açominas Gerdau SA	
Czech Republic	Important exporter to EU; sector under transformation (rationalization and privatization)	Nova Huta ZDB Vitkovice Trinecke Zelezarny	Czech Environment Inspectorate (Prague; Ostrava)
Poland	Important exporter to EU; sector under transformation (rationalization and privatization)	Huta im T. Sendzimira Huta Czestochowa Huta Zawiercie Huta Katowice Huta Ostrowiec	Not interviewed

6. Steel and environment: industrializing and transition economies

BRAZIL

Sectoral Development and Competitiveness

Despite the need to import most state-of-the-art production technologies, the level of process equipment in the leading Brazilian firms is on a par with other international producers. Once one considers the rapid improvements in areas such as tinning and galvanizing (for example, CSN) and in areas of special steels production (for example, Piratini) since the early 1990s, the level of diversity in Brazilian production can also be highlighted. The organization of the Brazilian steel sector is shown in Table 6.1, although actual production at 25.2 Mt in 1996 and 24.9 Mt in 1999 (IBS, various) reveals the excess capacity that exists.

Table 6.1   The steel sector: installed capacity (total 1996 - 28.0 Mt)

Integrated – 18.4 Mt (coal)		Integrated – 4.5 Mt (charcoal)	Semi-integrated (EAF) – 3 Mt
CSN	4.6	Cosigua	Piratini
Usiminas	4.2	Pains	Gerdau
Cosipa	3.9	Acesita	Villares
CST	3.7	Belgo-Mineira	Mendes Jr.
Açominas	2.0	Mannesmann	Cofavi
Others – all routes	2.2		Dedini

Source: IBS (in CSN, 1997b).

In recent years, the most important impacts on the sector have come from the 1990 Plano Real economic stability programme and the privatization process that was central to it. The privatization of the steel sector was an early target of the Plan. The dismantling of the national steel production organization, Siderbras, resulted in the piecemeal selling-off of its constituent parts, beginning with Usiminas (1991), CST and Acesita (1992) and finally CSN, Cosipa and Açominas (1993). The newly privatized companies attracted mainly domestic investment which has revitalized the sector following a period of low investment during the 1980s. This new investment enabled the purchase of new technologies, including environmental protection equipment. Prior to privatization, the steel companies had been managed with political and strategic objectives as well as economic and commercial ones and were beset with problems: production lines limited by insufficient inputs; subjection to supplier and transport cartelization; poor labour relations; steel prices indirectly managed by the government via buyer subsidies; and a negative and discredited image with respect to delivery times and quality (CSN, personal communication).

Post-privatization, firm objectives have changed considerably. An important area of development has been the attention to market demand, by improving client linkages, expanding product diversification and increasing value-added processes (for example, coating and painting). Much attention has been paid to the domestic market because of increased demand and uncertainties in the export market due to the fluctuating value of the *real* (Amann and Nixson, 1999). Another area is that of business opportunities emerging from the privatization process (shares in raw materials, energy, transport and related operations, for example CSN's 25 percent ownership of the Ribeirão Grande cement firm to profit from slag byproducts), and steel production optimization (CSN, 1997b). Similar strategies throughout the sector have led to significant productivity increases since the pre-privatization year, 1989.

In terms of trade, a particularly good recovery has occurred in semi-finished steel exports. These figure strongly in the trade balance of the sector where, against a general trend of reduced exports during the 1990s for reasons of domestic demand and the unfavourable exchange rate, the balance in these products has continued to improve (see Figure 6.1).

The privatization of the early 1990s led to a change in structure and direction for Brazilian firms as they sought to modernize their plants. The learning curve was steep, requiring reorganization (such as reducing labour requirements and increasing the efficiency of the remainder), heavy new investment in equipment, tighter controls over costs, and new strategies for marketing, sales, and materials and product development. Alongside these changes, the firms and the Brazilian steel association (IBS) have been pressurizing the government to reduce the 'Brazil Cost' which includes the perceived obstacles to competitiveness such as the national systems of finance, taxation, tariffs, working practices and infrastructure. Although the 'Brazil

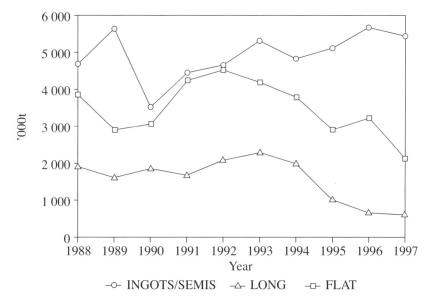

Figure 6.1   Brazil: trade balance by major product group

Cost' imposes additional burdens for steel firms, they are still favoured by an overall structure of costs which benefits considerably from advantages in other input costs, particularly labour, iron ore and electricity. Since these three areas account for approximately 60 percent of total costs for steel firms (Amann and Nixson, 1999), it is here that most of the competitive advantages are to be found for Brazilian producers operating in the global market place.

Regulatory Regimes and Impacts

As with steel plants worldwide, the focal areas for environmental protection are atmospheric emissions followed by water discharges and solid waste management. Different firms have different priorities, however, such as CSN and CST due to their proximity to residential areas, and Cosipa due to its location within the industrial complex of Cubatão. Upstream environmental impacts from iron ore extraction and charcoal use are further dimensions to the sector since they provide the Brazilian sector with international competitive advantages but also have significant environmental impacts, for example, currently over 650,000 hectares of native forest is destroyed annually for charcoal production (Medeiros, 1995). The use of energy is also high compared with international competitors, although several firms are in the process of constructing new power stations or buying into recently privatized energy suppliers (see Table 6.2).

Table 6.2   Gigajoule per tonne of steel produced (average)

France	20.0
US	20.1
Germany	17.6
Japan	18.1
Brazil	24.9

Source: CST (n.d.).

The development of environmental legislation and regulations in Brazil has accelerated since the 1970s, although government agencies in charge of regulations and implementation vary according to states and their regional economic activities. Resources, styles of monitoring and enforcement, and environmental performance strategies differ across boundaries, with the result that production sites with similar environmental impacts are treated differently within the national territory. The outcome is that the location of industrial sites is becoming increasingly responsive to environmental regulations and their enforcement in different states (FIESP, personal communication).

The separation of federal and state regulations has played an important role in industrial development. While federal regulations provide a minimum framework for environmental performance, states have the legal authority to enforce stricter limits and requirements. In the case of São Paulo, which has the highest concentration of industrial development, the demands of environmental regulations are of an order far removed from other states, such as its neighbours, Minas Gerais and Rio de Janeiro. The result is that different states have implemented federal regulations in different ways, in terms of monitoring and legal action, and in terms of resourcing state agencies to carry out federal policy.

Regulations with respect to the steel companies have in most instances been instituted within agreements – *Termos de Compromisso* – whereby the regulator and the firm have identified long-term programmes of priorities and investments. This approach was common during the 1990s and has been successful due to the environmental investment programmes of the privatized companies. The agreement identifies a time span for environmental improvements, specifying responsibilities, investments and actions, regularity and efficiency of equipment and the on-going costs of monitoring and maintenance. Naturally there are competitiveness implications of the negotiated style of the regulatory system since firms may escape non-compliance penalties or may have to invest in new technologies, but it is clear that this approach promotes awareness of environmental issues and makes regulatory management more sensitive to business and investment cycles. For instance, CSN signed an agreement of 325 items with FEEMA (the Rio de Janeiro regulatory agency) in 1994 to resolve its environmental problems before May 1998, and claimed that 80 percent were already achieved by 1997 (CSN, 1997a). For CST, the *Termo de Compromisso* was drawn up in September 1990, outlining 40 items which had to be accomplished by 1994; in October 1994, 45 more items were added due to the successful achievement of most of the original tasks (Guimarães, 1996). CST invested US$60 million to achieve the 1994 demands. For Usiminas, the 1990 *Termo de Compromisso* with COPAM (Minas Gerais regulatory agency) had the objective of instituting adequate operational facilities to meet environmental regulations. This was renegotiated in 1994 and 1996 with 37 actions to be undertaken at an associated cost of over US$170 million (Usiminas, 1996).

Although leading companies have taken positive steps, other companies have lagged behind. FEEMA is still critical of CSN and its environmental performance whilst Cosipa in Cubatão (São Paulo State) still has a long way to go before CETESB (the regulatory body) will reduce its high level of pressure on the firm. In these two cases there is apparent disagreement between regulators and firms in terms of their environmental achievements and current performance. The difference between the two cases is that FEEMA continues to struggle against low resources – which impedes inspections – while Cosipa is inspected regularly by the area branch of CETESB. A further difference is that penalties levied against CSN have been effectively returned to the firm for assistance with *Termo de Compromisso* objectives, whereas Cosipa receives none of its fines for such tied investment. The changes of the 1990s, with privatization, opportunities for establishing *Termos de Compromisso* and greater environmental awareness within the industries (in terms of community, market needs, and legislation), have ushered in a new wave of regulation that has sought more flexibility where possible, greater cooperation and improved assistance. This has been possible in most cases, but command and control has still been necessary where companies have been slow, or intransigent, in implementing necessary changes.

Firms Responses: Investment, Technological Change and Environmental Management

Despite these efforts [end-of-pipe technologies and raw material improvements], legislative compliance was not always reached, and when attained, the costs were very high and the benefits sometimes questionable. (IBS, 1990, p. 23)

New investments following privatization have enabled companies to adopt a more aggressive stance relative to expansion and development than in other steel producing countries where capacity is not increasing. The low current steel consumption per capita level (compared internationally) allows considerable scope in this respect. In the case of CSN, its strategy of expansion involves a new NUCOR mini-mill project to be constructed in Pecém, Ceará. While CSN has also focused on downstream finishing and product development, CST produces high-volume, low-price steel slabs almost entirely for export (98 percent). The company has concentrated its resources and now holds 18 percent of the international market in slabs and produces the lowest-cost liquid steel in the world (see Table 6.3). This contrast marks the division between the semi-finished steel export firms (CST, Açominas) and the other firms focusing on flat and long products for the domestic market.

Table 6.3   Comparative cost of liquid steel (no depreciation): indexed, 1997

CST	100
Mexico	134
Rep. Korea	155
Japan	163
USA	177
Germany	185

Source: CST (1997b).

A new post-privatization emphasis has also emerged in terms of environmental awareness. For CSN, for example, environmental protection was approached within its technical development strategy (1995–2000), taking 6 percent of the US$1.3 billion allocated. In CST, environmental protection has been included within all three post-privatization investment stages (1993–2000) totalling US$17.23–18.23 million. This expenditure has generated indirect financial gains from efficiency technologies such as pulverized carbon injection (PCI), top recovery turbine (TRT) in the blast furnace, and increased continuous casting (CST, 1997b). Most companies have increased environ-mental expenditure during the 1990s, even those which were private and not part of Siderbras, such as the Gerdau Group (1996) which has invested US$46 million in 'eco-efficiency' in order to reach international environmental parameters (see Table 6.4).

Investments in environmental performance improvements have been substantial since privatization, especially for older firms where the costs entailed are considerable due to issues of space availability, physical interference, and facility shutdown to allow for installation (IBS, 1990). It must also be pointed out that process technology developments have also led

Table 6.4   Investments, 1991-6 (US$ million): Gerdau Group[a]

	1996	Last 5 years	%
Machinery/equipment	60.3	580.1	59.6
Reforestation	5.4	31.1	3.2
Environment	3.4	46.0	4.7
Property	8.2	30.4	3.1
Others	5.5	36.0	3.7
Subtotal	82.8	723.8	74.3
Acquisitions	—	250.2	25.7
Total	82.8	974.0	100.0

Notes: Next 5-year investment programme: US$650 (Machinery/equipment 73%; Environment 12%; Information technology 8%; Automation 5%; Others 2%).

  [a] The Gerdau Group includes companies apart from steel producers, such as a reforestation company, hence high figures for that area. Its steel companies include Cosigua and Aços Finos Piratini.

Source: Gerdau Group (1996).

to environmental performance improvements; increased continuous casting and the installation of PCI are amongst the best examples of this. Most of these process developments across the sector are based on imported technologies and foreign technical advice for implementation and improvements. These international links have characterized the Brazilian sector since its inception and the situation is unlikely to change in the long term. This is the case for most developing economy steel firms, since technology development is both costly and R&D-intensive, therefore few firms have a strong capacity in this area. Those which have include Voest Alpine in Austria, Mannesmann in Germany, and Lurgi in Italy.

While technological developments are the conventional way to reduce emissions, the area of environmental management was the focus for a lot of work during the late 1980s and 1990s. In the 1990s, more emphasis was given to establishing environmental management systems, departments and personnel to oversee implementation, monitoring (including audit and evaluation) and effective environmental public relations and education. Amongst the environmental management tools, the ISO 14.001 standard has provided an important target for firms, especially those involved in international trade. For others focusing on the domestic market, Gerdau for example, ISO 14.001 has not been prioritized and they have focused instead on applying best available technologies.

Usiminas has been a leader in industrial environmental management. As early as 1979, technical assistance on environmental control was organized with Nippon Steel. To stay ahead of regulators and competitors in environmental affairs, Usiminas has clearly stated objectives and associated action plans that go beyond more basic technological installation intentions. These objectives are mirrored by other leading companies that have environmental statements, strategies and targets. Within CSN, the environmental management system has four areas: written procedures, monitoring, policies and institutional strategies. Measures have focused on priority areas such as particulate matter emissions from stacks, particulates in suspension in the air (around the plant and in the city), and measurement of effluents (especially pH, temperature, cyanide, phenols, ammonia, BOD and heavy metals) in water treatment and quality stations for the Paraíba do Sul river (CSN, 1997a).

Since 1992, CST has also adopted a positive approach to environmental management and has prioritized the formulation of an EMS which will lead the company towards ISO 14.001 certification. An important statement in the company's environment document is the recognition of the role of the environment in the cost structure of the company, and the need to establish a positive cost–benefit ratio from the EMS. Almeida e Silva (1995) notes the benefits accruing from the CST environmental policy: 90 percent atmospheric emissions reduction (1990–4); US$26 million saved by recycling and consequent reduced waste volumes; water recirculation of 91 percent; and reuse of gases for 90 percent of electrical energy production. Cosipa (1997) has invested in the environment in the form of its PAC (Projectos Ambientais Cosipa) fund, set up in 1997, which has invested US$160 million in pollution control (23 percent of a total investment plan of US$691 million) and achieved considerable reductions in particulate emissions and BOD, and improved capture of manganese, cyanide and ammonia.

ISO 14.001 certification has become a popular mechanism by which firms can reveal their environmental credentials. The principal driver for the take-up of environmental management outlined by ISO 14.000 has been the factor of international markets and the uncertainty about how ISO 14.000 might be employed in the future in order to restrict free trade, or in terms of consumer awareness and the pressures that this would have on steel customers to reveal competent, upstream environmental management.

Training of personnel and the organization of environment teams and departments is another area of environmental management that has been targeted and, as with 14.001, it varies between firms. The recent nature of environmental developments has led to wide-ranging company experiences in this regard, from fully fledged environment departments, through smaller environmental sub-departments, to decentralization of environmental responsibilities to facility level. In terms of training, experiences are varied although it is clear that environmental education is increasing and is now being incorporated into training at all levels within the companies. Environment managers appear to be convinced that, once this takes place, energy savings and greater environmental risk awareness will be both economically beneficial and reduce accidents.

Environmental auditing and accounting are also areas for future development by environmental managers. The concept of a 'pollution cost system' (Maciel, 1993) in the steel sector is still underdeveloped in Brazil, as it is in Europe. The consideration of pollution costs as a factor in production cost reduction and greater efficiency is gaining ground slowly although the difficulties associated with identifying and calculating specifically environmental costs, apart from production and labour costs, are problematic. CSN currently operates a basic environmental accounting system but it is not clear how influential it has been in contributing to environmental performance improvements.

The need to expand environmental activities into the community is another important area of development that is especially urgent for firms operating in close proximity to urban areas. IBS (1990, p. 25) makes this social communication function explicit when it states that: 'The company must emphasise that it is conscious of its social responsibility and is preoccupied with promoting and harmonizing the aspects linked with this responsibility, such as development and environmental protection.'

Mechanisms for increasing industry–community links are numerous, including: local newspaper information; company–residents meetings; school visits and competitions; 'hotline' phone numbers; and tree planting. Usiminas has one of the longest-established environmental education programmes in the country. Projeto Xerimbabo is an adult and children's environmental education programme that is linked with the company's own Zoobotanic Park and has been running for 12 years. For other companies, their close proximity to other firms and residential areas creates different tensions. In response to its proximity to the city centre and residential areas, CSN has developed a monitoring strategy for the city of Volta Redonda and it also maintains 131 hectares of land which is protected by federal legislation and is part of a wider greening policy (CSN, 1997a).

A planting programme has also been followed by Cosipa which has achieved 17m²/employee of green area (the WHO recommends 12m²/employee) (Cosipa, 1997). However, Cosipa's real problems lie in controlling its emissions, especially since it is located in such a sensitive area. As a response to the severe emissions in the locality, the company is part of the 'Road Bath' scheme (with CIESP, CETESB, DERSA and the traffic police) which is aimed at keeping roads damp in order to prevent resuspension of dust in the Vale do Mogi region (Cosipa, 1997). In terms of community developments, there is a strong push towards government–university–company networks. In the case of CST there has been collaboration with the Federal University of Espírito Santo in the area of industrial development (see Morandi, 1997) and environmental control (see Guimarães, 1995). An example of this is the establishment of the COEG (Organising Commission of Government Institutions) to link together municipal organizations and the state regulator in Vitória in order to oversee the fulfilment of the *Termos de Compromisso* of the two principal companies in the area (responsible for 90 percent of the atmospheric contamination of Greater Vitória): CST and CVRD.

Environmental Regulations and Sectoral Change

Brazil's steel sector is expanding and modernizing with the new investment generated from the early 1990s' privatization process. Privatization has provided an impetus to the sector to move ahead on several fronts, such as price competitiveness, rationalization of production, product development, quality, raw material and energy supply security, and also environmental investment and management. These changes have been costly to the firms in question but there are factors which suggest that the investments are sound ones. Brazilian steel is highly cost competitive on the international market – particularly CST's in the slab market. Low current steel consumption leads analysts to suggest that capacity can be expanded (bucking the general trend in international steel production) and environmental investments raise company profiles, protect 'stakeholders' such as workers and neighbouring communities, and improve market opportunities (the impetus for ISO 14.001 implementation).

Total investments in the sector continue to rise, although environmental investments are now stabilizing following intensive investment in the early privatization years. It appears that environmental protection will hover at approximately 6 percent of all investments. Although the international market is competitive at the moment, advantages in labour costs (if not offset by equally low labour productivity) and raw material availability (particularly iron ore, and charcoal for some firms) provide the sector with strong competitive advantages, particularly in semi-finished steel, which is increasingly the leading export product.

The obstacles to reducing environmental impacts revolve around company priorities and investment strategies. While regulators and legislation have impacts in terms of determining which media are important – highlighting water, then air for instance – the penalties in Brazil would appear to be insufficient deterrents for firms. The cases of CSN and Cosipa are examples where firms have been slow to meet regulatory demands, choosing to invest in other production areas rather than in environmental protection. Firms should be given credit for rapid environmental developments since the 1990s but the starting point was a low one and considerable work remains to be done. It is imperative that support for impact reductions comes from the executive level – as in the case of Usiminas – and that there is a strong working relationship with regulators to achieve clearly defined targets.

Beyond the commonality of federal environmental policy, there are wide variations between state regulatory agencies in Brazil. Resources for agencies also vary according to state funding and prioritization, and this may lead to different approaches, implementation and agency–firm relations across the country. Therefore, there may be small competitiveness impacts due to regulatory-based pollution abatement costs, including penalties, within Brazil, let alone in comparison with steel sectors elsewhere and particular international firms. However, as with firms throughout the world, the costs associated with environmental regulations are unlikely to be key concerns for firms in terms of their competitive position in domestic and international markets. In the cases of Cosipa and CSN, for example, the very gradual process by which the regulator has been able to encourage environmental changes suggests that any adverse impacts from regulatory-induced changes have been spread out over a long time horizon.

Two of the major shifts in the Brazilian steel industry in the 1990s have been in production technology – such as continuous casting – and environmental management initiatives. Privatization gave rise to a wave of investment that covered both these areas relatively well. Apart from the recognition of the need to be competitive in terms of price and quality, investment in state-of-the-art technology and environmental management have been notable developments. The production technology advances such as continuous casting and recycling initiatives (of production gases for energy savings, for example) have had positive environmental and cost benefits, therefore there has been a slight shift towards process and production methods (PPMs) and not solely relying on end-of-pipe systems. Since these technological developments are widely available and applied throughout the world, the environmental benefits are not always considered discretely, therefore the 'cleaner production' concept is not applied, despite that fact that they fit the bill very well.

In the area of environmental management, the enthusiasm for ISO 14.001 among steel companies is evident and it is apparent that significant progress is taking place in the systematization of environmental controls, the installation of management structures and procedures, and increased environmental awareness via training. A major caveat is that ISO 14.001 does not guarantee environmental performance improvements. For these to take place, regulators and firms must audit processes and reach agreed and practicable targets. These are evident in the *Termos de Compromisso*, however the penalties for not meeting agreed targets must also be evident and effective.

Since the early 1990s, Brazilian steel has become fully integrated into the international market place for steel products, although the most dynamic changes for the steel sector have been taking place within the country in terms of demand for flat products and it is here that most large firms are focusing their attentions. The sector is competitive and modern, revealing similar technologies to those in place elsewhere in the world. Environmental investments were extensive during the first five years of privatization, accompanying quality and increased competitiveness initiatives; however the impact of environmental investments on competitiveness is not made explicit by firms. Approximations of 5–10 percent per annum of investments and operating costs can be attributed to environmental costs, and these costs are widely considered as costs rather than benefits – although, exceptionally, Usiminas is attempting to benefit from its positive approach to environmental issues. What is critical to the environmental performance of the Brazilian steel sector is that this capacity expansion should take place alongside environmental safeguards, innovative and effective EMS, and a shift towards PPMs rather than capture systems in firm-level approaches to environmental protection and control.

REPUBLIC OF KOREA

Sectoral Development and Competitiveness

The Republic of Korea's steel sector is dominated by a single firm with two plants. In this respect it reflects the experience of other countries where a single firm has dominated the sector, such as British Steel in the UK and Usinor-Sacilor in France. Apart from Pohang Steel Co. (POSCO), the sector includes a range of small and medium-sized EAF firms which operate principally to fulfil domestic demand within their respective regions.

The cases of Inchon and Dong-Kuk, both in the port city of Inchon, are examples of such firms. As EAF firms, the principal preoccupation is the management of dust collected from fabric filters, and also noise due to their close proximity to residential areas. The Korean regulators brought pressure to bear on Inchon Steel Co. which was threatened with closure for excessive emissions levels; the company responded with technological changes that enabled it to fulfil regulatory requirements and avoid closure. In both cases, the firms have installed similar systems to other EAF plants worldwide and environmental issues do not provide the principal concern for Korean EAF firms in terms of competitiveness. High-quality, low-cost scrap and electricity costs are the determining factors in production, linked to productivity increases from reductions in steel-making (tap-to-tap) time and a shift towards near net shape casting of products (KOSA Management Research Division, personal communication). As with other EAF producers around the world, the problems of effective landfilling of dusts and other materials remains and this is managed by the government via its landfill policy, which categorizes wastes as special landfill, wastes for further treatment, and byproducts which may be used in road surfacing and cement-making. Although there may be on-going issues relating to the effectiveness of end-of-pipe control systems and dust management, these are not particular to Korean EAF firms, and investment in bag filters is a universal response.

Korea was late in developing an integrated steelworks. Prior to the 1970s, steel production was dominated by the smaller EAF plants concentrating on rolling mills for the production of bar and wire-rod steel. With the lack of a large integrated steel facility, ironmaking and steelmaking was limited. The state intervened as part of its GIO-oriented (growth- industry- and outward-oriented) Long Term Perspective Plan carried out during the 1972–81 period (Song, 1997), leading to the building of the Pohang steel plant with an investment of US$3.6 billion.

Many of the competitive advantages of POSCO were put in place during its construction. As a modern plant equipped with continuous casting and environmental technologies from the outset, production has been efficient and environmentally attentive. Swift construction and low construction costs have also been influential in making the company cost competitive and achieving a short maturation period between being an infant industry and becoming internationally competitive (see Table 6.5; Auty, 1991; Kang, 1994). This cost competitiveness varies according to steel product, which accounts for the Brazilian firm CST's ability to offer the lowest semi-finished steel prices in the global market despite their higher construction costs.

Table 6.5   Unit cost and construction period for overseas steel works

	POSCO 4th stage, Korea	CST, Brazil	CSC 2nd stage, Taiwan	PASMIC, Pakistan	OGISHIMA 2nd stage, Japan
Construction unit cost ($/t)	460	700	857	1 727	626
Construction period (months)	24	36	43	254	42

Source: POSCO, cited in Mal-Soo, 1987, p. 16.

In the late 1980s, demand in Korea continued to rise and the need for a further plant was clear. This new plant at POSCO's Kwangyang Bay site was constructed during 1987 and featured a 100 percent continuous casting ratio and high levels of computerization (Mal-Soo, 1987). As with the Pohang plant, construction costs and short completion time has enabled early competitive advantages; this has been recognized as an important factor in the competitiveness of both POSCO plants (POSCO, personal communication; Kang, 1994). By the end of 1986, even before Kwangyang's construction, the local cost of Korean coil was US$282 per tonne, as compared with US$444 in the US and US$520 in Japan; the new plant assisted in reducing this further (Mal-Soo, 1987). The high level of demand and low level of competition within the Korean market enables POSCO to maintain a high level of capacity utilization which is essential to lowering production costs within the integrated steelmaking route. Beyond the initial construction cost advantages, it is this high capacity utilization that provides POSCO steel with a competitive advantage in the global market (Lee, n.d.; Moody's Investors Service, 1996).

In the Korean steel sector taken as a whole, the major technological challenges lie in increasing the ratio of continuously cast output and in the degree of computerization of the process. New products (incorporating high strength, light gauge, high anti-corrosion, and endurance in high temperatures), resource or energy-saving technologies and environment technologies are all areas in which competitive advantages are sought. The steel and cement sectors have been especially active in developing their environmental technology capacities (MOTIE, personal communication). The challenge is being met with increased R&D investment and greater academic–industrial links, such as those between POSCO, POSTECH and RIST. Although there may be potential threats to future developments, such as the current up-to-date technologies mitigating against any revolutionary new technologies arising in the short-term (*vis-à-vis* Japanese steel plant modernization for example), a relative scarcity of quality scrap and its rising price during the late 1990s (KOSA Management Research Division, personal communication), and a high level of maturity in the Korean sector (see Juhn, 1998; D'Costa 1994), the outlook in terms of production and regional demand are, on balance, good.

The increased globalization of the steel industry via joint ventures and technological exchange are also likely to assist in this process, for example, POSCO's joint venture with US Steel, with POSCO supplying half of the capital (US$180 million) for this modernization, plus technology and expertise. POSCO is continuing its globalization strategy with projects such as a mini-mill in Indonesia, a pellet plant in Brazil, an HBI (hot briquetted iron) plant in Venezuela, and several steel processing plants in China and Vietnam; the globalization strategy expects to have 50 overseas steel production and sales bases by 2005 (POSCO, 1997; Table 6.6). Growth in demand in China and the Mekong Basin are recognized as important regional opportunities for the Asian steel sector generally into the twenty-first century, as is the emergence of regional and sub-regional commercial networks across the East Asian economic zone which links Japan, Korea, Taiwan and the coastal region of China, and with China and Vietnam due to their market liberalization (Masuyama, 1996; Toda, 1995).

Table 6.6   POSCO's major overseas projects in the 1990s

Location	Equity share %	Total investment (US$ million)	Completion date
Dalien, China	70	53	October 1997
Shanghai, China	70	59	Late 1997
Shanghai, China	80	180	Late 1998
Tianjin, China	100	8.4	December 1995
Haiphong, Vietnam	50	56.12	September 1995
Ho Chi Minh, Viet.	50	3.9	April 1992
Leong, Thailand	3	730	June 1998
Indonesia	[mini-mill]	n.a.	After 1999
Cairo, Egypt	13.4	220	December 1998
Brazil	50	215	June 1998
California	50	388	April 1996

Source: *The Economist*, 7 May 1996, cited in POSRI (1996).

Although the 1997–8 financial crisis in the region led to a reorientation of steel exports towards North America and Western Europe, the recovery has stimulated demand within the region once again. New products such as steel cans (80 percent of the domestic market, 1996) with its associated recycling activities organized by the Korean Metal Can Recycling Association, and steel framed houses are both initiatives to promote the versatility and recyclability of the material and to keep domestic demand high.

In terms of trade, the sector has a strong positive balance of flat products, importing ingots and semi-finished products to facilitate this and for domestic consumption (Figure 6.2). This negative balance for ingots and semi-finished steels reveals the high steel demand in the Korean market and for steel finishing for export, and the difficulty of meeting this demand with only two main integrated plants. This domestic demand has had a negative impact on export competitiveness relative to other manufactured products since it

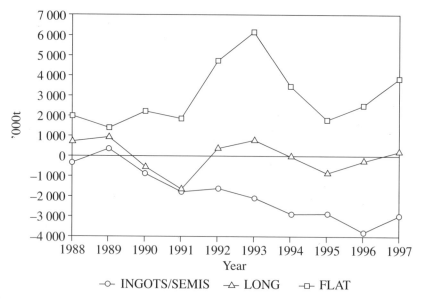

Source: IISI (various).

Figure 6.2   Korea: trade balance by major product group

restricts export volumes; nevertheless there has been relative stability in the
revealed comparative advantage of Korean iron and steel exports since 1980
when it reached a positive value, following the trend in trade liberalization in
the country from the mid-1980s (Kang, 1994; J.-M. Lee, 1995). The focus on
flat products is similar to the experience of the EU's integrated plants, and the
negative balance for ingots and semi-finished products is very different from
the Brazilian trade balance, and in long products very different from the
balances of the Czech Republic and Poland.

Regulatory Regimes and Impacts

In Korea, the environmental costs of rapid industrial growth were amongst the
highest in the developing world and the beginnings of environmental
governance did not emerge until legislation at the end of the 1970s (see Eder,
1995; You, 1995). The 1977 Environmental Preservation Act was the
precursor to the founding of the Environment Administration (EA) in 1980,
effectively a reorganization of the environmental affairs bureau of the
Ministry of Health and Social Affairs (MOE, 1996).

Increasing public awareness of environmental degradation and
environment-related health issues provoked the decentralization of the EA

with the establishment of regional Environment Branch Offices in 1986, separation of departments by pollution media, an environmental dispute settlement act, and upgrading to cabinet level in 1990 (Ministry of Environment). However, it was not until the late 1990s that the original command-and-control regulatory system began to shift towards more flexible instruments with greater government–firm agreement on targets and voluntary initiatives (POSRI Environment Team, personal communication). Developments in this area have been under-taken under the auspices of the Ministry of Trade, Industry and Energy (MOTIE) since 1995, such as soft loans for environmental technology acquisitions, and the promotion and support of cleaner technologies research and information, including life cycle analysis (MOTIE, personal communication).

In practice, the principal deterrent for producers is the 'polluter pays' policy of environmental management through the MOE's emission charge system. If limits are exceeded, the firm must comply and pay emission charges that are equivalent to the expenses for treating the actual volume of the pollutant emitted. Further charge systems include the deposit-refund system for waste disposal (established January 1992) which enables the MOE to collect deposits from producers and importers to cover waste collection and treatment costs for wastes which are designated as being recyclable (the deposits are reimbursed according to waste recycling performance), and a waste treatment charge system for wastes that are potentially harmful or difficult to treat or recycle, that was put in place in July 1993 (MOE, 1996). The standards relating to emission limits have gradually been tightened over time across most of the 26 regulated emissions, including further reductions during 1999–2000 (see Table 6.7).

During the late 1990s the limits came more into line with EU standards, although variations remain according to whether the limits are compared with the strictest regulatory targets in the EU such as the Netherlands and Germany or others. In the case of POSCO, there is always the intention to undercut the national regulatory limits by 20 percent in order to provide a safety net for compliance, therefore emissions are likely to be in the order of the better performing northern European steel firms. This can be achieved due to the relatively new equipment that is in place and the capture technologies that were installed at the time of construction. The government has recognized the positive steps made in the steel industry in terms of environmental performance. For example, the MOE and the Board of Audit and Inspection congratulated the Kwangyang Works on its activities in connection with the Kwangyang Bay, in 1990, 1991 and 1994. In 1995, the Pohang plant was selected as the most energy-efficient workshop in the metal industry in a MOTIE report (POSCO, 1997).

Currently there are strong penalties for failure to meet emissions targets.

Table 6.7   The trend in regulatory limits

Pollutants		1994	1996	2000	EU comparisons[a]	
Dust (mg/Sm2)	Sinter	200	70	50	50–100	Belgium
	EAF	30	20	10		
SOx (ppm)	Sinter	800	500	500	300	France
	Power plant	1 200	1 200	270		
NOx (ppm)	Sinter	200	200	200	500	Belgium
COD (mg/l)	Pohang	100	90	90	25	Netherlands
	Kwangyang	80	70	70		

Note: National emissions standards.

Sources: POSCO (1995); IISI/UNEP (1997).

There are various means at the regulators' disposal such as prosecution, the imposition of emission charges, or the option of shutting down operations. In terms of emission charges, only 10 of the 26 standardized contaminants are subject to charges. The charges that may be imposed range from US$650 to US$5,200 per infringement according to the size of the firm and the degree of excess (MOE, 1996). These were made stricter in 2000, having been announced in February 1991 in order to provide firms with sufficient warning.

In Korea, as in most countries, atmospheric emissions provide the focus of environmental management attention. Although air emissions are being reduced, they still do not compare as well as other companies on certain parameters, for example levels of SOx are higher than other companies due to the higher sulphur content of heavy oil, especially when compared with Japanese companies which operate flue gas desulphurization (POSCO–Pohang Environmental Management Team, personal communication). In the case of Kwangyang Bay, where POSCO operates its newer plant, a regulatory zone has been established to manage the atmospheric problems generated by the industrial processes in the area, particularly relating to VOCs (Korean Environment Institute, personal communication; POSCO–Kwangyang Environmental Management Team, personal communication).

The steel industry accounts for 19 percent of total water use in Korea, and discharges approximately 21 percent of that intake (1993) (Hong, 1996). In the case of Pohang, there were plans for a zero-discharge system to be operating by the year 2000, resulting in 10,000 tonnes of discharge water being recycled. By 1997 the firm was recycling 98 percent of water, making its waste water effluent volume the lowest in the world in relation to output (POSCO–Pohang

Environmental Management Team, personal communication). Due to the relatively recent construction of the sites, they comply relatively easily with the MOE Water Quality Management Bureau's industrial source standards on maximum allowable concentrations, which vary according to the discharge volume and the region where the wastewater is discharged (Water Management – MOE, personal communication; Yum, n.d.).

The third principal contamination medium is solid waste (see Table 6.8). The steel industry in Korea accounts for 25 percent of the total volume of industrial waste (1990). Slag is the largest volume waste item and is 100 percent recycled as a cement material or as an aggregate in construction and road building. Currently, recycling of byproducts is in the region of 93.7 percent (1996), up from 62 percent (1984); the remainder is landfilled or incinerated (Hong, 1996). Although hazardous waste appears to be effectively managed through government-controlled waste treatment facilities (Waste Division, MOE, personal communication), the fact that larger companies treat their own non-hazardous waste and that there are no landfill costs for this may lead to pollution abatement cost advantages relative to some firms in the EU for example.

Table 6.8   Environmental effects by process in Korea (per tonne of hot coil)

	SOx (NM^3)	COD (kg)	Waste (kg)
Blast furnace	0.84	0.0227	626
COREX	0.44	0.0016	549
EAF	0.24	0.002	88

Source: Hong (1996, p. 9).

The steel industry is an intensive energy consumer, utilizing 14 percent of total Korean energy consumption in 1995 (11.6 million TOE), and 28 percent of the energy consumption of all manufacturing industries. There has, however, been a steady 16 percent reduction in energy demand per tonne of steel between 1975 and 1995. Korea has one of the highest electricity costs amongst the principal steelmaking countries, so POSCO's ability to supply 80 percent of its own electricity since early in its existence has played an important part in its competitive position (Amsden, 1989).

The tightening-up of regulations throughout the 1980s and 1990s has led to POSCO improving its environmental performance indicators, but the key factor in terms of longer-term trends in these data is that the plants are of relatively recent construction, especially Kwangyang, which means that state-of-the-art cleaner and end-of-pipe technologies were fitted from construction and improvements are more closely related to eco-efficiencies and the maximizing of environmental technology capacities.

Firms Responses: Investment, Technological Change and Environmental Management

Beyond the management issues, there has also been considerable investment in technologies. From its establishment to 1996, POSCO set aside 10.8 percent of total investment for environmental improvements. This figure is amongst the highest in the world, and is considerably higher than the Korean national average of 3 percent (POSCO, 1997). The targets of the current POSCO environmental investment plan are shown in Table 6.9.

Table 6.9   Investment plan for environmental improvement (million won)

	1997	1998	1999–2003	Total
Water	3.068	14.112	24.512	42.242
Air	18.427	20.922	419.297	458.646
Waste/other	14.508	11.315	64.531	90.354
Total	36.543	46.359	453.940	536.842

R&D investment for environment	1987–94	1995	1996
External research	1.023	448	722
In-house research	10.492	5.562	7.106
Total	11.515	6.010	7.827

Source: POSCO (1997).

The principal technologies involved in productivity and quality improvements in Korea have been COREX, thin slab casting, strip casting, endless rolling, and mini-mill developments. Increased demand from users has also led to technologies which reduce steel product erosion and increase precision. Examples of increased product diversity are the light beer can which has been in the market since August 1996, and the steel framed house which has been promoted in the country following introductions in the US and Australia. From the development of the steel industry in the 1940s, Korea has depended on foreign expertise and technologies and this same trend has continued into the environment technology field.

The implementation of environmental management systems in Korea has been pursued principally by large chemical, construction and electronics firms. POSCO, as one of the larger companies in the country, took its first step towards strategic environmental management with the creation of an environment and technology team in 1983 and more recently received its ISO 14.001 certificate as a means of presenting itself as a world class firm in terms of environmental standards and also as a commitment to stakeholders' environmental needs:

> The implementation of the EMS enabled POSCO to take more preventive and systematic approaches. This change helps the company to continue its quest for environmental management, which in the long term translates into *sharpening competitive edge* as well as building an image of an environmentally friendly steel producer. (POSCO, 1997, emphasis added)

The environmental policy is part of this process and was announced in December 1995 (see Table 6.10).

The Environmental Policy is realized via a standardization of environment-related procedures, the activation of an EMS in February 1996, and Lloyds certification in July 1996 – BS7750 – and September 1996 – ISO 14.001. The process of certification was recognized by the certification organizations as unproblematic due to the 'front-line' technology that is employed by the firm and the fact that an environmental management system had been put in place by a POSCO ISO Taskforce set up in 1995 to standardize procedures (Lloyds Register Quality Assurance, Korea, personal communication; POSCO, 1997).

Learning and training have provided the backbone of much of the Korean industrialization programme from the 1970s. While the initial stages of construction and engineering depended on foreign expertise, POSCO's training programmes enable the replacement of external expertise by company-trained personnel and this has fed into technological developments also. For environmental education, there is systematic training of employees to increase awareness of the impacts of production. Beyond formal in-house training, there are also environmental initiatives taken by employee organizations: in Kwangyang, a group called 'The Song-Am Hoe' is involved in clean-up activities, environmental awareness, and links with local people to protect the surrounding environment.

As with many environmental management systems, an early element was the need to maintain a 'greening' policy in and around the steelworks. In response to Pohang residents' requests, a green belt to reduce noise and the transmission of emissions was established between the steelworks and the city and was called the 'Steelworks in the Park' (POSCO-Pohang Environmental Management Team, personal communication; POSCO, 1997). In terms of establishing links with communities, POSCO initiated two major projects for participation in 1991 organized by an Environmental Management Committee. In the case of Pohang, the Committee covers 250 firms and in

Table 6.10   POSCO's environmental policy, December 1995

Since the establishment of the company, environmental considerations have been one of the pillars of POSCO's management. Therefore, it has been implementing pollution prevention measures in addition to manufacturing steel products via environment-friendly methods. In order to further contribute to worldwide efforts to preserve the environment, POSCO hereby declares the following environmental policy which will be applied to all of the activities at both Pohang and Kwangyang Works:

- Recognize the environment as a major element of its management strategy and endeavour to harmonize it with other elements for the company's competitiveness.
- Continuously pursue pollution prevention and environmental improvement, bearing in mind that all our activities may influence the environment.
- Abide by the environment-related laws and regulations: set up and implement in-house standards in full consideration of the characteristics of the local area.
- Pursue resource saving and energy efficiency throughout the company's activities.
- Re-use and recycle wastes in an efficient manner and properly treat wastes in order to avoid causing secondary pollution problems.
- Set practicable targets and improvement plans for the environmental policy and routinely review and evaluate the operations by setting up an audit system.
- Endeavour to develop environmental technologies, in particular clean technologies.
- Educate and train all employees to participate actively in the environmental improvement programme and set up an extensive communication system with internal and external parties.
- Open POSCO's environmental policy and objectives to stakeholders and encourage all suppliers and subcontractors toward environment-friendly management.

Source: POSCO (1997).

Kwangyang, 60 companies. The Committees seek to monitor companies' environment-related activities and to assist in environment technology transfer. For the residential communities, POSCO has arranged plant tours for a wide range of groups, it has been involved (with the Green Federation) in a musical for children, and in 1995 assisted in the YMCA International,

Environmental Conference, a Photo Exhibition for Environment, and co-operated in a Local Agenda 21 programme with Pohang City Council (POSCO, 1997). Despite these developments, opposition from certain groups remains, due to noise and odour (Pohang) and criticisms of atmospheric emissions from a nearby fishing community and from bee-keepers who claim that emissions have killed their bees (around the Kwangyang Bay). A counter-argument of environmental managers is that the high profile of the plant in each location, as the largest in the area, leads to it being targeted by opposition groups (POSCO–Pohang/Kwangyang Environmental Management Teams, personal communication).

Environmental Regulations and Sectoral Development

There are three factors that have underpinned POSCO's profitability since its inception (Amsden 1989, pp.296-7): lower labour costs and increased productivity; low construction costs; and government support in the shape of infrastructure and services subsidies and low interest foreign capital. The Korean Advanced Institute of Science (KAIS) estimated that the government supported POSCO to the extent of US$42 million (1970 nominal exchange rate) in the early years.

Jai-Eun Lee, the managing director of POSCO, adds to these points by emphasizing the cost competitiveness advantages of high production efficiency (based on high labour productivity and high capacity utilization), and the up-to-date steelmaking facilities such as continuous casting which reduce costs by 10 percent relative to some competitors (Lee, n.d.). These elements have ensured the competitiveness of Korean steel; however, one can identify longer-term structural changes which will affect competitiveness, such as labour, technology and trade policy. In the Korean case, labour reductions in the steel industry alongside innovative and extensive technology developments (at least for POSCO) will continue to impact upon the sector in terms of productivity and costs. Apart from POSCO, other firms are considerably smaller and their development pattern and competitiveness is dependent on the health of their clients, although the collapse of Hanbo Steel and the problematic sale of Sammi Steel reveal that the sector has been under pressure for a considerable period of time. The imbalance between the scale of POSCO and other producers reveals that very different problems exist between the two.

In terms of the environment, one must differentiate between POSCO's high international reputation for innovation in this area and its realization of the need to pay attention to the whole life cycle of the business activity (B.W. Lee, 1995), and the low levels of environmental awareness and management among other producers. The gap between the two is wide and clearly greater dissemination of the POSCO model would appear to be useful for the sector as a whole. The principal obstacles to this dissemination appear to be lack of knowledge and finance, therefore the two other companies visited – Inchon and Dong Kuk – were operating a purely compliance approach to legislation. Due to the strict environmental legislation and command-and-control strategy of the government, this has led to improving environmental performance but few initiatives such as 'cleaner production' or ISO 14.001 implementation.

In the case of production and environmental technologies, one must differentiate also between POSCO's policy of innovation and its leading position in international developments, and other companies which are smaller in scale and have few innovations. Against POSCO's elevated status in international steel competitiveness, other producers of steel in Korea are struggling against different sets of priorities. Since their development is closely tied to the Korean economy, its 'boom' years have led to a proliferation of EAF producers around the country to supply the intermediate and heavy industrial sectors directly. As a result, their fate is closely tied to these sectors.

In terms of the environment, it is not clear that these firms have been burdened by the costs of legislation in recent years. The nature of the Korean regulatory system and a generally compliant business culture, for example, a business culture responsive to non-monetary rewards such as a close community relationship (see Song, 1997), has meant that investments in environmental technology have taken place, although apart from POSCO this has focused on capture systems. The current changes in regulatory approach, towards more voluntary initiatives, may assist the firms in becoming more innovative in terms of process and management approaches, although this is not yet clear. What can be said in conclusion, however, is that the regulations are generally complied with in the steel sector, that environmental costs have had to be internalized in the last ten years, and that companies remain competitive, and in the case of POSCO able to expand production beyond the country within a strategy of globalized trade and investment.

THE CZECH REPUBLIC AND POLAND

Sectoral Development and Competitiveness

While the changes in the European Union's steel sector during the 1980s were dramatic due to the extent of rationalization, they do not compare with the widespread collapse of the steel sector in the former Soviet bloc countries between 1988 and 1992. During this period, steel production in this region fell from 236.9 to 159.4 million tonnes and did not recover during the following five years, dropping to 130 million tonnes by 1997 (IISI, 1998). For Poland and the Czech Republic, the declines were not as marked as in the former Soviet Union, but between 1988 and 1997 both national production volumes had fallen by 31 percent (ibid.). The political changes in the Czech Republic and Poland from the late 1980s had overwhelming impacts on the national economies, and manufacturing industries in particular.

The early 1990s led to greater freedom for businesses, in the case of Poland under the 1990 Economic Transformation Programme (the 'Balcerowicz Plan'), but this was followed by a crisis with the loss of COMECON markets and poor exchange rates (Lubbe, 1993). In the Czech Republic a market-oriented economy was launched in January 1991 but the fracturing of the Czech Republic and Slovakia in 1993 added an extra complication in the case of these two countries. The steel sector has been a major player in the transition process. Due to its scale, trading potential and labour demand, the sector has been a barometer of the economic changes and has undergone extensive restructuring to reduce its open hearth processes contribution and to increase the proportion of continuously cast steel (see Table 6.11). The open hearth furnaces were central to the poor environmental performance of the sector and their phasing out has enabled a steadily improving trajectory of performance; a IISI/UNEP (1997, p.18) report regards the OHF as 'an obsolete process'. Due to secondary emissions management problems, the use of the open hearth process for many decades across the region has led to long-term environmental degradation. Although there are considerable environmental problems associated with the iron and steel sectors in Poland and the Czech Republic, the slow elimination of open hearth processes is an

Table 6.11   Capacity and production in the Czech Republic and Poland

Country	Capacity		Production		
	Total crude steel ('000 t)	Open hearth (% share)	Crude steel	Continuous casting (1989)	No. of plants
Czech Rep.[a]	19.000	40	11.700	1.420[b]	7
Poland	22.600	45	14.800[c]	1.150[b]	16

Notes: [a] Including the Slovak Kosice plant.
  [b] 1989 (it has risen rapidly since – in Poland 60 percent is continuously cast: OECD, 1998).
  [c] 1991.

Source: Ambler and Marrow (1998).

important step towards modernizing the sector and ridding it of an antiquated process that accounted for a considerable proportion of the environmental contamination in the steel-producing regions of the former Soviet bloc.

For the iron and steel sectors in both Poland and the Czech Republic, the changes have been similar. Apart from the domestic market focus, the remedies are similar to the restructuring principles adopted across Western Europe during the 1980s, with labour reductions, decreases in capacity, greater focus on steel quality and selected product lines, and improved marketing and sales. The origins of these changes are often more political than economic in origin, therefore the impacts have varied, with perverse effects such as greater negative impacts on better performing firms and lower productivity improvements than expected (Keat, 2000).

Table 6.12 is a Polish Steel Association overview of the 1990s development of the sector. Inevitably there are significant environmental repercussions from the changes. For instance, closure of obsolete technologies, capacity reductions and liquidations, especially of more heavily contaminating processes such as OHFs (from 70.9 percent of production in 1990, to 10 percent in 1995), have led to notable emissions and discharge reductions. The difficulty in this context is detecting the principal drivers for these changes, that is, national economic development and market factors versus environmental regulations and EU convergence factors. A further critical factor is the overall drop in economic activity, for example Poland had 13 operating blast furnaces in 1990 and only six by 1995 (Polish Metallurgical Chamber of Industry and Commerce, 1996).

Table 6.12   Major restructuring measures in the Polish steel industry, 1990-6

- **Liquidations**: approximately 7 Mt of capacity in open hearth plants; approximately 0.9 Mt of capacity in obsolete rolling mills; approximately 0.130 Mt of capacity in tube and pipe mills.
- **Modernization of blast furnaces** in Katowice, T. Sendzimira and Czestochowa works.
- **Installation of secondary refining facilities** in numerous steel mills.
- **Commissioning of eight continuous casting machines,** making it possible to use the CC route for 60 percent of crude steel output
- **Drastic reduction of harmful emissions** to the environment: gas emissions were reduced from 846,000 tonnes in 1989 to 327,000 tonnes in 1995 and dust emissions from 134,000 tonnes to 29,000 tonnes.
- **Employment** in steel industry reduced from 147,000 in 1990 to 91,000 in 1996.

Source: Metallurgical Chamber of Industry and Commerce (1997).

The most important phase of transition has been the privatization process. State ownership of the economy up to the 1990s has given way to the mass privatization of the leading industrial firms. By 1997, amongst the 25 Polish steelworks, 11 were privatized (state ownership less than 50 percent), six registered as 100 percent state-owned enterprises, and eight as state enterprises (Metallurgical Chamber of Industry and Commerce, 1997). A cherry-picking process has taken place and a large number of private owners have been found for many firms. Nevertheless, the state still controls many enterprises and continues to seek new owners, and there has been interest from firms such as British Steel, Thyssen (Germany) and Voest Alpine (Austria), despite evidence of certain difficulties. For example, in the case of Poldi Ocel steelworks (Czech Republic), a privatization scandal emerged involving the filing of bankruptcy proceedings against the new buyer. The Italian firm Lucchini also encountered difficulties following its $150 million investment in Huta Warszawa (Poland) when land ownership disputes and strikes over layoffs followed (*Business Central Europe*, 1996a, 1996c). One of the features of the restructuring process beyond privatization has been the shift from labour-intensity to capital-intensity with an aim to increase productivity. The Polish steel sector, for instance, has reduced its labour force from 147,000 in 1990 to 84,000 in 1997, with a target of 43,000 by 2002 (Polish Metallurgical Chamber of Industry and Commerce, 1997; British Chamber of Commerce, Poland, 1997a).

Privatization is based on the recognition that new investment will enable many run-down firms to regenerate, invest in more modern technologies, rationalize their activities and be able to trade competitively. An example is the European Bank for Reconstruction and Development (EBRD) investment in Stalexport, a metals trading company which has bought into steel production (Huta Ostrowiec, Huta Szczecin and Huta Lebedy) in recent years (Polish Metallurgical Chamber of Industry and Commerce, personal communication; *Business Central Europe*, 1998a). More generally, in Poland total continuous casting has jumped from 1 Mt in 1990 to 4.5 Mt in 1997, a sign that there has been significant new investment for productivity gains. Part of the privatization and restructuring process has been the fragmentation of firms into separate business units. Since the large firms were traditionally involved in wide-ranging activities associated with steel production, such as mechanical engineering and steel services, they have created a number of independent business units across the same steel plant site. For example, between 1992 and 1996 Huta Sendzimira (Poland) established 17 commercial companies based on the production and service departments of the steelworks (*Annual Report*, 1996).

Due to the recent changes in the national economies of Central Europe, the competitiveness of the steel sector is altogether unclear although some general statements may be made (see Table 6.13).

Table 6.13   Competitive strengths and weaknesses of the iron and steel sector

	Poland	Czech Rep. and Slovakia
Strengths	Small plants still profitable; privatization already started	Low wages costs and low exchange rate increase; competitiveness on export markets
Weaknesses	Outmoded and inefficient equipment; strong impact on environment/bad plant location (close to urban areas); high energy and raw materials consumption	Very low capital and labour productivity; high dependence on low quality raw materials imported from former Soviet Union combined with extremely high costs of switching to alternative supplies
Restructuring	Conversion of some companies into joint stock companies; restructuring projects identified based on Western direct participation commercial cooperation	Split of the large integrated steel works into smaller operating units; withdrawal of subsidies and closure of inefficient mines; promotion of energy-efficient and environmentally friendly production techniques
Prospects	Medium	Medium/good

Source: Ambler and Marrow (1998).

If one considers the principal elements lying behind costs and thus competitiveness, one must address the raw material, energy and labour costs of the industry, and also the technological and product considerations. While access to raw materials inputs has provided an important competitive advantage, the availability and price of energy is also advantageous. The difficulties that lie ahead in terms of this synergy between Central European coal and steel production will be significant since there is already some change in the coal sector. In the Czech Republic, for example, the Ostrava region has seen the closure of much coal mining capacity. This impacts on both the local coke oven firms and also the steel firms. It is likely that the Polish coal mining, coke oven and steelmaking sectors will be considerably rationalized during the next 10 years: there was a plan to close 24 coal mines, reducing output by 17 percent by the year 2000 (OECD, 1998a).

In terms of trade, it is clear that flat products, which are generally higher-value products, are not well developed (Figures 6.3 and 6.4). In the case of the Czech Republic, the Slovakian firm VSZ Kosice registered a positive trade balance in flat products until the Czech and Slovak republics separated in 1992. What remains is a strong focus on long products, also mirrored by Poland, and a generally positive balance in ingots and semi-finished products. In the case of Poland, the exports of ingots and semi-finished products, especially to Germany, remains an important feature of the sector.

Regulatory Regimes and Impacts

During the command economy years there was environmental legislation but

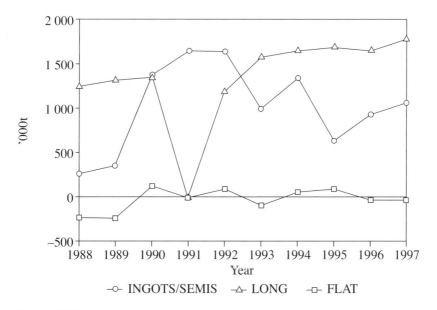

Source: IISI (various).

Figure 6.3   Poland: trade balance by major product group

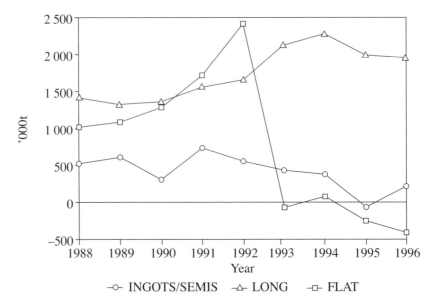

Note: ªCzechoslovakia to 1992; Czech Republic from 1993.

Source: IISI (various).

Figure 6.4   Czech Republic:ª trade balance by major product group

it was weak and ineffective (see Alcamo, 1992). However, during the mid-1980s there were improvements as pollution control and nature conservation (as in Western Europe) were considered and new legislation was established, such as the 'polluter pays' principle. However, until the market transition, environmental regulation and enforcement was not a high priority of the authorities and widespread environmental degradation was tolerated, as it was across the region (IIASA, 1992). Although legislation existed, such as stack height for emissions dispersal, the demands of production and the nature of the command economy overrode the principles of environmental management.

The transition has brought with it stronger environmental administration, in line with similar authorities which have come into existence throughout Europe to administer more modern environmental legislation (see Caddy, 1997). For instance, in the Czech Republic 14 pieces of environmental legislation were enacted between 1990 and 1995 in order to move towards greater harmony with the EU environmental legislation. The arrival of new legislation has raised criticism from the business sector that there was little consultation (hence existing implementation difficulties), although the Business Council for Sustainable Development and the Czech Environmental

Management Centre seek to act as mediators with government in order to influence environmental policy (Czech Environmental Management Centre, personal communication). Corrective action in the immediate or near term (3–5 year period) was activated by the new legislation, including various elements of economic and institutional reform, regulations and enforcement systems (IIASA, 1992).

Much of this was made possible by valuable support from Western Europe and the OECD via the PHARE programme that includes environmental protection, as well as from the World Bank and the European Bank for Reconstruction and Development. Between 1989 and 1993, Central and Eastern Europe received US$500 million for environmental protection, but for Poland alone it is estimated that $260 billion is required to reach a sustainable path of economic development, while the Czech Republic estimates $30 billion (Zylicz, 1993; Hewett, 1995; Kolk and van der Weij, 1998). A significant recognition of the need for international environmental cooperation and new sources of environmental protection investment was the 1991 meeting of World Bank, UNECE, OECD, EBRD and national representatives at Dobris Castle in the Czech Republic. The Dobris assessment led to an Environmental Action Programme for Central and Eastern Europe.

In the Czech Republic, environmental protection is the responsibility of the Ministry of Environment and industrial control is operated via a State Environmental Inspection Agency. The Ministry was set up in 1990 and the Agency, set up in 1991 by law, and separating from the forest management and protection division in 1993, has 30 regional inspectorates. The National Environment Fund established in 1991 is an important basis for environmental protection since emissions charges, groundwater abstraction and environmental fines are directed into it. Nevertheless, the problem for Environment Funds throughout the region is that levies are generally too low in relation to the damage caused, and they do not keep up with inflation, firms therefore prefer to pay the levies rather than invest in preventative measures (Kolk and van der Weij, 1998).

In Poland, there is considerable control at the regional and municipal government level where responsibility for environmental control is established. In the case of Katowice, where the steel industry is concentrated, the voivodship operates 10-year environmental plans. During 1985–95, planned reductions of 15 percent in dust and gas emissions were surpassed to reach 40 percent, mainly via economic mechanisms within the industry, better quality fuels and improved environmental technologies. As Anna Zawiejska of the Environment Department (Katowice Voivodship) notes: 'The greatest effect as far as air pollution is concerned was achieved in the metallurgical industry' (British Chamber of Commerce, Poland, 1997b).

The National Fund for Environmental Protection and Water Resources Management is an important mechanism in Polish environmental protection, and in 1991 it accounted for $400 million of environmental expenditures, one-third of the national total (Zylicz, 1993). An additional mechanism utilized in Poland is a national 'black list' of most polluting firms. In 1990 the Ministry for Environment compiled the list and forced the firms to present an environmental action plan. By 1996, only 17 of the 80 had fulfilled their environmental obligations although a quarter had gone out of business or been fragmented (*Business Central Europe* 1996a; Millard, 1998); in the metallurgy sector, Huta Czestochowa was erased from the list in 1998 following improvements.

Beyond emissions charges, penalties are small and the closure option is rarely considered. The closure of Vitkovice's (Czech Republic) iron-making division is, however, an example of where this has happened. In the cases where penalties have been paid, it is for persistent failure to address a problem that has been recognized by the inspection team. Nevertheless, it would appear that penalties *per se* do not provide a deterrent, apart from the administrative difficulties such as late or non-payment due to firm liquidity problems. In Poland in the late 1980s, the fine collection ratio only reached 40 percent (Statisches Bundesamt, 1995; Bates *et al.*, 1998).

Rather than a command-and-control system of environmental inspection in Central Europe, the systems appear to be flexible and to encourage change, mainly via economic instruments and considerations of eco-taxation alongside sectoral policies (see ECE, 1998; Kloz et al., 1998). The negative side of this is that firms may not always meet strict limits but will be treated lightly as long as they are seen to be improving and investing. The positive side is that firms are responding to the environment agencies, they do have environmental management objectives (some of them innovative, such as landfill remediation) and they are establishing longer-term targets to change processes and improve environmental performance. Huta Czestochowa (Poland), for example, has invested heavily in becoming a semi-integrated process firm with environmental systems incorporated as part of this development, whilst Nova Huta is building a mini-mill with the assistance of the US firm Kaiser.

The major challenge in the near future is convergence with the EU. For that to happen, a wide range of environmental performance improvements will have to be made, and this will also have to take place in terms of regulations and targets (see Table 6.14). The table outlines the gaps that exist at present and also shows that these two countries are leading the field of other Central and Eastern European countries. Legislation is likely to continue to be upgraded apace and fees and fines were expected to rise 20–50 percent by 2000. In Poland, for instance, there are currently amendments to the

Environmental Protection and Management Act, the Waste Act, a new Water Law, and a Framework Act of Environmental Management.

Table 6.14   Assessment of the compliance levels of the European Union environmental legislation in ten Central and Eastern European countries (%)

Legislative fields	Czech Rep.	Poland	Average (10)
General environmental policy regulation	77	63	57
Air	60	47	46
Chemicals, industrial risks and biotechnology	31	33	27
Nature conservation	67	100	65
Noise	17	50	32
Waste	56	26	33
Water	61	78	61

Source: Regional Environmental Center for Central and Eastern Europe (1996).

There is still a considerable gap between the state environmental protection agencies and firm environmental performances among the integrated firms of Central and Eastern Europe and the EU. Although atmospheric emissions limits have been tightened in Poland and the Czech Republic during the 1990s, there are numerous areas in which this tightening up has to take place. The fact that OHFs are still operating in several plants and that ironmaking takes place in older technologies that have only been subjected to stricter regulatory scrutiny during the 1990s suggests that the argument that there has been lower investment in environmental protection to date in these firms is valid and that there may be advantages accruing from this fact. However, it is also evident that the steel sectors in both countries have undergone wholesale changes during the 1990s in response to stricter regulations and national development and market circumstances. The closure of Vitkovice's ironmaking operations and the reduction in blast furnaces operating at the Sendzimira plant are signs of this taking place. Significant changes to operational management such as these have led to dramatic reductions in total emissions loads from these plants and others.

Firm Responses: Investment, Technological Change and Environmental Management

Much of the Central European steel industry is Soviet-built. The development of the industry in isolation from the steel industries of Western Europe and elsewhere led to heavy R&D investment and Soviet designed equipment. This equipment has been successful and in some cases it was highly advanced, such as in vertical continuous casting (Huta Zawiercie, Poland). From the end of the 1980s, intensive investment in environmental technologies was required, as well as investments in updating process technologies. A problem that is not limited to the steel sector is that much of the environmental technology development has continued to focus on end-of-pipe palliative measures. For example, of the $250 million of bilateral EC aid to 1992, only five of 140 projects involved renewable energy or cleaner technology: all were funded by Denmark (Manser, 1994).

Generally speaking, there is a wide range of technologies across the Czech Republic and Poland. The outmoded OHF system still survives in these countries, despite developments such as Nova Hut's 'tandem furnaces' which lead to considerable energy savings as heat from one in operation pre-heats the other. Against this openhearth tradition, albeit declining rapidly, can be weighed many of the newer EAF plants that have been set up and which reveal few differences from EAFs in EU countries.

Newer technologies that are considered state-of-the-art across the world, such as the alternative ironmaking technologies, pulverised carbon injection and turbines for gas recycling, are not common in Eastern Europe although the larger and more buoyant firms may well invest in such technologies in the near future. Currently, there are examples of the construction of new 'mini-mills', increased continuous casting, and more product-related investments in the downstream areas of the plants. Despite firm level developments, there is little state support. It is only recently that the Czech Business Council for Sustainable Development has been promoting the 'win–win' concept as a way of encouraging greater interest and investment.

Due to the strong recent history of local R&D during the Soviet period, there remains a pronounced academic, technical and engineering tradition that has moved on to environmental technologies as part of its own evolution. For this reason, there is currently a balance between imported technologies and those which are being developed by domestic firms (for example, OPAM in Poland), the steel firms themselves or in collaboration with local institutions. When imported technologies are required, it is often neighbouring countries such as Austria and Germany that are turned to (Kazmierczyk, 1997; *Business Central Europe*, 1996a).

Steel companies have only taken a systematic approach to environmental management in the last 10–15 years at most. In Western Europe, for example, most large firms only instituted an environment department during the 1980s. In Central Europe the changes have been more recent, with the development of environmental management – as opposed to unintegrated water and air emissions control teams performing basic monitoring and maintenance functions – from the late 1980s and into the 1990s. A problem during the 1990s was that initial business enthusiasm for the environment led to studies that revealed only difficulties, therefore managers rapidly became sceptical. Currently, the Czech Ministry of Environment is attempting to promote environmental management. During 1998, a government decree on EMAS implementation was passed and an accreditation system is already in place. It is a voluntary scheme and two firms have already been accredited. The objective is part of the general shift in policy to the EU directives. In the Czech Republic, IPPC/BAT implementation is taking place and is likely to be made compulsory from 2007 (Ministry of Environment, personal communication).

The ISO 14.000 system of establishing environmental management has only been in operation for five years, therefore it is not surprising to find a mixed reaction to the system and its implementation. Since it is not commonplace in Western Europe, one must ask the question, why should one expect to find it in Central Europe? The reason is market access. For the same reason that firms in developing economies, such as Korea and Brazil, have moved towards 14.001 (EMS) certification, the transition economies can also be expected to have seen it as a market driver. Nova Huta was only the second company in the Czech Republic to gain ISO 14.001, for its rolling mill plant. Huta Czestochowa's coke oven batteries received the first ISO 14.001 certification in Poland.

Within the Czech Republic, it is the business sector's Czech Environmental Management Centre and the Czech chapter of the Business Council for Sustainable Development which have promoted a positive response to proactive environmental management. To date, 10–12 Czech firms have certification and numerous others are undergoing the implementation process (Czech Environmental Management Centre, personal communication). One of the strategies is for implementation to take place amongst groups of firms; this is currently the policy of INEM (the International Network for Environmental Management). Accreditation companies perceive market opportunities in this area. Lloyds, for example, set up an office for accreditation in Prague in 1993 for ISO 9.000, but from 1998 an environmental consultant was posted to deal with the rise in 14.000 demands. Lloyds is itself competing against several German accreditation firms (such as RWTUV); by July 1997 RWTUV had accredited five firms in the Czech Republic.

Despite the very high levels of contamination around the principal steel regions of Central Europe, public opposition to heavy industries is not intense. Clearly the environmental legislation of the early 1990s, such as stricter air emissions limits and rising landfill taxes, have had an impact on firms; however, for residents near the steel firms one must question to what extent the levels of contamination have fallen. As with firms in Western Europe and elsewhere, there are few set mechanisms to improve links with 'neighbours' and stakeholders, such as the municipal government, residents and other commercial operations. The outcome is often a range of activities that involve educational programmes, improved dialogue and communication, and 'sweeteners' to those neighbours who claim to have been affected by firm operations.

If there is one area that would facilitate improved assessment of steel firm environmental performance it would be auditing and accounting. Since this is the next step in the ISO 14.000 range of norms, it is likely that significant developments will take place in this area in the short term; however, until comparative information is constructed at a firm level, it is exceedingly difficult to compare like with like across the sector and then to make international comparisons. In Poland, Huta Czestochowa has been working on a model with a technical university and has presented its model at a seminar for other Polish steel firms. If successful, the firm hopes to establish 'first mover' benefits and gain from any environmental services opportunities that may result.

Environmental Regulations and Sectoral Change

The Central European steel sector has undergone major restructuring in the last decade. The most extreme example is Huta Sendzimira (Poland) which has closed two of five furnaces, decreased output from 6 Mt to 2.6 Mt and reduced labour from 40,000 to 17,000. The focus now is on competition based on increased continuous casting and other machinery (an investment of $400 million), a shift towards products in demand domestically such as flat steels (now 90 percent of output), and increased productivity (*Business Central Europe*, 1997). Foreign consultancy reports on restructuring in both Poland and the Czech Republic envisaged output figures at approximately half their 1989 levels by the year 2000, with accompanying labour reductions and specialization, quality and productivity efforts (Ambroz, 1997). In Poland the cost of this process was estimated at $4.45 billion (Polish Metallurgical Chamber of Commerce, personal communication).

Beyond the pressure for convergence and more open competition for products across Europe, Central European firms must also be aware of increasing competition from further east, from those countries which are not investing in new equipment, which retain low-cost labour inputs, and which also have abundant subsidized energy. It appears that Central and Eastern Europe will develop into a region of lower labour costs and basic low-technology production for export into the European Union (until convergence takes place). Steel production is likely to follow a similar path, especially in terms of the orientation of export production. Low labour costs and energy costs are likely to prevail compared with Western European competitors, but the gap in environmental costs (charges and fines) will decline as convergence intensifies. Another outcome may be the increase of sub-contracting by Western European firms to the east, and even joint ventures or buy-outs (UNIDO, 1995).

Technology is both a saviour of Central European industry and a hurdle for it. It can provide the means by which strict new limits can be reached, but also the cost of up-to-date technology can be prohibitive, especially during the uncertainty of this transition phase. Of the two difficulties cited for Czech harmonization for EU environmental protection, the introduction of new and advanced technologies is highlighted; the second is the passing of new environmental legislation. For Poland, it is the difficulties associated with emissions law, such as the reductions in emissions limits, and the movement towards a BATNEEC concept (Regional Environmental Center, 1996). Despite these considerations, the modernization process in many steel plants reveals the need to move beyond traditional technologies, open hearth furnaces in particular, towards more efficient production technologies and effective capture systems.

In terms of the directions firms may take, much will depend on the relevant governments' balancing of economic imperatives and environmental needs. Opinions are mixed about how successful they have been to date during the 1990s. Fagin and Jehlicka (1998) are critical of the second transition Czech government in terms of how it favoured end-of-pipe approaches rather than sustainable development considerations, to the extent that the term 'sustainable development' does not appear in the 1995 State Environment Policy document. Francis Millard (1998) is also critical of a 'clean-up' rather than damage prevention approach in Poland.

It must be noted that the steel sectors in both countries underwent major restructuring during the 1990s. This included heavy environmental investment. While there are wide variations between firms, in that some have closed some operations whilst others have invested in upgrading and process change, there are similarities in that technological change has been required to meet new legislation. Although regulatory pressures are often flexibly enforced at present, the new demands of legislation and the movement towards convergence and the need to be conscious of IPPC has required greater firm awareness. These changes have been undertaken within environmental management structures that have advanced considerably during the 1990s to deal with the new demands. With restructuring leading to a 50 percent capacity loss, it is likely that the firms that survive will be those which have invested in more modern technologies, such as continuous casting to improve productivity. Older technologies such as open hearth furnaces will be closed alongside other 'dirtier' technologies. In this respect, the 1995–2005 period in Central Europe will have almost imitated the 1980s changes in the Western Europe steel sector. The environmental benefits emanating from such a restructuring process will be considerable.

GLOBALIZATION, STEEL AND ENVIRONMENT

It is apparent that environmental protection measures are not employed evenly at national or international levels across the steel sector. The firms which are most proactive in this area are those which are part of larger groups, those which produce for export, and those with environmental strategies generated from an executive level. Perceptions of future trade restrictions based on environmental factors, whether as suppliers or directly from consumers or financial pressures derived from shareholder activities or affected communities, are apparently drivers in this regard. Independent firms and those producing for domestic markets appear less motivated to introduce environmental technologies or management measures. Although there is a general consensus across firms that 5–10 percent of investment and operating costs are committed to the area of environment, this figure varies considerably year on year and from plant to plant.

Due to this comparatively low figure *vis-à-vis* energy, labour, transport and raw materials costs, firms remain less concerned by the influence of environmental costs in terms of competitiveness than they do of other factors. It therefore receives low priority within firms although there is a commitment to compliance (to avoid penalties and public relations difficulties) and in certain cases a commitment to environmental issues as a proactive rather than reactive firm strategy, for example POSCO and Usiminas. Nevertheless, it is clear that the factor of environment increased in terms of profile and awareness within EU firms during the 1980s, and during the 1990s in particular in the transitional and industrializing economies. For this reason there is a lag in terms of environmental responses by EU firms and those of firms in competitor economies, but the regulatory standards in the latter economies are being strengthened continually to be increasingly on a par with the EU. This is the case, for example, in the Central and Eastern European economies seeking convergence with the EU and harmonization of environmental regulations. Of more significance, due to the wide variations in terms of regulatory implementation and firm performance both within the EU and within these other economies, is the environmental performance of individual firms rather than of national steel sectors *per se*.

The firms at the cutting edge of environmental management are pursuing process technology developments, raw material, energy and product research, and a more comprehensive approach to environmental issues, which includes not only prevention and control but also communication of activities. By taking a longer-term view and a strategic approach to environmental activities, these firms seek to turn the costs of control into competitive advantage, either in terms of compliance cost reduction, market access or the public perception of the firm (and in turn its market value). The point to make here is that these firms are relatively few, and although they support Porter and van der Linde's 'win–win' concept in terms of investing in the environment and attempting to generate commercial advantages from doing so, there is no evidence to suggest that there are competitiveness benefits from pursuing this strategy versus other more conventional competitive strategies, such as product development or niche market specialization. Only in the even fewer cases where steel firms have invested in process technology and environmental technology development for the subsequent sale of these technologies is there an explicit link between stricter environmental regulations, initial environmental investments and subsequent commercial gains. Mannesmann (Germany) and Voest Alpine (Austria) are examples of firms that have taken this approach.

In the case of 'pollution havens' and firms relocating to avoid stricter environmental regulations, it is necessary to investigate processes and products rather than the aggregate data for the sector. At the aggregated level, it is clear that demand is increasing in developing economies more rapidly than in developed and transitional economies. For example, China's share of global consumption has risen from 8.9 percent in 1988 to 16.5 percent in 1997, and the share of 'Other Asia' (which excludes China and Japan) has increased from 9.2 percent to 14.7 percent (IISI, various). The result has been an attempt by developed economy firms to globalize, by establishing new plants and joint ventures in areas of potential demand. It is not for reasons of labour costs or weak environmental regulations that these firms are expanding their operations, but rather to gain market access. Although it is possible to export products to these growing markets, the high transport costs of finished products makes it more profitable to establish new plants. In many cases these plants are EAF operations, specializing in value-added products that are not currently offered by domestic producers.

Technological take-up, both of process and environmental control equipment, is highly variable beyond a basic level of almost universal applications. The differences between integrated and EAF routes are clear and in the latter the options available to firms are fewer than those existing for integrated plants but at the same time they have fewer problem areas. In integrated firms, the presence of the 'dirtier' processes of ironmaking (sinter plants and coke ovens) poses an added problem, alongside the sheer volumes of emissions and wastes produced along the route from raw materials to finished product, and the toxicity of certain emissions, such as dioxins, benzene, toluene, and so on. Despite significant reductions in energy use, solid waste recycling, atmospheric emissions and water discharges from the 1970s, there is still room for improvement despite lower returns. The new wave of environmental control developments are to be found in process changes, such as the switch from conventional ironmaking to direct reduction iron (DRI), and also in continuous casting. Although continuous casting is being applied on a broad front across the world, other technologies remain at a pilot phase and will need to demonstrate their cost effectiveness before more firms make the extensive capital commitment that is required. Most large steel firms remain 'second movers' rather than 'first movers' in terms of major technological changes since the factor of risk is excessively high under current global market conditions.

At the level of products and processes, the impacts of environmental regulations on the globalization of the sector become more apparent. It is evident that the pollution-intensive processes of steel production, such as ironmaking via sintering, coking and blast furnaces, have been affected by increasing environmental pressures and subsequent regulations. The increased share in EAF route steel, the collapse of the 'dirty' open hearth furnace route, and the increases in alternative ironmaking technologies all bear witness to this shift away from traditional ironmaking. It is significant that coke and sinter production has declined in heavily regulated economies and that this is not so elsewhere; China provides the most remarkable example of this shift. Although environmental technologies can provide safeguards (to a certain extent) in both these processes, such as electrostatic precipitators in the sintering process, it is the fugitive emissions and the toxicity of certain byproducts (dioxins, benzene, toluene, polycyclic aromatic hydrocarbons (PAHs) and so on) that continue to make environmental management problematic and costly.

The desire to seek alternatives to these traditional ironmaking processes is apparent throughout the sector. To date, these alternatives to traditional ironmaking are not proven at large volumes and are not leading to shifts away from the sinter and coke inputs. What appears to be happening is that there is a reduction in coke per tonne of liquid steel production accompanied by a global shift to increased trade in coke, with demand in developed economies being met from developing and transitional economies, such as Poland. In this way, there has been a subtle process of industrial flight within the steelmaking process. This can be defined as a 'hide and source' strategy by developed economy firms as a response to a tightening of atmospheric environmental regulations for an industrial process which suffers from various environmental management problems.

The global iron and steel industry has changed significantly since the 1970s.

Alongside extensive restructuring and changes in technologies and products, consideration of environmental issues and investment in technologies and management systems has increased. Despite wide variations across firms and countries, there have been universal improvements in energy use and emissions loads. Nevertheless, the sector remains one of the most pollution-intensive industrial sectors and rising environmental awareness within governments and civil society will bring further pressures to bear in terms of stricter and new regulations, economic instruments, technology benchmarks and voluntary initiatives. It is clear that there are competitiveness implications that are derived from these developments since pollution abatement costs will be different and are highly variable year on year due to major long-term technology investments.

To assess the level of these competitiveness impacts is a complex process due to the range of variables involved, yet overall variations are unlikely to be more than ±5 percent of investment and operating costs. When considered relative to the key competitiveness factors in the sector, such as raw materials, energy, transport and labour costs, and related factors such as productivity and capital costs, and the age and location of plants, the environment as a factor in competitiveness must be contextualized and its relative importance given sufficient recognition without exaggeration.

It is not clear that transitional and developing economy firms generate advantages in their competitiveness positions from poor environmental performance. Although investment in pollution abatement, take-up of environmental management systems and technological innovations in cleaner technologies have generally been introduced in EU and other developed economy firms prior to their competitor firms in transitional and developing economies, there are eco-efficiencies and productivity gains that can be established as a result of these innovations, therefore such developments should not be considered as a purely negative impact on competitiveness. It is also the case that there is a flow of technological and service innovations from firms in more developed economies to those elsewhere, apart from exceptions such as POSCO which is a newer firm and has a large R&D organization (that is, POSRI, POSTECH, RIST) to support innovation and transfer.

There is a time lag between take-up of technological and management changes in EU firms and those in transitional and developing economies (also within these regions between similar types of firms), but it is difficult to claim that this delay creates a medium- or long-term competitive disadvantage for those who innovate or modify their activities first, as a response to regulation or market pressures. This is not to say that the 'win–win' scenario is alive and well, but rather to emphasize quite different points: that environmental issues are not *determining* factors in firm performance and competitive positions; that environmental regulations will inevitably lead to additional costs for firms but that these may be recovered to some extent from advantages established through eco-efficiencies, and increasingly, market opportunities and improved community and wider public relations; that firms do not migrate to avoid environmental regulations, but rather relocate to take advantage of market access opportunities; and finally, that rather than observing changes in production and trade in the final product, there are more important issues to address in terms of 'hide and source' strategies (such as cokemaking) and potential gains from process technologies (such as continuous casting, PCI) rather than from environmental technologies *per se*.

Although many firms in the EU perceive themselves to be disadvantaged by environmental regulations compared with their competitors in transitional and developing economies, and claim that these competitor firms generate competitive advantages from lax regulatory regimes and subsequent poor environmental performance, this picture is oversimplified and consequently inaccurate. There are wide variations in firm environmental performance and regulatory implementation and enforcement across the EU as there is across national steel sectors in transitional and developing economies.

Different licensing arrangements, different regulatory resourcing and foci, different plant vintages and processes, different products and markets, and different locations all lead to a highly complex pattern of regulatory impacts and responses. However, it is overwhelmingly the factors of raw materials, energy and labour costs, market dynamics and national economic conditions that determine steel firm competitiveness. Environmental regulations and their costs and benefits for firms are the icing on the cake. Firms may seek strategic ways of reducing these costs, such as outsourcing problematic products or processes, or enhancing the benefits such as capitalizing on the public relations and market advantages that may be derived from cleaner production, but they are unlikely to determine the success or failure of a firm in domestic or international markets.

In the highly competitive markets of the late twentieth and early twenty-first centuries, it has been a rational strategic decision for firms to pay more attention to environmental issues in terms of controlling the costs and enhancing the benefits that result from responses driven by environmental regulations. Additionally, firms have been increasingly sensitive to client demands in these areas, and to community, environmental group and media pressures. However, there remain wide variations between different scales, processes and orientations of firms in terms of these responses. Current and future environmental regulations in the EU and elsewhere should encourage *all* firms to be more responsible in terms of environmental management, and ensure that environmental performance is not considered merely as a supplement to economic performance.

Steel production can be less pollution-intensive. The industry itself has proved this and continues to strive in this direction. Regulations, whether via indirect or direct instruments, or with increased voluntary dimensions or technological elements (such as the technological benchmarking of IPPC), can assist in this drive towards a cleaner manufacturing sector. Steel firms are not unadaptable and slow to innovate. They have adapted with considerable flexibility to changes in global process, product, price and market trends during the 1980s and 1990s, and they are able to respond with equal vigour to the challenges of societal demands for cleaner manufacturing. A few firms will experience a 'win–win' scenario in the process, via innovations in new technologies, but most will internalize the costs of the response and adapt to reduce them. Steel firms will not be uprooted and forced to relocate to reduce these costs although the demands for more flexible and globalized steel corporations will lead to new joint ventures and new plants. The internationally competitive steel firms of the twenty-first century will be attentive to their environmental responsibilities; but more importantly, they will be concerned with market access, high levels of productivity and technological and product innovation. It is these factors rather than environmental regulations or other environmental pressures which will determine the changing make-up of global steel production.

PART III

Leather tanning: environmental regulations, competitiveness and locational shifts

Jan Hesselberg and Hege Merete Knutsen

DR STOCKMANN ... such as all the pollution seeping down into the bath house [the only tourist attraction in the small town] from the valley [with a tannery] above. ... Yes, I love my home town so much that I would rather see it destroyed than blossom on a lie.

A PERSON IN THE CROWD This is to speak of a pure enemy of the people!

(Henrik Ibsen, *En folkefiende* (1882), Oslo: Gyldendal, 1992, p. 88; authors' translation)

7. The global tanning industry: a commodity chain approach

The leather tanning project comprises a number of case studies in Germany, Italy, Portugal, Poland, the Czech Republic, Brazil, Mexico and India. The case studies are based on interviews in combination with other information and are presented in a way that highlights and discusses different aspects of competitiveness and environmental pressure and practice in the industry. The analytical framework and the state of the global tanning industry are presented in this chapter.

OBJECTIVE

The tanning industry was selected to attain knowledge on how *competitiveness* in a pollution-intensive, technologically mature, raw materials and labour-intensive industry is affected by changes in environmental regulations. In a broader context this implies that we want to shed light on the causes of changes in the international location of leather tanning since the 1970s. To what extent and how can these changes be attributed to increasing *environmental pressure* in Europe?

The 'Porter hypothesis' suggests that environmental regulations are good both for the environment and for competitiveness. Environmental regulations drive innovation and technological change, which lead to product and process-innovation offsets (Porter and van der Linde, 1995). In respect of product-innovation offsets, the costs of technological change that reduce environmental damage are offset by the fact that the products are improved and/or become more attractive to consumers and attain higher prices in the market. Process-innovation offsets refer to more efficient use of inputs, such as chemicals and energy, which reduce the cost of production. It is argued that resourceful and internationally competitive companies are *best* placed to achieve such offsets. An essential question is: what explanatory power does this hypothesis have in the technologically mature tanning industry? Furthermore, what mechanisms are at work in the tanning industry, facilitating or restraining more environmentally sound production?

What makes leather tanning of particular interest are the *spatial and*

functional changes that have taken place since the 1970s. In the period
1969–71 to 1994–6, the share of developing countries in global production of
light leather increased from 35 percent to 56 percent and from 26 percent to
56 percent in heavy leather.[1] The shares of both North America and Europe
declined (Tables 7.1 and 7.2). The decline is substantial in Northern European
countries such as Germany and the UK, whereas impressive growth rates level
out in Italy and Portugal.

*Table 7.1   Output of bovine hides and leather (wet salted weight) (% share
of the world)*

	Raw hides		Heavy leather		Light leather (area)	
	1969–71	1994–96	1969–71	1994–96	1969–71	1994–96
Europe	23	16	26	16	37	27
North America	24	16	13	8	14	5
South	36	47	26	56	35	56

Source: FAO (1994, 1998).

A similar trend has been evident in exports, particularly of light leather,
where the share of developing countries has increased considerably,
particularly since the late 1970s, while that of the developed countries,
especially Europe, has declined (see Tables 7.3 and 7.4).

There has been a decline in production and employment in the leather
industry in most developed countries in recent years (see Table 7.5). One-
fourth of the production units and one-third of the workforce have been lost in
the EU tanning industry since the beginning of the 1980s. There are only 3,000
tanneries left, and these employ some 50,000 workers. Of the total turnover of
the tanning production in the EU, Italy accounts for 54 percent, Spain 15
percent, Germany 7 percent, UK 6 percent and France 5 percent. Italy has
2200 tanneries,[2] Spain 278, Portugal 115 (120 according to our sources, see
below) and Germany fewer than 80 (Stanners and Bordeau, 1991; Rydin,
1997). Having said this, there has not been a *dramatic* decline in the *turnover*
of the tanning industry in the EU in recent years. In 1989, which was
considered 'a good year' for the industry, the turnover amounted to 8 billion
ECU, against 7.5 billion in 1994 (Stanners and Bordeau, 1991; Rydin, 1997).

Functional changes observed in the tanning industry are:

1. specialization takes place in the various *stages* of the production process
    resulting in increasing use of sourcing;[3]
2. tanneries specialize in production of leather for certain product types and

market segments; and

3. some former tanneries are now only involved in coordination and marketing.

For practical reasons the latter form of functional change was not examined as part of the study.

Table 7.2 *Production of bovine hides and leather (wet salted weight) (% share of the world)*

	Raw hides		Heavy leather		Light leather (area)	
	1977–9	1997	1977–9	1996	1977–9	1996
Brazil	4.6	9.3	5.8	5.2	4.7	4.8
India	6.1	6.3	8.5	11.0	5.7	5.4
Mexico	1.6	2.1	1.2	1.2	3.6	3.8
South Korea	—	—	3.1	2.7	2.5	13.8
Germany	3.9	2.4	1.7	—	5.8	1.3
Italy	2.5	2.4	9.2	11.5	10.5	16.1
USA	21.3	17.0	9.5	7.3	7.8	4.3
China[a]	—	10.0	2.0	22.0	2.0	10.0
Europe	22.0	15.0	24.0	16.0	38.0	27.0
North	64.0	51.0	67.0	42.0	62.0	43.0
South	36.0	49.0	32.0	58.0	38.0	57.0

Note: [a] China includes Hong Kong.

Source: Based on FAO (1996, 1998).

Table 7.3 *Exports of bovine hides and leather (wet salted weight) (% share of the world)*

	Raw hides		Heavy leather		Light leather (area)	
	1969–71	1994–96	1969–71	1994–96	1969–71	1994–96
Europe	28	34	59	63	48	26
North America	37	36	20	9	5	9
South	25	12	12	18	42	60

Source: FAO (1994, 1998).

Table 7.4   *Exports of bovine hides and leather (wet salted weight) (%
               share of the world)*

	Raw hides		Heavy leather		Light leather (area)	
	1977–9	1997	1977–9	1996	1977–9	1996
Brazil	—	1.1	4.2	2.6	5.2	4.2
India	—	—	4.2	—	7.0	2.1
South Korea	—	—	—	—	—	20.0
Germany	5.9	6.0	17.8	13.0	4.7	2.6
Italy	—	1.3	13.6	26.1	12.9	15.9
USA	39.2	32.8	8.1	9.8	9.4	9.1
China[a]	—	5.0	—	1.0	1.0	26.0
Europe	30.0	34.0	59.0	69.0	37.0	26.0
North	90.0	90.0	69.0	89.0	61.0	40.0
South	10.0	10.0	31.0	11.0	39.0	60.0

Note: [a] China includes Hong Kong.

Source: Based on FAO (1996, 1998).

THE TANNING INDUSTRY

Tanning is part of the leather industry. The leather industry consists of three
sub-segments: (a) those who produce hides and skins, that is, by animal
husbandry and slaughtering; (b) *the tanning industry*,[4] that is, the leather
production segment of the industry; and (c) the manufacture of leather
products, such as shoes, bags, garments and upholstery.

The three main stages of production in the tanning industry are (a) pre-
treatment (dehairing, remove flesh, pickling); (b) tanning *per se* where the
tanning agent is applied; and (c) finishing (after-treatment: drying, dyeing,
mask defects, add shine). The first two stages are wet processes. Traditionally,
all three stages have been carried out in the same production units. However,
with the on-going specialization that takes place in the branch, there are a
number of 'tanneries' that only do the finishing.

A Pollution-intensive Industry

Often *pollution-intensive* industries are defined as industries characterized by
high levels of toxic release after efforts have been made to control the
pollution and/or high levels of pollution abatement costs, compared with other

Table 7.5 Production and employment: leather and fur products (ISIC 323)

	Index of production 1990 = 100 (value)		Employment (thousand)	
	1985	1995	1985	mid-1990s
Belgium	146	45	3	3
France	119	82	24	14
Germany	112	67	25	17
Greece	118	79	4	2
Italy	112	94	27	32
Netherlands	144	77	2	1
Portugal	65	77	5	8
Spain	109	71	17	16
UK	78	99	24	16
USA	105	80	52	36
China	—	—	850	1491
India	84	139	40	46
South Korea	72	47	31	25

Source: UNIDO (1995, 1997, 1998).

industries. This implies that pollution-intensive industries can be understood as industries that are *potentially* polluting, that is, there are high levels of toxic discharge in production units of the industry in question *unless* high levels of investment are made to control the pollution. Tobey (quoted in Ballance *et al.*, 1993) classifies industries with pollution abatement costs of 1.85 percent or more of the production costs as pollution–intensive. Typically, environmental protection costs in the European tanning industry amount to 5 percent of the cost of production and 2–4 percent of the turnover (Stanners and Bordeau, 1991; Rydin, 1997). In other words, the tanning industry can be considered a pollution-intensive industry.

Wastewater contains dissolved and suspended organic and inorganic solids, potentially toxic metal salts, chrome and electrolytes such as sodium chloride and sulphide (see Figure 7.1). The biological oxygen demand (BOD) and chemical oxygen demand (COD) are high. Chrome-containing sludge and solid waste represent problems of disposal. Chrome is a controversial issue in the industry. It is not disputed that hexavalent chrome is highly toxic and carcinogenic. However, representatives of the industry are concerned that it has not been proved that trivalent chrome is hazardous: 'Numerous studies have been made on the toxicity of trivalent chromium. These studies include

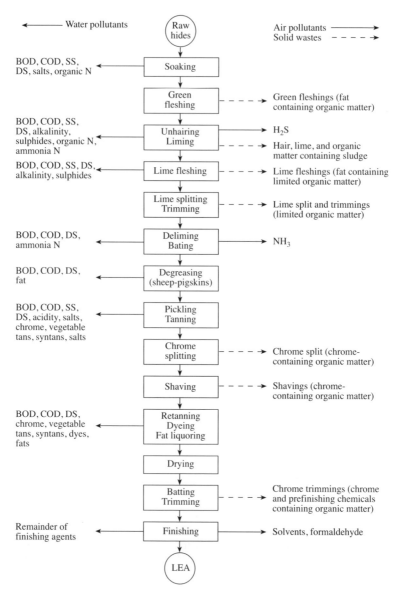

←——— Water pollutants

Raw hides

Air pollutants ——————→
Solid wastes – – – – →

BOD, COD, SS, DS, salts, organic N ← Soaking

Green fleshing – – – → Green fleshings (fat containing organic matter)

BOD, COD, SS, DS, alkalinity, sulphides, organic N, ammonia N ← Unhairing Liming → H₂S
– – – → Hair, lime, and organic matter containing sludge

BOD, COD, SS, DS, alkalinity, sulphides ← Lime fleshing – – – → Lime fleshings (fat containing limited organic matter)

Lime splitting Trimming – – – → Lime split and trimmings (limited organic matter)

BOD, COD, DS, ammonia N ← Deliming Bating → NH₃

BOD, COD, DS, fat ← Degreasing (sheep-pigskins)

BOD, COD, SS, DS, acidity, salts, chrome, vegetable tans, syntans, salts ← Pickling Tanning

Chrome splitting – – – → Chrome split (chrome-containing organic matter)

Shaving – – – → Shavings (chrome-containing organic matter)

BOD, COD, DS, chrome, vegetable tans, syntans, dyes, fats ← Retanning Dyeing Fat liquoring

Drying

Batting Trimming – – – → Chrome trimmings (chrome and prefinishing chemicals containing organic matter)

Remainder of finishing agents ← Finishing → Solvents, formaldehyde

LEA

Source: UNEP 1994, p. 20.

Figure 7.1   The production process of tanning

human, aquatic animal, plant subjects in great detail. The results conclude that chromium in the trivalent state is not a significant toxic.' (Thorstensen, 1997, p. 55) In the US trivalent chrome has been removed from the list of heavy metals which it is illegal to discharge. Tanners nowadays use trivalent chrome, which is also more economic in use, and tanners in Europe are frustrated about strict discharge limits on trivalent chrome and the fact that regulating authorities rarely distinguish between the two types. Having said all this, it has been found that even in modern trivalent chrome tanning there is a formation of hexavalent chrome during the wet processing. Wolf (2000) maintains that the way to prevent this formation is to eliminate *all* use of chrome salts. However, he admits that with most types of leather, it is impossible to dispense completely with trivalent chrome salts due to their excellent tanning action. Moreover, municipal or ordinary incineration of chrome-containing leather waste is not an option due again to the formation of hexavalent chrome (trivalent chrome is oxidized to hexavalent chrome) (*World Leather*, November 1999).

Finishing treatment may result in much air contamination due to the use of organic solvents in lacquers and pigments. It is now common to shift to water-based solvents. Bad odour is due to hydrogen sulphide and compounds containing sulphur, ammonia and nitrogen (Ballance *et al.*, 1993; Nordisk Ministerråd, 1993; Mensink and Lange, 1996). It is important to note that as much as 80 percent to 90 percent of the pollution, but only 15 percent of the value added, are usually generated in the wet processes (Miljøministeriet, 1992).

METHODOLOGY

The point of departure of the analysis is that spatial and functional changes in the division of labour result from *restructuring* in the industry, that is, closures and measures taken by the industry to remain competitive. Against this backdrop the role of environmental pressure in spurring and shaping the process of restructuring is examined (Knutsen, 1998a). Two types of pressure are considered: (a) environmental requirements, that is, environmental regulations and enforcement by the authorities; and (b) market pressure.

As qualitative data were required to analyse the on-going processes of restructuring in the industry, the case study approach was chosen. This approach is also the best way of obtaining data on delicate issues such as environmental strategies, since it allows for cross-checking of information from a wider range of sources (Knutsen, 1997). Our primary data are from in-depth interviews with tanners, and information from branch associations, institutions (such as, tanning schools and centres that render technical services

to the tanners) and suppliers of machinery and chemicals (Hesselberg, 1997).
In line with the case-study approach, selection of countries and tanneries was
made according to selected criteria relevant to the focus of the analysis. In
Western Europe, Germany was selected as a *best case* in terms of strict
environmental regulations and enforcement and Portugal as a possible *worst
case*. Italy is of interest, being the largest tanning nation in Europe. Poland and
the Czech Republic were selected because interviews in Germany and Italy
revealed increasing sourcing of wet-blue (semi-finished leather) from these
two countries. Moreover, Poland and the Czech Republic are liberalizing their
economies on the one hand and harmonizing their environmental regulations
with the EU on the other, in order to become members of the Union. Likewise,
Italian involvement in the Brazilian tanning industry was important to the
selection of Brazil. Moreover, the size and level of export of the Brazilian
tanning industry were important considerations. Mexico imports raw hides
and wet-blue from Brazil and has experienced increasing exports of leather
and leather products with economic liberalization. At the same time, the
country's inclusion in NAFTA (North American Free Trade Area) may have
enhanced the strictness of environmental regulations and enforcement. India
was selected as a possible worst-case developing country. Tanning is on the
verge of extinction in Scandinavia. Hence, tanneries in Norway, Sweden and
Denmark were included to supplement the data from Germany and Italy in
order to obtain more knowledge on causes of survival and success in the
increasingly sharp global competition. In the various countries the tanning
industry is not uniform. Tanneries typical of the main sub-segments of the
tanning industry in the respective countries were selected. Relevant criteria in
this respect were product type (upholstery leather, shoe leather and leather for
fashion/fancy products); market niche (the top and bottom end of the market);
degree of specialization in certain stages of the process versus sourcing of
components; whether sourcing wet-blue or not; whether foreign ownership or
not; and size of tannery (production/employees). In practice, it was mostly
best-case tanneries in the respective branch segments and countries that were
willing to participate in the study. As argued in the conclusion, this does not
jeopardize the main findings. The in-depth data are supplemented with
quantitative data/statistics on production and exports collected from secondary
sources. Data on regulations were obtained mainly from our interviewees in
the branch and to some extent from secondary sources, due to a limited time
schedule.

The Commodity Chain Approach

It is not possible to examine and assess the role of environmental regulations
and enforcement in the competitiveness of the tanning industry without also

looking into processes and factors of the 'non-environmental' type that affect competitiveness, such as technological change in the industry, trade and industrial policies, and access to markets, raw materials and labour. The restructuring–commodity chain approach developed in Knutsen (1998a) opens up the inclusion of 'non-environmental' aspects in the analysis of the tanning industry.

At the *international level* and at a high level of abstraction, restructuring can be attributed to processes such as the erosion of the Fordist mode of production and/or the introduction of a new techno-economic paradigm. This very abstract level of explanation is only briefly touched upon in this book. We are more concerned with lower levels of abstraction where restructuring is linked to economic globalization[5] and liberalization processes, as well as increasing pressure to reduce polluting production at the international and national level. Globalization here signifies the combination of geographical extension of economic activity across national borders and the functional integration of these activities. Functional integration, which is necessary in considering globalization, is signified by different forms of coordination and control. At the firm level it refers to a strategy of worldwide intra-firm division of labour where firms source inputs, semi-processed goods, knowledge and so on from wherever it is judged to be most beneficial and profitable.

Globalization in the world economy and at the firm level is understood as a restructuring response to the erosion of the Fordist mode of production, facilitated by the new opportunities offered by new technology to coordinate economic activities in distant places. The new technology *per se* may also spur restructuring, as it offers possibilities of productivity enhancement through automation, and more flexibility in responding to variations in demand and quality improvements (Knutsen, 1998b, 2000).

Economic liberalization generally makes it easier for firms and branches to pursue a globalization strategy. Furthermore, when firms go global, this is often used as an argument by industry and politicians to pressure for increasing economic liberalization. When some firms go global, the competitive environment of the supplier and client industries in the commodity chain change, and these industries too may have to restructure. Economic liberalization implies, among other things, that the tanning industry is subject to changes in trade policies.

At the *branch level*, branches and branch segments are affected differently by the above processes. Branch specific factors, such as technological characteristics (technological change is easier to attain in some branches than other) and characteristics of the commodity chain of the branch in question, explain this. Commodity chains signify the sequence of value-adding activities that make up the final product, where each activity can be considered a node in the chain, and the power relations between the parties that interact

(Gereffi, 1996). The former dimension of value-adding activities reflects economic linkages merely in terms of input–output structures. It is the latter dimension of power relations, which is sometimes referred to as governance structures of coordination and control, that make the input–output structure interesting. Power relations determine what activity is going to take place and where; in what node of the chain surpluses are generated and/or appropriated; how much of the surplus is reinvested in what node; and what nodes cover adjustment costs when surpluses are low or zero. The significance of place and time for the activities in question are intrinsic to the concept of commodity chains as, for example, industrial policies and regulations affect power relations between the business interests represented in the respective nodes. The commodity chain approach visualizes the aspect of coordination and regulation of geographically dispersed activities, and hence the above-mentioned functional aspects that are necessary in order to speak of globalization.

The input–output structure of the commodity chain of the tanning industry begins at the input end with the agricultural sector that provides the raw hides via slaughterhouses and their agents and dealers. In addition, machinery, equipment, chemicals and knowledge are supplied by the machinery and chemical industry. At the output end, footwear and upholstery manufacturers are the main markets for the tanners.

The hypothesis of Gereffi, Korzeniewicz and Korzeniewicz (1994) is that capital from the North[6] coordinates and controls the links that keep the commodity chain together, and tend to extract surplus value from the South or the periphery. The potential to do so is perhaps more in *buyer-driven* than *producer-driven* commodity chains. In a buyer-driven commodity chain it is the buyers, who are brand-name companies and retailers, who have the authority to determine 'where and how global manufacturing takes place' (Gereffi 1994b, p. 99). High profit levels may be attained when low-cost production in low-cost locations are combined with premium prices in the final market, due to the attraction of a brand-name. In the producer-driven commodity chain, control is in the hands of giant firms with a long history in the world economy. They control backward and forward linkages in capital and technology-intensive goods.

Gereffi's distinction between buyer-driven and producer-driven commodity chains is similar to the more narrow distinction of Rosenberg (1976) between *consumer-* versus *producer*-initiative, referring to the *initiative to innovate*. When the initiative to innovate resides among the consumers (or client industries), innovations tend to be incremental in character, while producer-initiative more often leads to radical innovations (Gjerdåker, 1999). As argued below, the commodity chain of the tanning industry is predominantly buyer-driven.

At the *firm level*, technological competence, financial resources, coordination and marketing skills are considered the main sources of power in the commodity chain. Polluting production can be externalized to the weaker parties in the commodity chain. However, functional integration in the chain through sourcing agreements, that contain technology collaboration, may also up-grade the weaker party technologically, which in turn results in positive effects for the environment (Knutsen, 2000).

The *place-specific level* deals with how the local context (national or sub-national) conditions the nature of the restructuring in the branch. As already implied, relevant factors are industrial and trade policies and regulations; environmental regulations and their enforcement and timing; consumer pressure; local business culture and so on.

COMPETITIVENESS AND ENVIRONMENTAL PRACTICE

In its most simple form *competitiveness* refers to the ability of a firm to earn profits, survive and grow in the market. Low profits and mere (temporary) survival usually give connotations of weak competition, which is based on a competitive strategy of cost cutting and price leadership. Strong competition, in contrast, requires constant innovation and often leads to growing market shares. It is based on a competitive strategy where firms, for instance, compete in uniqueness in the market and with superior quality products for which customers are willing to pay premium prices. Hence, the argument is that strong competition is more profitable and more viable in the longer run than weak competition (Storper and Walker, 1989; Porter, 1990). It is important to keep in mind that weak and strong competition, or put differently, competition in cost cutting/price leadership on the one hand and superior quality and uniqueness in the market on the other, are generic strategies, that is, they represent two different classes of strategies with internal variations and sub-categories. In practice, firms rely on combinations of cost cutting and quality, but the dominant element of the two determines what generic strategy a firm pursues. Moreover, as the case of the tanning industry illustrates, below, it is possible to compete in superior quality and uniqueness in the market and still earn low profits.

In line with the 'Porter hypothesis' above, one may expect that the more quality-orientated firms are in their competitive strategy, the more likely they are to perform well in terms of environmental practice. This is due to the possibilities of process and product-innovation offsets. In the same vein, the more dependent firms are on cost cutting and price competition, the more important it may also become to make use of opportunities to pollute. All cost cutting matters and there may not be sufficient surplus available for investments in cleaner technology that would otherwise have been profitable in the longer run. In such cases externalization of polluting stages of production to weaker units in the commodity chain through sourcing relationships is an option. The more externalized the sourcing relationship is, both from a functional and a geographical point of view, the better the opportunities of hiding pollution. The point is that the less formalized the relationship and the more remote the supplier, the more difficult it is to hold the core firm responsible for the pollution that is caused. Moreover, when suppliers bid for contracts with core firms in competition with other low-cost suppliers, they may end up cutting costs to such an extent that they cannot afford environmental measures. On the contrary, when core firms cater to demand for eco-products in the top end of the market, they may put pressure on their suppliers to improve their environmental practice and even assist in the required technological up-grading. Customers are generally much more concerned with how harmful it is to consume a product than whether the production process has been polluting, especially when production takes place far away. It is, however, not uncommon that measures to make a product safer for the consumer also result in some improvement in the environmental practice of the producers.

TECHNOLOGICAL CHARACTERISTICS

As mentioned in the objective of the study above, leather tanning is a *raw materials-intensive*, *labour-intensive* and technologically *mature* industry. The typical cost structure in Europe is that raw materials account for 55 percent of production costs, labour 12 percent, chemicals 10 percent, energy 3 percent and 'other production costs' 20 percent. The latter includes 5 percent pollution abatement costs (Rydin, 1997). Having once been a profitable industry in Europe, margins are now generally low. In interviews profits are held to be about 3 percent in Germany and 2 percent or below in Portugal. Some are even happy to earn profits at all. A lot of capital is tied up in raw hides. Tanning may take 20–25 days from pre-treatment to completion of the finishing processes, and a medium-scale tannery may well have £1 million tied up in raw materials at any time. Being a byproduct of meat production, supplies of raw hides of a quality that can be used by the tanners fluctuate. High-quality hides in particular are scarce, and prices are high.

Incremental technological changes take place in the production process, but there has not been any *significant* reduction in the unit cost of production. Neither have the changes that have taken place in the finishing processes been sufficient for the industry to escape sharp price competition even in higher quality market segments. At present the industry appears to be bumping against a technological ceiling. The properties and costs of the raw materials constrain radical technological change. There are many steps in the production process and the chemicals applied in the various steps have to be compatible. Hence, the tanners are reluctant to experiment with chemicals for fear of ruining the expensive raw material. The scope of mechanization and automation is restricted due to the fact that the hides are of different sizes. To cut them to standard shapes would result in a lot of wasted material. High quality raw material for the best quality leather is processed individually, based on craftsmanship and tacit knowledge built through generations. Tanners in this niche are reluctant to collaborate closely with chemicals and machinery suppliers, fearing that their secrets will leak out to competitors. This mainly applies to German tanners, whereas Italian tanners tend to use new finishing technology which has to a large extent been developed by German and Swiss suppliers of chemicals. Portuguese tanners also collaborate with such suppliers but are more reluctant than the Italians to collaborate with each other due to mistrust.

Although the chemistry of the tanning process is complex, standard technology is simple in the sense that it is possible to produce leather on the basis of recipes from the suppliers of chemicals. Standard technology diffuses easily to 'new' competitors with the help of suppliers of chemicals and machinery. However, in the high quality tanneries that remain in northern Europe, tacit knowledge and artisan skills, as well as creativity and sense of fashion pertaining to the finishing of the leather, give a competitive edge. Although some tacit knowledge is applied in standard technology, it is not as important to competitiveness as in the high quality niche, where appearance and durability matter more.

RESTRUCTURING AND PRESSURE IN THE COMMODITY CHAIN

Historically the tanning industry in the North has 'followed' the more labour-intensive footwear industry to developing and other low-cost countries (Tables 7.6 and 7.7). This is first and foremost signified by a locational shift where expansion of footwear production in 'new countries' has spurred the establishment of a domestic tanning industry. In addition, some tanners in the North relocated production to these countries. This was done to circumvent tariff barriers, cut costs and to be located closer to the customers so that they could respond more easily and quickly to their demands. The footwear industry in low-cost countries competes fiercely in price. The pressure trickles down to tanners in the lower-cost segments in high cost countries who are then 'compelled' to relocate so that they too can exploit the place-specific low cost advantages. Even manufacturers of leather products who are located in developed countries and compete in higher quality niches shop around for cheap leather of reasonable quality. Due to the profit squeeze this represents, tanners in the North source semi-processed leather from low cost countries in Eastern Europe and the developing countries as a means of cost cutting. As expressed by one of the famous upholstery manufacturers in Germany who caters to the top end of the market, customers accept a price differential of 10 percent, but not 20 percent.

*Table 7.6   Production of leather footwear (ISIC 324), index 1990 = 100
          (value)*

	1985	mid-1990s
Germany	145	60
Italy	116	95
UK	114	73
USA	133	81

Source: UNIDO (1998).

*Table 7.7   Exports of leather footwear (ISIC 324), % share of the world
          (value)*

	1977–9	1994	1996
Germany	4	2	4
Italy	38	21	25
Portugal	1	6	6
US	—	2	1
China[a]	1	26	25
Europe	88	52	55
North	90	54	58
South	10	46	42

Note: [a] China includes Hong Kong.

Source: Based on FAO (1994, 1996, 1998).

As already mentioned above, raw hides are expensive, supplies fluctuate and high quality hides are often scarce. On top of this, developing countries with domestic supplies of raw hides imposed embargoes and restrictions on exports of these in the late 1960s and the 1970s. This was part of their industrial policy to support the development of more value-added exports. Export embargoes also reduced the prices of raw hides in these countries. Hence, relocation of production and outsourcing are means to ensure better access to raw materials as well as to reduce the cost of the raw material. Sourcing of lower quality raw materials and semi-processed leather from developing countries reduces the cost of the final product. Despite the fact that incremental changes have resulted in more advanced finishing so that lower quality inputs can be processed into relatively high value finished products, the raw materials end of the commodity chain still represents a profit squeeze to the tanning industry at large.

Suppliers of machinery and chemicals are the main innovators in the branch. They are sensitive to the locational changes that take place and up-grade tanners in the 'new' countries to secure future markets. This is borne out by our findings in Brazil and Mexico. Thus the locational shift is to a large extent outside the control of the tanning industry itself. However, tanners also up-grade tanneries in 'new' countries to protect their own competitiveness in the short run, that is, to get access to reasonably good quality raw hides and semi-processed leather. This sharpens the price competition in the industry.

Together the two squeezes, at the raw materials and the market end respectively, result in low profits that are an obstacle to investment in technological change which could otherwise have improved profits. Put differently, the industry is trapped in a vicious circle of price competition that is difficult to break out of. As already mentioned, tanning is labour intensive and labour costs are lower in Eastern Europe and the South than in Western Europe. Generally speaking it is a problem that price competition limits how much the tanneries in Western Europe can afford to pay for labour, although some tanneries may balance out higher labour costs with higher efficiency (Knutsen, 1999).

The *power relations* in the leather commodity chain have increasingly turned in favour of the client industries. Hence, the commodity chain has become increasingly buyer-driven: 'the imbalance of power between offer and demand is all in favour of the latter, which is able not only to haggle or impose prices but also to determine the relocation of production centres' (*World Leather*, May 1996, p. 23). Due to intense competition in the tanning industry, buyers are able to squeeze the tanners for lower prices, increased performance standards, shorter delivery times and smaller production runs. The clients demand more, but want to pay less. The result is an increased profit squeeze on the tanners. The bargaining power *vis-à-vis* their client industries is reduced, and lower profits imply reduced financial means to demand more advanced technology from suppliers of machinery and chemicals.

The changes in the commodity chain have led to a situation where the initiative[7] to innovate to an increasing extent comes from the client industries:

'Strong international competition makes it impossible to divert much capacity from this everyday fight for market positions to basic research' (Taeger, 1996, p. 223). The lack of producer initiative has made it easier for newcomers in the tanning industry to catch up with established producers. As the tanning industry has been 'maturing' and the pace of technological development has slowed down, it has become increasingly difficult to create competitive advantage based on process offsets: 'The high level of technological globalization means that leadership based on technology is likely to be short lived' (*World Leather*, June/July 1996, p. 32). Skills and technology are spreading to an increasing number of producers, making it difficult to maintain a technological leadership over competitors: 'innovations are becoming few and far between and the technological edge of the industrialized countries is shrinking' (Taeger, 1996, p. 212).

NOTES

1. Light leather is used for shoe uppers and a number of different leather products, whereas heavy leather is used for items such as shoe soles, belting, straps and mechanical leather. Heavy leather is made from unsplit cattle hides.
2. They are mostly small scale.
3. Sourcing refers to a core firm buying semi-finished or finished products from the supplier, off the shelf or according to specifications on a contractual basis. The semi-finished products are completed and both categories of products are marketed as a part of the product range of the core firm (Bergstø *et al.*, 1998).
4. Technically speaking, number 441 in EU's NACE classification scheme refers to tanning and dressing of leather, which includes the following: tanning and dressing (441.1); manufacture and imitation of leather based on natural leather (441.2); and currying, dyeing and finishing of leather (441.3) (Stanners and Bordeau, 1991)
5. The process of globalization also has political, social and cultural dimensions.
6. North and South are used interchangeably with developed (industrial) and developing countries.
7. When clients of the tanning industry demand certain product qualities, the message is conveyed to the suppliers by the tanneries or it reaches the suppliers in other ways. The suppliers innovate and sell their new solutions to the tanning industry.

8. The tanning industry in Western Europe

This chapter provides country-specific analyses of the contraction of the tanning industry in Germany, Italy, Portugal and Scandinavia. The main focus is the impact of environmental requirements on the contraction that has taken place in Western Europe and how environmental requirements affect competitiveness in the industry at present.

REGULATORY PRESSURE IN THE EU

There are differences in environmental regulations and enforcement in the tanning industry in the EU. Tanners in Spain and Italy are subject to stricter regulations on discharge of salt in the wastewater, whereas tanners in Germany have bigger problems with the disposal of sludge and solid waste. Effluent discharge limits on chrome to surface water and sewerage are stricter in Germany than in Italy and Portugal. Limits on emissions of volatile organic compounds (VOC) are stricter in Germany than Italy, and the Italians negotiate for more lenient VOC emission standards in the EU than current German levels. There is also a difference in timing. Germany was the first country to impose stricter regulations and enforcement in the tanning industry. Italy has followed, but in Portugal the process has only just started.

Germany

In 1989 tanning ranked fourth in environmental protection costs among German manufacturers. The authors claim that environmental protection costs have further increased in the 1989 to 1993 period, when regulations became stricter. At present, Verband der Deutschen Lederindustrie (VDL) holds that environmental protection costs of the tanning industry in Germany are between 3 percent and 5 percent of the total cost of production. One of the tanners interviewed had estimated the cost of sludge disposal as 3.5 percent and wastewater treatment as another 2 percent of the cost of production. Another tanner complained that his total environmental cost is as high as

10 percent of turnover, which was partly attributed to strict regulations and enforcement by local authorities. In Germany the share of environmental protection investments in total investments amounted to 14.7 percent in 1989, and the tanning industry ranked the highest, followed by the chemical industry at 12.6 percent. The average for all German manufacturing industries is 4.6 percent. In addition to these costs, tanners complain about the amount of management that compliance with environmental requirements involves, and about 'indirect' costs of time and efforts that could have been 'better' spent in production (Haid and Wessels, 1996).

Technological changes have to be documented and continuously approved by different authorities. The authorities also regularly check that effluent standards are complied with. It is not uncommon for tanners to be fined for non-compliance with certain parameters, such as the pH level and chrome contents of the wastewater. When solid waste and sludge are disposed of, the tanners have to document that it does not affect the groundwater. The tanners complain about the time that has to be spent dealing with these issues. Small tanneries have the biggest problems with the time frames because they have few employees (Haid and Wessels, 1996).

The tanners often complained about the way they had been treated by the authorities. There had been little understanding of their problems. In one of the tanneries it was emphasized that it had been a big mistake to attempt to be technologically ahead of the environmental regulations. It only made the authorities require even more, until it became impossible to comply. Having learnt from experience, today they only do what they have to. In respect of the requirement to use the best available technology, another tanner complained: 'It applies even when the technology does not benefit the environment, and in this way we are subject to unnecessary investment.' Having said this, more of the interviewees mentioned that with the increasing problems of unemployment in Germany over the past couple of years (since 1995–6), they had experienced less pressure to improve their environmental standards.

The federal government is responsible for the development of the national framework of environmental legislation. The states may then add to or strengthen the national legislation and are responsible for the overall water resource management at the state level. At the lower administrative levels within the state, the districts are responsible for water supplies, wastewater treatment and public works; whereas the municipality or county issues permits and carries out the monitoring and inspections (Krüger Consult, 1995).

In the 1960s and 1970s regulations on emissions of wastewater into municipal sewerage plants were established at the municipal level. In 1986 federal minimum standards for discharge of wastewater from industry and sewerage plants were established, and the standards have gradually been tightened. A permit is required to discharge wastewater, and 50 industry branches as well as sewerage treatment plants are subject to specific regulations. The actual standards for discharge of hazardous substances are based on what is possible with the best available technology. Otherwise, the standards are based on commonly acknowledged technology. The minimum requirements are the same in all of the states and do not take into consideration the ambient environmental standard. However, there are certain river projects where the requirements are stricter than the federal minimum standards. There are also taxes to be paid on discharge to water. Threshold levels have been established that express how much of the various substances the environment can absorb without causing damage. If the discharge exceeds the threshold levels established by the authorities, the firms are given control values to comply with. The tax is calculated on the basis of the deviation between the threshold level (how much nature can absorb) and the control values (how much the firm has permission to discharge). When a firm does not comply with the control levels issued to it, it is subject to an additional, heavier tax. The amount depends on how much and for how long a time the firm exceeds the prescribed levels (NOU, 1995, p. 4). The German legislation is stricter than the EU's dangerous substances directive (76/464/EEC), in the sense that in Germany 'all discharges are illegal unless a permit is granted for releasing the discharges from this prohibition' (Krüger Consult, 1995, appendix 1, p. 17).

Waste disposal is problematic and expensive in Germany. Industry generates large amounts of waste and there is public resistance against the establishment of new disposal sites (the so-called NIMBY effect – Not In My Back-Yard). Germany introduced a federal law on waste and sludge disposal in 1974. It contains regulations pertaining to pre-treatment before disposal, and the disposal itself. There are strict standards on how much is permitted of the various pollutants, and hence the treatment costs of hazardous wastes are considerably higher than in other countries. In addition, some of the states have introduced taxes on disposal of other types of industrial waste.

When Germany introduced the above mentioned minimum standards for wastewater to be discharged into water in 1986, the concentrations of chrome and sulphides[1] in the wastewater had to be reduced (Besserer, 1996). The tanners could no longer discharge their wastewater directly to a communal effluent treatment plant, but had to undertake pre-treatment themselves to separate out sludge containing chrome. The tanners are also responsible for the disposal of the sludge (Haid and Wessels, 1996). The latter is a problem, since chrome-containing sludge is not accepted as a fertilizer in agriculture. The limit of total chrome in the wastewater of the chrome process has been reduced from 4 mg/l in 1968 to 1.0 mg/l in 1995 (Besserer, 1996). Actually, the practical limit is 0.5 mg/l since the chrome process water is mixed with other wastewater after the cleaning. Hexavalent chrome is banned. In comparison, the Italian limit for total chrome is 2 mg/l for discharge to surface water and

4 mg/l for discharge to sewers (*World Leather*, November 1996). The Portuguese limit is 2 mg/l for both (*Diario da Republica*, 1992, Ch. 9, table 10).

VDL claims that the chrome regulations that were introduced in Germany in the 1980s led to closure of half of the German tanneries in operation at that time. Construction of effluent treatment plants incurred high investment costs and required more land. Some of the tanners built such plants and went bankrupt later. Others suffered from higher costs of treatment in the common effluent plants. The industry had little time to adjust and did not manage to convince the authorities of the problems caused by the new regulations. VDL ascribes this to the fact that in 1980 the industry was already small, with only about 7,000 employees (VDL statistics). It describes the industry as 'a guinea pig and victim'.

Backnang is known as the tannery town of southern Germany. At the beginning of the twentieth century 200–300 tanneries were located there. At present only two or three are still in operation. Tanners from Backnang relate their more recent problems of 'survival' to the way in which environmental regulations have been implemented by the local authorities over time. A common wastewater plant that the tanners had constructed was donated to the local municipality in the 1960s when the municipality was required to treat sewerage. The municipality was required to undertake even more advanced treatment in the 1970s. At this time the tanners wanted to build their own treatment plant, something the municipality would not permit. Instead they wanted the tanners to pay for the treatment in the municipal plant. To serve the needs of both the city and the tanners, an advanced chemical treatment plant was erected. The final cost of it grew to five times higher than initially planned, yet it was a failure in operation. The tanneries had to pay very high fees to have their effluent treated. Even 15 years ago, the treatment costs were two to three times higher per cubic meter of effluent (DM6 than the common rate DM0.50-1). In addition, the authorities decided to build a costly incineration plant for solid waste, despite the warnings of the tanners. This project also turned out to be a failure, since the trivalent chrome was converted to the more hazardous hexavalent chrome during incineration. The chemical wastewater plant was later made into a biological treatment plant, as the tanners had suggested in the first place. However, when the federal wastewater requirements of 1986 were effected, the tanners had to build their own treatment plants, and 9 out of the 12 remaining tanneries decided to close down.

As already mentioned, it is the sludge problem which is held to be the most difficult for tanners in Germany at present. The cost of disposal varies from state to state. There are also regulations to prevent transport of solid waste and sludge from one state to another. In one of the tanneries it was explained that the local cost of disposal had increased from DM60 per tonne in the 1980s to the present level of DM240 per tonne. However, since the tannery in question is unable to dry the sludge to the required moisture level of 45 percent, it has to pay DM360 per tonne. Hence, in practice, it experienced nearly a sixfold increase in disposal costs in the 1980s, and was forced to close down pre-tanning activities.

Regarding environmental product standards, Germany has stricter limits on pentachlorophenol (PCP), a fungicide used in hide preservation, than other countries. Imports of leather products to Germany containing 5 ppm or more of PCP are banned. Certain azo dyes that, among other things, are applied in leather dyeing can form carcinogenic and/or mutagenic properties (Mensink and Lange, 1996). Germany and most Western industrial countries have prohibited the use of such dyes in consumer products that are in contact with the skin for long periods.

Italy

In 1976 Italy introduced law no. 319: 'Framework legislation for environmental protection and the regulation of wastewater discharges', also referred to as the Merli law. The laws on wastewater that were introduced in the 1980s focused on promotion and incentives to achieve waste minimization. By a law of 1992 the EU directives on water which were not already covered by the national framework legislation were transposed into national law. Discharges from industrial sites are covered by the national framework legislation. In practice, it is the municipality or Health Department that grants discharge permits at the local level. The permits are media specific and should be valid for four years. There are large regional differences in environmental enforcement, particularly between the north and south of the country (Krüger Consult, 1995).

The Merli law gave the tanners until June 1979 to comply, but nothing happened and pressure from the industry resulted in a revised Merli law which was introduced in December 1979. The point was that the government should finance part of the wastewater treatment plants to be established (see Sbrana, 1981, and Florida, 1995, in Gjerdåker, 1998). However, the industry still complained that it was difficult to comply with the discharge limits, and UNIC, the branch organization, suggested a revision of the salt, sulphur, ammonia and COD standards in 1991. As shown above, the COD standards are stricter than in Germany. The ammonia standard for discharge to surface water is 10–15 mg/l in Italy, 10 mg/l in Germany and 15 mg/l in Portugal (*World Leather*, November 1996; *Diario de Republica*, 1990).

According to one of the Italian tanners interviewed, it is only since about 1990 that the authorities have required them to do something to reduce pollution: 'Ninety percent have done almost nothing', he said. Yet other tanners claimed that they are given little time to adjust to the environmental requirements. In Arzignano the tanners are subject to restrictions both on the use of water and the discharge of effluent. The tanners have permission to use a certain quota of water per day; whatever they do not use they can sell to other tanners. The sourcing and sub-contracting relationships between the tanners in the district are, among other things, a way of sharing the water resources. One of the tanners reported that the effluent is checked by the authorities every other day. If the pollution loads are too high, he is fined: 'If you want permission to do something you have to pay,' other tanners held.

The common wastewater treatment plant, which has been co-financed with the authorities, is under-dimensioned. This was because the tanners were required to contribute financially to the project according to how much they emitted, which led them to underestimate the quantity that they generated. As a result they have had to build underground tanks where they store the effluent until the treatment plant gets added capacity to receive it. In the meantime it is not uncommon for some of the wastewater to find its way into the river at night. The tanners regard the cost of wastewater treatment as affordable, which they attribute to the concentration of the industry and the economies of scale in having a common treatment plant.

The tanners were concerned about the high cost of removing salt from the wastewater. The high content of salt is mainly due to the fact that it is used to preserve the hides, but some is also added in pre-tanning and the tanning process itself. To use more water to lower the salt concentration is an option they mentioned, but, as already explained, there is limited access to water in Arzignano. Measures taken at present are to shake off some of the salt before the processing starts and then to filter some of the remainder out of the wastewater. The chloride and sulphate discharge limits in Italy are 1000 mg/l to surface water and 1200 mg/l and 1000 mg/l respectively when discharged to sewers. In comparison, the sulphate limit in Portugal is 2000 mg/l (*Diario da Republica*, 1990).

One of the tanners held that it is the treatment plant which is responsible for the disposal of sludge. Other tanners in Arzignano, however, complained that sludge disposal is a problem. Some of them dig pits in the ground which they line with cellophane. When the pit is full, they seal it with cement. The disposal sites are filled within 2–4 years, and it is becoming more and more difficult to find new ones. In Santa Croce they now transport sludge to southern Italy for disposal (Gjerdåker, 1998).

In Arzignano 70 tanneries have joined together to set up SICIT, a company that recycles organic waste and sells it as animal feed and fertilizer. Ital Gelatine is another company that manufactures gelatine and glue out of the waste. Sala turns hair into fertilizer and Ilsa is a company that turns waste containing chrome into fertilizer. In contrast, fertilizer made from such waste is not acceptable in Germany. According to SICIT, an incineration plant for hazardous wastes that incinerates waste and sludge at extremely high temperatures (+2000° Centigrade) may be a solution to the chrome problem. The high temperature makes the substances inert and prevents the conversion from trivalent to hexavalent chrome.

The EU directive on air pollution from industrial sites (84/360/EEC) was due to be complied with by 1 April 1994, but Italian tanners claim that no air pollution law is yet in operation. However, they fear a proposed VOC directive and are negotiating with the EU for standards that are considerably laxer than those which apply in Germany. Since their competitive edge lies in the finishing processes where they convert low quality hides to good quality leather, they are reluctant to change to water-based finishing agents. With higher VOC standards they feel they would be at a disadvantage *vis-à-vis* the Germans, who compete in high quality aniline leather which requires very little finishing. Water-based finishing is acceptable for car leather which is rough, but not for furniture and garment leather which is manufactured in Arzignano. Some claim that it remains to be seen whether the water-based alternatives are more environmentally friendly than solvents. Manufacturers of chemicals think it is only a matter of time before the Italian tanners get used to the new finishing agents and achieve the necessary experience and skills in applying them. Manufacturers of machinery express more scepticism regarding water-based agents, and claim that they are in the process of developing machines to make the use of solvent-based agents more environmentally benign.

In line with German tanners, the Italians are quite clear that the cost of complying with environmental requirements are not compensated by innovation offsets. The old chemicals render better leather than the 'new' less polluting ones. Ecological leather is of lesser quality and more expensive. Customers are concerned with price, not ecology. It is risky to experiment with new chemicals, both because expensive raw material may be damaged, and because the customers may not appreciate the quality and appearance of the product.

Portugal

The environment ministry was established in Portugal in 1990. Since 1993 it has had overall responsibility for water management. Five regional directorates are responsible for practical implementation and enforcement, supervised by the Directorate of the Environment. In addition, 305 municipalities and 4,200 parish councils collect local taxes and manage the regulations. A law of 1990 provides quantitative and qualitative limits for wastewater discharges and contains a framework for the establishment of branch specific discharge limits. In 1994 a law on a permit system for the use and discharge of water was established. Permits for the discharge of wastewater can be granted for 10 years at a time.

Commenting on the effectiveness of the law, Krüger Consult (1995, appendix 1, p. 35) writes:

> The Ministry and the municipalities have their area of responsibility and the authority to sanction pollution. However, the weakness of the pollution monitoring and compliance systems, the frequent absence or imprecision of standards, and a prejudice in favour of economic activity and employment have made successful prosecutions rare.

According to the tanners, the environmental regulations came with membership of the EU in 1986. From 1990 onwards they have been constantly subject to new regulations, and in the last few years authorities have also become stricter and more consistent in their enforcement of the regulations. Since 1992 they have been subject to restrictions on water consumption. One of the tanneries had a permit to use 40 litres of water per kg of hide. According to UNEP (1994), water consumption of tanneries in general ranges from 25 l/kg to 80 l/kg. Water conservation down to 50 l/kg is considered acceptable to most tanners.

In Alcanena the EU and the Government have funded a common effluent treatment plant for primary, secondary and tertiary treatment. It was established in 1988 and the treatment was free of charge to the tanners until 1995. Before the effluent flows through a system of pipelines to the treatment plant, the tanners have to separate the waste streams into three: chrome-free and sulphide-free; chrome-free with sulphide; and sulphide-free with chrome. Then they neutralize the effluent and remove coarse particles. In the treatment plant, the primary treatment is a physical/chemical process for particle sedimentation and removal. In the secondary treatment oxygen is added to enhance the degradation and reduce the BOD. Tertiary treatment to oxidize nitrates was due in the second half of 1997. Chrome is recovered in a specialized plant and then mixed with new chrome so that it can be reused by the tanners. The wastewater that the plant emits contains less than 1 mg/l of chrome. There is no collaboration in respect of chrome recovery and recycling between tanners in Porto and Alcanena. The chrome sludge of the former is claimed not to be wanted in Alcanena (*World Leather*, August/September 1997).

In Porto an agreement of 1992 between the city and APIC, the Portuguese leather tanning association, gave the tanners until 1999 to adjust to environmental requirements. In Porto there is no common effluent treatment plant for sewage in general. Although one tannery has recently erected its own effluent treatment plant, it happens that effluent is discharged into the sewer. One of the tanners who were fined for this won a court case against the city. The authorities cannot require him to treat his effluent as long as it does not have a treatment plant for the sewerage of the city. Since the city is now building a sewerage treatment plant, the tanner tells that he too has to construct one. However, he will only build one for the finishing processes, since he intends to move the wet processing to another location. The general view in the industry, however, is that most of the tanneries in Porto will close down, at least their wet processing facilities, when stricter environmental regulations are imposed. The city authorities of Porto did not permit the establishment of a wet-blue plant in a peripheral industrial area of the town three years ago. This may be a sign that they do not wish to give priority to this type of industry.

Tanners both in Alcanena and in Porto estimate their environmental control costs to be 2–3 percent of their turnover. The cost was expected to double by 1998 with the forthcoming requirements for tertiary treatment and stricter EU regulations, among other things. Recycling of chrome and more efficient use of water, chemicals and energy are among the measures they take. They complain that the environmental requirements affect their competitiveness *vis-à-vis* low cost producers in developing countries. Sludge and solid waste from trimmings are deposited in Alcanena or kept on the tannery premises. According to the interview at Lusagua-ETAR, the salt content of the wastewater poses no big problem to the common effluent treatment plant in Alcanena since the tanners remove some of the salt before they start processing. In contrast, one of the tanners is concerned that an eventual removal of salt from the wastewater will become expensive since such a process will require membrane technology. As already indicated, the limits on discharge of sulphate and ammonia are stricter in Italy, which also has a standard on chlorides that Portugal does not have. Problems of wastewater and solid waste were the main concerns of the Portuguese tanners and only one of them complained about requirements pertaining to air pollution. He had been required to construct a higher chimney. Some of the tanners reported that they make use of water-based solvents.

Many of the tanners and other industry representatives held that the environmental regulations are becoming unrealistically strict. This is both a matter of investment, requirements, cost level and access to space. Portugal is in the difficult situation of competing, on the one hand, with countries that have already taken on the burden of adjustment to stricter environmental regulations and, on the other, with countries that have not yet become subject to environmental costs. Like the tanners in Germany and Italy they cannot compensate for the increasing costs by more efficient use of inputs and/or higher profits. The refrain is that eco-leather does not sell. One of the tanners had experienced this in practice. Likewise, the Portuguese association of shoe and leather articles indicated that measures taken in Alcanena to improve environmental practices have had no positive image effects for the shoe industry at all. However, some of the tanners are optimistic that the attitude of the customers will change in 10–15 years. Even today there are instances in which the customers are concerned with their environmental practice. Exports to Germany are a case in point: they have to sign contracts with their customers regarding the non-use of particular hazardous chemicals. This is due to the above mentioned product standards that have been introduced in Germany. One of the tanners had also been subject to inspection by representatives of a chain of retail stores. He claimed that the so-called green image of this customer was hypocritical since the customer had admitted that similar controls were not carried out among its suppliers in Asia. The Portuguese tanners find themselves in a difficult position. They face increasingly stricter regulations but, contrary to Germany, they do not have access to the market segment that is prepared to pay the highest prices and hence they have even less opportunity to pass the increasing costs on to the customers. Having said this, even the German tanners find it difficult to absorb the increasing environmental costs in their product prices.

PLACE-SPECIFIC RESTRUCTURING AND ENVIRONMENTAL PRESSURE IN THE EU

Germany: Two Waves of Contraction

Germany's share of global production of hides and skins has decreased from 3.9 percent to 2.4 percent between 1977–9 and 1997 (by weight). The country's shares of global production of heavy leather (by weight) and light leather (by area) decreased, from 1.7 percent to 0.004 percent, and from 5.8 percent to 1.3 percent respectively (1977–9 to 1996). Germany's share of global leather exports also decreased quantity-wise. Heavy leather decreased from 17.8 percent to 13.0 percent, and light leather from 4.7 percent to 2.6 percent in the same period. Contrary to the decrease in production and exports of leather, Germany's share of global exports of hides and skins (that is, the raw material) increased from 5.9 percent to 6.0 percent (1977–9 to 1997) (FAO 1994, 1998; see also Tables 7. 5 and 7. 6).

The tanning industry in Germany has been the largest and most prosperous in Europe. It benefited from large markets, experienced firms and easy access to raw materials of high quality. The contraction started in the 1960s when the number of tanneries was reduced from 800 to 300. In 1996 there were fewer than 80 tanneries left, 37 large (with more than 20 employees) and 30–40 small-scale tanneries. Since the mid-1980s there has been a substantial decline in the number of large units: there were 86 in 1976, 71 in 1986, and only 37 in 1996 (VDL, 1997). The latter figure includes the two remaining large tanneries in the former German Democratic Republic (GDR), where there were 19–20 large tanneries.

Moreover, the decline in production was substantial from the 1960s until the mid-1970s. From 1984 to 1994 production declined from 36,167 tonnes to 15,989 tonnes. The changes in the value of output were also substantial, decreasing from DM1.5 billion to DM1.0 billion from 1984 to 1994 and further down to DM0.8 billion in 1996 (VDL, 1997). The figures for 1994 and 1996 include tanning in the former GDR. From 1976 to 1996 the number of employees in tanning units with 20 and more employees decreased from 8,284 to 3,023, the number of workers declining from 6,652 to 2,336. As these figures imply, there has only been a slight decrease (three percentage points) in the share of workers in the total number of employees.

Also qualitatively speaking, there have been changes in the German tanning industry. In the 1960s leather for footwear represented the largest share of the production (Ballance *et al.*, 1993). At present, shoe leather accounts for only 30 percent of production. The industry has shifted to production of upholstery leather for automobiles, aeroplanes and furniture, which accounted for 60 percent[2] of the production in 1996. Of the remainder, 7 percent is for 'leather products' and 3 percent for 'garments, gloves and other uses' (material obtained from VDL).

German tanners were the first to be hit by stricter environmental requirements by the authorities and they are also subject to the strictest requirements at present. The first wave of contraction in the German tanning industry which started in the 1960s is closely linked to the introduction of synthetic shoe-sole material replacing much of the demand for heavy leather and to the locational shift of the footwear industry that represented a loss of markets. Although the industry was subject to environmental regulations, they were not strictly enforced in the 1970s. The second wave starting in the mid-1980s, however, can be attributed more directly to the increasingly strict environmental requirements, as these were imposed on an already weakened and vulnerable industry. Tightening of the chrome regulations took place in this period. In the first part of the 1990s, 25 percent of those who closed down production in Germany relocated to developing countries and Eastern Europe (Haid and Wessels, 1996).

The fact that German tanners have not benefited from first-mover advantages in respect of having to adjust early to stricter environmental requirements can be attributed to the general barriers to technological change and to price competition in the industry. As will be further elaborated below, pressure in the market for more environmentally sound production processes in the tanning industry is negligible. The surviving German tanners mainly cater to markets for high quality expensive products. The fact that these niches are small is corroborated by the price sensitivity German tanners experience and the competition from Italian tanners.

Italy: Design Intensity, Flexibility and External Economies

Italy has the largest share of bovine leather production in the world, closely followed by South Korea (FAO, 1996). During the last 30 years, production has increased by 400 percent. Italy's share of the global output of bovine leather increased from 4 percent in the mid-1960s to 15 percent in 1996 (figures obtained from branch organization in Italy; Gjerdåker, 1998). The 1970s saw the most expansive period of the Italian leather industry, with a large increase in the number of production units and employment. This was linked to the growth of the Italian footwear industry. Actually, in the period 1981 to 1991, there was a slight decrease in the number of production units and employment in Arzignano.[3]

In the period 1977–9 to 1996, Italy's share of global production of both heavy and light leather increased (FAO, 1994, 1998). Both in terms of heavy and light leather production, Italy already far outstripped production in Germany in 1977–9. The two countries' share of global production of hides and skins, however, are identical in 1997. Regarding exports, the share of heavy and light leather has increased from 13.6 percent to 26.1 percent and from 12.9 percent to 15.9 percent respectively. Italy's share of world exports of light leather had a downturn to only 7.8 percent in 1992 with a gradual increase thereafter.

Santa Croce and Arzignano are the main centres of bovine leather tanning in Italy; 70 percent of the leather production in Santa Croce is for the shoe industry. The production process is divided between a large number of small and highly specialized sub-contractors.[4] Fashionable and artisan type products, differentiation, small batches of each product and relatively high prices are characteristic of Santa Croce. In Arzignano 70 percent of the production is upholstery leather. Classic high quality leather is manufactured at a larger scale and in a more industrial (as opposed to artisan) manner than in Santa Croce. In both places, but more so in Arzignano than Santa Croce, a major competitive advantage lies in the ability to manufacture fashionable leather from medium to low-quality hides. The split[5] is made to look like full grain leather. The same is done to low quality grain. 'Stuccu' is a chemical innovation used to correct the grain of furniture leather. Santa Croce, as already implied, is better known than Arzignano for creativity and fashion. Both districts are characterized by a gradual move upmarket towards higher quality products and a gradual change to being more and more involved in the finishing processes only. The latter is facilitated by extensive sourcing of semi-finished leather from abroad.

Italian tanners benefited cost-wise from the time-lag between the sharpening of the environmental requirements in Germany in the mid-1980s and the fact that it was not until the late 1980s that Italian tanners really started to experience stricter requirements. Moreover, environmental requirements are still stricter in Germany than in Italy. As Italian tanners work in order to obtain EU emission standards for the finishing processes that are more lenient than the present German standards, they may not even in future have to comply with the same degree of stringency that the German tanners must live with today. Furthermore, due to geographical concentration of production in industrial districts, Italian tanners have been able to absorb some of the environmental costs by 'external economies of scale' in effluent treatment. The Italian sense of design and fashion and incremental innovation in finishing processes give them a competitive edge in design-intensive products. This in combination with lower pollution control costs represents a challenge to the premium quality and more costly German products, particularly in the upholstery segment.

Portugal: Between Two Stools

In the global context, Portugal's shares of production and exports of hides and skins and leather are still too small to detect changes over time of any relevance.

Tanning is a traditional industry in the country and is carried out mostly by family-owned firms. About 90 percent of the leather is made for the shoe industry, the remainder for clothing and 'fancy goods'. As in Italy, the impressive growth rates in the Portuguese tanning industry coincided with the take-off and expansion of the domestic footwear industry. The growth set in a little later than in Italy, that is, in the second part of the 1970s, culminating in the golden years of the tanning industry in 1986–9. The tanners took advantage of this to upgrade their machinery. According to APIC, the number of tanneries has 'always' remained between 100 and 150. From 1980 to 1997, 12 to 15 new tanneries were established, whereas 20 had to close down in the early 1990s. Of the 120 tanneries in operation at present, about 100 are located in and around Alcanena and 20 in Porto and the nearby areas.

From 1990 onwards production has been erratic. Measured in square meters, production declined by 7 percent from 1990 to 1996, but it increased by 2 percent in value (APIC, 1997). There was a slight increase in the quantity of production in the 1993–5 period, from 31,000 to 34,000 tonnes, and an increase in exports from 6,000 to 8,000 tonnes. Most of the exports go to Spain, the UK and South Korea. Compared with domestic production, imports of leather are substantial. In the 1993–5 period it increased from 60,000 to 67,000 tonnes. The most important countries that Portugal imports leather from are the US, Brazil and Spain (*World Leather*, March 1996). The large discrepancy between domestic production and imports signifies that the Portuguese tanners are not able to keep pace with the demands of the shoe industry. The levelling out of growth rates in the quantity of production of tanned leather, while the client industries increase their imports of the same, implies that the Portuguese tanners are not sufficiently competitive *vis-à-vis* tanners in other countries. This is further corroborated by the above mentioned fact that 20 tanneries had to close down in the 1990s. The tanneries that closed down tended to be the smaller ones, with 10–15 employees.

So far there has not been much environmental pressure on Portuguese tanners compared with the Germans and Italians. Environmental requirements by the authorities have increased since 1992, but at this time the Portuguese tanners had already started to lag behind the domestic shoe industry. From a competitiveness point of view the Portuguese tanners fall between two stools. They compete in standardized products with low-cost tanners from developing countries and in quality with tanners from Italy and Spain. The price competition in standardized products makes them subject to a hard squeeze by the footwear manufacturers. To cope with this and the high prices of raw hides, they source lower quality raw hides and semi-processed leather from Eastern Europe and developing countries. However, lacking the Italian design-intensity it becomes difficult to advance to high quality niches with inferior quality raw hides (Knutsen, 1999).

As environmental requirements now increase and the profit squeeze intensifies, Portuguese industry sources believe that most of the small family units and other financially weak units will have to close down. In this perspective the potential late-comer advantage of access to cheaper and more reliable end-of-pipe solutions does not make much difference.

Sourcing: Cost Cutting and Externalization of Pollution

Price competition in the industry implies that stricter environmental requirements are among the factors that lead to an increase in sourcing from lower cost countries. When speaking in general terms of a locational shift of tanning to developing countries, tanners in Germany, Italy and Portugal explained this by lower labour and environmental costs. It is, however, the case that sourcing of semi-processed leather to cut environmental costs appears to be more prevalent in Germany and Italy than in Portugal. Being under less environmental pressure so far, Portuguese tanners were more concerned about the sourcing of wet-blue as a means of securing reasonably priced raw materials.

In Germany only half of the remaining 37 tanneries are tanneries in the conventional sense doing everything from pre-treatment to tanning and finishing. Both in the literature (Ballance *et al.*, 1993) and in the interviews it was emphasized that stricter environmental regulations have contributed to an externalization of the wet-processing, particularly wet-blue production. Wet-blue is semi-finished leather which has gone through the first tanning process where chrome is applied. At present there are only two tanneries in Germany that process wet-blue only. Most of the wet-blue which is imported to Germany comes from Eastern Europe, where, as expressed by a German branch person: 'Employment is more important than the environment'.

It is not uncommon for German tanners to collaborate with wet-blue producers abroad. There are examples where German tanners provide hides, know-how, machinery, recipes and chemicals. One example of extensive sourcing of semi-finished leather is a tannery that buys wet-blue from Brazil and gets it processed to crust in Poland (both are wet processes). The Polish sub-contractor, who only works for this German tannery, is provided with the above mentioned inputs. The German tannery has trained a Polish tanner who monitors the production with the Polish counterpart. The externalization started around 1995. According to the owner, it was the requirement of the local authorities that he construct a wastewater treatment plant which spurred the externalization. Even with imports of wet-blue, he thinks environmental regulations in Germany are too strict. He is critical of the authorities' establishment of emission standards *before* the problems of waste disposal have been solved.

One of the large German producers of upholstery leather for furniture has also closed down the production of wet-blue in Germany. This was done in 1995 because of the high increase in the cost of sludge disposal (3.5 percent of the production costs), but also because they had to cut labour costs. The closure resulted in the loss of 100 jobs. In the interview it was held that the main competitive disadvantage of the German tanning industry is the high cost of labour and strict environmental regulations: 'Environmental regulations are as disadvantageous as the labour costs.'

Sourcing of wet-blue is profitable because the tanners avoid the most polluting stages of production. At the same time they retain the stages of production with the highest value added. However, it is argued that the sourcing of wet-blue is not uncomplicated because it requires a close relationship between core firm and supplier. Knowledge of the process and chemicals used is important for the finishing and final quality of the product. It is often claimed that tanners who cater to premium quality market niches tend to prefer to do the wet-processing themselves. In contrast, one of the tanners who caters to such markets and purchases wet-blue explained that it is easier to control the quality when buying wet-blue than the hides and skins with hair. The traders in hides and skins are considered difficult to deal with, and the tanners can easily be deceived. Having said this, two of the tanners interviewed were involved in wet-blue production in Germany as a niche activity to ensure supplies of raw materials of the highest quality.

Italian tanners, like the Germans, consider sourcing of wet-blue a strategy to cope with stricter environmental requirements. Fifty percent of the raw materials used in Arzignano are imported wet-blue. In the interviews, tanners explained that they both save water for the finishing processes and avoid pollution. Wet-blue is imported from a wide range of countries: the US, Argentina, Brazil, South Africa, Australia, Russia and Eastern Europe.

At present it makes sense to conclude that sourcing of wet-blue to avoid environmental costs is more prevalent in Germany and Italy than in Portugal. Most tanneries in Portugal are still involved in all the stages of processing, and sourcing of wet-blue is more a strategy of securing lower priced raw materials to meet the low cost competition in general. It is sometimes also mentioned in the interviews that they buy wet-blue and crust from Latin America because these countries have embargoes on exports of raw hides, implying that they would rather have had access to the raw hides. Some of them did, however, express the view that sourcing of wet-blue is the solution to the increasingly stricter environmental regulations, and hence that the incidence of wet-blue sourcing is bound to increase in the near future. Others were of a different opinion, and held that quality improvement is the most viable strategy. To ensure high quality, they have to do the wet processing themselves and hence source less rather than more of the wet-blue. Contrary to German and Italian tanners, the Portuguese did not usually go into technological or other agreements with their suppliers of wet-blue, preferring arm's-length relationships.

SCANDINAVIA

As in Western Europe in general, there has been a clear contraction of the Scandinavian tanning industry. The process has been tougher than in Germany in the sense that even fewer tanneries remain. There are only five large tanneries left in Norway, Sweden and Denmark. As in Germany, environmental regulations and enforcement have become much stricter. Those that remain do fairly well, but struggle hard to be able both to survive in the market and to comply with the stricter environmental requirements. In-depth interviews have been made in four of the five[6] tanneries, and the findings corroborate the data from Germany and Italy (Gjerdåker, 1999). The purpose of the following presentation of three of the tanneries is to provide more details on competitive strategies. Data on the fourth tannery is not included here because it does not bring any new aspects into the analysis.

ScanLeather A

ScanLeather A is the Scandinavian tannery which comes closest to establishing a brand name. It concentrates on a limited product range and has reached a position where it can afford to turn down orders which do not suit the profile of the firm. The question remains: how did the tannery manage to reach this position in the first place? Two decades ago ScanLeather A was described as one of the least profitable firms in Scandinavia. In the mid-1970s the tannery was on the verge of bankruptcy, because the product range was too wide, the products were old-fashioned and the firm had to deal with severe environmental problems.

Flexibility and diversification are positive for competitiveness, but not when applied excessively. Producing a wide range of leathers puts stringent demands on know-how both in product development and the evolution of markets. In order to gain a competitive edge it is necessary to become skilled at doing one thing. The strategy which enabled ScanLeather A to survive the crisis was to focus exclusively on the production of upholstery leather for export markets. Upholstery leather is a high quality niche with opportunities for development. The tannery abandoned the production of leather for clothing, shoes and bags, and dedicated its production exclusively to upholstery leather.

ScanLeather A chose the relatively virgin US market. This was a deliberate strategy in order to avoid competition from established German and Italian tanners who for a long time had been strong in the production of furniture leather on the European market. Furthermore, US tanneries are predominantly large scale, producing a restricted variety of leathers at high volumes. The medium-sized ScanLeather A had an advantage *vis-à-vis* their North American competitors in terms of greater flexibility. The diversification into automotive leather is another important explanation for the success of ScanLeather A. Automotive leather is a more stable segment of the market than furniture leather. The customers are larger and the seasonal cycles are less pronounced, which makes it easier to secure a stable production volume and to better exploit the existing production capacity.

Their first customers for the automotive segment were the North American Ford and Chrysler. After a while they also started to produce automotive leather for the Lear Corporation, a large firm which makes seats for Saab and Volvo. Today ScanLeather A has between 1,000 and 1,500 different customers, divided among three segments: *technical leather* (leather for cars, trains, aeroplanes and boats that demand specific technical specifications of durability and wear resistance), *residential leather* (leather for private houses), and *public leather* (leather for official buildings, offices, bars and restaurants).

ScanLeather A operates with a service stock from which customers can place orders for as little as one hide, to be delivered the next day. Of a batch of 400 hides one customer may want 300, while the remaining 100 are divided between 10 to 20 customers. The firm has a standard collection of 200 colours. Approximately 200,000 m^2 of leather (40,000 hides) is in stock at any time.

In order to obtain a competitive advantage, it is important to have a company culture where quality ranks above quantity. A focus on quality is necessary since the raw material is so expensive. The individual hides are followed through every step of the production process. Workers have personal responsibility in the production process, which is what the ISO system builds on; each worker controls the job which is done before him and the job which is passed on. Another factor of vital importance for the competitiveness of ScanLeather A is that they have pursued a global production strategy.

ScanLeather A bought a factory in the US in order to expand production. The plant was bought inclusive of employees and customers, which were important factors in choosing to buy this particular plant. The production taking place in the US is mostly for furniture. Now they have developed towards what is called the 'car aftermarket', consisting of individual customers buying particular upholstered seats to fit the car according to personal taste.

The production unit in the US is a finishing plant equipped to do part of the wet-processing only. Production at this plant is based on further processing of European and US wet-blue. Large scale specialized wet-blue producers can perform the process much more efficiently and economically than an integrated tannery. Furthermore, it would have been difficult for ScanLeather A to get a concession from the environmental authorities to do the complete wet-processing because these processes are polluting and the environmental regulations are stricter the closer the factory is located to densely populated areas. The US wet-blue producers are generally located in states where environmental regulations are less stringent (such as Kansas), and the factories are often located close to slaughterhouses in order to get access to fresh hides, thus reducing the amount of salt in the effluents.

The reason for imports of wet-blue from the South to the production unit in Scandinavia is strict environmental discharge restrictions. In addition, ScanLeather A used to buy wet-blue from another Scandinavian tannery before it obtained a concession from the environmental authorities to increase its own production.

Sourcing of wet-blue is a widespread response to environmental regulations among North European tanners in order to reduce the costs of effluent treatment and sludge disposal. A problem with such a strategy is that part of the control of the production process is lost. Another risk is that the condition of the semi-processed hides will change slightly while in transport, making it difficult, for instance, to produce consistent and homogeneous aniline dyeing.

Thus, many tanneries with high quality requirements are reluctant to out-source. Other Scandinavian tanneries choose not to import wet-blue for fear of losing control over the quality of the product, and thus all their leather is processed from the raw hide stage. Problems of quality control can be overcome by transferring technology and expertise to sub-contractors. There are also specialized and skilled producers of wet-blue that offer to do contract tanning based on company-specific recipes.

It could be interesting to know to what extent the competitiveness of ScanLeather A is dependent on the practice of out-sourcing. It is a fact that the two Scandinavian tanneries with the most optimistic views of the future are those who engage in this strategy.

ScanLeather B

Since the early 1980s the main focus of the firm has been production of furniture leather. ScanLeather B owns several subsidiaries, most of them located in Asia. More than half of their furniture is sold on the Asian market, mainly in Japan and Hong Kong, representing the medium-quality segment of the market. A small share of the production goes to the European market. China is growing rapidly as a market for furniture leather, and it is an important market for ScanLeather B. Other important markets are Taiwan, Australia and Japan.

The production of furniture at ScanLeather B was for many years based on imported leather from Germany and Italy, but the firm decided to diversify upstream into tanning. A finishing plant was established in Asia, where production was based on further processing of imported wet-blue. The necessary expertise and know-how was obtained through cooperation with a German tannery. The diversification into tanning has been a profitable business. The minimum order accepted by ScanLeather B is 50 hides per customer. They have three large and ten small to medium sized customers. The firm is concerned with obtaining economies of scale.

Approximately 80 percent of the leather finishing is done at the plant in Asia. Being located there is an advantage in order to get established in the Asian market. Shipping the leather from Europe takes three weeks, which implies three weeks of storage costs while at sea and a corresponding increase in time of delivery.

ScanLeather B does not process Scandinavian raw hides because they are too expensive. In the first period of production the main activity was wet-processing of German hides, which then were shipped to Asia for finishing. However, this practice stopped. Now the activities have been reduced to a minimum, and finishing activities have replaced wet-processing. There has been a simultaneous reduction in the number of workers. ScanLeather B buys the raw hides which are then sent to German contract tanners for wet-processing. The firm has for a long time had close relations with these contract tanners. They also buy wet-blue directly from Germany and crust from Brazil. ScanLeather B has an agent in Brazil checking hide quality before buying. South American hides are much cheaper than Scandinavian hides, and more suited for lower quality markets. European wet-blue costs 30–50 percent more than Brazilian wet-blue. Due to the lesser grain quality of the Brazilian hides, the hides need to be more heavily coated.

About 80 percent of the finishing activities in Asia are based on imported low quality wet-blue and crust from Brazil. Thus, if access to high quality hides were the prime motive for producing in Scandinavia, it must either be as a long-term strategy for the future, or indirectly as a matter of image for marketing purposes. 'Scandinavian leather' has become a concept that vouches for quality. It is possible to buy Brazilian wet-blue, do some of the finishing in Europe and claim that the leather is European. It is worth a lot of money to be able to market European products. 'Europe' sells on the Asian market.

The case of ScanLeather B is interesting as it clearly illustrates that there is a tendency in the industry to sacrifice quality for price. Its success is due to the fact that the average buyer of leather is not sufficiently demanding, at least not regarding quality. What the average buyer of leather demands is a competitive price. ScanLeather B also seems to have benefited from the financial crisis in Asia. As Asian buyers can no longer afford to purchase European leather, this leaves the firm with an opportunity to increase their market share of less expensive leather.

The experiences of ScanLeather A and B suggest that a focus on upholstery leather seems to be a prerequisite for survival in high-cost countries. The reason why other Scandinavian tanneries have disappeared is precisely because they failed to shift to upholstery leather. However, the example of ScanLeather C below is an exception because it still produces leather for shoes, bags and clothing.

ScanLeather C

Levels of productivity and automation have increased in European tanneries, and new chemicals have been developed which make it possible to produce a wider range of variations in the leather than ever before. However, the basic technological characteristics remain the same. As tanning still involves an element of craft, the use of the most advanced technology does not necessarily give the best product quality (technological leadership does not necessarily bring *product*-offsets). Being in the technological forefront is thus not necessarily a goal; the important thing is daring to take new routes, to risk experimenting with new strategies. It is necessary to seek markets that are willing to pay for quality.

ScanLeather C specializes in niche markets. It produces tailor-made products for foreign brand producers. Today all of the production is made to order. Close to 90 percent of production is exported, with the US as the largest market. The tannery has specialized in the production of leather for footwear (uppers), belts, purses and bags. About 50 percent of the production is for leather goods other than shoes, which is a segment of the market less vulnerable to seasonal variations in fashion than footwear leathers.

The diversification strategy of ScanLeather C does not just apply to products, but also to the production process itself. The motive is to spread risk. In order to prepare for the cyclical fluctuations of the industry, the firm has resorted to contract work. The contract work functions as the shock absorber which makes it possible to have stable production.

The strategy of ScanLeather C has changed from processing imported raw materials for the domestic market, to processing indigenous raw material for export markets. Export restrictions in Latin American countries effectively stopped imports of raw hides from that continent, and for the last 15 years ScanLeather C has predominantly used salted, Scandinavian hides. The initial disadvantage of restricted access to cheaper hides may in the long run be to the advantage of the firm, as it has put pressure on the firm to upgrade quality. It is the repeated ability of ScanLeather C to deliver leather of high quality that makes the customers continue to entrust new orders to them. The explanation of the continued existence of the firm lies not only in the type and quality of the products produced, but first and foremost in the kind of relations they have established with their customers. The greater the demands in terms of product quality and special features, the greater the demand for service, and good customer service is the foundation for the development of stable customer relations.

ScanLeather C has gained a reputation of being 'nice people to do business with', which is very important in a small industry where a bad reputation spreads quickly and can be devastating to a firm. ScanLeather C has succeeded in developing a network of stable relations, not only with clients but also with suppliers of hides and technology. Common to all the links in the network is that they are all concerned about *quality*. Being linked to demanding or sophisticated clients, to producers of top quality raw material, to suppliers of the most advanced technology, undoubtedly does something to the *image* and the reputation of a firm. The continued existence of ScanLeather C stems from its ability to nourish and take care of its network relations. It meets regularly with its suppliers of technology. The suppliers offer service and adjustments, while the tannery receives new technology for testing.

Having a production unit isolated from other tanneries, as is the case with

ScanLeather C, is a disadvantage in terms of environmental protection. A cluster of tanneries can share the expenses of treating the effluents by constructing a common treatment facility and dividing the costs among them. In the absence of such a solution, tanners elsewhere have had recourse to municipal treatment facilities, getting their effluents treated together with communal sewage.

Although ScanLeather C has constructed a treatment facility on the factory premises, the problem of waste disposal remains. The tannery has been promised a local disposal site for hazardous waste by four successive mayors, but so far nothing has happened, most probably because nobody wants a waste disposal site in their vicinity. Thus, ScanLeather C has been forced to construct a mountain hall for disposing of the waste. This hall was expensive to make, and it is about to be filled up.

The ideal solution to the waste problem would be to use the sludge as farmland fertilizer. In the US sludge containing chrome can, after a court decision in 1994, be used as fertilizer. In Scandinavia such a practice is prohibited unless the sludge contains no more than 100 ppm (parts per million) of chrome in the dry sludge (Denmark) (equivalent to the natural occurrence of chrome in the soil), or 150 ppm in Norway. The equivalent limit in Germany is 950 ppm, 1,700–1,800 ppm in Italy and 5,000–7,000 ppm in the US. The sludge generated at the treatment facility at ScanLeather C contains 7,362 ppm. The problem is said to be that the more the problem is tackled, the more stringent the demands from the authorities become. In order to find a solution to the waste problem the firm is planning to construct a waste treatment plant which will treat all solid waste from the tannery as biomass. The plant will produce energy through a gasification process which, due to high temperatures, prevents the trivalent chrome being converted into the carcinogenic hexavalent chrome. This is a pilot project. No other tannery in the world has tried this. If it succeeds, it may be a profitable project which could lead to a 95 percent reduction of the waste volume, resulting in a 100 percent loop where the waste is used to produce energy. The production of energy will be equivalent to the present bought electricity and diesel oil which the tannery consumes annually. The facility will be costly to operate, but it is expected that costs of waste treatment and earnings from the sale of energy will balance.

COMPETITIVENESS IN WESTERN EUROPE: SUCCESS OR SURVIVAL?

Generally speaking, the remaining tanneries in the higher cost countries in

Europe cater to the top end of the market and there has been a shift from production of shoe leather to upholstery leather. The tanneries that survived the contraction have upgraded production technologically with more advanced chemicals and machinery and compete in higher quality niches, but some gain access to this market as artisans employing old-fashioned methods. Creativity and improvement in the finishing of the leather are also important to competitiveness. However, this is not sufficient. The tanners maintain that nobody is safe in any niche any longer, and in any niche they must keep a sharp watch on price competition. The tanning industry is small in most of the countries and the market for high quality products is limited. Based on changes in the volume and value of production over time accounted for in international and national statistics, as well as the low profit margins, sharp price competition and future challenges reported by the tanners, competitiveness appears to be more a sign of survival than of grand success.

Environmental requirements are not the root cause of the problems the European tanning industry has suffered over the last three to four decades. Historically the contraction started with the relocation of the labour intensive footwear industry, which in turn can be linked to the erosion of the Fordist mode of production (Knutsen, 1998a). Moreover, the tanning industry has not yet been able to exploit opportunities in the new techno-economic paradigm of microelectronics. Structural factors such as the properties and high costs of raw hides are the main explanation for this. Against this backdrop the tanning industry was vulnerable when environmental requirements were tightened in the 1980s. Closure and restructuring of the tanning industry in the North was speeded up by stricter environmental requirements. Because of the limited scope for innovation-offsets, environmental requirements by the authorities become costly. In combination with sharp competition in price it is, however, obvious that stricter environmental requirements, when imposed, represent a challenge to competitiveness in the European tanning industry today.

In the EU countries where the tanning industry is small, the tanners complain that they have been met with little understanding of the techno-logical and cost challenges that stricter environmental regulations and enforce-ment involve. German tanners complain that they have been the guinea pigs for the introduction of stricter environmental regulations in the manufacturing sector. Regulations and enforcement are considered inflexible (Germany) and unrealistically strict (Italy and Portugal). In order to survive, competition in high quality niches combined with a constant eye on opportunities for cost cutting are necessary. This is most likely to increase the incidence of outsourcing of the wet processes. Environmental pressure and the polluter pays principle in the tanning industry lead to the fact that the polluter moves unless customers pay.

NOTES

1. Sulphides rapidly deplete oxygen in the receiving water. In solutions with pH lower than 10–13, more of the sulphide is present as hydrogen sulphide. Hydrogen sulphide is odourless at lethal concentrations and highly corrosive to iron and concrete (Thorstensen, 1997).
2. 50 percent according to Ballance *et al.* (1993).
3. The field study was carried out in Arzignano. The data from Santa Croce are based on the M.Phil. thesis of Gjerdåker (1998).
4. Sub-contracting is a sub-category of sourcing. When it is clear that the supplier has a contractual relationship with the core firm and hence the product in question is made to order, the supplier can be referred to as a sub-contractor.
5. Hides are split in slices to give uniform thickness to the grain side, that is, the top layer. The lower layer is called split. Split can be finished into suede or finished with imitation grain (*Leather Dictionary*, Norwegian furniture manufacturer, Internet).
6. The fifth tannery was not included for practical reasons.

9. Tanning in Eastern Europe, Brazil, Mexico and India

This chapter presents case studies of the tanning industry in countries in Eastern Europe and the South, that is, countries to which the tanning industry has been shifted. The key questions are: what attracts the tanning industry to these countries, and how is competitiveness affected by economic liberalization and environmental pressure?

THE CZECH REPUBLIC AND POLAND

Tanning in Poland and the Czech Republic declined in the 1980s with the loss of the footwear market in COMECON (Gjerdåker and Odegard, 1999). Large, inefficient tanneries that had previously been protected by the government found it difficult to adjust to competition in the free market throughout the 1990s. The low quality image combined with restricted access to credit and high interest rates made it difficult to finance the need for raw material, not to speak of technological and environmental upgrading.

On paper, tanneries in both countries are subject to limits on discharge of pollutants to surface water. Generally speaking, the limits are lenient and few in the Czech Republic compared with Germany, Italy and Portugal. In Poland discharge limits have been established for more pollutants and the levels are also more on a par with those in the three Western European countries (*Leather*, November 1996). Having said this, the limit for discharge of total chrome in the Czech Republic is 2 mg/l as in Italy and Portugal. In Poland the limit is 1 mg/l. In order to fulfil requirements to become part of the EU, pollution control authorities in both countries are in the process of tightening the environmental regulations.

The Czech Republic and Poland are known for good quality hides. The scarcity of raw materials on the global market has increased and so has the price of high quality domestic hides. High quality hides are exported. Although quota restrictions on exports were imposed, the price of raw hides continued to rise, and the Czech Republic abolished the quotas in 1995. The result of high prices for raw hides is that the local tanners have to source low quality hides from Russia and the Ukraine or engage in contract work for tanners from Western Europe. The key is that the richer foreign counterparts advance capital to purchase the expensive raw materials. For example, some 60 percent of the private tanneries in the Czech Republic are joint ventures with German and Italian firms. The contract work is basically for semi-processed leather, and there are large increases in the exports of wet-blue from both countries. For the Western European firms, costs can be substantially reduced by wet-processing in a country with cheap labour and lenient environmental regulations. To them this is a way to avoid export quotas on raw hides and gain access to high quality raw hides. Moreover, transport costs of wet-blue are lower than for the heavier raw hides. There are examples where contract work contributes to technological upgrading of the tanneries to improve the quality of the wet-blue. However, this does not solve the pollution problems. Such quality upgrading can be made without the installation of pollution abatement equipment. Very few tanneries have effluent treatment plants and there is little enforcement of environmental regulations. In one of the interviews a German tanner dryly commented that the river Elbe returns pollution that has been shifted by outsourcing to the Czech Republic.

The local tanners are subject to a profit squeeze caused by the high price of raw materials and pressure from what remains of the local footwear industry. The prices of shoes in Poland rise faster than inflation while the price increase of leather remains below inflation. On top of this, environmental regulations are becoming stricter. Polish and Czech tanners fear the combined effect of the cost increase that stricter environmental requirements involve and the abolition of export quotas. They assume the Western Europeans will purchase the entire stock of high quality raw hides, preferring to process it in lower cost countries. The Polish and Czech tanners will then have to resort to the use of low quality hides from the former Soviet Union. This will deprive them of developing a competitive tanning industry directed at the top end of the international market, based on their domestic supply of high quality raw hides.

BRAZIL

Increasing Production and Exports of Wet-blue

By the end of the 1980s Brazil had become virtually self-reliant in leather and leather shoes, and was one of the main exporters in the world. During the last two decades Brazil produced and exported about 5 percent of all world leather. From the late 1960s until 1986 the output of light bovine leather almost doubled, and from 1986 to 1994 output grew by another 40 percent (FAO, 1996). By the early 1990s, Brazil was the largest producer of light bovine leather in Latin America, and the fifth largest producer in the world. Production was carried out exclusively by domestic tanneries, mostly family owned. More than 95 percent of the bovine raw hides used were Brazilian. The number of tanneries reached a peak in the mid-1980s with more than 700 companies employing 70,000 people. Together with about 4,000 shoe manufacturers,[1] the leather industry employed directly and indirectly about 1 million people (Odegard, 1999).

As with the demise of communism and economic liberalization in Poland and the Czech Republic in the 1980s and 1990s, liberalization of the Brazilian economy in the 1990s affected the tanners via the footwear industry. Increased competition from imports reduced the market for Brazilian tanners. A number of footwear manufacturers and tanners were not internationally competitive. Liberalization exposed latent problems in the industry. Huge profits in the tanning industry in the 1980s had, to a large extent, been wasted by mismanagement and luxury consumption. Moreover, many tanneries were coming of age, the third generation was often not willing to take over and family members were fighting over resources. An advantage of liberalization was increasing competition in the chemical and machinery industries. Because of the competition, tanners gained access to more advanced technology, making the production process more efficient and improving the properties of the final product. The other side of the coin is that dependence on externally generated innovations reduces the bargaining power of the tanners in the commodity chain.

The restructuring of the industry implied closures and concentration of production in large groups where foreign investments, Italian in particular, are strongly involved. Italians source wet-blue for finishing in Italy. Unlike Poland and the Czech Republic, Brazilian raw hides are of relatively low quality. With Italian design and finishing technology, however, leather made from Brazilian hides is competitive in the international market. Although the number of tanneries was dramatically reduced from more than 700 in the mid-1980s to 250 in 1998, out of which only 20 are held to be well-functioning, production and exports have increased throughout the 1990s. While 20 percent of all leather was directly exported in 1987, this increased to 27 percent in 1990 and doubled to 50 percent in 1997. Indirect exports, mainly of leather shoes, decreased from 39 percent to 26 percent and further to 22 percent in the respective years.

The increase in direct exports is closely connected with a 32 percent growth in the availability of domestic hides from 1990 to 1997. The total export of salted hides, crust and finished leather has remained stable or has declined since 1993. It is wet-blue that accounts for the increasing exports. In 1997 wet-blue accounted for 72 percent of the direct exports by weight, and as much as 90 percent of the growth of the direct exports (Abicouro/Aicsul, 1997; Abicouro, 1998).

Tanning in Brazil was initially located in the southern states, but has followed the domestic footwear industry to the Central Western region (during the last 15 years) and northern Brazil (in the last 5 years). Industry sources refer to this as a process of interiorization. What attracts the industry northwards is lower production costs, financial incentives, proximity to the cattle industry, slaughterhouses and the footwear industry.

Environmental Requirements

Environmental regulations in Brazil were virtually non-existent until the mid-1980s according to the interviewees. The new constitution of 1988 introduced important elements to improve the protection of the environment, but most of these proposals remained at the level of good intentions. The unstable political and economic situation of the 1980s pushed long term environmental issues aside. This had serious consequences for the environment. Highly contaminated water was released directly into waterways and on to the topsoil, and organic and toxic solids were being dumped as regular waste. Only in the most extreme cases of contamination, such as in areas with a high concentration of tanneries, were efforts made to clean up. Estancia Velha (in the southernmost state of Rio Grande do Sul), a small village near the shoe district of Novo Hamburgo, is an example. With close to 20 medium and large tanneries, pollution reached unbearable levels in the 1970s, and the area was one of the most polluted of the entire country. With pressure from the local population and more stringent environmental regulations by the southernmost state from the early 1980s, the companies were forced to start to clean up.

It was not until the early 1990s that increased national and international environmental awareness resulted in stricter environmental regulations that also influenced the tanneries outside the tanning districts in the southern states. With the 1992 Earth Summit in Brazil (Rio de Janeiro) there was an increasing domestic debate on environmental issues, environmental legislation was updated and political practice improved. Since then environmental law at the federal level has become much stricter. The federal law requires regulations at state level to be as strict or stricter than the federal standards. In 1994 a new comprehensive environmental law was presented to the Congress, but many parts of it took years to get through the political bureaucracy of the country. Only in April 1998 was the law on environmental crime finally passed.

At the company level, environmental consciousness was reasonably high among the directors. Smaller or bigger efforts were made in all of the tanning companies to improve the environmental performance. Both national and foreign chemical companies held that solutions to pollution problems were the main field in innovation of the tanning industry. An environmental expert claimed that 'the industry and government have the knowledge [necessary to eliminate the environmental problems of the tanneries] – the rest is affordability'.

Many sources claimed that only in the southernmost state of Rio Grande do Sul are tanners subject to environmental regulations on a par with the EU level. There are several indicators that the general level of stringency in enforcement of environmental regulations in Brazil is substantially lower than in Europe. Tanners in the South claimed that their environmental expenses were 0.5–2 percent of the production costs. This is confirmed by the results of an environmental investigation carried out by Abicouro in 1998. The level of environmental costs is significantly lower than the typical 5 percent in Europe. Despite strict environmental regulations on paper since the mid-1990s, enforcement is lenient. In practice, a number of companies do not have to comply with the regulations because they are economically fragile.

Wet-blue and the Environment

Increasing exports of wet-blue to Europe in the 1990s have had a positive environmental effect in so far as it has restricted the use of hazardous preservatives, such as PCP. So far, however, the overall environmental effect is clearly negative.

More importantly, tanners and other industry sources generally hold that specialization in exports of wet-blue is not profitable if you have to treat the pollution according to regulations. Many of the environmental problems in the South have been solved not by introducing cleaner production technology, but by outsourcing the pollution intensive wet-blue production to the *bluseiros* in the west-central and northern regions. An environmental expert said without hesitation that 'many [tanners in southern Brazil] do finishing just to avoid environmental problems'. In other words, the most polluting part of the process has been shifted internally in Brazil and to a region where the state government puts much more emphasis on attracting industry than enforcing environmental regulation. Several informants who had knowledge of the area could confirm that environmental pressure from the authorities and the NGOs in the interior is much lower and there is almost no enforcement. Although there are some significant environmental advantages to the relocation of wet-blue production closer to the raw material sources,[2] these are offset by lower standards in the enforcement of the regulations of the pollution-intensive wet-blue process. Treatment facilities, even in the newer and modern tanneries, are inadequate since most of them only do primary treatment.[3] It is also claimed that effluent treatment plants are often only turned on when foreign visitors or factory inspections are expected.

In Brazil environmental control costs are one-third of those in Italy. Yet the total processing costs of leather (excluding the cost of raw materials) are 'only' 10 percent lower than in Italy, that is, at the same level as the above mentioned price difference that customers of high quality German upholstery leather accept. However, to this should be added the lower costs of raw hides that contributes another 10–20 percent cost advantage. Moreover, Brazilian industry sources claim that the main competitive advantage of their exports of wet-blue to the EU is trade policies. Brazilian wet-blue is not subject to any import tariffs in the EU, unlike crust and finished leather. Neither is wet-blue subject to quota regulations. Even at the Brazilian end, wet-blue is not subject to tariffs when exported.

The Brazilian case confirms the general assumption that sourcing wet-blue from the point of view of the core firms is to a large extent one way to access raw hides and implement a cost cutting strategy. Since Brazilian tanners face severe competition from other low cost tanners for sourcing relationships and access to markets in the North, all cost cutting matters in order to attain a competitive edge. In this perspective the importance of low environmental control costs should not be underestimated. Moreover, since sourcing of wet-blue takes place in an industry where little has been achieved in the development of cleaner process technology that *radically* reduces the problem of wastewater and solid waste, sourcing is unlikely to have significant positive effects on the environmental practice of the suppliers. More concretely, the technology that is transferred to improve the quality of wet-blue is not of the type that reduces pollution in the production process to any significant degree. This is in line with the findings from Poland and the Czech Republic.

Growth of Brazilian production and exports of wet-blue is a result of economic liberalization. This is negative to the environment because most of the pollution is generated in the wet-processing and because wet-blue renders little value added and profits to be reinvested in end-of-pipe and cleaner technology. On the one hand, costs of compliance with stricter environmental regulations in Brazil were not the reason for disinvestment of the companies, but rather appeared as an additional cost at a time when the tanneries were economically very fragile. Here are clear similarities with the German case. On the other hand, lower environmental costs in Brazil than in the North contribute to the explanation of why the Brazilian tanning industry is competitive at present, after the restructuring.

MEXICO

Increasing Exports after the NAFTA Agreement

Tanning is an old traditional activity in Mexico. Electrical machinery was first introduced in 1902, and industrial production of leather was strongly stimulated by high demand for leather products in the US during the second world war (Rodriguez-Abitia, 1997). In more recent times, production of light leather has increased gradually throughout the 1980s. The increase was quite impressive from 1990 to 1996, from 346 million to 400 million square feet (FAO, 1998). However, according to Rodriguez-Abitia (1997) there is no significant growth in production concomitant with the introduction of the NAFTA. On the contrary, it seems that expansion of production was discouraged by uncertainties due to the political and economic problems Mexico experienced in 1994. Nevertheless, the country belongs in the top ten of the world leather producers. Mexico's share of world production is about 4 percent by area (see ibid.). According to statistics from the UN, Mexico accounted for 3 percent of world exports of leather and ranked number 19 among the leading exporters in 1995. In exports of leather products, Mexico ranked as high as number nine (http://www.intracen.org/, downloaded December 1998). Having said this, export earnings from leather at US$150 million are significantly higher than export earnings from leather products at US$28 million. As opposed to the more gradual increase in production, Mexico experienced an impressive increase in exports of leather in the 1990s, particularly after the NAFTA agreement. Exports of leather shoes at 6.5 million pairs in 1994 is minuscule compared with Brazil's export of 129 million pairs and Italy's 262 million pairs. Although exports of shoes increased somewhat in the 1990s, Mexico imported more shoes than it exported in 1992–4. Mexican shoe production in this period is lower than in the mid-1980s, but higher than in the early 1980s (FAO, 1996).

In Mexico tanning is concentrated in Guanajuato, where the town of León is located; in Mexico City; and in Guadalajara. According to CICUR, 70 percent of the leather tanned in Mexico is tanned in the state of Guanajuato, where there are 650 tanneries (http://www.cicur.com.mx/fepel98, downloaded February 1999). The bulk is located in León and its outskirts. Most of the tanneries are small, processing fewer than 100 hides per day. In Mexico as a whole, it is estimated that 80 percent of the tanneries can be categorized as tiny with 15 or fewer employees (Rodriguez-Abitia, 1997). In León there has been a gradual expansion in the number of tanneries, usually as family members and relatives of established tanners have set up new units. Over time the concentration of tanneries has attracted shoe factories, suppliers of raw hides and suppliers of chemicals and machinery/equipment which in turn has further stimulated expansion of tanning. Contrary to Brazil, Mexico does not have any indigenous supplies of raw materials to speak of to explain the establishment and growth of the tanning industry. However, access to raw hides from Brazil and the US is good.

Environmental Requirements

Apart from a boom in pollution control in the mid-1990s, NAFTA has not really resulted in stricter enforcement of environmental regulations in the tanning industry, implying that pressure from the Mexican government is weak. The exception was due to the fact that Canadian geese of passage died from drinking contaminated water in León. The pollution control authorities then undertook physical control of a number of tanneries and initiated a plan to locate the tanneries in an ecological park with common effluent treatment. This was not realized, allegedly because the government did not make the necessary investments in infrastructure. Although discharge limits to water are not significantly laxer than in the North, there is little enforcement and the tanners complain that there are no designated disposal sites for solid waste (Table 9.1).

There is furthermore no environmental pressure in the local market. Less than 10 percent of the tanneries in Mexico have effluent treatment plants (see Rodriguez-Abitia, 1997). However, those who indirectly or directly cater to the export market experience some environmental pressure, but not of the kind that means much to the local environment. With a pollution-intensive production process it is still possible to comply with the environmental product standards that the market requires.

In an in-depth study of eight chrome tanneries in León, Wiik (1999) revealed that six manufacture wet-blue, and that only one of the six has a wastewater treatment plant. However, both Wiik and Rodriguez-Abitia (1997) have data indicating that pressure from the authorities in the mid-1990s and the cost of buying water have encouraged a shift in interest from internal production of wet-blue to sourcing of wet-blue. Exports of leather from Brazil to Mexico quadrupled from 1992 to 1997, and the bulk of this is most probably wet-blue.[4] When wet-blue production is shifted from Mexico to Brazil, this also implies that pollution is shifted to Brazil where effluent treatment is often inferior (see above).

Strategies of Competition and Environmental Practice

Based on Porter's (1990) generic strategies of competition in quality and cost-leadership, three types of tanneries were identified:

1. quality based on durability and appearance for the automobile upholstery market;
2. quality based on appearance and flexibility for the fashion-product market; and
3. cost-leadership for simple shoes and various other products.

Table 9.1 Effluent discharge limits, selected parameters, mg/l (excepting pH)

	Germany		Italy		Portugal		Mexico: rivers	
	Surface	Sewer	Surface	Sewer	Surface	Sewer	Agriculture	Protected
PH units	6.8–8.5[1]	6.5–10[1]	5.5.–9.5	5.5–9.5	6–9			
BOD	20–25[2]		40	250	40		150	30
COD	≥15[2]		160	500	150			
Sulphide	1.0–2.0[3]	1.0–2.0[3]	1.0	2.0	1.0			
Chrome tot.	0.5–1[2,3]	0.5–1[3]	2.0	4.0	2.0	2.0	1.0	0.5
Chloride		600[1]	1000	1200				
Sulphate			1000	1000	2000			
Ammonia	5–10[1,3]		10–15	30	10		Total N = 40	Total N = 15

Notes: Surface refers to discharge to surface water, that is, discharge directly from the tannery. The limits are the maximum concentration of pollutants permitted for discharge. It is important to note that the figures are collected from different sources and that the limits are frequently changing. The Mexican limits selected for presentation here are monthly averages. The two categories of rivers in agricultural areas and protected rivers reflect the most lenient and the strictest of the emission limits. Mexico has established effluent limits on more parameters than listed here. N is nitrogen.

Sources: Germany: 1) UNEP, 1991, in Ballance et al., 1993; 2) VDL interview; 3) World Leather, November 1996. Italy: World Leather, November 1996. Portugal: Diáro da República, 1990, 1992. Mexico: NOM-001-ECOL/1996 ref. in Rodríguez-Abitia, 1997.

Then environmental practice was quantified on the basis of five parameters:

- wastewater treatment,
- environmentally sound use of chemicals;
- efficiency in use of water and energy;
- housekeeping; and
- other measures and projects to reduce pollution.

Contrary to expectation, the tanneries that rely on appearance and flexibility for the fashion market have as low an environmental practice as those with a cost cutting strategy (Knutsen and Wiik, 1999; Wiik, 1999) (Table 9.2).

The best tanners in the sample, both in terms of technology and environmental practice, are upholstery tanners. They score much higher than the other tanners as they do more for the environment on all of the parameters. The upholstery tanners produce for indirect exports to German, US and Japanese automobile manufacturers via local seat manufacturers. However, the automobile manufacturers deal directly with the tanners in controlling both the quality of the products and the production process. They are even claimed to pressure for cleaner production. Nevertheless, only one of the three upholstery tanners has an effluent treatment plant. Moreover, the automobile manufacturers do not check on the environmental practice of those who supply the Mexican upholstery tanners with wet-blue.

Demanding automobile companies are by no means sufficient to explain the environmental practice of the upholstery manufacturers. Automobile companies prefer to link with large tanneries to ensure large supplies of leather of consistent quality and appearance. The three upholstery tanneries are large. This reflects economies of scale that reduce the unit cost of environmental measures. All three possess financial and technological resources, such as departments of technological development and well-educated employees. Like the upholstery tanners, the fashion tanners who export their products stress that their customers are concerned with the pollution loads in the finished products. In contrast to the upholstery tanners, they are crystal clear that their customers do not care about the production process. The fashion tanners have modern technology to meet the customers' demand for quality. They do, however, insist that they cannot invest in and increase the cost of production of 'something' that the customers are not willing to pay for, such as cleaner production for the sake of the environment. In one of the tanneries they claimed to have sufficient capital reserves to invest in cleaner production, but would not do this since the market does not require it. With no pressure, it is better to secure the position in the market by investing in technology to improve the characteristics of the products. To survive in the market, the other fashion tanners also expressed that they have to direct all their attention to

Table 9.2 Competitive strategy and environmental practice

Competitive strategy (relative)	No. of units	No. of employees	Product type	Market	Technological level	Environmental practice[a] (relative)
Quality: durability and appearance	3	135, 370, 750	Automobile upholstery	Indirect exports	Modern-advanced	High, scores: 11, 13, 19
Quality: appearance flexibility	2	65, 85	Fashion bags, shoes	Direct exports	Modern	Low, scores: 2, 5
Cost-leadership	3	25, 25, 5	Crust, shoes, misc.	National customers, some small-scale	Standard	Low, scores: 3, 4, 4

Note: [a] Number of scores is indicative of the potential of the respective measures to reduce pollution, which in turn is based on Mensink and Lange (1996). The variables and values are as follows:

1. Wastewater treatment: no: 0; mechanical: 4; chemical: 6; biological: 8.
2. Environmentally friendly use of chemicals (type and quantity): no: 0; yes: 2. Comment: common measure, less potential for pollution abatement than a wastewater treatment plant.
3. Efficiency in use of water/energy: no: 0; yes: 1. Comment: common measure, less potential for pollution abatement than a wastewater treatment plant.
4. Housekeeping: range: 0–4. Comment: based on observations in the respective tanneries. Examples of indicators are use of safety equipment, cleanliness and tidiness labelling and storage of chemicals, instructions on machines, safety routines and emergency exits. This applies both to discharge and accidents that may affect nature, workers and people in the vicinity of the tannery.
5. Other environmental measures: no: 0; yes: 6. Comment: this refers to different combinations of projects such as: wet-white production, hairsaving systems and disposal systems of solid waste.

The system of allocation and the number of scores obtained by each of the respective tanneries are accounted for in more detail in Wiik (1999).

Sources: Knutsen and Wiik, 1999; Wiik, 1999.

product requirements and to cutting costs where it does not affect the ability to respond quickly to the changing demands of their customers.

The tanneries that compete on costs are small and have little or no contact with the international market. They all claim that they have had to pay more attention to the quality of their products. This is because economic liberalization results in increasing imports of competing products, including plastics. This has also stimulated price competition. There is no demand for environmentally sound products in the local market, either in terms of product properties or the nature of the production process. They also report that when their customers export leather products, they are not concerned with the environmental practice of the tanneries at all. The tanners agree that they would have priced themselves out of the market by giving higher priority to the environment. They have made some smaller changes in their production process. Measures have been taken to reduce water consumption and apply more environmentally sound chemicals. Both are considered cost-efficient, as water is expensive and the high cost of the new chemicals is offset by the fact that smaller quantities are required per unit of production. The essence of the Mexican case study is that those who comply with environmental requirements do so in order not to lose markets.

In line with the findings from Brazil, economic liberalization has led to better access to products and services of the supplier industries. In Mexico access to more advanced chemicals has improved environmental practice somewhat in all three categories of tanneries. In this respect functional integration in a *global* commodity chain can be considered positive to the environment, when measured in pollution per unit of production. However, changes in the use of chemicals are not sufficient in order to comply with existing standards on discharge of wastewater, unless the wet-processes are externalized. When tanneries shift to more environmentally sound production in their own unit by externalization of wet-blue production, they hand the pollution problem over to another place or country. This means that pollution continues in Mexico and/or increases in Brazil where much of the imported wet-blue comes from. A substantial amount of wet-blue production still takes place in Mexico and the Mexican tanning industry is expanding. This implies that the overall pollution problem in sum is aggravated.

INDIA

From Protection Towards Liberalization

There are about 2,500 tanneries in India, of which 80 percent are small, employing only a few people. In addition, it is said that there may be another

3,000 very small tanneries spread around the country. These tanneries carry out only the first and most polluting stages of production. During the last decade there has been a growing process specialization among the tanneries. The industrial tanneries are mainly located in Tamil Nadu (more than half of total Indian leather production), Calcutta (15 percent) and Kanpur/Agra (12 percent) in Uttar Pradesh (Hesselberg, 1999).

Today India uses only 20 percent of the hides of fallen (natural death) and slaughtered cattle. Only about half of the yearly off-take of cattle is slaughtered. This is important because the hides of fallen animals are of inferior quality. This fact, together with the fact that India is the country with the largest cattle herd in the world (and 53 percent of the world's buffaloes), points to an enormous potential for leather production in both quantitative and qualitative terms. The country has only 6 percent of the world's production of leather and only 4 percent of the exports of leather and leather goods. Still, this production (2 percent of GDP) and exports (7 percent of the country's total exports and the fourth largest export sector) are important. Unfortunately, export is mainly of components for shoes that are made in Europe. India also has to import chemicals and machinery for the tanning and leather goods industries. There is, in other words, a huge potential for improvements in these sectors, and thus for national economic growth and foreign exchange earnings.

Figures 9.1 and 9.2 illustrate this growth potential. In order for India to take advantage of this, the country must increase the share of exports of quality products ready for sale to end-consumers. The Indian government in 1975 banned the export of raw hides in order to force private business to increase the level of value-added in the tanning and leather goods industries. Again in 1995 a ban was imposed on exports of semi-processed leather with a similar intention. In order to reduce exports of finished leather, the government imposed an export tax of 10 percent in 1997. In 1999 the tax on imports of chemicals and machinery to the tanning sector was removed (*World Leather*, no. 2, 1998 and no. 2, 1999). The government has undoubtedly achieved a positive development through its industrial policy towards tanning. Kumar (1997) reports a change in the leather industry from 1974–5, when 85 percent of exports in the industry was leather (all stages from raw hide to finished leather), to 1989–90 when the percentage had decreased to 35 percent. There was a corresponding increase in the industry's exports of leather *products* from 15 percent to 65 percent. Today the major share of exports is *semi-*processed leather *goods* (although mostly of low quality). The challenge for the future is to find ways to improve the quality and to be able to compete internationally regarding finished leather *goods*.

However, the EU has brought India's policy on leather production and exports to the World Trade Organization. The criticism is against the ban on exports of raw hides and particularly against the wet-blue export ban. To meet

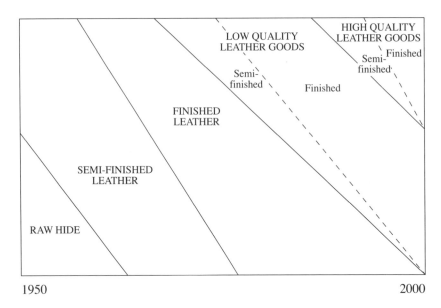

Note: In the ideal model, exports of semi-finished leather finish in 1979. The exports then
          change mostly to finished leather (73 percent). There are some exports of semi-finished
          leather goods (20 percent) and a minimum of finished leather (7 percent).

*Figure 9.1   Percent distribution of exports from low to high value added:
               export - ideal model*

WTO compliance, India has agreed to remove all *quantitative* restrictions on
imports by the year 2003 (*World Leather*, no. 3, 1999). Still, the country has
high import tariffs and can be said to be highly protectionist, although
gradually less so. The pressure now brought to bear on India makes it very
difficult for the country not to comply with the WTO in future on tariffs as
well. It is necessary in order to sustain international competitiveness over time
for industry to have its own R&D and thus a continuous innovation process. It
is almost impossible for a country to achieve lasting industrialization without
an ability to export industrial goods. Furthermore, the EU market is protected
by quota restrictions on imports of leather *goods*. This makes it difficult for
countries in the South to advance from exports of components to finished
consumer goods. It is essential for development to be able to reach higher
levels of value-added in industry. This is close to impossible to do without
trade restrictions in the South during a transition period. Development cannot
be achieved by subjecting countries at *different* levels of industrialization as
well as general economic development to the *same* rules, that is, to trade
liberalization and reductions of state interventions. For instance, the process of

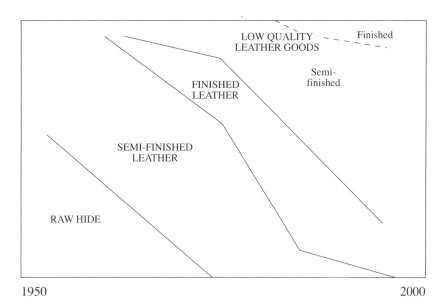

1950   2000

Note: The distribution in 1995 was: almost complete cessation of exports of semi-finished leather; finished leather: 18 percent; semi-finished leather goods: 71 percent; and finished leather goods: 10 percent.

Sources: Based on Chandramouli (n.d.); Thyagarajan *et al.* (1994); Central Leather Research Institute (1998).

Figure 9.2   Percent distribution of India's exports of leather and leather goods

globalization, operating through import liberalization and devaluation, has important implications for low-income groups because prices normally rise and there is a recessionary impact on the economy, and thus their real incomes decline. The international pressure to conform to what benefits the North may be termed *global imperialism*. Furthermore, Germany recently imposed an import ban on leather and leather goods containing PCP. Other countries in the North have followed Germany's example. Although this may be an environmentally sound step to take, it hampers exports from India because the substitute chemical is ten times more expensive and has to be imported. This may be called an example of *green imperialism*.

There has so far been no demand from Europe that Indian tanners should stop using child labour. At present, half of those employed in tanneries in India are male children. (Most labourers in tanning belong to so-called backward castes, especially to Chamar. Due to religious prejudice, tanners have a social stigma.) No girl child or woman works in tanning. (In contrast, in leather goods production 80 percent of the workers are female.) In future, import restrictions may be imposed on goods produced by processes involving children. If this becomes the case, and the North thus decides not only how the production processes should be carried out in the South but also *who* should work there, we could speak of *social imperialism*.

Heavy Pollution

In India, tanneries have been proven to reduce crop yield on farms in the neighbourhood (Varadarajan and Krishnamoorthy, 1993). There are furthermore many cases of *salting* of wells and of fish deaths in streams. The presence of sodium sulphite, chrome and other tanning agents removes oxygen from the water, and thus stops the self-purification process in streams and rivers by killing the biota. The river Palar in southern India is a case in point. The water is heavily polluted for as far as 100 km and 35,000 hectares of farmland are affected. Agricultural yields are reduced by 40 percent. Several illnesses have become more prevalent, especially among children (Kjellberg and Prasad, 1997). In a study of the groundwater in Kanpur, the result is that the content of chrome, fluor, DDT, lindane and chlorine, among others, is far above safe standards (Central Pollution Control Board, 1996). The same is the case with the main river, Ganga. The 300 tanneries in Kanpur are a large part of the city's pollution problem. In the Jajmau part of the city a new CETP (common effluent treatment plant) was recently built with Dutch assistance. Jajmau has a concentration of tanneries. However, the Central Pollution Control Board found that this CETP is insufficient and is not functioning well. Often the effluents are sent untreated or only partially treated into the Ganga. Effluents from the other tanneries in Kanpur are either floating out on to paths outside the small factories or piped down to the groundwater through boreholes on the factory site (Pandya, 1998).

The state of Uttar Pradesh has threatened to close down tanneries (and other polluting industries) that do not adhere to standards on effluents. This has not led to adoption of new technology in the production process, that is, *cleaner* technology, nor to the use of more end-of-pipe technology, that is, *cleaning* technology. Instead a process of shifting from wet-blue to the finishing stages of leather production is now taking place. More and more tanneries are sourcing wet-blue from remote areas in India and from Nepal. Thus, the major pollution problem is to some degree shifted out of Kanpur into rural areas and poorer neighbouring countries, therefore this is not a decrease but only a 'relocation of pollution'. These processes can be called *interiorization of pollution* and *trickle-out of pollution* respectively. In addition to the pressure to reduce pollution by cost-increasing measures, that is, an environmental squeeze since the cost of complying with regulations cannot be absorbed by more effective resource utilization, tanneries experience pressure to reduce total production costs due to the increasing price competition following trade liberalization, that is, a profit squeeze. Competition from especially Brazil, China and Pakistan in markets in the North as well as in the home market in India necessitates cost cutting in order to maintain market shares for the Indian tanning and leather goods industries. The environmental pressure from government regulations in the two mentioned countries is presently clearly less than is the case in India (even if enforcement of regulations is weak at the moment).

The typical tanneries in India are today sub-contractors to global firms. The attraction for these firms is mainly cheap labour, less cost on pollution abatement and a huge and growing Indian market. Semi-skilled labour in tanneries is paid only US$0.4 an hour in India (1996) compared to US$3.5 in South Korea, US$6 in the US and US$14 in Italy (*World Leather*, no. 3, 1996). The global firms can source leather components from a number of countries. They have many options. Still, they often compete among themselves on price rather than on quality and design in the mass consumer goods segments of international markets. Thus, they are constantly looking for places where there are opportunities for lower costs. The double pressure to which Indian tanners are exposed from state environmental legislative activism and from globalization of the Indian economy makes for a very uncertain future indeed regarding sustained utilization of the huge potential for leather making in the country. This uncertainty also applies to maintenance of real wages, and thus levels of living, and to reductions in pollution, and thus to improvements in health. In sum, a large part of today's tanneries in India is probably only economically viable because of weak enforcement of environmental as well as work place regulations.

Possible Solutions

Presently, there are four particularly relevant ways in which industrial pollution may be reduced in India. All cost money, and they are thus not likely to be carried out in the short term.

Relocation

The tanneries in Calcutta will probably at some time be forced to move to a new planned industrial site outside the city. There a CETP will be built with government subsidies, cheap loans and external expertise. The problem elsewhere in India is the shortage of adequate land, and the fact that the many small tanneries cannot even afford the 15 percent of the cost of building a CETP that they must cover, let alone the daily running cost. In addition, a

CETP does not solve the problem of safe disposal of sludge containing chrome. Relocation out of cities without any change in technology and/or environmental performance will of course only be a geographical shift of pollution. However, it may result in fewer people being adversely affected health-wise.

Adoption of cleaner technology
The technology used in tanneries in India is old-fashioned. Thus, there is considerable scope for improvements that will both increase the quality of the products and decrease pollution. This technology is well-known and accessible from foreign machine companies. Again, the small as well as the medium-scale tanneries cannot normally afford such investments. They often compete in a so-called poverty market where the low buying-power of the people requires the lowest possible price. Inferior quality is a way to achieve such a price. Thus, a need for innovation in process technology does not arise. This is called the low quality trap.

For the tanners who sell to firms making leather goods components for exports, demanding customers might force them to adopt new technology, with a pollution reducing effect. At present, there is not much pressure of this kind. There is also little demand in the North for so-called eco-leather, that is, leather made with a minimum of adverse environmental impact. Traditional vegetable tanning is no real alternative because it uses a number of chemicals (although not chrome). In addition, the production time is quite long, making it less profitable. The conclusions are that innovation in the production process is difficult to achieve and that environmentally friendly leather is not in demand at the moment. However, joint ventures between Indian firms and foreign companies may involve transfers of knowledge and direct investments in technology upgrading in order that companies from the North can obtain cheap but somewhat improved quality leather. This may result in reduced pollution as a kind of environmental improvement into the bargain, an unintended positive side-effect. The problem of industrialization, poverty alleviation and development in general in India with such a process is that it becomes very difficult for the Indian industry to climb the ladder of value-added, to produce and export higher quality goods. It is a danger that the Indian industry may be kept at the intermediate level through the interest of the dominant foreign partners.

Enforcement of environmental regulation
At present the authorities try to enforce the environmental laws and regulations through inspections to ensure adherence to the standards which have been set. Violations are fined. This system allows opportunities for corruption, which is said to be a major problem in the tanning sector. Tackling

this problem in a country with low wages in the public sector is extremely difficult. It may therefore be sensible to change over gradually to greater reliance on the market as a mechanism to transform the behaviour of the private firms. To introduce bans and taxes on, for instance, the use of toxic chemicals can force tanners to adopt new ways of production that are less polluting. Of course, this can only be an addition to public knowledge and control of what hazardous substances each and every small and large production facility emits to air and water. Undoubtedly, there exists a huge knowledge gap not only on the part of public authorities but also among many small tanners regarding the toxicity of the chemicals they use.

Judicial activism

In view of the lack of will among most politicians to do something about pollution and its severe health effects, the Supreme Court as well as judges in the High Courts of some states in India decided from 1996 onwards to use legislation to close heavily polluting industries. This has become known as judicial activism. Not many industries have actually been closed down. The threat of closure has led some firms (also some tanneries) to relocate out of cities, some to reduce pollution, and many to continue as before. Of the last group, a few have had to pay fines of insignificant amounts. Another way of continuing production as before is reported in *Down to Earth* (15/1–99):

> There is a notice in bold, red lettering on the gate of Super Leather Industries ... It says that the factory has been closed following the ... order by the Supreme Court, which directed the closure and relocation of 168 polluting industrial units in Delhi by November 30, 1996. Take a walk around the boundary wall and there is another notice at the back of the premises which announces business as usual: A K Leathers. The name has changed. What has not changed is the dark grey sludge – replete with dangerous chemicals – that flows mockingly towards ... the Yamuna.

At the same time, the government has encouraged people and interest groups to report polluting firms to the courts. This is called public interest litigation. Thus, pollution-intensive industries are pressured to become more environmentally sound both from above and below.

In Tamil Nadu the High Court closed 235 tanneries for a few months in 1996. The pressure from the private sector and the workers forced the authorities to allow a reopening without reduced pollution but with a promise from the tanners that in future there would be primary treatment of effluents or that they would organise themselves and build CETPs. Obviously, there is a conflict between environmental improvement and the need for employment and economic growth in the short term. However, the important question is whether continued pollution will hamper long-term sustained economic growth and social development. Industrialists are however more concerned about competitiveness and short-term survival. In such a highly complex and vast country as India, with its enormous development problems, a changing attitude amongst those running and owning industries is essential. This is probably the only politically feasible way of achieving lasting environmental improvement. The most important impact of judicial activism may thus prove to be increased awareness of and positive opinions about the need to reduce pollution among private business managers.

India's Supreme Court decided in 1999 that if a public interest litigation brought against a firm was unsuccessful and thus delayed production unnecessarily, the party (for instance, a voluntary green organization or a community) had to bear the cost, that is, pay the firm in question for lost profit (*Down to Earth*, 15/1–99). This will undoubtedly limit the willingness of popular organizations to use the option available in the legislation to stop pollution from industry.

CONCLUSION

According to our findings environmental regulations and enforcement represent a cost problem and an 'absolute problem' to the tanning industry in developed countries. Examples of the latter are constraints on the use of water in Italy and limited access to waste disposal/landfill sites in Germany. However, the tanning industry has not yet experienced any process-innovation and product-innovation offsets to speak of *à la* Porter and van der Linde (1995). Low profit margins both in high and lower cost countries are an obstacle to investment in technological change which may have intended or unintended positive environmental effects. Competition is so severe at present that firms will not invest in cleaner production unless it is quite clear that it pays off. Low profits are of course also a big obstacle to investment in end-of-pipe technology since this technology does not render economic offsets.

Modern technology in the tanning industry that ensures efficient production and high quality products does not at the same time significantly reduce pollution. The main concern of the customers is good quality at reasonable prices and timely supplies. The tanners hold that the market is not ripe to pay premium prices for eco-labelled products. From a product quality point of view, industry sources stress that there is no viable alternative to chrome tanning when flexible and soft leather with a high shrinkage temperature is required. The market for chrome-free upholstery leather in the automobile industry is so far limited, and the tanners themselves are reluctant to promote chrome-free leather as eco-leather, fearing the negative consequences this may have for the image of the industry at large.

What all this boils down to is that stricter environmental requirements have not so far been an engine of significant improvement in environmental practice. On the contrary, the tanning industry is subject to an environmental squeeze resulting from the combination of profit squeeze and demanding regulators whose requirements are costly. The technological ceiling exacerbates the problem of environmental squeeze. The technological ceiling and profit squeeze signify structural problems, although not necessarily eternal problems for the branch. A solution among more tanners in the EU is thus to outsource the more polluting stages of the production process. The fact that the bulk of our interviews have been made in best-case tanneries both in the EU and the lower cost countries underscores this line of argument.

Not only are we experiencing a step-wise shift in the location of tanning from Northern Europe to Southern Europe, Eastern Europe and developing countries. There is also an on-going *interiorization* of the more polluting segments of the industry within the lower cost and developing countries to which tanning has been shifted. It is the technological ceiling and profit squeeze that lead to externalization of the most polluting processes. Unfortunately for the receiving end, these processes are also those that generate least value-added. It is also unfortunate that sourcing relationships which improve the quality of the product do not *per se* solve environmental problems. It is possible to obtain the required good product quality without process changes that radically improve environmental practice. The bottom line is that end-of-pipe measures are still required to treat the bulk of waste and pollution. Our findings imply that such facilities are often inferior in Eastern Europe and developing countries. This also explains why economic liberalization is not conducive to the environment as far as the tanning industry is concerned. Pollution may decline in some locations only to increase elsewhere when the most polluting stages of production are interiorized or trickle out to locations where 'nobody bothers'. It is also food for thought that economic liberalization in the case study countries may actually deprive the tanners of the possibility of building up competitive advantage in higher quality products.

NOTES

1. One of the higher estimates, including artisan home industries (Schmitz, 1995).
2. The advantages are that the use of salts and chemical preservatives for the preservation of hides for transport are almost eliminated, and less energy is used for transport since wet-blue weighs half as much as raw hides.
3. Primary treatment refers to a physical/chemical process for particle sedimentation and removal.
4. This is based on interviews Odegard (1998) made in Brazil. Wet-blue is not singled out as a separate category in national and international statistics. See also Knutsen and Wiik (1999).

PART IV

Environmental regulation and industrial restructuring: the case of the fertilizer industry

Anthony Bartzokas

10. Technological trends and industrial organization in the European fertilizer industry

INTRODUCTION

This chapter examines how environmental regulation has influenced technological change, corporate strategies and the competitiveness of the fertilizer industry in Europe.[1] The fertilizer industry is a mature, pollution-intensive process industry. Major innovations have been introduced in the past and the current allocation of investment on research and innovation is limited. The market shares of advanced countries and especially those of European Union member states in this sector have been declining in the last 20 years. The manufacturing of some products and downstream processing of many raw materials have been transferred to developing countries. A closer look, however, reveals some additional interesting trends that will bring the environmental dimension into the picture. First, the European fertilizer industry went through a significant restructuring process and the remaining firms have managed to retain their position in the European and international market in some areas of final products. Second, final products are being produced by different production processes and that implies different structures of input requirements and value-added shares. The production of nitrogen fertilizers, for example, is an energy-intensive manufacturing process that depends on the supply of natural gas while the production of phosphate fertilizers uses phosphate rock imported from developing countries, incurring high transport costs. Third, the final product of the industry is an input to agriculture. That makes the environmental implications of fertilizer production much wider, compared to other sectors, and the link between producers (fertilizer firms) and users (farmers) an interesting one.

After the selection of the fertilizer industry as one of the case studies for this book, we took a closer look at environmental problems in various stages of the production process of different groups of final products. In order to assess the importance of inter-regional differences in environmental compliance costs on production and trade patterns in the fertilizer industry, we examined how the industry has been developing in several countries and different regions. This process helped identify comparative trends in the relative importance of environmental legislation in the overall performance of the fertilizer industry. In this chapter, we first review the technological trends and the overall performance in the European fertilizer industry in the context of the general trends in the world fertilizer industry. The declining demand for fertilizer application in European agriculture due to environmental regulation is also analysed. In addition, we look closely at what kind of corporate strategies have been pursued and how European firms are trying to incorporate economic and environmental factors into their corporate strategies.

THE PRODUCTION PROCESS AND THE ENVIRONMENT

Mineral fertilizers are made from naturally occurring raw materials containing nutrients which have normally been transformed into a more plant-available form by industrial processing. While the chemical components of finished products are relatively simple, the manufacturing technologies are highly developed, and production plants are very capital-intensive. Fertilizers are produced as straight or multi-nutrient products, and the production processes vary in accordance with the nutrients produced. The main pollutants emitted to the atmosphere from fertilizer production units are ammonia, fluorine, nitrogen oxides, carbon dioxide, dust and fume. On most modern units, the abatement plant is part of the production process. All liquids and dust from scrubbers, cyclones and filters are fed back into the production process (France and Thompson, 1993). Fertilizer production consumes approximately 1.2 percent of the world's energy and is responsible for approximately 1.2 percent of the total emission of greenhouse gases, including CO_2 and nitrous oxide (N_2O). The main energy requirement for the production of fertilizers is linked to the nitrogen component: 92.5 percent for N, 3 percent for P_2O_5, and 4.5 percent for K_2O on a global basis (Kongshaug, 1998).

As competition in the fertilizer industry has become increasingly international, manufacturers have diversified their production in many different directions aiming at better quality and increasing value-added for the customer. Fertilizers are grouped by nutrients provided. Fixed nitrogen (N), water-soluble phosphorus (P) and water-soluble potassium (K) are the primary fertilizer nutrients. Sulphur (S) is considered the most important secondary nutrient. The various steps involved in the manufacture of finished fertilizer products, from raw materials through intermediate products, are shown in Table 10.1.

Table 10.1   Products of the fertilizer industry

Nutrients	Source	Intermediates	Fertilizer products
Nitrogen (N)	Nitrogen from air (hydrogen from natural gas)	Ammonia	Urea
		Nitric acid	Ammonium nitrate Calcium ammonium nitrate Nitrogen solutions Ammonium sulphate
Phosphorus (P)	Phosphate rock	Phosphoric acid	Ammonium phosphates Superphosphates
Potash (K)	Potash		
Sulphur (S)	Sulphur source	Sulphuric acid	
			Multi-nutrient fertilizers (NPK, NK, PK)

Source: EFMA (1997b).

Ammonia

Ammonia (NH_3) is the intermediate product for nitrogen fertilizers. The further processing of ammonia produces straight nitrogen fertilizers such as ammonium nitrate (AN) and calcium ammonium nitrate (CAN), urea, urea ammonium nitrate (UAN), as well as solutions of the above fertilizers and ammonium sulphate (AS). Ammonia is also the main component of many multi-nutrient fertilizers. Combining nitrogen extracted from the air with hydrogen derived from hydrocarbons produces ammonia. About 85 percent of world ammonia production is based on steam reforming processes, and most of them use natural gas as feedstock. In Europe, approximately 85 percent of ammonia plants use natural gas (EFMA, 1995a and 1997b).

Since ammonia synthesis requires a large amount of energy, energy saving has been the prime concern of technological development. The history of the modern ammonia technology started in 1913 when the Haber–Bosch process was developed for the synthesis of ammonia from atmospheric nitrogen. No fundamental innovation has occurred since then. Traditionally, partial oxidation of heavy fuel oil was used. Since the oil crisis in the 1970s, however, steam reforming of natural gas became relatively competitive.

Table 10.2 shows that total energy use, including raw materials, for the production of ammonia improved significantly from 88 GJ/t NH_3 in 1940 to 40 GJ/t NH_3 in the 1960s and to around the current value of 28 GJ/t NH_3, which is already close to the thermodynamic minimum. It is expected that the present ammonia production technology will not change fundamentally, at least in the near future. With the available concepts, the margins of additional improvements have become rather small after years of intensive research and development. Only relatively low cost retrofitting of existing plants should be expected, including the redesign/replacement of the ammonia converter to achieve more contact with the catalyst and decreasing pressure losses (Appl, 1993 and 1997).

Table 10.2   Energy consumption requirements of ammonia plants

	1940	1966	1973	1977	1980	1991
Energy consumption (GJ/t NH_3)	88	40	38	34	30	28

Source: Appl (1993).

Nitric Acid

Nitric acid (HNO_3) is mainly used for the production of straight and compound fertilizers. It is also used, on a smaller scale, in the chemical industry and for the production of explosives. The production of nitric acid across Europe utilizes the same basic chemical operations. First, oxidation of ammonia with air to give nitric oxide, and second, oxidation of the nitric oxide to nitrogen dioxide and absorption in water to give a solution of nitric acid (EFMA, 1995b). The main environmental factor affecting the process selection is the NO_X level in gas emissions.

Extended absorption and selective catalyst reduction (SCR) are generally recommended as best available techniques for NO_X reduction (EFMA, 1995b). Technical and economic considerations will influence the choice between the extended absorption and the SCR techniques for an existing plant. The SCR technique has been preferred to extended absorption among fertilizer manufacturers.

The technologies mentioned above have been well established and are readily available from engineering firms. While it is generally considered that new opportunities for technological development are relatively limited, other technological possibilities are being investigated. For example, synthetic zeolite could be used to adsorb NO_X and other processes which use NO_X to oxidize SO_2 to sulphate in an ammonia solution and use NO_X with limestone slurry to give gypsum and ammonia (IFA, UNEP, and UNIDO, 1998).

Urea

Urea ($CO(NH_2)_2$) is the most concentrated solid nitrogen fertilizer available. In Europe, the use of urea is generally limited to heavy soils, where it is incorporated into the soil after application. Urea is also used for manufacture of cattle feed and synthetic resins.

Technology innovations related to the urea synthesis process are aimed at decreasing capital costs for new plants. For example, the low-profile pool-type reactors and horizontal condensers are reported to decrease the capital cost of a urea unit by about 10 percent compared with the conventional (vertical) designs. Flash evaporation of 90 percent solution to over 99 percent helps to decrease fouling of the evaporator heat transfer area, thus decreasing the cost of operation and, to some extent, the capital cost of the evaporator unit (Schultz and Harris, 1998). Some or all of these improvements have been used in updating existing plants. Modern processes have very similar energy requirements and nearly 100 percent material efficiency (EFMA, 1995e).

Another innovation that has been adopted, especially in new plants, is the production of granular urea instead of prilled urea. The conversion to granular urea is mainly driven by the market demand for a high-quality product (larger particles) that is more resistant to breakdown and caking, easier to handle and apply, and compatible in size with other conventional granular materials used to make high-quality, physical blends (bulk blends) (Schultz and Harris, 1998).

Phosphoric Acid

Varieties of production processes with different raw materials are being used in the manufacture of phosphoric acid. The thermal process uses phosphorus as its raw material. Because of the amount of energy that is needed, this process has been abandoned. The wet processes use phosphate rock decomposed with an acid. Currently, they are the only economic alternative way to produce phosphoric acid, accounting for 95 percent of world production (EFMA, 1995d).

There are three possible sub-groups of wet processes, depending on the acid which is used for the acidulation, namely, nitric, hydrochloric or sulphuric. In Europe, normally the sulphuric acid route is used in the production of fertilizers. These different processes are needed because of different ores available and gypsum disposal systems. Most phosphate ores have to be concentrated before they can be used or sold on the international phosphate market.

The disposal of phosphogypsum poses a serious problem, especially with the large-scale phosphoric acid production units of over 1,000t/d capacity which are now being built. Around 5 tonnes of phosphogypsum are generated per ton of phosphoric acid expressed as P_2O_5. This phosphogypsum contains some of the trace elements from the phosphate rock, including cadmium and some radioactive elements. Although it was previously a common practice for phosphoric acid plants situated on coasts to pump gypsum into the sea, where it rapidly dissolves, recent restrictions on the disposal of phosphogypsum into the sea have been introduced, subject to restrictions on the cadmium content of the gypsum.

Three methods are available to deal with phosphogypsum, namely, use as saleable products, discharging into water, and dumping on land (Benchekroun, 1992; EFMA, 1995d; Davister, 1996).

Use as saleable products

The use of phosphogypsum for other purposes has been widely encouraged, but economic and quality problems and low demand for the resulting products frequently inhibit this solution. These problems relate not only to the impurities in the phosphogypsum, but also to its relatively high moisture content. Plaster-board, plaster and cement are the main possibilities, but it is also possible to reuse phosphogypsum in sulphuric acid production. Gypsum and phospho-gypsum are also used in large quantities as a soil amendment for saline soils. The ready availability of natural gypsum and the high cost of gypsum-based sulphuric acid are the main obstacles to its use. Presently very little phospho-gypsum is reused in the EU countries, due to the low costs of the current disposal methods and the high costs for purification of phosphogypsum. However, in countries where gypsum and other sulphurous raw materials are scarce, phosphogypsum has been successfully used for these purposes.

Disposal to water

The gypsum can be pumped through an outlet into the sea at coastal sites. In other cases it is pumped into rivers, but this mode of disposal becomes economically less attractive if the receiving water is far away. Disposal of gypsum into the sea has the advantage that gypsum is more soluble in seawater than in fresh water. However, some of the impurities in the gypsum should be controlled. Gypsum itself is fully soluble and is not harmful to the environment. High efficiency (above 97 percent) of phosphoric acid production is essential for this method of disposal, and good quality rock phosphate should be used in the plant, if the pollution is to be kept within local environmental quality standards.[2]

Disposal on land

Disposal on land is not possible everywhere because it requires space and certain soil qualities where the gypsum stack is situated. Belt conveyers to the gypsum storage pile transport dry gypsum from the filter in some plants. A ditch that collects the run-off water, including any rainwater, surrounds the pile area. In other plants the filter cake is slurried with recycled pond water and pumped to special storage areas where phosphogypsum eventually dries in stacks. The area receiving the phosphogypsum slurry is sub-divided into smaller areas, with each section being used in rotation. Slurry is discharged on top of the storage pile, and the phosphogypsum rapidly settles out of solution. Clear water runs off and drains to the adjacent cooling ponds. The water is recycled within the system to ensure that the contaminants are kept within the plant. The phosphogypsum stack is surrounded by a ditch, which can contain not only this water but also any water that might spill accidentally. The system should be designed to prevent any contaminated water from reaching the surrounding ground water system.[3]

The problem with cadmium

During the processing of phosphate rock, cadmium is partitioned between wastes from the beneficiation process of phosphate rock and phosphogypsum from the further processing into phosphoric acid. The percentage of the elements that is transferred from the phosphate rock to the phosphogypsum depends on the type of process and the rock used. The cadmium level in product fertilizers is increasingly causing concern in Europe (*Phosphorus and Potasium*, 1989, no. 162, p. 23; OECD, 1995; and Lin, 1997).

Regulations or voluntary limits on the cadmium content in fertilizers vary from country to country in Europe, as shown in Table 10.3 (OECD, 1996a; UNIDO and IFDC, 1998). While the EU directive on cadmium emissions to water in 1988 explicitly recognized the desirability of reducing inputs of cadmium to soils as part of an overall strategy for reducing environmental contamination by cadmium, it also acknowledged that there was still no feasible process to remove cadmium from phosphate rock and that exports of rock phosphate represented a significant source of revenue for a number of developing countries in Africa (EFMA, 1997b).

In 1991, the members of the European Fertilizer Manufacturers Association decided that they would try to discuss an agreement based on self-restraint, rather than wait for EU regulation. In 1995, the members agreed to make efforts to reduce the cadmium content of the fertilizers they deliver to Western Europe to a maximum level of 60 mg cadmium per kg P_2O_5, which is roughly equivalent to 137 mg cadmium per kg phosphorus. It was also agreed that this reduction should take place by 2007, in line with the implementation of the IPPC directive for existing plants (EFMA, 1998a). The European Commission recently decided not to formalize a negotiated agreement or a regulation for the time being, but to assess the risk to humans from cadmium in fertilizers more carefully before taking any regulatory action.[4]

Table 10.3   Limit values on cadmium content in fertilizers in Europe

Country	Limit values (mg Cd/kg P_2O_5)
Austria	120
Belgium	90
Denmark	48
Finland	22
Germany	75
Netherlands	18
Norway	44
Sweden	22 (NP-NPK), 44 (PK)
Switzerland	22 (NP-NPK), 44 (PK)

Source: OECD (1996).

NPK and Other Fertilizers

Fertilizers containing more than one of the primary nutrients, namely, nitrogen (N), phosphorus (P) and potassium (K), are known as multi-nutrient fertilizers. There are three types:

- complex fertilizers, which contain at least two of the nutrients, N, P and K, and are obtained by chemical reaction;
- compound fertilizers, which contain at least two of the three basic nutrients and are obtained by chemical reaction, by blending or by both. The granules produced may contain the different nutrients in varying ratios;
- blend fertilizers, which are produced by the dry mixing of several materials. No chemical reaction is involved.

The majority of multi-nutrient fertilizers applied in the EU are of the complex type. Complex NPK fertilizers are usually manufactured by producing ammonium phosphates, to which potassium salts are added prior to granulation or prilling. PK fertilizers, on the other hand, are generally produced as compounds by the steam granulation of superphosphates (SSP or TSP) with potassium salts (EFMA, 1997b). Blend fertilizers are obtained by the mechanical mixing of several fertilizers and granular potash to give the desired analysis. Most producers of multi-nutrient fertilizers in Europe are producing nitrate-based fertilizers, namely, NP or NPK. These are being produced with either the mixed-acid or the nitrophosphate production process. The mixed-acid process involves processing of raw materials with mixed acid and the granulation or prilling process (EFMA, 1995c, and 1995h). The nitrophosphate route involves the dissolution of the phosphate rock in nitric acid and uses all the nutrient components in an integrated process without solid wastes and with minimal gaseous and liquid emissions (EFMA, 1995g). Since the process is not dependent on sulphur, no sulphur oxides are emitted. Furthermore, the process produces no phosphogypsum and no gypsum wastewater. Also, as byproducts are upgraded to commercial products, there is no solid waste.

Leaching of nitrates from agriculture

Recently there has been a growing concern that mineral fertilizers used in agriculture have adverse effects on the environment. When nutrients are applied to crops, they might not all be taken up by the plants immediately. In addition, farmers might be applying inappropriate quantities of fertilizers. Depending on the type of nutrients and the existing soil conditions, different kinds of fertilizer input are required in order to maintain a given level of soil fertility. The nutrients applied may leak over time to the environment, where they could cause pollution.

Agriculture is the main source of nitrate in drinking water, either directly to surface waters through surface run-off or through land drains or by infiltration to groundwater. Most of this nitrate originates from agricultural inputs. Nitrate occurs naturally in soils and becomes vulnerable to loss when supply exceeds crop requirement, particularly if the imbalance develops at times when water is draining through or over the soil. The essential legislation about nitrate in water in the EU is the 1980 Drinking Water Directive. This set legal maximum allowable concentrations in drinking water for many chemical and biological determinants, including nitrate. The 50 mg/l nitrate level became binding on all member states in 1985 (Archer and Marks, 1997). By the late 1980s, several member states were pushing further EU legislation to tackle the main sources of nutrient input to waters. Consequently, in December 1991 the Council of the EU adopted a directive, often known as the Nitrates Directive, concerning the protection of waters against pollution caused by nitrates from agricultural sources. This directive recognizes that, while the use of nitrogen-containing fertilizers and manure is necessary for EU agriculture, any over-use of fertilizers and manure constitutes an environmental risk. It emphasizes that common action is needed to control the problem arising from intensive livestock production, and that agricultural policy must take greater account of environmental policy.

Basically, two types of measures could be considered to deal with this problem. The first is improvements in fertilizer products. Improvements in fertilizer products induced by environmental factors correspond, to some extent, to the trends in fertilizer products shown in Table 10.3 (see also,

EFMA, 1995f). Complex and compound fertilizers account for 83 percent of all phosphorus, 67 percent of all potassium, and 25 percent of all nitrogen consumed in the EU. They are normally classified according to the ratio of their nutrient content, in the order N, P_2O_5 or P, and K_2O or K. Given the range of soils and crops in the EU, a wide variety of grades should be available to meet the different agronomic and environmental requirements.

Slow and specifically controlled release fertilizers are aimed at plant nutrient use efficiency and at minimizing nutrient losses. The effectiveness of such fertilizers requires a good match between the release rate and the plant needs. Therefore, fertilizers that are designed to provide better control over the release in soils are expected to provide high use efficiency and minimize adverse effects on the environment. The most acceptable types of slow or controlled release fertilizers in practical use are organic nitrogen compounds and fertilizers protected physically by encapsulation with hydrophobic materials, mainly coating. The potential of these fertilizers to serve as controlled release nutrient sources has led to a steady and significant increase of their use (Trenkel, 1997; Shaviv, 1999).

The second type of measure is to improve the practices of fertilizer application to the agricultural field. The leaching of excess nitrates can also be prevented by farmers' appropriate practices of fertilizer application (Persson, 1998). In many countries, new legislation or codes of good farm practices have been developed to improve nutrient efficiency and reduce the load on the environment (IFA and UNEP, 1998). Farmers are encouraged to make fertilizer plans for their crops, taking account of the total input of nutrients from mineral fertilizer sources. A mineral book-keeping system enables farmers to monitor the nutrient flow on their farms. Nutrient efficiency would be improved as a result of optimal dosing, coupled with an informed fertilizer choice, new application techniques and more appropriate timing. EFMA has published the Code of Best Agricultural Practice of Nitrogen for farmers (EFMA, 1997a). The recommendations provided by the code encourage appropriate application rate, correct timing of the application, the use of a suitable type of fertilizer and a correctly calibrated fertilizer spreader. The recommendations are aimed at achieving good crop yields while minimizing the loss of nutrients by leaching or volatilization. Farmers are also encouraged to choose a suitable type of fertilizer: selection should include an assessment of likely environmental impact and agronomic efficiency. Both chemical form and physical characteristics are important. The choice of fertilizer and chemical form of the nutrient components depends on the chemical properties and analysis of the nutritional requirements and physiological sensitivities of the crop (Baldock, 1996).

Appropriate application of fertilizers also depends on factors such as the skill of the operator; the correct calibration and maintenance of the spreader; and adjustment for fertilizer spread pattern. The fertilizer industry, in cooperation with fertilizer spreader manufacturers, performs regular tests to ascertain the most appropriate form and properties for fertilizer granules and prills in order to achieve optimal spreading. The industry also offers farmers the special service of checking, and if necessary recalibrating, fertilizer spreading equipment (EFMA, 1997b).[5]

THE STRUCTURE OF THE FERTILIZER INDUSTRY

Considering the technical characteristics of the production process and the large quantities of raw materials used and byproducts produced, the fertilizer industry has a significant potential to create environmental problems. Various forms of environmental regulation, mainly related to the manufacturing process of fertilizers, have been introduced in Europe. Also, since the early 1980s, there has been considerable concern about the impact on the environment of fertilizers used in agriculture, particularly about the level of nitrates in water supplies and the cadmium content in fertilizers. On the other hand, the European fertilizer industry is facing stagnating demand in the European market and increasing imports of low-cost fertilizers from foreign producers, especially those in Central and Eastern Europe, the former Soviet Union and North Africa. Profitability has been very low for the European producers for many years. This has led to a considerable restructuring of the industry. Production capacity and employment were reduced drastically, and a wave of mergers and acquisitions took place. In what follows, we will discuss the main trends in the international fertilizer industry and the response of European manufacturers.

The Demand for Fertilizers

In 1960, 88 percent of world fertilizer consumption was taking place in developed countries, Eastern Europe and the Soviet Union. From 1980 to 1990 fertilizer consumption in the developed countries stabilized, except in the Soviet Union where it increased until 1988. Then fertilizer consumption fell sharply, by 70 percent in Central and Eastern Europe and in the former Soviet Union. While consumption in developed countries has declined, the developing countries have increased their share, which accounted for only 12 percent of the world total in 1960. In 1992, fertilizer consumption in developing countries has for the first time exceeded that of the developed countries and reached 61 percent of the world total in 1998. The increase was particularly strong in the case of nitrogen fertilizers (IFA, 1999).

Currently the European Union accounts for 13 percent of the total world consumption (ibid.). The plant nutrient applied widely in Europe is nitrogen: 10 million tons of nitrogen were used in 1998. The consumption of phosphorus and potassium in the same year amounted to 3.7 million tons P_2O_5 and 4.3 million tons K_2O (EFMA, 1998b).[6] The trends in fertilizer consumption since 1970 show that the sharp rise in prices in the 1970s had a negative impact on phosphate consumption, which never fully recovered. By 1994, phosphate consumption in the European Union had fallen 35 percent from its 1980 level. On the other hand, nitrogen benefited from the considerable increase in cereal production and from the more intensive fertilization of grassland in countries with favourable climatic conditions for this crop. However, nitrogen consumption has also fallen by 4 percent since 1980 (own calculations based on Table 10.4). By 2008, fertilizer nutrient consumption is expected to decline further in the EU 15 countries: a decline of 8 percent for nitrogen, 9 percent for phosphorus and 7 percent for potassium is expected (EFMA, 1994 and 1998c).

France is the largest single mineral fertilizer market, accounting for 24 percent of nitrogen fertilizer consumption in Western Europe. Germany accounts for about 18 percent, the UK for 15 percent, Spain for 10 percent and Italy for 9 percent. There are also differences in the intensity of mineral fertilizer application rates per hectare throughout the EU. Relatively high application rates are found in the Netherlands, Belgium, Finland and France. Generally speaking, a trend of declining application rates per hectare has continued recently, and large reductions have been observed in Denmark, the Netherlands and Finland (EFMA, 1997b).

The main reasons for the decline in consumption is the reform of the Common Agricultural Policy (CAP). This reform, implemented in 1992, abandons price support mechanisms in favour of compensation paid directly to farmers. It has had a particular impact on the arable land sector. The intervention purchase prices of cereals have dropped by almost 25 percent, and these reductions have been compensated by direct aid per hectare. At the same time, aid payment is contingent on freezing the surface area devoted to cereals, oil and protein-yielding crops. Consequently, as the production of crops was reduced, demand for fertilizers declined by about the same proportion (European Commission, 1997b).

Production Capacity

There have been significant shifts in the distribution of world fertilizer production over the past two decades. Total production of fertilizers in developing countries increased almost threefold between 1979 and 1998, while production declined in the developed countries, and fell by a half in the former centrally planned economies after 1989 (see Table 10.5). As a result

Table 10.4   Consumption of fertilizers in the European Union, 1970-94

	1994	1993	1992	1991	1990	1985	1980	1975	1970
Nitrogen fertilizers ('000 t N)									
EU15	9600	9207	9058	9877	10218	10869	9994	8227	6826
Belgium	168	169	152	161	166	178	180	169	167
Denmark	316	326	333	370	395	382	374	339	289
Germany	1787	1612	1680	1720	1788	2286	2303	1906	1642
Greece	334	338	393	408	427	450	333	275	201
Spain	919	929	818	999	1063	962	902	722	578
France	2308	2222	2154	2569	2492	2408	2147	1708	1453
Ireland	429	401	353	358	370	314	275	153	87
Italy	879	918	910	907	879	1055	1006	724	595
Netherlands	380	370	390	392	390	500	483	453	405
Austria	122	124	124	132	135	165	160	121	126
Portugal	137	130	127	135	150	137	137	141	77
Finland	198	173	174	166	207	202	197	199	169
Sweden	210	226	211	175	212	246	244	258	226
United Kingdom	1412	1268	1219	1365	1525	1568	1240	1045	801
Phosphate fertilizers ('000 t K$_2$O)									
EU15	3717	3605	3688	4102	4412	5106	5680	5275	5812
Belgium	51	51	50	59	72	85	97	113	143
Denmark	51	54	64	76	89	106	111	129	127
Germany	451	415	490	519	609	1055	1226	1221	1323
Greece	144	133	178	176	187	180	158	160	118
Spain	504	496	423	502	534	462	476	422	432
France	1030	1014	1029	1253	1349	1466	1773	1664	1809
Ireland	143	136	137	136	139	133	145	135	183
Italy	585	589	613	662	645	692	748	490	518
Netherlands	64	68	68	75	74	81	83	81	109
Austria	59	61	65	72	74	90	99	76	123
Portugal	69	71	77	75	80	70	81	74	35
Finland	90	82	82	76	117	155	150	171	180
Sweden	55	53	46	44	58	86	123	141	146
United Kingdom	421	381	360	371	380	439	404	391	558

Source: EUROSTAT, CRONOS: Environment Database.

the share of world fertilizer production located in the developing countries was greater than that of the developed countries at the end of the millennium.

Table 10.5   World fertilizer production, 1979-98

	Developed countries		Developing countries		Transition economies		World
	Volume ('000 Mt)	% share	Volume ('000 Mt)	% share	Volume ('000 Mt)	% share	Volume ('000 Mt)
Total fertilizer							
1979	64 769	54.5	23 964	20.2	30 007	25.3	118 740
1984	64 338	46.1	36 132	25.9	39 210	28.1	139 680
1989	61 685	40.3	48 601	31.8	42 636	27.9	152 923
1994	60 831	44.8	55 110	40.6	19 815	14.6	135 755
1998	59 408	40.3	66 503	45.2	21 341	14.5	147 253
Nitrogenous fertilizers							
1979	27 254	45.7	17 724	29.7	14 646	24.6	59 625
1984	28 260	37.9	26 767	35.9	19 481	26.1	74 508
1989	28 663	33.8	35 457	41.8	20 742	24.4	84 862
1994	39 069	48.5	39 816	49.4	1 668	2.1	80 553
1998	29 024	32.8	48 243	54.5	11 183	12.6	88 451
Phosphate fertilizers							
1979	18 337	55.1	6 200	18.6	8 726	26.2	33 263
1984	17 519	48.0	9 019	24.7	9 953	27.3	36 491
1989	15 902	40.0	12 169	30.6	11 661	29.3	39 733
1994	15 167	47.2	13 966	43.4	3 031	9.4	32 164
1998	13 641	41.3	16 192	49.0	3 208	9.7	33 040

Source: FAO STAT.

Production of nitrogenous fertilizer in the developed countries increased slightly over this period, but their share of world production declined from almost a half at the end of the 1970s to a third in the 1990s. The developing countries increased their share of world production at the expense of the developed countries in the 1980s and of the transition economies in the 1990s, so that by the end of that decade they accounted for over half of world production.

Production of phosphate fertilizers in the developed world has actually fallen during this period, particularly in the European Union. Again the North's share of world production has declined significantly, while that of the developing countries has increased to overtake production in the North in the late 1990s.

From its earlier large share of 40 percent in world mineral fertilizer production in the mid-1950s, the EU has experienced a drop in its share of the world total output. Table 10.6 presents the allocation of world fertilizer production among the main producers. Germany and the Netherlands are two of the main producers of nitrogen fertilizers. During the heavy restructuring of the industry in the early 1990s, the European fertilizer industry reduced nitrogen fertilizer capacities by 25 percent. Western Europe's share of the world nitrogen fertilizer production fell from 20 percent in 1981 to 11 percent in 1997 (IFA, 1999). For ammonia production its share declined from 14.9 percent in 1980 to 8.8 percent in 1998 and for urea production from 12.3 percent to 4.9 percent (EFMA, 1998a).

Almost all the world's nitrogen supply is produced from ammonia. About three-quarters of world ammonia production is based on natural gas, and this proportion has increased steadily from less than 60 percent in 1970. In 1996, the most important producers of natural gas were the former Soviet Union, accounting for 25 percent of total world production, and the US, which contributed 24 percent. Western European countries produced 11 percent of the world total. The UK produced 32 percent of the Western European total, the Netherlands 29 percent and Norway 19 percent. The cost of feedstock accounts for two-thirds to three-quarters of the total cost of producing ammonia. In the case of urea production, natural gas accounts for more than 80 percent of all input costs (IFA, 1999).

About two-thirds of phosphate fertilizers are derived from phosphoric acid, which is obtained by processing phosphate rock with an acid, mainly sulphuric acid. Overall, mineral fertilizers account for approximately 80 percent of phosphate use. While over 30 countries are currently producing phosphate rock, the top 12 producing countries account for nearly 95 percent of world phosphate rock production. The main producers in 1996 were the US (31.7 percent), China (20.5 percent) and Morocco (14.7 percent) (Table 10.6). Within Western Europe, there are only small reserves in Finland.

Over the past two decades, there has been a distinct trend towards the processing of phosphate rock in countries with substantial natural resources of this material. In 1997, the US accounted for 43 percent of the world phosphoric acid production, Northern Africa (Morocco and Tunisia) for 15 percent, the former Soviet Union for 8 percent, and Latin America and the Middle East for 6 percent each (IFA, 1999). Phosphoric acid production capacity in Western Europe has fallen by 60 percent since 1980, with a drop in its share in world capacity from 14 percent in 1980 to 4.7 percent in 1998 (EFMA, 1998a). From the mid-1980s to the mid-1990s there was little investment in new phosphoric acid plants and several plant closures in Western Europe.

Potash is produced in the few countries where the ores are located. In 1996

*Table 10.6   World fertilizer production: ammonia (N), phosphate rock (P)
and potash (K) ('000 metric tons), 1992-6*

	1992	%	1994	%	1996	%
Ammonia						
China	18 000	19.3	20 075	21.2	24 483	23.4
United States	13 400	14.3	13 397	14.2	14 564	13.9
India	7 452	8.0	7 503	8.0	8 549	8.2
Russia	8 786	9.4	7 264	7.7	7 932	7.6
Canada	3 100	3.3	3 474	3.7	3 840	3.7
Indonesia	2 690	2.9	3 012	3.2	3 647	3.5
Ukraine	3 908	4.2	3 004	3.2	3 302	3.2
Germany	2 110	2.2	2 170	2.3	2 512	2.4
Netherlands	2 590	2.8	2 479	2.6	2 353	2.2
Mexico	2 200	2.4	2 028	2.1	2 054	2.0
Trinidad	1 570	1.7	1 649	1.8	1 801	1.7
Poland	1 490	1.6	1 607	1.7	1 796	1.7
All other	26 104	27.9	26 678	28.3	27 734	26.5
Total	93 400	100.0	94 340	100.0	104 567	100.0
Phosphate rock						
United States	47 000	33.8	41 650	32.6	44 665	31.7
China	21 400	15.4	24 761	19.4	29 000	20.5
Morocco	19 145	13.8	19 765	15.5	20 830	14.7
Russia	11 500	8.3	8 021	6.2	8 680	6.1
Tunisia	6 400	4.6	5 699	4.4	7 100	5.0
Jordan	4 300	3.1	4 216	3.3	5 355	3.8
Israel	3 600	2.5	3 961	3.1	3 840	2.7
Brazil	2 850	2.1	3 938	3.1	3 823	2.7
Togo	2 083	1.5	2 149	1.7	2 731	1.9
South Africa	3 080	2.2	2 545	2.0	2 655	2.0
All others	17 642	12.7	11 183	8.7	12 631	8.9
Total	139 000	100.0	127 843	100.0	141 310	100.0
Potash						
Canada	7 270	30.4	8 040	34.8	8 170	34.2
Germany	3 460	14.5	3 290	14.2	3 200	13.4
Belarus	3 310	13.8	3 021	13.1	3 200	13.4
Russia	3 470	14.5	2 498	10.8	2 800	11.7
United States	1 710	7.3	1 400	6.1	1 390	5.8

Table 10.6   *(continued)*

	1992	%	1994	%	1996	%
Israel	1 300	5.4	1 260	5.5	1 320	5.5
Jordan	794	3.3	930	4.0	1 200	5.0
All others	2 586	10.8	2 661	11.5	2 620	11.0
Total	23 900	100.0	23 100	100.0	23 900	100.0

Source: US International Trade Commission, Office of Industries, *Fertilizers Industry & Trade Summary*, March 1998, table 7.

the former Soviet Union (Russia and Belarus) accounted for 25 percent of world potash production, North America, mostly Canada, for 40 percent, Western Europe for 21 percent and Israel and Jordan together for 9 percent. These regions thus accounted for a total of 92 percent of total world production (IFA, 1999). In Europe, the merger of two German potash companies resulted in a large reduction in production capacity. Potash mines in France will be closed by the year 2004, when the deposits will be exhausted (EFMA, 1997b).

Trade Patterns

Although not as marked as the trends in the global production of fertilizers, trade patterns have also changed in the past two decades with the share of the developed countries falling from almost three-quarters in 1979 to about 60 percent in the late 1990s. Developing countries have increased their share of world exports, but in contrast to what has happened in production, the transition economies also gained an increased share of world fertilizer exports during the 1990s (see Table 10.7). The developing country share of exports has been particularly marked in the case of phosphate fertilizers, where it increased from around a fifth in 1979 to between a half and two-thirds in the 1990s (FAO STAT).

About 90 percent of world ammonia production is processed or used locally, and the remaining 10 percent is exported. The major exporters in 1997 were Russia and Ukraine (using Russian gas for production), accounting for 49 percent of world exports, Trinidad for 19 percent and the Middle East for 18 percent. The major net importers were the US (46 percent) and Western Europe (31 percent).

Total nitrogen fertilizer exports from Central and Eastern Europe and the former Soviet Union increased from 18 percent of the world total in 1980 to

Table 10.7   Exports of manufactured fertilizer, 1979-99

	Developed countries		Developing countries		Transition economies		World	
	$ mn	%	$ mn	%	$ mn	%	$ mn	%
1979	6 018	74.1	947	11.7	1 156	14.2	8 122	100.0
1984	7 037	67.1	1 553	14.8	1 891	18.0	10 481	100.0
1989	8 779	65.3	2 449	18.2	2 216	16.5	13 444	100.0
1994	8 209	62.4	2 477	18.8	2 464	18.7	13 150	100.0
1998	8 269	58.8	2 705	19.2	3 092	22.0	14 067	100.0
1999	8 369	60.3	2 556	18.4	2 954	21.3	13 878	100.0

Source: FAO Statistical Database.

about 33 percent in 1996 (IFA, 1999). The significant decline in fertilizer consumption in the CEE countries and the FSU in recent years has led to a sharp increase in the quantity of low-priced nitrogen fertilizers imported into the EU. The share of imports in European nitrogen consumption reached 23.5 percent in 1998, and the CEE and the FSU countries accounted for 71.4 percent of total nitrogen imports (EFMA, 1998d). Other important sources of imports to the EU are Libya and Morocco.

Previously the main form of phosphate was phosphate rock, which was mainly processed in developed countries. Over the last 20 years, as vertically integrated industries have developed at the site of rock mines, the role of phosphate rock as an intermediate input for the phosphate industry in the international market declined sharply from 53 million tonnes in 1979 to 31 million tonnes in 1996. Currently only 25 percent of phosphate rock is exported from the countries of origin, and two countries, Morocco and the US, account for nearly half of the exports (IFA, 1999). Because of that trend, the international trade of processed phosphate, including ammonium phosphate, triple superphosphate and phosphoric acid, has increased substantially in recent decades, at the expense of phosphate rock. From the mid-1970s to the early 1980s, most of the increase in processed phosphate trade was in the form of phosphoric acid. A more recent trend has been the increase in the trade of ammonium phosphate, which currently accounts for approximately 60 percent of the world phosphate trade, compared with 46 percent in the mid-1980s; while Morocco accounted for 41 percent of the world exports of phosphoric acid, Tunisia for 15 percent and the US for 11 percent, the US accounted for 60 percent of the world exports in ammonium phosphate, the FSU for 17 percent, and Morocco and Tunisia for 11 percent in 1996 (IFA, 1999). The major suppliers of phosphate fertilizers to Western Europe were Russia, Morocco, and Tunisia. (EFMA, 1997b).

World trade in potash, mostly in potassium chloride also called muriate of potash, increased slightly during the past decade. From 1994 to 1996, North America, mostly Canada, accounted for 47 percent of world exports, the FSU for 22 percent, Western Europe, mainly Germany, for 19 percent, and Israel and Jordan for 12 percent (IFA, 1999). It is expected that the European potash industry will continue to maintain the capacity fully to meet potash demands in Europe (EFMA, 1997b).

Fertilizer exports from the Western European countries mainly consist of NPK, byproduct sulphate of ammonia, and some nitrates and urea. The main markets are China, Thailand and the Americas. In 1968, net exports amounted to over 2 million tonnes, whereas in 1996 net imports increased to more than 1.4 million tonnes of nitrogen. The trade balance indicates that Western Europe changed from being a net exporter of nitrogen fertilizer from the 1960s to the early 1980s, to being a net importer in the 1990s. In other words, the trade balance deteriorated by 3.4 million tonnes of nitrogen (EFMA, 1997b). The market for phosphate fertilizers is another area of increasing trade deficit for the European Union in recent years.

Table 10.8 presents the import specialisation pattern in EU member states and other industrialized countries. The table reflects the diversity of the performance of the fertilizer industry in industrialized countries. It is interesting to note from a careful examination of these data that two different groups of EU countries are emerging. The first group includes Germany, the Netherlands, Austria, Portugal, Sweden and the UK, with low dependence on imported fertilizers in comparison to the average market specialization in the OECD. Recent trends have indicated that this point is still valid. The second group includes Denmark, Greece, Spain, France, Ireland and Norway, with heavy dependence on imported fertilizers. These trends have been stabilized in recent years after the restructuring of the European fertilizer industry. Our firm-level fieldwork examined case studies in the first group of countries in an attempt to highlight the elements of successful corporate strategies that led to the survival of fertilizer production in these countries.

CORPORATE STRATEGIES IN THE EUROPEAN FERTILIZER INDUSTRY

The European fertilizer industry employed about 110,000 people in 1983, but by 1992 the number of employees had reduced to only 40,000. In the 10-year period leading up to 1990, the number of ammonia plants decreased from 74 to 41, and production capacity declined by 12 percent. The number of phosphoric acid plants was halved during the 1980s, and capacity was reduced

Table 10.8   *Fertilizers and nitrogen compounds: country import*
                specialization relative to same share for the OECD

	1995	1994	1993	1992	1991	1990	1989	1988
Belgium	117.88	123.55	154.81	112	105.89	121.58	128.9	128.15
Denmark	168.01	193.23	204.07	220.74	206.35	258.48	216.65	221.05
Germany	85.29	73.85	76.65	85.15	76.34	80.72	77.24	85.85
Greece	210.31	213.87	175.53	160.85	188.84	89.31	133.36	115.16
Spain	154.25	164.25	127.16	161.63	175.01	162.85	160.61	177.71
France	145.76	138.62	126.13	152.99	145.31	170.48	175.43	166.07
Ireland	322.51	283	313.8	359.05	367.09	390.59	371.71	372.84
Italy	112.76	116.83	97.73	93.4	96.05	79.39	83.88	89.69
Netherlands	84.52	73.33	68.33	71.04	63.01	67.06	63.52	71.76
Austria	33.52	38.3	37.26	38.79	41.55	41.5	118.86	127.44
Portugal	73.11	99.29	70.84	69.67	70.13	69.61	71.4	75.74
Finland	81.11	157.05	153.6	125.21	130.91	121.58	109.85	125.04
Sweden	111.12	73.49	112.77	89.29	107.74	109.88	93.33	114.82
United Kingdom	70.71	70.83	64.15	73.39	73.27	66.34	65.83	53.39
Norway	159.39	162.57	170.67	148.03	156.2	128.96	116.88	96.9
Canada	42.96	44.18	54.73	53	51.97	48.79	41.17	50.16
United States	94.72	100.81	95.24	90.76	92.72	92.04	89.32	NA
Japan	55.12	67.71	74.41	77.15	78.79	71.54	73.98	83.53
Australia	213.62	196.47	186.47	165.94	174.07	151.46	116.23	108.48
New Zealand	319.85	283.12	300.68	247.01	172.41	142.39	171.21	115.24

Source: Eurostat, CRONOS: Competitiveness Database, 2000.

by 35 percent. The level of concentration of ownership increased and it was estimated in 1992 that eight major companies owned 80 percent of European fertilizer production capacity (IFA, UNEP and UNIDO, 1998). Low growth or even negative growth in consumption is expected, and competition with imports of fertilizers based on cheap raw materials has been intensified, particularly for upstream products such as ammonia, nitric acid and phosphoric acid. In this difficult market environment, the European fertilizer industry went through major structural changes with mergers and acquisitions of companies.

In an attempt to obtain detailed information on corporate strategies and adjustment patterns in this restructuring process, we conducted interviews with six major firms, namely, Norsk Hydro, Kemira, Agrolinz, Badische Anilin & Soda Fabrik (BASF), DSM, and Imperial Chemical Industries (ICI).[7] In what follows, we present detailed profiles of restructuring at the firm level and then we identify three types of corporate strategies in the restructuring process of the European fertilizer industry.

Norsk Hydro

Norsk Hydro has four main business areas, namely, oil and energy, agriculture, light metals and petrochemicals. Energy supply, in the form of hydroelectric power and petroleum, is at the root of the business activities of Norsk Hydro. Hydro is Europe's largest integrated energy company, playing a major role in the production and marketing of energy based on oil, gas and electricity in Europe. With its 25-year experience from the North Sea, the company is now stepping up its international oil activities, particularly in Angola and Canada, while it remains the largest energy processor in Europe. Hydro is also involved in both primary production and the semi-fabrication of aluminium and magnesium. The company is a major aluminium supplier in Europe, and its shipments to the United States are growing. Vertical integration is maintained, from raw materials to the manufacture of aluminium extruded sections and sheet, connected to the building and automobile industries. Light metal production in Norway is based on electrical power, mainly from the company's own hydroelectric power stations. The company considers it essential to utilize its broad expertise in energy production and processing. With access to cheap oil and gas supply, the company focuses on energy-related activities as core business, namely, fertilizer (based on natural gas), light metals, including aluminium and magnesium (which consume large amounts of electricity), and petrochemicals (based on oil) (Norsk Hydro, 1999).

Following the strategic choice to pursue competitiveness based on oil and natural gas, Hydro made a decision in the 1980s to expand the fertilizer business, resulting in the acquisition of plants in the UK, France and the Netherlands. Currently the company is the largest fertilizer producer in the world. In 1995, Hydro Agri was divided into Hydro Agri Europe and Hydro Agri International, which deals with business in other parts of the world. Hydro Agri Europe is one of the major fertilizer producers in Europe. Its annual production capacity is 12 million tonnes measured in finished products, and its market share is 25 percent, the largest in Europe, followed by Kemira and Grand Paroise. Nitrogen fertilizer represents more than half of the company's sales in Western Europe. In 1996, Hydro acquired two Italian fertilizer companies: Arnyca and Nouvo Terni Industrie Chimiche. Norsk Hydro also acquired most of the fertilizer plants of Enichem in Italy in 1997. Currently the company has production sites in seven European countries, including Norway, Sweden, the UK, the Netherlands, Germany, France and Italy. New marketing and distribution systems are being further developed in

Central Europe. The company supplies these markets with fertilizer from its production plants in Western Europe and through purchases from other producers.

Hydro is pursuing a global-oriented strategy. Hydro Agri International trades and supplies ammonia and is responsible for Hydro's fertilizer operations outside Europe. In 1998, this division sold 7.8 million tonnes of fertilizer. The company's share in a number of markets in Africa, North America and South America has increased markedly. Hydro's long-term focus is on growing markets outside Europe, and its strategy is aiming at the global fertilizer business with strong local presence, often together with local partners. The firm has a strong global network with local market positions, a large number of production sites and an extensive terminal and transport system, supporting its products from the raw material stage to the farmer's field. Hydro intends to develop further the local markets with brand-named goods, agronomic expertise and product development, as well as with speciality products from Hydro's fertilizer plants in Europe. Hydro's fertilizers are currently sold in more than 100 countries in the world.

The Middle East is regarded as very important for Hydro's product sourcing strategy (Soerbotten, 1998). Qatar is a rich source of natural gas, and Hydro has a 25 percent ownership of a plant that produces ammonia and urea. A marketing agreement was made for approximately 800,000 tons of urea in 1998. More than half of the urea and most of the ammonia are exported to Asia. In Jordan, a joint venture, Hydro Agri Jordan (HAJ), was established between Norsk Hydro ASA and Jordan Phosphate Mines Company (JPMC) to study the viability of phosphoric acid and Di-Ammonium phosphate (DAP) production in Jordan with local raw materials. Hydro regards Jordan as an ideal location for producing NPK because it has extensive reserves of good quality phosphate rock and potash, and it is close to target markets in Asia and Africa. Hydro has also established a joint venture in Morocco, Hydro Agri Trade Moroc. In addition, Hydro has affiliated interests in a large ammonia plant of Tringen in Trinidad and Tobago, and Farmland Hydro, a phosphate fertilizer company in Florida and three plants in Canada with favourable sources of raw materials. In 1995 new marketing units opened in Cairo, New Delhi, Johannesburg and Buenos Aires. Norsk Hydro also has a bulk blending plant in Thailand as an NPK supplier to Thailand. Usually plants on the coast are acquired because of the direct access to transportation of natural gas and fertilizers. Hydro has a strong market position in ammonia trading and shipping through an integrated system of factories, terminals and tankers.

Ammonia production is undergoing an extensive upgrading, with particular emphasis on energy efficiency. In the spring of 1999, the ammonia plant in Porsgrunn, Norway, entered the final phase of an extensive expansion and modernization project. A plant in Le Havre in France was also upgraded in

1999. On the other hand, the company has decided to discontinue production at its phosphoric acid plant in Vlaardingen, the Netherlands. The company also has a division of Industrial Chemicals, which supplies technical nitrates, nitrogen-based chemicals and industrial gases. Most of them benefit from economies of scope by utilizing the production and marketing facilities of fertilizers.

In 2000, Hydro's European fertilizer production plants are expected to achieve compliance with the European Fertilizers Manufacturers Association's Best Available Technique requirements for 90 percent of their processes. The remaining 10 percent will be completed by 2005 (the original goal was full compliance in 2000). Investments were made at the ammonia plants in Trinidad and Sluiskil in the Netherlands, with the intention of achieving better energy efficiency, lower emissions and higher production. The three ammonia plants in Sluiskil are the first plants in Europe without nitrogen discharges to water. Hydro is examining ways to reduce N_2O emissions from existing nitric acid production plants. The company thinks that more time will be required before appropriate technology is developed.

In 1988 the Dutch government and Hydro Agri Rotterdam (HAR) agreed a covenant concerning phosphoric acid production. In this covenant, HAR committed itself to a phased decrease in emissions of phosphate, cadmium and other heavy metals. For cadmium, a fixed end level of maximum 0.6 tonnes/year and 0.5 mg/kg gypsum was agreed, though the technology to achieve this was not yet available. It was recognized that the decrease in emissions with gypsum should not lead to an increased environmental burden from products based on the intermediate phosphoric acid. In 1994, a maximum level for fertilizers of 55 mg Cd/kg P_2O_5 was fixed, and a value of 15 mg Cd/kg P_2O_5 for fertilizers was included in the covenant as a goal for the year 2000.

After three years, however, Hydro announced plans to close its 160,000 t/y P_2O_5 phosphoric acid plant in the Netherlands (*Fertilizer Week*, 1999). Hydro took over the 53-year-old plant in 1986, before making upgrades in 1991 and 1992. In a statement announcing the closure, Hydro affirmed its commitment to Vlaardingen as a production base to target what it sees as a growing market for liquid and soluble fertilizers. At the same time, 12-year price lows continue to affect international markets for straight nitrogen fertilizers. Aside from environmental difficulties, Hydro cited costs and fertilizer market developments as reasons for the closure. The total plant closure cost is estimated at NOK170 million ($22.9 million). Total manpower at Hydro's Vlaardingen site was reduced from 167 to 82 employees as a consequence.

Hydro chose to close the plant in the light of revised Dutch regulations on phosphogypsum disposal. The present disposal permit from the Dutch authorities expired at the end of 1999, when stricter requirements were introduced. Hydro said it had pursued ways of continuing phosphoric acid production to meet the new disposal requirements. However, it concluded that the necessary capital expenditure would make the operation unprofitable. Since Hydro intends to strengthen its downstream speciality fertilizer production at the complex, the closure means it will have to import significant quantities of phosphoric acid. In order to substitute the phosphoric acid raw material source, the company is said to have made preliminary approaches to two major producers in North Africa: Morocco's Office Chérifien des Phosphates and Tunisia's Groupe Chimique Tunisien (Alperowicz, 1999).

Hydro Agri's product development strategy has identified three key environmental issues related to agriculture: (a) leaching of nutrients to water; (b) greenhouse gas emissions from fertilizer field applications; and (c) N_2O emissions from nitric acid plants.[8] As the requirement for continual improvements in fertilization methods has been increasing with regard to better quality, advice and environmental properties, Hydro began to work on the development of knowledge, services and tools to assist farmers in efficient fertilizer application as well as on conducting research programmes to reduce N_2O emissions. In 1987 Hydro Agri started to develop instant in-field methods to determine N fertilizer rate (Wollring *et al.*, 1998). And in 1998 the company launched the Hydro Precise fertilizer system. This system, combined with the appropriate products, minimizes nutrient losses during and after application.

Hydro is therefore focusing on research and development of speciality products in the form of tailor-made fertilizers. On the other hand, the focus on product differentiation is also intended to reduce the vulnerability of fertilizer products to fluctuations in the raw materials market. It also regards precision farming as beneficial for farmers because of the cost savings achieved, and at the same time it hopes that this will consequently lead to an increase in the attractiveness of Hydro's product combined with good service. While old farmers tend to maintain long-term relationships with suppliers, young farmers are more sensitive to price, service and technology and are more likely to switch between one supplier and another. Therefore, Hydro believes that it is crucial for the company to offer good service and technology to farmers to maintain the close linkage with them and increase their loyalty to its products.

Kemira Agro

Kemira Agro is a Finnish company, one of the world's major producers of mineral-based fertilizers. Kemira's share of the fertilizer market has increased, following the recent acquisition of BASF's phosphate business. Its main products are complex and nitrogen fertilizers used in agriculture and horticulture and special products for forestry. Kemira has production plants in six countries in Europe, including Finland, Denmark, Belgium, the Netherlands, France and the United Kingdom. Its main markets are in the European Union. Ammonia production of Kemira (6 million t/y) is the second largest in Europe, following Norsk Hydro (10 million t/y). The company's plants at Ince, UK, which Kemira acquired from DSM in 1988, produce 1 million t/y and are its biggest production site.

At the production site in Ince, ammonia is produced by conventional steam reforming, 1,000 t/d, and nitric acid is produced, 1,000 t/d, inhibiting flexibility. AN prilling and three NPK plants (600,000 t/y) producing 20 different kinds also exist at the site. Imports of ammonia are 10 percent of the necessary raw materials. Business target is mainly the UK market, and 10 percent of the products go to Ireland. While naphtha was used as raw material until 1970, it has been replaced with natural gas due to price, efficiency and sulphuric emission problems. Another change concerns storage. Previously the company had 30 dispersed places, but the central storage site was created, with implications for shifts in shipping from bag to bulk. In 1984, the AN plant was equipped with 100 percent filtration, making the effluent the cleanest possible, that is 10 mg/m^3. Ammonia losses were reduced significantly by modifying condensing systems at the ammonium nitrate solutions plants. The company estimates that the capital costs are 20 percent higher for old plants due to considerations of environmental protection.

About two-thirds of Kemira Agro's sales consist of NPK fertilizers. The company's main products are granular complex NPKs, low-chlorine NPKs, potassium sulphate and granulated/prilled straight nitrogen fertilizers. The company also produces a growing number of speciality products, often with added secondary or micronutrients to meet the demands of special crops or soil deficiencies. The horticultural fertilizer business further expanded its operations energetically in the Baltic countries and Eastern Europe. Sales of the product range for professional growers also rose significantly in Germany and Southern Europe. As a further shift is being made towards production tailored to customer needs in the European market, the company is emphasizing differentiated products to meet defined customer needs and currently sells 20 different grades of fertilizers. New units were set up in Germany, the Netherlands and Switzerland to obtain information on customer needs (Kliski, 1998).

For precision farming, Kemira Agro developed a computer program, Kemira Loris. This program imports site-specific data, displays it visually using maps, and processes them as site-specific plans. Overlaying maps and processing respective data according to customizable calculation models perform this. While a researcher outside the company initially designed the concept of the program during the early 1990s, Kemira assumed responsibility for the software development. This program is now commercially available in

Germany, Denmark and the United Kingdom. The company pays particular attention to the quality of the support service provided to the software users (Grandzinski, *et al.*, 1998).

Kemira Agro also published a customer-orientated report on farming, quality and the environment in Finland. The report is part of the extensive customer environmental advice programme, which deals with several aspects of sustainable farming. Close links have been established with the Danish fertilizer trade and agricultural advisory service, enabling the company to give specific advice to farmers on the management of both soil and crops, within Denmark's increasingly stringent environmental programmes. Kemira Agro in Benelux has developed the 'Kemistar' system to produce NPKs and other fertilizers, in response to very stringent quality standards. These are finally processed further into tailor-made fertilizer grades to suit farmers' individual requirements for specific crop nutrients. Changing demands have led to the recent introduction of 'Double Top', a sulphur-rich top dressing for oilseed rape and cereals, and Kemira 'N-Min', a user-friendly system of measuring available mineral nitrogen in the soil, which enables farmers to tailor nutrient applications to individual crops.

Fertigation is the main segment for Kemira Horticulture. Fertigation is defined as the application of fertilizers through irrigation water and is considered an integral part of plant nutrient management under pressurized irrigation (Hagin and Lowengart-Aycicegi, 1999). The customers are supplied with a wide range of water soluble solid fertilizers as well as nutrients in liquid form. Kemira Agro actively develops fertigation concepts and uses in emerging markets (for example, South East Asia) through agronomic trials in cooperation with experts. Several alliances have been formed with companies delivering related inputs to growers. Kemira has developed a complete range of granular NPK fertilizers with all necessary trace elements for open field horticultural crops.

Traditionally, the company has provided nutrients for Finnish forestry. Their long-term experience and knowledge has been utilized for practices in nurseries and especially in short rotation plantations worldwide. In forest fertilizer products, all main nutrients can be delivered in slow release form. Organomineral fertilizers are a novel development which complements Kemira's product ranges in the amateur gardening and professional horticultural segments of the market. The organomineral fertilizers are based on recycled materials. Environmental issues drive many of the developments by Kemira Horticulture. The latest innovations include slow release nitrogen fertilizers based on its own methylene urea production, biological fungicides, and 'Reciclean', a unique concept for disinfecting and cleaning in horticulture.

In the autumn of 1996, a new business unit, Kemira Agro Global, was formed to establish production sites outside Europe. In line with its global strategy, Kemira made significant investment commitments in developing its business operations in the Far East as well as in the Baltic countries and Poland. Several marketing companies have been established in these strategic areas. In Asia the company has developed sales and customer service offices in Thailand, Malaysia, Indonesia and China. Kemira Agro has also established new local sales and marketing offices in Russia, Estonia, Latvia, Lithuania and Poland. Markets through local agencies have been established on the African continent and in Central America as well. In these market areas, products are identified under Kemira Agro's own brand.

Recently, several joint ventures for fertilizer production have been established in Lithuania, China and Malaysia. They are aimed at achieving flexible response to local needs and access to raw materials (Törmälä, 1998). Kemira-Lifosa, the joint venture established in Lithuania, began the production of PK fertilizers in 1998. Joint ventures were also established in China and Malaysia in accordance with the company's strategy. Kemira Agro will have a minority holding in the Chinese company as well as in Malaysia. The plants were expected to go into operation in mid-1999 in Malaysia and during 2000 in China. New projects in both countries focused on special product sales (such as fruit and vegetable cultivation as well as rubber and oil palm plantations).

As regards the byproduct of phosphogypsum, opportunities to use it in the rehabilitation of eutrophicated lakes were investigated and discussed publicly in Finland, following pilot tests by other parties. Most of the company's CO_2 emissions originate in the production of ammonia from natural gas in Western Europe. The recovery of CO_2 from this production has increased significantly. In Finland, Kemira's emissions of greenhouse gases have decreased by about 15 percent since 1990. The role of nitrous oxide from nitric acid production is significant, even if the actual amounts emitted are relatively low.

Agrolinz Melamin

Agrolinz Melamin belongs to OMV (Austrian Mineral and Oil Company), which is Austria's largest quoted industrial company. It is one of the largest oil and gas groups in Central and Eastern Europe. OMV maintains international exploration and production activities and operates international polyolefin and chemicals companies. The company has five segments: Exploration and Production; Gas; Refining and Marketing; Plastics; and Chemicals. OMV intends to expand its Exploration and Production, Gas, Marketing and melamine businesses (OMV Aktiengesellschaft, 1998). The Chemicals segment consists of Agrolinz Melamin in Linz, Austria, and Agrolinz Melamin Italia in Castellanza, Italy (Agrolinz Melamin, 1998). Agrolinz Melamin has existed in its present form since 1994. An extensive restructuring process directed towards concentration on the company's key competencies marked the early years of the new entity. Since 70 percent of the equity of Chemie Linz was sold to DSM in 1996, Agrolinz has been concentrating on fertilizers and melamine/urea, mainly for resins, with its strengths based on the complete process integration of gas, fertilizer and melamine. While Agrolinz is the world's second largest melamine producer, it maintains a share of approximately 70 percent of the Austrian plant nutrient market. Its business concentrates on the markets of Austria, southern Germany and northern Italy, mainly due to the low transportation costs based on geographical proximity. The distribution of fertilizers is combined with that of plant protection chemicals, including pesticides and herbicides. BASF is the distribution partner for the southern German market, to which calcium ammonium nitrate (CAN) produced at the fertilizer plants of Agrolinz in Linz is sold.

Agrolinz is expanding its export activities to neighbouring countries, including the Czech Republic, Hungary, Slovenia, Italy and Switzerland. In Eastern Europe, production costs have continued to rise as they are aligned with those in Western Europe. As this constant increase in production costs together with sustained growth of demand in the Eastern European countries caused their exports to level off, Agrolinz has increased its shares in their markets. The acquisition of a majority stake in a Hungarian warehouse indicates a well-established presence in Hungary and the Czech Republic, where sales companies represented Agrolinz previously. The company's entry to the distribution stage of the agrochemical supply chain is intended to make it easier to sell to major distributors and customers, with low freight costs due to the short distances involved.

Currently the company is producing ammonia in two plants, nitric acid in two plants, ammonium nitrate (AN), granulated calcium ammonium nitrate (CAN), and granulated NPK with bagging and loading. Agrolinz Melamin's products are basically based on natural gas, and about 490 mn Nm^3 of gas was used in 1996. More than 90 percent was used as feedstock, and the rest as a source of process energy. In the past, emissions of air pollutants, including NO_X, NH_3, SO_2 and CO, represented the prime environmental problem. In addition, dust emissions occur from CAN, urea, and NPK production processes. As the production site is close to the city centre of Linz, improvements in environmental protection were particularly necessary. A combination of improvements to existing plants and new installations designed to prevent air pollution resulted in a 90 percent reduction in total emissions between 1984 and 1995 (OMV, 1997).

A conventional steam reforming process is used for ammonia production. NO_X reduction is achieved with the non-selective catalytic reduction (NSCR) technology developed by Agrolinz. NO_X is also emitted from two nitric acid plants. Selective catalytic reduction (SCR) is used to reduce the emissions of NO_X. In the most successful case, NO_X emissions were reduced from 900 kg/h to 30 kg/h. For the melamine and urea plants, preparations were initiated in 1994 for the reduction of contaminants in water, particularly for further reductions in nitrogen loading.

Cadmium content in phosphate fertilizers has already been regulated in Austria. Previously phosphate rock from Togo was used for fertilizer production. However, as it contains a high concentration of cadmium, Agrolinz currently uses phosphate rock with low cadmium concentration, mainly imported from Morocco, Tunisia, Jordan, Israel and the Czech Republic.

For precision farming, Agrolinz provides users of its products, including warehouses, dealers and farmers, with a computer program (InfoDesk 95) for the precise calculation of the nutritional requirements of crops. This program also includes a module for the calculation of nutrition and manure yield in animal husbandry. Agrolinz Melamin is committed to the recommendation of low nutrient dosage, which depends on particularly efficient use of fertilizers. Advice is printed on the bag to help farmers to use an appropriate amount of fertilizer. Consequently, the fertilizer use per agricultural area (ha) has been reduced, and also the total amount of fertilizer applications in Austria has declined from 165,000 ton N/year to 120,000 ton N/year.

BASF

BASF consists of five segments: Health and Nutrition; Colorants and Finishing Products; Chemicals; Plastics and Fibres; and Oil and Gas (BASF, 1998). The Health and Nutrition segments encompass pharmaceuticals, fine chemicals, crop protection agents and fertilizers, whereas ammonia is produced in the Basic Chemicals Division.

The company has five production sites in Europe, including Ludwigshafen and Krefeld in Germany, Antwerp and Ostend in Belgium, Ottmarsheim in France, and Seal Sands in the UK. Since its foundation in 1865, Ludwigshafen has been the centre of production for BASF. The production of ammonia by the Haber–Bosch process started here in 1913. The fertilizer products manufactured at this integrated production site include NPK compound; straight nitrogen fertilizers such as ammonium sulphate nitrate (ASN); and speciality fertilizers. The fertilizer division also produces products for plant care in home gardening.

In the 1960s, end-of-pipe technologies were mainly adopted for emission abatement. New facilities for waste treatment of pollution to the river Rhine started to operate in 1974. In the mid-1970s the German Federal Emission Control Law (FECL) granted an emissions permit. Since 1976, the report of emission data has been given to the government authority. In 1989, the first

Environmental Report was published, and currently the report provides information on the production site as a whole. Permit applications must by law be disclosed to the public, and environmental groups can make objections. The company also conducts Environmental Impact Assessment (EIA). As a large chemical company, BASF can utilize its expertise in various disciplines, including ecological, epidemiological, toxicological and medical studies.

Until the early 1980s, the benefits from the reduction in energy and raw material use were relatively high. However, as the concentration of emissions and effluents is getting lower, benefits are no longer high enough to cover the investment. The company thinks the increasing level of purification of waste gases and wastewater entails an exponential increase in the treatment costs.[9] As regards the leaching of nitrates, 'intelligent' fertilizers and counselling are now emphasized. The company expects fertilizer application planning by computer to enable farmers to conduct mineral fertilizer application more accurately at the suggested rate and at the optimal time. Satellite-assisted field application is an economically as well as ecologically important research project. The application of an optimal fertilizer mixture to individual sub-sections of large fields is envisaged for the future. Instructions to farmers on fertilizer application started in 1996. A CD-ROM on efficient use of fertilizers is distributed to farmers; the company thinks this would be beneficial economically as well as environmentally.

BASF has two ammonia plants, 1,200 t/d (since 1971) and 1,360 t/d (since 1982), using natural gas as raw material, and four nitric acid plants, two producing 270 t/d (since 1975) and two 270 t/d (since 1977), with pressures lower than 7.3 bars. Technological changes in ammonia production include the improvement in energy efficiency to 32 GJ/t N, recirculation of process water and connection of various processes. One of the ammonia plants was converted at the end of 1996 to co-produce methanol. In the case of nitric acid production, the company's own technology was introduced for selective catalytic reduction and low-pressure process, and the production capacity was cut down. Regulations in Germany are stack-based (for example, NO_X emission limit of 200 mg/m^3 for ammonia production, and of 220 ppmv, 450 mg/m^3, for nitric acid production). The company is proposing the so-called Bubble Concept, which allows the emission limit to be achieved at one production site as a whole, aggregating different production processes. BASF has experienced the closure of phosphoric acid plants because of economic as well as environmental reasons, namely the disposal of phosphogypsum. In fact, all of the phosphoric acid plants in Germany were closed. The company's plant for calcium ammonium nitrate production was also closed.

BASF's current focus is on NPK compound and speciality fertilizers with higher returns in its portfolio. In developing these specialities, the company is trying to take advantage of its expertise in plastics and process technology. For example, the company has developed fertilizers that control the release of nutrients to meet plant requirements. The composition of these NPK fertilizers needs to vary depending on soil conditions, climate, farmers' demands, and so on. As it is costly to maintain the production of a large number of different compositions, the company is pursuing an optimal balance between the variety of products and efficiency in the production process.

DSM

DSM's activities have been grouped into three areas: Life Science Products; Performance Materials; and Polymers and Industrial Chemicals (DSM, 1999a). These areas were established in May 1998, following DSM's takeover of the Dutch biotechnology firm Gist-Brocades. DSM is trying to focus on core activities in which the company can achieve a leading position in the market. As part of this strategy, the company is working on a shift in its product portfolio, particularly towards Life Science Products and Performance Materials. The activities in the third cluster, Polymers and Industrial Chemicals, are more cyclically sensitive, but on average they show excellent profitability, and the cash flow derived from this cluster is used to realize growth in the other two clusters.

The Polymers and Industrial Chemicals cluster consists of DSM Polyethylenes, DSM Polypropylenes, DSM Hydrocarbons, DSM Fibre Intermediates, DSM Melamine, and DSM Agro. DSM Agro produces high-nitrogen fertilizers (such as calcium ammonium nitrate) for grasslands and agricultural crops and, supplies agricultural wholesalers. DSM Agro is the largest fertilizer supplier in the Netherlands and ranks among the major players in Germany, France and Belgium. In the field of calcium ammonium nitrate, DSM Agro is the second largest supplier in Northern Europe.

In the past DSM had production sites in the US, Ireland, the UK, France, Belgium and the Netherlands and exported all over the world. However, with the trend towards higher gas prices in the Netherlands in mind, the company made a decision in 1988 to withdraw from the world market and to concentrate on Western Europe. The company's production plants in Ince, UK, were sold to Kemira in 1988. In addition, two plants in Rotterdam were sold to Kemira and a plant for TSP in Amsterdam to ICL of Israel. DSM currently maintains a small range of fertilizer products, and only nitrogen fertilizers are produced. The company's NPK production was stopped in 1993. In addition to the economic reason that the production of NPK fertilizers is costly, two environmental factors are also cited for that decision, namely, the disposal of gypsum as a byproduct and the cadmium content in fertilizers. As a result of this management decision the R&D activity on fertilizers has decreased since the late 1980s and is currently very small. While DSM as a whole spends

4 percent of turnover on R&D, only about 0.5 percent of its turnover is allocated to the fertilizer business, mostly for applied research. Computer software is distributed to farmers for appropriate applications of fertilizers. A service for the adjustment of spreaders is also provided to farmers.

DSM operates two ammonia plants, one of 1,360 t/d (1971), the other of 1,360 t/d (1986) at Geleen, the Netherlands, which is the largest production site of the company. There are also two nitric acid plants of 1,300 t/d as well as plants for CAN (1 million t/y), urea and caprolactam, which is a byproduct of ammonium sulphate (600,000 t/y). The ammonia, produced from natural gas, forms the basis for various types of downstream products such as fertilizers, urea, melamine and acrylonitrile. The older ammonia plant was revamped in 1996. The ratio of steam to carbon was reduced, and the technique for CO_2 removal was changed resulting in a reduction in energy consumption by 7.5–7.8 percent. The revamping of ammonia plant No. 2 at Geleen was completed in the spring of 1997. That project has reduced natural gas consumption by more than 25 percent (DSM, 1999b). In 1998 DSM Agro initiated the revamping of its fertilizer plant in Ijmuiden, the Netherlands. Moreover, preparations were made for modifications to be carried out to one of the nitric acid plants in Geleen in 1999–2000. The company expects these modifications to reduce the plant's nitrogen oxide emissions considerably. In 1998 the company opened a new urea plant in Geleen. This plant features 90 percent lower nitrogen discharges to surface water and a lower cooling-water and energy consumption. As regards CO_2 produced from the ammonia plants, half goes to urea production and the other half to beverage production.

DSM produces nitric acid and fertilizers at Ijmuiden. NO_x is the main emission to the air from the nitric acid production; emissions are currently within the limit values. Old plants, constructed in the late 1960s, are equipped with de-NO_x reactors with ammonia and methane. Currently there are discussions on implementing a reduction in NO_x emissions from 200 ppm to 50 ppm with new catalysts. In new plants established in the 1980s, NO_x absorption is achieved at high pressure (10–20 ppm) and also a de-NO_x reactor is adopted, resulting in a reduction in the NO_x concentration from 200 ppm to 50 ppm. At present there are no suitable technologies for achieving further reductions in the emissions of nitrous oxide (N_2O), which is released during the production of nitric acid from existing plants. DSM is collaborating with other companies on the development of catalysts that can be used for converting N_2O into the harmless nitrogen gas.

ICI

Since the incorporation of Imperial Chemical Industries plc in 1926, ICI has been one of the major industrial chemical companies in the world. Having made a strategic decision to focus on speciality chemicals, ICI is currently in the process of significant restructuring. The business activities of ICI now comprise Industrial Specialties; Coatings (paints); Materials (which consists of acrylics); and Industrial Chemicals (which covers petrochemicals, halochemicals, and a number of regional businesses) (ICI, 1999). The polyurethane, titanium dioxide and selected petrochemicals businesses were sold in 1999 to Huntsman of the US. ICI has been actively pursuing the sell-off of most of its Industrial Chemicals business, consistent with its strategic shift to speciality chemicals. Following this strategic decision to withdraw from bulk chemicals, the ICI group was looking for a company that would be interested in acquiring the fertilizer division. Kemira tried previously to acquire ICI fertilizers, but the UK government did not approve this acquisition because the authorities feared that the merger would create a monopoly in the fertilizer industry in the UK. On 31 December 1997 the fertilizer segment was finally sold to Terra Industries.

ICI Fertilizers has over a 25 percent share of the UK nitrogen fertilizer market. The main finished product is ammonium nitrate fertilizer. The majority of sales were in the UK, where the company maintained strong relationships with distributors and blenders. Its fertilizer production was supported by the manufacture of ammonia and nitric acid based on natural gas from the North Sea. Ammonia was also sold to ICI Acrylics for the production of methyl methacrylate, and to external customers as a raw material for acrylonitrile. The carbon dioxide which was produced in ammonia production was sold abroad; the main customer was Norsk Hydro, which acquired ICI's retail carbon dioxide business in 1995. ICI Fertilizers was not active in foreign direct investment. The company only had a shareholding in IFI in Ireland, which was producing ammonia, nitric acid, CAN, urea and NPK fertilizers. It had its headquarters at Teeside in the north-east of England and manufacturing sites both at Teeside and at Severnside in the south-west of England. Ammonia and nitric acid were the main products at Teeside. The ammonia was used for the production of nitric acid, together with ammonia from external sources.

An environmental report was published in 1990 for the first time in ICI. Since then, the contents have become more detailed and more open, providing information on environmental projects in the company. ICI has introduced a Safety, Health, Environment (SHE) Challenge 2000 programme with the corporate environmental priorities to be achieved by the end of 2000. Among the examples are: to halve the environmental burden (ecotoxicity, aquatic oxygen demand, acidity, and potentially hazardous emissions to air), using 1995 as the baseline; and to improve energy efficiency per tonne of production by 10 percent of the 1995 level. The company also publishes an Environmental Report and Chemical Release Inventory for specific production sites such as Teesside. What is specific to ICI's approach to the environmental issues is the introduction of Environmental Burden, a method to evaluate the potential environmental impact of wastes and emissions. NO_x is the primary emission from nitric acid production. A high-pressure process was adopted for the production of nitric acid, and non-selective catalytic reduction (NSCR) was used for NO_x reduction. In the UK, the National Network of Nitrogen Oxides (NO_x) observes emissions at various industrial sites. The value of the NO_x emissions from the ICI plant at Teesside was amongst the lowest in the UK.

Concerning accurate applications of fertilizers, ICI particularly emphasized that high quality of solid fertilizers is important for even spread. The Spread Pattern (SP) scheme aimed at offering a quantitative as well as qualitative measurement of the standard of products has been administered by the Fertiliser Manufacturers Association (FMA), which consists of fertilizer manufacturers in the UK and Ireland. The SP scheme is run independently by the Silsoe Research Institute, which evaluates straight nitrogen fertilizer using a specifically designed instruments (EFMA, 1997). It confirms the uniformity of the prills in the bag in terms of size and density, and indicates the evenness of spread of those prills independently of the type of fertilizer spreader. ICI's fertilizers have the highest spread rating. The Silsoe Institute also recommends the maintenance and calibration of the spreader.

CORPORATE RESPONSES TO ENVIRONMENTAL CHALLENGES

Based on our fieldwork, it is possible to identify three different corporate strategies in the restructuring process of the European fertilizer industry. The exit strategy: firms such as ICI, Hoechst and Enichem have decided to leave the fertilizer industry. These firms are relatively large and produce various kinds of chemical products other than fertilizers. These firms consider that their core competence is not in sectors based on the availability of cheap natural resources, including fossil fuels and mineral ores. Believing that the trend of declining profitability of the fertilizer business will continue, they have chosen a strategy of moving out of bulk chemicals to fine and speciality chemicals, which would require more intensive research and development.

Second, the regional orientation strategy: companies following this strategy include Agrolinz, BASF, DSM, Grande Paroisse, IFI and Fertiberia. Facing fierce competition from imports from Russia and Central Europe, in the case of nitrogen fertilizers, and from the North African countries such as Morocco and Tunisia, in the case of phosphoric acid, their strategy is basically to secure their own local markets within Europe. There are two types of firms included in this category. On the one hand, there are large, diversified firms such as BASF and DSM: their corporate characteristics are close to those of the firms which have already withdrawn from the fertilizer business. On the other hand, there are also relatively small, specialized firms such as Agrolinz. Close relationships with local farmers are regarded as very important for pursuing this strategy in regional markets within Europe.

The third type of corporate strategy is global expansion. Norsk Hydro and Kemira have decided to go beyond the European market, which has reached maturity. One of the characteristics of these firms is that they have their own natural resource bases. Norsk Hydro possesses oil and natural gas resources, and Kemira has its own reserves of phosphate rock with low cadmium content. With their core competence in areas related to the processing of natural resources, they are pursuing vertical integration in the fertilizer business. These firms have started to make foreign direct investment in the upstream segment in an attempt to secure access to cheap raw materials, including natural gas and phosphate rock, in the Caribbean and the Middle East. At the same time, they are also shifting to production in high-demand developing countries, such as South Asia and China.

In addition, we would like to consider how environmental issues have influenced corporate strategies in the European fertilizer industry. Among the various sources of environmental pollution, we identify major issues, including energy consumption and its related emissions of carbon dioxide, emissions of nitrogen oxides, disposal of phosphogypsum, cadmium content in fertilizers, and leaching of nitrates to waters (Schultz, 1992 and 1997). The production technologies that are used today have reached maturity and have remained essentially unchanged since the late 1960s. Most subsequent innovations focused on optimizing energy and intermediate inputs needed for the manufacturing of relatively simple fertilizers. Technologies have been more or less standardized, and R&D activities are relatively limited.

In the nitrogen sector, especially in the upstream segments of the fertilizer business, for example, ammonia, the production technologies have been well established, and many specialized engineering firms can readily provide these technologies in the world market. The key is high efficiency in energy and material use for manufacturing, and it has been relatively easy to enter the fertilizer business. In this technological trend, the investment made from the mid-1970s to late 1980s was aimed at modernizing old plants to use more efficient processes. Since energy saving could lead to reductions in emissions such as NO_X and CO_2, it was possible to achieve both economic and environmental objectives with the same technological measure. However, as efficiency in energy consumption is approaching the theoretical limit, the scope for further technological progress is expected to be very limited.

As regards reductions in NO_X emissions from the production of nitric acid, various types of technologies are well established and readily available from engineering firms. Although investment for pollution abatement normally does not produce direct economic benefits, the scale of costs required is not significant. For a new 1,000 t/d plant, the capital cost of an integrated SCR unit is estimated to be around 1.5 percent of the total, and a typical reduction in NO_x emissions from 1,000 ppmv to 150 ppmv using an SCR unit will add 1.1 percent to the operating cost of the nitric acid plants. Therefore, the overall impact of NO_x regulations on firm competitiveness would be relatively small. The major issue facing the nitrogen sector thus would be increasing imports based on cheap natural gas from Central and Eastern Europe and the former Soviet Union.

The recent focus of environmental regulations related to fertilizer application has been on the leaching of nitrates to surface and ground waters. Product differentiation in the composition of NPK fertilizers and sophistication of products such as speciality fertilizers, which are adjusted to specific conditions such as soil, temperature and moisture, special coatings for fertilizers and fluid fertilizers would be important to prevent excessive leaching of nitrates. The increasing requirements of environmental regulation has enlarged the scope for new product innovation. In addition, as precision farming in the agricultural field is emphasized, customers' dependence on the fertilizer manufacturer for tailor-made fertilizers, instructions about fertilizer spreading and the monitoring of fields using satellite systems is increasing. Consequently, the linkage between farmers and manufacturers is likely to become closer and that would make it difficult in practice for farmers to switch from one fertilizer supplier to another. This would in effect create entry or mobility barriers against other fertilizer manufacturers.

In the phosphate sector, one of the most serious issues regarding process wastes is phosphogypsum, which contains heavy metals such as cadmium. As we have discussed, at present there still remain technological and economic difficulties in removing cadmium from phosphate rock or phosphoric acid. One effect of environmental regulations on cadmium in phosphogypsum as well as in phosphate fertilizers is the shift in raw material use from phosphate rock with high cadmium content to that with low cadmium content. While some firms have already switched the source of phosphate rock from Togo to other countries such as Jordan and Morocco, this option may not always be possible, as the supply of phosphate rock with low cadmium content is limited.

A more significant effect of stringent regulations on phosphogypsum is firms' withdrawal from the production of phosphoric acid. In fact, there have been several plant closures in Western Europe, and phosphoric acid production capacity and output have fallen by 60 percent since 1980. More than 60 plants were operating in 1980 and the total production capacity was approximately 4.9 million tonnes P_2O_5 per year. In 1997, the number of operating plants was 11 and the total capacity had declined to about 1.9 million tonnes P_2O_5 per year. In 1977, there were 11 phosphoric acid plants in the UK. Now there are none. On the other hand, the average plant size has increased from 80,000 tonnes P_2O_5 per year to 176,000 tonnes P_2O_5 per year, suggesting that the decline in production capacity was mainly due to the closure of smaller units (Poulet, 1997).[10]

With regard to the issue of the cadmium content, we should underline the difference in implications between regulations on process wastes, that is, phosphogypsum, and those on products, that is, fertilizers. Since regulations in Europe on cadmium in phosphogypsum do not directly influence the production processes of phosphoric acid in other countries, these regulations would create an advantage to exporting countries such as Morocco. On the other hand, in the case of regulations on cadmium in phosphate fertilizers, the maximum concentration of cadmium, say, 60 mg cadmium per kg P_2O_5, have to be achieved by any fertilizer, whether it is produced within Europe or imported from outside. One consequence is that exporting countries trying to comply with regulations on product quality might shift the cadmium content from fertilizer products to phosphogypsum wastes ('pollution shift'). While clean phosphoric acid with little cadmium content would be exported to Europe, phosphogypsum with most of the cadmium originally contained in phosphate rock would be dumped in the exporting countries.

CONCLUSIONS

Facing stagnating demands for fertilizers and increasing pressures from cheap imports, the European fertilizer industry has been going through a significant restructuring process. At the same time, five major environmental issues have influenced technologies in the industry, namely, improvement in energy consumption in ammonia production, reduction in nitrogen oxides emissions from nitric acid production, disposal of phosphogypsum, cadmium content in fertilizers, and the leaching of nitrates from agricultural fields.

Under these circumstances of increasing competition from abroad and stagnating demand in the European fertilizer industry, there has already been an increasing focus towards the downstream segments of the sector. Overall, it seems that environmental regulations have influenced some firms in ways in which the pursuit of their corporate strategies is reinforced and strengthened. The increasing difficulties of the disposal of phosphogypsum have induced firms to withdraw from phosphoric acid production. At the same time, the requirement to limit the leaching of nitrates to waters has encouraged firms to pay particular attention to product quality and differentiation and to seek closer ties with farmers. In particular, environmental regulations on fertilizer products and their application have created close producer–user relationships between farmers and local fertilizer manufacturers, and this is becoming an effective 'mobility barrier' against new entrants to the European fertilizer market.

Under these economic and technological trends, firms in the European fertilizer industry are pursuing different corporate strategies. Several firms have already left this bulk chemical sector and shifted their focus to high value-added, fine and speciality chemical segments. Some others are concentrating on local markets, while there are also firms which are actively expanding their business globally. Those firms which decided to stay in the fertilizer industry are pursuing corporate strategies of moving from the upstream to the downstream segments of this sector, trying to turn environmental issues to their business advantage.

NOTES

1. Chapters 10 and 11 draw on four background reports: a report on the European fertilizer industry (Bartzokas and Yarime, 1999); the Chinese fertilizer industry (HuTao, 1999b); the Turkish fertilizer industry (Cetindamar, 1999) and the world phosphate industry (Demandt, 1999). These studies have reported the research findings of interviews with fertilizer manufacturers, industrial associations, technical experts, regulators and policy makers in Europe, China, Turkey and Morocco. Dr Bartzokas would like to thank Rhys Jenkins for his comments and suggestions and his overall contribution in the preparation of the final text of the chapters on the fertilizer industry. However, he is not responsible for any remaining errors and omissions.

2. The 76/464 EC Framework Directive on the discharge of dangerous substances into the aquatic environment identified cadmium as one of the most dangerous substances. The 83/513 Daughter Directive on cadmium fixed emission standards (limit values) and quality objectives on cadmium emissions from various sources. However, no limit values were set for the manufacture of phosphoric acid or fertilizer from phosphate rock, because 'at present there are no economically feasible technical methods for systematically extracting cadmium from discharges'. At the same time, it also stated that 'the absence of such limit values does not release the Member States from their obligation under Directive 76/464/EEC to fix emission standards for these discharges'. North Sea Declaration of 1990 called for a 70 percent reduction of cadmium to the North Sea by 1995 on a 1985 baseline, and a further target has been set to a 90 percent reduction by the year 2000. The target set for plants around the North Sea is 0.5 g cadmium per ton of phosphogypsum disposed to the sea, and this could serve as the preferred target elsewhere.

3. The investment for dumping the phosphogypsum to land with the transport water being recycled depends on the distances involved and the height and surface of the pile. The initial investment would be about 1.3 million ECUs, which represents about 8 percent of the phosphoric acid plant investment. The annual costs of phosphogypsum storage and water recycling would be 0.6 million ECUs or approximately 3.9 percent of the total operating costs of the plant. The cost of closing a gypsum stack depends on the site but is estimated to be 6.4 million ECUs. The overall cost of gypsum ponds could range from 3 to 17 ECU/t P_2O_5/year. Management of the phosphogypsum deposits would also be required for many years after the phosphoric acid plant ceased production, with additional treatment of run-off of waters (EFMA, 1995d).

4. For a recent report on the potential implications of the introduction of charges on high-

cadmium phosphate rock, see Oosterhuis *et al.* (2000).

5. Recently, it has been argued that modern, sophisticated technology could provide the farmer with new opportunities to adjust the application of nutrients to the needs of crops and to the potential crop yield. Examples of measures in which the European fertilizer industry is involved include (EFMA, 1997b):

- Advanced advisory computer programmes for fertilizer planning, which take account of inputs from all fertilizer sources, organic as well as inorganic, application techniques, good fertilizer practice and local regulations;
- precision farming, which uses satellite communication and detailed field and crop information to improve farm operation and nutrient efficiency by means of the site-specific application of fertilizers;
- integrated crop management, which is a comprehensive system of modern farming husbandry that balances economic production with environmental responsibility. The system seeks to integrate improved crop nutrition, crop protection techniques, soil management, and crop rotations to maximize energy efficiency; and
- development and promotion of soil analysis and crop deficiency diagnosis to facilitate the fine-tuning of fertilizer rates to actual crop requirements.

6. In many cases quantities or percentages of the primary nutrients, except nitrogen (N), are expressed in terms of phosphorus pentoxide (P_2O_5) and potassium oxide (K_2O), instead of elementary phosphorus (P) and potassium (K).

7. Interviews were conducted by Masaru Yarime and Ivo Demandt from August to October 1997.

8. Hydro has conducted life-cycle analysis to evaluate the environmental impacts of agricultural production. Hydro Agri Europe's research centre in Hanninghof, Germany, analysed wheat production in Europe, from the manufacture of agricultural inputs to activities in the fields. The results show that close to 90 percent of the environmental impact from wheat production in Europe stems from the activities in the field, primarily the use of fertilizer. Incorrect use of fertilizers, whether they are mineral fertilizer, manure, organic composts or plant residues, can lead to excessive leaching of nutrients, deterioration of soil fertility and soil erosion. In addition, excessive greenhouse gas emissions during growth may occur (Kuesters and Jenssen, 1998).

9. The following rule of thumb is applied: a reduction by 90 percent, from 90 percent to 99 percent and from 99 percent to 99.9 percent, requires approximately the same expenditure in each case (BASF, 1993).

10. Recent examples of plant closures include: the closure of a plant of Société Chemique Prayon-Rupel in Belgium in 1992 because its phosphogypsum landfill permit has been cancelled by the Flemish authorities; the closure of a plant of Kemira in Rotterdam in 1992; the closure of a plant of BASF in Antwerp in 1993 because of stricter regulation on phosphogymsum disposal; and the closing down of a plant of Hydro Agri in Rotterdam at the end of 1999, citing the environmental regulation on phosphogypsum as a major reason for the decision.

11. The fertilizer industry in developing countries

The development of the fertilizer industry took place in the developed countries of Western Europe, North America and Japan until the late 1960s. However, in the 1970s and early 1980s, the construction of new plants shifted to locations where cheap natural gas was available, such as countries of the Caribbean and Middle East. In recent years, there has also been a trend towards the production of nitrogen fertilizers in high-demand developing countries such as China, India, Indonesia and Pakistan. In this chapter, we present the main findings of our case studies on environmental regulation and fertilizer production in two developing countries with a large fertilizer industry, which are undergoing a restructuring process driven by import penetration and market liberalization (China and Turkey). In the last part of the chapter, we focus on phosphate fertilizers, a sub-sector in which European firms are facing increasing competition from developing countries. After an overall discussion of sectoral trends in the phosphate industry, we examine in more detail the case of Morocco, one of the leading producers of phosphate rock and the main supplier of the European fertilizer industry. Finally, in our concluding remarks, we draw some policy conclusions based on our findings regarding the impact of environmental regulation on industrial restructuring and competitiveness.

THE CHINESE FERTILIZER INDUSTRY

Introduction

China is a developing country with a rural population of 870 million. China's production of chemical fertilizers is the largest in the world, accounting for approximately 15 percent of total world production. When it comes to the consumption of chemical fertilizers, China is ranked first in the world, with more than 25 percent of total world consumption. With the expansion of agriculture in recent years, China is becoming increasingly dependent on chemical fertilizers and pesticides.

Chinese Agricultural Policy

The agricultural policy of China has a very strong influence on the local demand for chemical fertilizers. Changes in agricultural policy exercise direct influence on their total consumption. A review of this policy and its priorities will provide a basis for the discussion of current developments and the future of domestic fertilizer production.

Food self-sufficiency is the core of Chinese agricultural policy; narrowly, this means grain self-sufficiency policy. Other policies supporting this objective are trade policy, subsidies and the official quota system for the distribution of fertilizers. After the implementation of the 'Household Responsibility System' in the early 1980s, China came out of the period of shortages in food supplies and was able to export agricultural products. Furthermore, in order to encourage farmers to produce more grain, pricing policy has been used as an incentive. Consequently, grain prices have been increasing rapidly. Due to the increasing demand for agricultural products, the consumption of chemical fertilizers by farmers is also very large and is increasing rapidly (Jingru, 1992). According to recent estimates provided by the World Bank, China's dependence on imported fertilizers has increased to 5 million tons since 2000 despite the large-scale investment programme in large plants. Any attempt at further improvement of the self-sufficiency rate will require the establishment of at least 12 new 400,000 ton nitrogen fertilizer plants with an investment of about US$4.4 billion (World Bank, 1997, p. 17).

Table 11.1 presents the total consumption of chemical fertilizer and the breakdown by groups of products in China.

One of the priorities of trade policy in China is to support the food self-sufficiency objective. One dimension is that trade policy sets up barriers to limit grains and other agricultural products from being imported to China. At the same time, trade policy encourages imports of materials which are being used in the production of agricultural products within China, such as chemical fertilizers and pesticides (Cao, 1998). Due to the increasing demand for agricultural products, the consumption of chemical fertilizers by farmers is very large and is increasing. At the same time, trade policy encourages farmers to use imported chemical fertilizers and pesticides. China set up very low custom tariffs for chemical fertilizers for several decades. The tariffs vary according to the different kinds of chemical fertilizers. Normally the higher the quality, the lower the tariff. Because of this tariff policy, China is ranked first in the world in terms of imported fertilizers and in recent years it has spent about US$3 billion annually on them. North American companies are supplying China and have managed to capture more than 75 percent of the market in recent years (Table 11.2). The European presence is limited and has declined considerably recently. China has been the main export market for US

Table 11.1   Total consumption of chemical fertilizers in China

Year	Consumption of chemical fertilizer (10^4 tons)	Nitrogenous fertilizers	Phosphate fertilizers	Potash fertilizers	Compound fertilizer
1980	1 269.4	934.2	273.3	34.6	27.3
1985	1 775.8	1 204.9	310.9	80.4	179.6
1986	1 930.6	1 312.6	359.8	77.4	180.8
1987	1 999.3	1 326.8	371.9	91.9	208.7
1988	2 141.5	1 417.1	382.1	101.2	241.2
1989	2 357.1	1 536.8	418.9	120.5	280.9
1990	2 590.3	1 638.4	462.4	147.9	341.6
1991	2 805.1	1 726.1	499.6	173.9	405.5
1992	2 930.2	1 756.1	515.7	196.0	462.4
1993	3 151.9	1 835.1	575.1	212.3	529.4
1994	3 317.9	1 882.0	600.7	234.8	600.6
1995	3 593.7	2 021.9	632.4	268.5	670.8
1996	3 827.9	2 145.3	658.4	289.6	734.7
1997	3 980.7	2 171.7	689.1	322.0	798.1

Source: State Statistical Bureau (1998).

fertilizers, especially DAP, urea and potassium sulphate. US fertilizer exports to China in value terms have increased more than 50 percent since the early 1990s, largely because of the purchasing policies of the Chinese government.[1]

The fertilizer market is controlled by the central, provincial (including city and autonomous region) and county governments, according to the policy of 'national planning and different government management'. The fertilizer products, which are sold through state-owned marketing networks, are about 85 percent of domestic fertilizer consumption. The current market network of chemical fertilizers is being used as an instrument for the control of the agrochemical market, in order to avoid speculation, price rises, counterfeiting and other practices that might harm farmers.

The State Development and Planning Commission (SDPC) sets the basic retail prices of imported chemical fertilizers and the maximum fluctuation zone of the prices. For example, according to a document (code 164, 1998) issued by SDPC on 7 February 1998, for imported urea and ammonium biphosphate the basic prices are 1,700 Yuan and 2,200 Yuan respectively. The prices could be changed only within a 10 percent zone. For domestic chemical

*Table 11.2   Country share of exports of fertilizers and nitrogen compounds
to the Chinese market (%)*

	1995	1994	1993	1992	1991
United States	77.3	73.4	59.5	70.1	67.3
European Union (15 countries, excluding ex-GDR)	2.5	5.4	9.9	9.3	8.3
Federal Republic of Germany (excluding ex-GDR)	2.3	3.7	4.7	5	3.5
Greece	0	0	0.6	0.8	0.3
France	0	0.01	0	0	0.4
Italy	0	0	0.01	0.9	0
Finland	0	1.3	4.5	2.4	3.6
Sweden	0.1	0.1	0	0.3	0.5
Norway	0	3.34	6.3	5.7	5.0
Turkey	0	0.5	0	0	0.2
Canada	14.4	12.3	14.6	7.6	11.0
Mexico	0	1.2	0	0	0
Brazil	0	0	0	1.3	0.7
Chile	0.8	0.4	2.3	0.9	0.4
Japan	0.1	0.1	0.3	0.1	0.2
Korea (South)	1.4	0.8	0.5	0.2	1.3
Malaysia	0.5	0	0	0.3	1.3
Singapore	0.02	0.02	0.01	0	0
Israel	0.3	0.3	4.0	3.1	0
Australia	0	0	0	0.2	0.3
Others	2.7	2.3	2.8	1.2	4.1
Total	100.0	100.0	100.0	100.0	100.0

Source: Eurostat, CRONOS: Competitiveness DataBase, 1999.

fertilizers, the government also controls the prices. For example, the highest price of urea in Yantai City in 1998 is fixed at 1,800 Yuan.

There used to be many direct subsidies to fertilizer production. With the transition to the market system, many of these subsidies were abolished. However, indirect subsidies are still in place. For example, the Yantai Chemical Fertilizer Company pays 0.32 RMB/kWh for electricity while the market price is 0.56 RMB/kWh (US$0.07/kWh) for other industries (HuTao, 1999). In addition, according to the regulations issued by the State Council as well as SDPC and the Ministry of Railways, the freight rate for chemical fertilizers, unlike other sectors, did not increase to 0.0415 RMB/t/km from 0.0365 RMB (Lin and Zhang, 1998).

Sectoral Trends

Nitrogen fertilizers (75 percent) and phosphate products (24 percent) dominate the Chinese fertilizer industry. For example, in 1997 total fertilizer production was 28.53 million tons, of which nitrogen was 21.53 million tons and phosphate 6.5 million tons. The distribution of fertilizer plants is 62.9 percent nitrogen, 37.0 percent phosphate and only 0.1 per cent potash plants.

Chemical fertilizer firms in China are mainly small-scale nitrogen chemical plants. In every one or two counties, a small nitrogen fertilizer plant operates for the needs of local agriculture (see also Table 11.3). Small-scale chemical fertilizer plants contribute 64.5 percent of total production, so these plants are extremely important to China. In the past, the small-scale plants only produced NH_4HCO_3 as well as a limited amount of urea. In recent years, the Chinese government has invested in small-scale urea and ammonia phosphate plants, and up to 1996, 77 plants had been set up with a total capacity of 3.2 million tons of urea and 2.47 million tons of ammonia phosphate.

Small-scale factories produce low-grade nitrogen and phosphates using locally developed technologies. The use of ammonium bicarbonate for the production of nitrogen fertilizers involves a simple technology based on anthracite coal deposits. This production process has been widely adopted in small plants. However, it is highly polluting and energy inefficient (World Bank, 1997, p. 18). Although the volume of production of China is ranked first in the world, the productivity of Chinese fertilizer plants is very low. The

Table 11.3   Size of China's chemical fertilizer plants

Size	Production capacity of plants ('000 tons)	Number of enterprises	Percentage of total chemical fertilizer industry enterprises	Estimated % of total production
Large	≥300	22	1.59	25
Medium	Mainly 40–80	55	4.78	25
Small	<25	1 057	93.63[a]	50

Note: [a] Of which, over 70 percent are very small plants with capacity lower than 15 thousand
        tons.

Source: Ministry of Chemical Industry (1998).

overall labour productivity is only half that of western countries, but energy consumption is almost double. The equipment for small-scale chemical fertilizer plants is mainly made in China, but that of large and medium plants is imported. The age of the machinery in existing plants varies; some was made in the 1990s with new technologies, but some dates back to the 1960s. The details are given in Table 11.4.

The equipment for large-scale fertilizer plants is mainly imported from the US and Europe. The following technologies of chemical fertilizer production are already widely diffused in China: US Kellogg with lower energy consumption; US Brown with deep cooling and energy saving; UK ICI-AMV; and the German Wood-AMV technology. The role of local equipment suppliers before the 1990s was limited to the support of imported equipment. After the early 1990s, some Chinese equipment and technology has been used as well, but the amount is very limited. The motives behind management decisions for the adoption of cleaner technologies need further clarification. Especially in the case of simple pollution abatement equipment, demand was initially created by the introduction of regulation but the combination of simple recycling and reuse as well as energy saving has yielded significant economic benefits that created additional demand through the 'demonstration effect' to other managers in rural areas (Ding, 1995a, 1995b).

Environmental Regulation and the Chinese Fertilizer Industry

Although there are many general environmental laws in China, environmental management is mainly based on the regulations issued by SEPA. Compared to environmental laws with general provisions, SEPA regulations have more details for implementation as guidelines. A series of environmental policies and regulations suited to its national conditions, such as Environmental Impact Assessment and the Pollution Levy/Charge system have been implemented across the country. China has many environmental laws, regulations and standards; however, enforcement is the essential problem. In the future, environmental regulation will become stricter, due to the worsening environmental conditions and the increasing environmental awareness of the population

Since 1991, all provinces, autonomous regions and municipalities directly under the central government (NEPA) have carried out a pollution charge system. If pollutants discharged exceed the national standard, the polluter must pay a fine, depending on the amount and concentration of the pollutant; this has been standardized across the country. The pollution permit system is based on the volume control of pollutants, taking the improvement of environmental quality as its target; it specifies the category, quantity and discharge course of the pollutants discharged by the enterprises, which obtain

Table 11.4 Chemical fertilizer production equipment

	Locally-produced equipment				Imported equipment			
	No. of production units	When manufactured (%)			No. of production units	When manufactured (%)		
		1990s	1980s	Pre-1980s		1990s	1980s	Pre-1980s
Urea	133	68.4	15.8	15.8	23	17.4	21.7	60.9
Nitramines	45	8.9	17.8	73.3	1	0	0	100
Phosphate	1966	23.9	56.5	19.6	0	0	0	0
Potash	75	65.0	34.0	—	4	100	0	0

Source: Ministry of Chemical Industry (1998).

verified 'permits' for pollutants. The registration of the pollutant discharge is the base of the implementation of the pollutant discharge permit system. The system is the quantitative specification for the pollution discharge from production units according to the existing regulations and the local situation. The registration of the pollutant discharge is universal and it must be implemented in all the pollution discharge units. The pollution permit system for air pollution control and other aspects are on trial. Indeed, a new policy on Total Emissions Amount Control is being prepared by SEPA, which is actually an extension of the pollution permit system.[2]

The main pollutants of the chemical fertilizer industry in China are described mainly as wastewater and air emissions. Limited solid waste is being produced (PRCEE, 1997). Normally, the affected polluted areas are around the manufacturing plants. Most of the air emissions, except dust, could be re-used by adding new equipment. Coal-based plants have some additional TSP and SO_2 emission problems. Natural gas and other resource-based plants have smaller problems, compared with coal-based factories. Wastewater results in extensive organic pollution of water.

Due to the reconstruction of SETC, there are no special data on the emission of pollution available for the chemical fertilizer industry. The information provided in Table 11.5 is about emissions and treatment of wastewater and gas from raw chemical materials and chemical products in 1997 and the very low level of treatment gives a rough estimate of the scale of the environmental problems in fertilizer manufacturing plants (which is a sub-sector of this industrial branch).

Table 11.5   Treatment of wastewater and gas from raw chemical materials and chemical products in 1997

	Enterprises (unit)	Treatment facilities (sets)	Waste emission	Wastes treated or purified	Rate of treatment (%)
Wastewater (10^6 t)	6 522	8 288	4 277.5	1 088.2	25.4
Air emissions (billion cu m)	6 522	11 882	938.0	296.9	31.6

Source: *China's Environmental Protection Yearbook 1997.*

The indirect environmental consequences of fertilizer products, that is, the consequences of using chemical fertilizer, are also significant. The impact is

very wide, including aquatic body pollution, decreasing soil fertility, land
degradation, soil erosion, deforestation, wetland disappearance and others.
The use of chemicals has contributed significantly to the eutrophication of the
aquatic body in rural China. According to researchers studying Lake Taihu
and Lake Dianchi, for example, the contribution of fertilizer application to
eutrophication is over 50 percent of the total pollution effect. According to
FAO, chemical fertilizer used per hectare in China is 2.6 times the world
average and 3.4 times the average for developing countries (FAO, 1996;
HuTao, 1999b).

The Chinese fertilizer industry is facing pressures from the introduction of
environmental regulations and has to improve its environmental performance.
At the same time, clean technologies could also improve the efficiency of
energy and materials consumption at the firm level. The State Economic and
Trade Commission (SETC) is also considering the introduction of incentives
to encourage the adoption of environmental technologies. As environmental
problems are becoming increasingly important, clean technology has a big
potential and it will be used more and more in the future. Among the clean
technologies, the most important are energy saving applications.

In order to promote cleaner production, SETC is also issuing some policies
to encourage firms to shift to cleaner production. In the future, as in the case
of the large fertilizer plants, new technology will be used, especially low cost
and high efficiency technology, some of which will be produced domestically.
In the case of new plants, production capacity should be larger than 20–30
thousand tons of ammonia to reach economies of scale, according to SETC's
estimates. More and more technological innovations will be focused on small
and medium chemical fertilizer plants, especially in an attempt to increase
the installed capacity of small plants to between 40 thousand tons of ammonia
and 60 thousand and from 60 thousand to 80 thousand tons. The capacity of
110–130 thousand tons of urea per plant is also a direction of development.

Compared with large fertilizer plants, pollution abatement equipment in
small plants is not as widely diffused, mainly because almost all the small
plants are located in counties where the environmental awareness of
local people is not as strong as in urban areas and where the capacity for
the enforcement of environmental regulations is relatively low. Pollution
abatement equipment installed in small fertilizer plants are simple devices
for recycling and reuse of water and air emissions as well as some
equipment for noise control which are required by labour protection laws
(Wang, 1998).

In order to improve the productivity of small chemical fertilizer plants,
cleaner technologies have been introduced. For small-scale chemical plants,
after the adoption of cleaner technologies the average consumption of coal as
input materials, coal as fuel, and electricity are respectively 1,245 kg, 298 kg

and 1,300 kWh, an improvement of 48 kg, 43 kg and 12 kWh respectively. For small nitrogen fertilizer plants, energy consumption per ton of ammonia is 14.48 million Kcal and 0.48 million Kcal less than before.[3]

According to the State Development Planning Commission (SDPC) and the former Ministry of Chemical Industry, the policy for the development of the fertilizer industry could be divided into two areas: policy for new projects and policy for existing projects. The aims are to establish new fertilizer plant projects of large and medium scale and to introduce incremental technological innovations for small and medium scale fertilizer plants.

Imported products with lower price and higher quality are challenging the existing chemical plants. How to improve the quality of locally produced fertilizers and reduce the production cost are the main problems to be solved by managers in existing plants. Technological innovation is an important factor in any attempt to solve these problems. For existing plants, technological innovation for small-scale fertilizer plants will be stressed. As described above, China will also adjust its structure of chemical fertilizer manufacture towards large-scale plants.

Overall, nitrogen fertilizers produced in small-scale plants dominate the structure of the chemical fertilizer industry. The Chinese government is implementing a policy for structural change in the sector and the aim is to shift from small to larger size plants and from the specialization in nitrogen to a diversified production base which will include phosphate and potash fertilizers. The performance of most of the chemical fertilizer firms is not good enough. Ownership is one of the main reasons: the government, either through central government or at provincial level, owns all of the chemical fertilizer firms. At present, small-scale plants are in a very difficult position. In the fertilizer market, imported high quality fertilizers and large-scale domestic plants challenge them, and some have already been bankrupted. They are also facing pressures from the introduction of stricter environmental regulations due to increasing environmental concerns (Qin, 1996).

THE TURKISH FERTILIZER INDUSTRY

Sectoral Trends

This section aims to analyse the impact of environmental regulations and standards on the Turkish fertilizer industry's pattern of development. The general aggregate analysis will be followed by a firm-level analysis. The impact of environmental regulation on production and technological change will be investigated in depth by introducing the research findings of fieldwork with six Turkish fertilizer companies.[4]

Turkey has a well-developed fertilizer industry. At present, there are six major fertilizer-producing firms in the local market, including two private firms. Due to high domestic demand and export possibilities to neighbouring countries, Turkey still needs new investment in the industry. Local demand is expected to increase in the next 5-10 years particularly due to the Southeast Anatolia Project (SAP), which will increase demand by 25 percent. When this project is completed, it will increase arable land in Turkey by 1.7 million ha. By 2005, it is planned that 55 percent of the project will be finished and this will add 894 thousand ha of land for agricultural production (Kazgan, 1992).

Production of fertilizers increased by 23 percent per year during 1962-72, 18 percent during 1973-8, 16.7 percent during 1979-84, and 6.5 percent during 1985-9 (TUMAS, 1987). In the 1990s, the fertilizer industry suffered from the deterioration of macroeconomic conditions in Turkey and its output experienced fluctuations. Fertilizer production in Turkey reached its highest level in 1993 but then experienced a radical drop in 1994 due to both changes in the subsidy system and the devaluation of the Turkish currency. Since then, the industry has been trying to recover. According to the seventh five-year national plan, fertilizer production was projected to grow at an annual rate of 4.5 percent in the period 1996-2000 (SPO, 1996).

In terms of consumption, nitrogen fertilizer is the most important fertilizer product. At 631,000 tons, nitrogen consumption was 53 percent of all consumption in 1976; this increased to 1,148,000 tons in 1996, corresponding to 64 percent of all consumption. Phosphate consumption has increased slightly from 522,000 tons in 1976 to 578,000 tons in 1996. The consumption of potash is supplied by imports. Although the consumption of potash increased 255 percent in terms of *volume*, its 1996 level is only 74,000 tons, representing only 0.04 percent of total fertilizer consumption (Eyüpoðlu, 1992). (For more details on these trends, see Table 11.6.) The volume of imported fertilizers is increasing, especially in the area of compound fertilizers. Our analysis of import trends at the four-digit SITC 3 level points to an increasing market penetration by European exports in this area of fertilizers.[5]

The Turkish fertilizer industry is highly dependent on imported raw materials and energy. This is one of the main handicaps for the competitiveness of the industry. Many domestic resources, however, can be utilized and the State Planning Organization tries to provide incentives for firms to invest in these areas. The imported energy cost is very high in Turkey compared to many developed countries. Local firms have been pressing the government for cheaper energy prices. Energy prices are undermining the competitiveness and any potential for exports by Turkish fertilizer companies; in fact, energy savings appeared to be one of the main considerations for new technological investment by Turkish firms.

Environmental Regulation and Technological Change

The Environment Act of 1983 is the first environment law in Turkey. It charges for pollution, based on the 'polluter pays' principle, by supplying a detailed list of fees for all types of pollutants. This Act requires industrial establishments to report their pollution levels according to follow-up regulations that came into being in 1986, 1988, 1991, 1993 and 1995 as air quality protection, noise, water pollution, solid waste, medical waste, and hazardous materials regulations. The fertilizer industry's production process is controlled through specific regulations that cover the area of air emissions and wastewater. Although the solid waste of the fertilizer industry is hazardous, no

Table 11.6   Trade and production[a] of fertilizers in Turkey ('000 tons)

	1976	1980	1985	1990	1991	1992	1993	1994	1995	1996
Nitrogenous fertilizer										
Production	211	600	770	1 026	852	969	1 027	702	939	924
% of total	38	63	56	66	69	65	65	67	71	68
Imports	480	349	270	386	359	341	460	143	363	342
Exports	0	0	15	111	83	69	40	19	30	1
Consumption	631	782	916	1 200	1 104	1 206	1 335	1 007	1 054	1 148
Potash fertilizer										
Production	0	0	0	0	0	0	0	0	0	0
Imports	39	20	41	62	47	81	93	64	78	85
Exports	0	0	0	2	11	2	0	4	3	1
Consumption	29	30	34	64	48	63	85	56	67	74
Phosphate fertilizer										
Production	344	348	604	538	386	527	557	345	392	425
% of total	62	37	44	34	31	35	35	33	29	32
Imports	146	414	138	178	198	135	304	91	192	107
Exports	0	0	155	43	52	39	18	8	17	13
Consumption	522	483	477	625	618	658	787	444	580	578
Total fertilizer production										
Production	555	948	1 374	1 564	1 238	1 496	1 584	1 046	1 331	1 348

Note: [a] To avoid double counting, the production statistics relate to primary production.

Source: AFP (1998).

special regulations yet exist. Turkey and the EU countries have largely similar regulations and standards for wastewater and air emissions. However, Turkey has no special regulation for the solid waste in the fertilizer industry, which is mainly phosphogypsum.

Overall, the Turkish environment legislation seems to be similar to that of the EU. Only in some details does the Turkish legislation seem lacking. This result could be due to the fact that even prior to Turkish application for full membership of the EU, Turkey drew heavily on the experiences of the Western European countries, particularly Germany, in formulating its own environmental legislation. Today, it continues to bring its laws into line with the EU. The existing plan of the Ministry of the Environment is to complete the harmonization of the Turkish environment laws with EU ones by 2001. One of the motivations behind this endeavour is to prevent any trade impediment to Turkish firms that might occur because of the evaluation of environmental factors in trade. When it comes to the application of fertilizers in agriculture and the promotion of agricultural production methods compatible with the requirements for the protection of the environment and the maintenance of the countryside through measures such as technical assistance, cost sharing for trial installation, and conservation compliance, Turkey has no regulation or policy instruments in place.

The main conclusion of our case study indicates that, although environmental issues and regulations are recent in Turkey, they are becoming increasingly effective. In parallel with the regulations, public awareness is increasing and environmental technology suppliers are flourishing. Nevertheless, all these developments do not mean that there are no problems. Only one firm out of six is actually operating under regulatory limits while two other firms satisfy limits partially and the remaining three fail to comply with regulations at all. If environmental laws were applied to fertilizer firms at their official levels, at least half of the firms would be closed down. This, in turn, could reduce the production of local firms by more than 70 percent.

None of the firms has a complete pollution prevention system at the firm level, but rather partial systems at their different production units. Firms start to invest in cleaning and treatment technologies for their most polluting production units so that they can decrease their pollution to acceptable limits. As firms are not eager to invest in new equipment, almost all environmental investments are pollution cleaning technologies rather than pollution-preventative technologies. We observed only three firms adopting pollution-prevention technologies for some of their production units, but these firms were undertaking new investments, and when they chose a production technology, they concentrated on those with embedded environmental technologies. Another reason for the type of environmental investments is that in four cases (firms F1, F3, F5, and F6) firms received financial support from the World Bank for their energy transformation from fuel oil to natural gas. These investments brought the complementary environmental investments that are related to water consumption and air emissions.

As the majority of investment projects are aiming at pollution-cleaning purposes, they usually consist of emission cleaning systems and water saving technologies. The main reason why investment focuses only on these two waste types and does not include solid waste is that regulations concerning solid waste have not yet been prepared for the fertilizer industry. All firms with solid waste simply stack it on open land at their production site.

It was clear from interviews that none of the producer firms (including state owned ones) is willing to invest in clean technologies unless they are forced to do so. In areas where the local authority is active and forces firms to comply with regulations, firms act. This was clearly observed by the behaviour of firm F1 which stopped its phosphoric acid production in Izmit while it continued production in its plant 2 location, where local authorities are weak in monitoring the implementation of environmental regulations.

How regulations were effective in determining firms' investment behaviour can also be observed by analysing their attitude towards environmental management. As regulations do not bring any requirement to set up environmental management, none of the firms has an environmental statement/report, environment management systems, ISO 14.000, or environment cost accounting. Except for two firms, F2 and F3, firms do not have environmental training either.

Although environmental regulations could not directly affect how production is carried out, it has forced firms to invest in waste treatment utilities. The majority of firms (four out of six firms) have invested in wastewater treatment systems for industrial water use in 1994. Also all firms invested in waste cleaning systems both in 1988 and in 1994. These are the years when regulations were becoming increasingly evident. After 1992, the establishment of the Ministry of the Environment (ME) further accelerated the workability of regulations. For example, Izmit municipality region, which is chosen as a pilot application by the ME, increased its enforcement power significantly. The selection of this region is not a coincidence. It is the most concentrated industrial district in Turkey: thousands of firms have production facilities in the area including two of our case study firms. The ME encourages other municipalities to follow this successful example.

When fertilizer firms were asked about their technology investments, they listed water saving, energy saving and waste reducing technologies as the main categories of investment (see Table 11.7). Fertilizer firms' limited response to regulations and their neglect of environmental policies could be explained mainly by the fact that they produce for the local market and they do not face any pressure for cleaner products from the demand side. Only one firm, which aimed to increase its product quality and at the same time prevent and control environmental pollution, invested simultaneously in new waste reducing technologies in 1980. However, in later years we see that although all firms aimed to prevent and control environmental pollution, they invested in water and energy saving technologies that indirectly led to improvements in their wastes and emissions.

Table 11.7   Technology investments in Turkish fertilizer firms

Pollution problem	Number of firms	Objectives[a]	Year	Cost (million TL/year)
Water saving technologies	2	1, 2, 3	1994	247 320
	2	1, 2, 3	1995	104 340
	1	3	1995	200
	2	3	1996	1 700 000
Energy saving technologies	1	1, 2, 3	1988	16 353
Waste reducing technologies	1	1, 3	1980	19 987

Note: [a] Objectives: 1 increasing production quality; 2 economic savings; 3 preventing and controlling environmental pollution; 4 customs union.

Source: SIS, unpublished data.

The overall analysis of firms' management practices reveals that they do not have any formal environmental policy at the firm level. Nevertheless, more importantly, many of them do not plan to have environmental policies either. As Turkish fertilizer firms tend to respond only to regulations, the starting point for any policy should be to transform this management culture (*Nokta*, 1997). This, however, requires not only training of firm management in environmental issues but also increasing customer pressure that will demand environmentally friendly products. In the case of fertilizers, farmers who have limited resources and low levels of education could be a problem. That is why the government's agricultural policy plays a crucial role in forcing fertilizer firms from the demand side as well as through regulation.

At the government level, significant work has been done in regulating the environmental impact of the fertilizer industry. Only the solid waste issue, namely the disposal of phosphogypsum, is not dealt with from the regulation point of view. Although there is considerable success in terms of preparing regulations, as indicated by the authorities at the ME, there are problems regarding their enforcement. In our study, both the government institutes and firms complained that the laws are not applied evenly to all local producers. On the one hand, private firms argue that state companies often do not pay fines for pollution, because they are either too poor or else politically too powerful, and the logic is that it is the same budget anyway. On the other hand, state owned firms argue that private firms have more flexibility in being able to avoid fines because they can use other means (by securing the support of local officials or buying the land of complaining farmers) to solve disputes. As the aim is to change firms' attitudes towards the environment, the ME should make it clear that firms cannot get away with their pollution and that they will all be punished equally.

Half the firms, F4, F5 and F6, indicated that they would like to export abroad. Among them, firm F2 is seriously considering taking a share in European markets when European fertilizer firms start to close down their plants in Europe because of environmental problems. However, none of these firms is successful in exports. They all failed largely to export abroad after export subsidies were cut in 1993. The main reason behind this failure lies in the fact that the Turkish fertilizer firms are locked into old technologies. Although they need radical changes in total production, they do not invest. The main obstacle, according to fertilizer companies, is the government's pricing policy that keeps profit margins very low and makes the market unstable. In that respect, our review of corporate priorities indicates that there is a clear need for government policies, such as investment incentives rather than price subsidies for fertilizer products that could create an incentive structure for technological modernization investment in the direction of more efficient and cleaner technologies (Yýldýrým, 1997; Çetindamar, 1999).

Although the government liberalized the fertilizer market in 1987 and allowed private firms to trade fertilizers, it still keeps control of its marketing and distribution organization, which is still an intermediary between farmers and fertilizer firms, since its members comprise 40 percent of all farmers in Turkey. The government first buys fertilizers from producers at open bids; it then adds charges on top of that price and then reduces the price by the subsidy amount (40 percent of the final price) and sells them to its members through the intermediary organization. This system looks quite problematic, since having such an intermediary organization increases prices.

Despite the private firms' exaggeration of the problems created by state intervention, it is true that government intervention as a fertilizer producer and distributor prevents the healthy development of the industry, particularly its technological development. The government forces state owned firms to operate irrationally in many ways and, as these firms constitute the majority of the market, it affects the whole industry. First, state owned fertilizer firms are not allowed to invest due to political concerns, although these firms want to. For example, a state owned firm wished to invest in a new ammonia plant in the Izmit region. It aimed to invest $150 million for a capacity of 550,000 tons of ammonia. It was calculated that this would save $40 million of otherwise imported ammonia each year (Sabah, 1995). The Turkish government, however, did not approve this investment due to privatization discussions. Not only long-term plans but also short-term plans and even urgently needed investments are not approved, since none of the political parties want to commit resources to the industry.

Our case study analysed three influential ministries and three research institutes as well as five non-governmental organizations. Our observations show that although environmental issues are new in Turkey, a few very professional institutions are active in the area. While government institutions are creating the legal framework for environmental regulations and standards, non-governmental organizations are focusing more on the formation of interest groups around the issue of increasing environmental awareness. Both streams of developments are new but promising.

The Turkish case study provides some illuminating insights into the links between environmental regulation and fertilizer manufacturing in developing countries. The impact of environmental regulation on production cost and investment decisions is still rather limited to investment incentives and small additions of end-of-pipe equipment in existing plants. However, the regulatory framework and the existing distribution network are the main sources of inertia for new investment in the local fertilizer industry.

PHOSPHATE FERTILIZER PRODUCTION IN DEVELOPING COUNTRIES

Phosphate fertilizer production has been concentrated in developed countries, mainly in the US and Western Europe, for many years. This was justified not only by their level of industrial development, but also by the large scale of domestic demand. However, while the US phosphate fertilizer industry was using domestic phosphate rock deposits, the European industry was dependent on imports of phosphate rock. These imports initially came from the US, as it was the only country exploiting its phosphate rock reserves on a large scale. Over the past three decades, however, the US has lost market share in Western Europe to emerging suppliers from developing countries. This trend was the beginning of an increasing involvement of developing countries in the global phosphate industry. Initially this involvement was restricted to exports of phosphate rock, but they eventually expanded into the production of processed phosphates (Gregory, 1992; Bumb, 1995; and USITC, 1998).

The emergence of phosphate fertilizer production in developing countries has changed the geographical pattern of trade in basic materials, intermediates and finished phosphate products. For many years, phosphate rock was the main item that was being exported to processing plants in major consuming countries. Over the last two decades, however, trade in processed phosphates has increasingly replaced phosphate rock trade and processing of natural phosphates is being vertically integrated near mining sites (Louis, 1997). This trend is illustrated in Figure 11.1.

As former exporters of phosphate rock prefer to continue with downstream processing, exports of phosphate rock have been decreasing. Consequently, world phosphate rock exports fell from 53 million Mt produced in 1979 to 27 million Mt in 1993. Since then there has been a slight increase, to reach 31 million Mt in 1996. At the same time total exports of processed phosphates increased from an average of 8 million Mt P_2O_5 between 1984 and 1986 to 13.7 million Mt P_2O_5 between 1994 and 1996, despite a fall in total phosphate consumption during this period (IFA, 1999).

The main destination for phosphoric acid exports is Western Europe, where

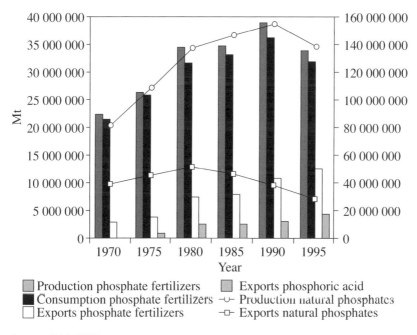

Production phosphate fertilizers   Exports phosphoric acid
Consumption phosphate fertilizers   –○– Production natural phosphates
Exports phosphate fertilizers   –□– Exports natural phosphates

Source: FAO-STAT.

Figure 11.1   Phosphates in the world market

most phosphoric acid plants were closed down for economic and environmental reasons, and India, which uses phosphoric acid for its phosphate fertilizer plants. The main exporters of phosphoric acid are Morocco, Tunisia and the US, as is shown in Figure 11.2.

Due to declining transport costs and economies of scale in processing offered by vertical integration of mining and processing, export-oriented producers are in a very good position to compete with the traditional phosphate producers. In addition, the phosphate industry in the US and Western Europe is facing increasing operational costs due to the introduction of environmental regulation. This further strengthens the competitive position of the newly emerging resource-oriented phosphate producers (Edmonson, 1995).

In what follows, we will briefly present two patterns of emerging phosphate fertilizer producers. The first pattern is a typical resource processing strategy, which builds on the availability of indigenous phosphate resources. The second strategy is being followed by countries with large rural populations and increasing demand for fertilizer consumption. Furthermore, we will elaborate on the process of technological capability building that has been associated with the increase in value added in phosphate production in developing countries.

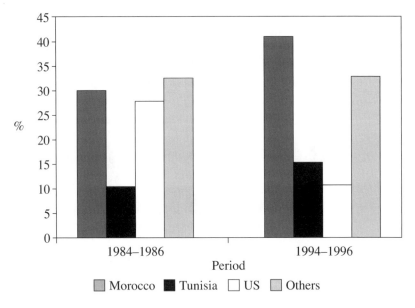

Source: FAO-STAT.

Figure 11.2   Exports of phosphoric acid

Countries concentrating on export-oriented production are mainly found in North Africa and the Middle East, such as Morocco, Tunisia and Jordan. They have large phosphate reserves but lack significant domestic demand for phosphate fertilizers. Consequently, these countries initially choose to export phosphate rock to foreign processing plants. However, when they started to realize the potential for export-oriented production of intermediates and finished fertilizers, they decided to develop downstream capacity themselves, increasingly replacing exports of phosphate rock by exports of processed phosphates. For many of these countries, the lack of any significant alternative sources of foreign exchange provides a strong incentive for investment in downstream production. Usually, they integrated phosphate processing with already existing mining operations in large phosphate fertilizer complexes, allowing for large scale, export-oriented production.

An important feature of export-oriented production in developing countries has been the growth of state-owned enterprises (for example, OCP in Morocco and JPMC in Jordan). This is due to the strategic importance of the industry and the large capital outlays required for fertilizer production, which often called for considerable government support. Without this active support, investment opportunities may fail to be transformed into viable projects for fertilizer production in these countries. An alternative way of stimulating domestic fertilizer production has been to attract foreign direct investment, in the form of joint ventures. Although investments by transnational corporations in fertilizer production in developing countries have been quite limited, it has been important in some countries with sufficient resource endowments to support a substantial export-oriented industry (UNCTC, 1982).

A phosphate fertilizer industry developed to serve the needs of the local market is found mainly in Asian countries. The significant growth in fertilizer consumption in most developing countries followed an unprecedented growth in population in most of these countries and put increasing pressure on their natural resource base to produce additional food on limited cultivable land. In order to prevent the resource base from degrading and also to increase food production to meet the requirements of the growing population, consumption and demand for chemical fertilizers has increased considerably (Bumb, 1992; *Phosphorus and Potassium*, 1990).

In response to this growing domestic demand for phosphate fertilizers, government policies in these countries have been twofold. First, to ensure that fertilizers are provided at reasonable prices that farmers can afford and, second, to ensure that adequate quantities of various fertilizers are available every season. In order to achieve the first objective, governments have introduced price regulation and financial incentives to increase the use of chemical fertilizers by farmers. The second objective, however, requires either a constant flow of foreign exchange for imports of fertilizers or major investments in domestic fertilizer production. Considering the broader welfare implications, many countries eventually chose the latter option and decided to develop domestic fertilizer production capacity.

Concerning technological capability building, transnational corporations have played an important role. Whereas their part in providing capital to developing countries through foreign direct investment (FDI) has been relatively small, they do provide technology and technology services, including for project design and implementation. The nature of technology and knowledge transfer, including supply of process technology, detailed plant engineering, supply and installation of plant and equipment and plant construction differs in various developing countries. In many cases turnkey projects are awarded to one foreign company, using either the supplier of a process technology or a specialized chemical engineering consultant. In other developing countries where domestic engineering capability may be available and where government policies are oriented to maximum utilization of domestic engineering capacity, the foreign contractor may be given only very limited responsibilities, with local engineering firms undertaking substantial responsibilities and construction work. The role of governments in this process of acquisition of foreign technology and expertise is and will likely become increasingly important. As such it will have considerable influence on the pattern of relationships with foreign engineering corporations and be able to stimulate the growth of indigenous technological capability. In general, however, there continues to be considerable dependence on transnational corporations for process knowledge and basic designs, together with detailed plant engineering of fertilizer plants. In order to reduce such dependence significantly, much greater efforts are necessary in most developing countries in order to develop design and engineering capability and for greater absorption and development of process know-how, through increased R&D activities in these countries.

Besides governments and transnational corporations, the World Bank has also been particularly instrumental in providing financial support for fertilizer projects in developing countries. As a result, capital resources became a less important constraint on fertilizer capacity development, except in the case of exceptionally high infrastructure costs (such as railroads, ports and harbour facilities).

The Phosphate Industry in Morocco

Phosphates are one of the key minerals produced by the mining industry in Africa. Production of natural phosphates in Africa is concentrated in the north and north-west. Morocco possesses an estimated 70 percent of the world's total deposits. South Africa has about 21 percent of the world's known reserves although its industry is still modest. Other producers are Togo, Senegal, Tunisia and Algeria. Because Morocco owns about two-thirds of the world's reserves of phosphate rock, its chemical industry is dominated by downstream phosphate chemicals. The main products manufactured are phosphoric acids and phosphate based fertilizers. Morocco is Africa's leading producer and the world's largest exporter of phosphate rock and phosphoric acid.

In the 1960s Morocco decided to start processing an increasing part of its phosphate rock locally, in order both to satisfy domestic demand for fertilizers and for the export market. The Office Cherifienne des Phosphates (OCP) has implemented a series of projects in the field of the processing of phosphate rock and managed to become one of the leading world exporters of phosphoric acid.

OCP employs 27,235 people including 700 engineers and other professionals. The company posted a net profit of 800 million dirham in 1996 after losing 1.3 billion in 1994 and 14 million in 1995. With an output of 20.8 million tonnes in 1996, compared to 20.3 tonnes in 1995, it is in the process of reducing debt accumulated because of the major capital investment in the 1980s (11.6 billion dirham at the end of 1996). In 1997 OCP produced over 23 million tonnes of phosphate rock, 2.7 million tonnes of phosphoric acid and in excess of 2 million tonnes of solid fertilizers, taking its share of the world phosphate market to 31 percent. Nevertheless, OCP's debt to turnover ratio remains at a high level (at around 66 percent at the end of 1997). However, further improvement of this ratio should be expected during the next three years. OCP anticipates that the level of debt will not exceed 10 percent of turnover by 2001.

OCP increased its export sales to \$1.55 billion in 1997, which is 15 percent higher than the year before. Rock exports increased 14 percent while phosphoric acid export volumes increased by 9 percent. The company's TSP exports fell in 1998 due to phosphoric acid supply constraints caused by extremely high acid demand from India in particular. DAP export sales recovered, on the other hand. For 1998, OCP was very cautious, but overall they expected to see some improvement in their export sales. OCP continues to see a strengthening in its position in the phosphate rock market. In 1997 OCP's share of the world export market amounted to 37 percent, while Mexico and the US between them accounted for over 30 percent, as did Western Europe. OCP is currently undertaking an ambitious investment programme worth more than \$1.39 billion which will strengthen its phosphate processing capacity with the expansion of existing mines, through the 'debottlenecking' of existing units at Safi and Jorf Lasfar and the development of new plants as new joint ventures with foreign partners.

OCP has invested in the debottlenecking of the complex's eight 500 t/d P_2O_5

lines, which are based on Rhône Poulenc's single dehydrate process with a double gas scrubbing system. Two of them have already been completed and the end of 2000 will complete a further two. The increased output resulting from the debottlenecking will be used to support downstream production at Jorf Lasfar, both in already operating plants and in the new joint venture plants. Once the debottlenecking of the remaining phosphoric acid lines is completed, OCP plans to revamp the six existing sulphuric acid units in order to meet increasing demand.[6] Some of the sulphuric acid demand may well be met by imported products, as OCP has recently constructed receiving and storage facilities for sulphuric acid at the port of Jorf Lasfar. This forms part of OCP's new strategy to further diversify sulphur procurement options; the company has also begun to import liquid sulphur for the first time. OCP's current annual sulphur requirements amount to more than 2.7 million t/a, which traditionally have been met by imports of solid sulphur. Jorf Lasfar alone accounts for 1.4 million t/a, and requirements are rising as phosphoric acid production has been increasing.

Also at Safi, OCP plans to revamp its phosphoric acid production capacity. A new 2,300 t/d sulphuric acid unit is due for completion at the Maroc Chimie site in 2000. The phosphoric acid revamp, when it is completed, is expected to raise capacity by up to 200,000 t/a P_2O_5, bringing total phosphoric acid production capacity at Safi to 1.6 million t/a P_2O_5. As part of its expansion plans for the Safi complex, OCP recently added a new 475 t/d phosphoric acid concentration unit as well as two new phosphoric acid storage tanks of 10,000 P_2O_5 each. The new sulphuric acid unit under construction at Maroc Chimie will use the double absorption process (Monsanto), which in addition to the greater production efficiency achieved will also result in lower SO_2 emissions.

In 1996, OCP started a joint venture known as EMAPHOS (Euro-Moroc-Phosphore) together with Prayon-Rupel and Germany's phosphates company, Chemische Fabrik Budenheim. The plant is based on Prayon technology and is one of the largest of its kind worldwide. They built a production unit at Jorf Lasfar for pure phosphoric acid, with a capacity of 130,000 t/a P_2O_5. OCP is supplying the phosphoric acid for the plant from its Jorf Lasfar facilities. Budenheim takes two-thirds of the output, whilst Prayon and the US company Solutia are taking most of the remaining tonnage. Within the context of this joint venture OCP is also looking into the possibility of establishing a sodium tripolyphosphate plant at Jorf Lasfar (Lin, 1997).[7]

Another joint venture between OCP and the Indian company Chambal Fertilizers was scheduled to start up in July 1999. The joint venture is a 50:50 split between OCP and Chambal and involves the construction of a 330,000 t/a P_2O_5 merchant grade phosphoric acid plant, employing Prayon technology, with associated sulphuric acid production facilities, using Monsanto's double absorption technology. At a design capacity of 3,200 t/d the sulphuric acid unit will be the largest Monsanto unit in existence. Two-thirds of the acid produced by the plant will be taken up by Chambal (Lin, 1997).

Environmental Problems

The state of environmental regulation in Morocco is in sharp contrast to the situation in Europe. In Morocco, there are numerous valid laws that are being applied. However, these laws only refer to products and none of these norms belong to the category of what we would call environmental regulation of the production process. In short, we can conclude that besides hygienic norms and those related to products, which are of direct consequence to the environment, there is a lack of any environmental regulation. The technical resources to monitor compliance with these norms are limited. A number of environmental laws are in the process of being promulgated. They particularly concern air quality, effluents, solid wastes and environmental impact assessments. Furthermore, the ministerial department responsible for the environment, established in 1994, has chosen a strategy of consultation with industry instead of a command-and-control strategy. Norms will be executed at a sectoral level and determined after consultation with the mediators in the sector concerned. In the case of the phosphate industry, the commission will consist of people representing the Department of Environment and people acting on behalf of OCP.

Some industries, however, voluntarily apply a number of environmental norms which, because of the lack of national norms, are based on European or international standards. The majority of the other industries, and notably those who export their products, only pursue product quality control. It is not recommended, though, that Moroccan authorities adopt international environmental standards in order to reinforce their environmental management. According to information coming from developing countries that integrally adopted legal norms produced by industrial developed countries, these norms practically paralysed their environmental efforts, as the norms could not be applied under any circumstance. A preferable method would therefore be to take small steps, evaluating companies individually. Confronting them with their own strengths and weaknesses, every plant could be subjected to temporary legal norms. Eventually this system will also result in a system of national legal norms, but then a more realistic one because of the adaptation to the specific needs of Morocco.[8]

The environment has a high priority for OCP, especially when it comes to the technical standards of new investment. In setting up its mining and processing operations, including the choice of technology and equipment and during their operation, OCP always takes into account the protection of the environment. Hence, much of the current investment made at Safi is aimed at reducing emissions, particularly concerning improvements in primary filtration and effluent washing. Before disposal of the phosphogypsum produced at the Safi and Jorf Lasfar complexes into the sea, it is washed prior to disposal, and disposal points have been chosen to take advantage of the best currents in order to ensure material is carried away from the shoreline. Having said that, we should point out that there is no limit on the cadmium per tonne of phosphogypsum disposed of to the sea.[9]

With regard to cadmium, OCP's R&D subsidiary has also developed a decadmiation process, which it is improving with the support of the World Phosphate Institute and the EU. Earlier this year, OCP signed a partnership agreement with the Moroccan government aimed at further reducing emissions from phosphate operations, and began the construction of an air quality laboratory at Jorf Lasfar.

In the long run, the phosphate industry in Morocco will have to adjust to the internationally evolving norms and standards concerning the phosphate industry through the introduction of new technologies. OCP is being confronted with an evolution of European legislation towards increasingly restrictive specifications, in terms of product quality. An example is the norms regarding heavy metals (such as cadmium), natural radioactivity and the phosphates in detergents. If this development is going to spread among all the countries of the European Union, it could seriously destabilize the market for phosphates and its downstream products and, in the process, the economies of a large number of countries including Morocco. One other consequence is that Morocco and other phosphate exporters from developing countries, in trying to comply with regulations on product quality, might shift the cadmium content from fertilizer products to phosphogypsum wastes ('pollution shift'). While clean phosphoric acid with little cadmium content would be exported to Europe, phosphogypsum with most of the cadmium originally contained in phosphate rock would be dumped in the exporting countries.

This perspective has led to two different responses among export-oriented producers. One of them is research into decadmiation technologies for phosphoric acid. Although several processes are shown to be technically applicable, their cost is the primary constraint. The most interesting project is currently under development at OCP and is jointly financed by the EU. However, due to the increased operating costs involved in decadmiation, a shortage of phosphate rock with a low cadmium content and a subsequent price increase is regarded as a requirement before any commercial decadmiation could take place on a large scale. The other response is to discontinue exports to those countries in which cadmium limits are prohibitive and look for other markets with less restrictive or even no cadmium regulation, for example in Asia. This has already led to the formation of many joint ventures between newly emerging export-oriented producers, such as Morocco and Jordan, and Asian countries such as India, Pakistan and Japan. Some Asian countries either supply themselves domestically with finished fertilizers, as in the case of Japan, or they secure their supply of phosphoric acid to feed their domestic production base, as in the case of India.

OCP's intentions for the marketing of downstream products, after its inauguration of further downstream phosphate capacity at Jorf Lasfar which enhanced its ability to supply key markets at a favourable price, complicated the outlook for P_2O_5 production in Western Europe. Morocco is endowed with over three-quarters of the world's known phosphate reserves. This is an important source of the country's wealth. When Morocco began to develop its downstream capability, initially in the form of phosphoric acid, OCP was careful not to provoke any hostile reaction from the established Western European P_2O_5 producers, which could have jeopardized the Moroccan move into higher added-value markets. OCP continued to supply several Western European phosphoric acid producers which had under-utilized capacity. By choosing not to undercut the Western European phosphate manufacturers in their home market, OCP acknowledged that its long-term interests would be better served by working in close collaboration with European phosphate manufacturers. Also on the side of the Western European phosphate manufacturers, there was a continuing preference for close contacts with raw material suppliers who could potentially be strong competitors in the downstream markets.[10]

These developments suggest that Western European producers, instead of trying to preserve market share at all cost, chose to specialize in sectoral niches where their competitive advantage could remain unchallenged. This essentially meant that regional production of phosphoric acid became increasingly confined to those producers who still enjoyed exceptionally favourable unit costs or managed to secure long-term preferential agreements with phosphate rock suppliers (for example the OCP–Grande Paroisse joint venture). At the same time, OCP and other North African phosphate rock producers have their own interest in ensuring that a downstream P_2O_5 sector will survive in Western Europe.

CONCLUDING REMARKS

For many years, consumption and production of fertilizers were concentrated in the developed regions of Western Europe and the United States. During the past few decades, however, fertilizer consumption has increasingly shifted towards developing regions. The main forces held responsible for this shift are:

1. the introduction of environmental legislation restricting the use of fertilizers in many developed countries; and
2. a significant growth in fertilizer demand in developing regions as a result of an unprecedented growth in population in most of these regions, particularly Asia.

Developing countries also gained importance in fertilizer production, underlining the dominance of consumer-oriented production in the global fertilizer industry. Production increased most in Asia, particularly in China and India, because for these countries the development of domestic fertilizer capacity was the only way to meet increasing demand at home. While China's phosphate fertilizer industry is based on indigenous resources, India depends on joint ventures with countries in North Africa and the Middle East to secure its supplies of phosphates, mainly as phosphoric acid.

However, while fertilizer production started to move towards developing countries, export-oriented production also increasingly gained importance. Resource-oriented producers are found in those regions endowed with large reserves of natural phosphates, such as North Africa and the Middle East. Countries in these regions are developing downstream phosphate production capacity near their phosphate mines, responding to the potential to exploit their abundant reserves of natural phosphates by adding value to their processed phosphates. This trend is likely to continue as the integration of mining and phosphate processing, practised in these countries, offers obvious advantages as a result of:

1. reduced transport costs by shipping highly concentrated processed fertilizers instead of phosphate rock; and
2. economies of scale in processing as a result of vertically integrating the manufacturing process allowing for large-scale, export-oriented production.

In summary, the world fertilizer industry has gone through major changes. It started with the emergence of significant fertilizer production capacity in developing regions. For some of these regions, mainly Asia, this was pure necessity as they were under pressure to meet increasing domestic demand for fertilizers which resulted from an unprecedented growth in population in these countries. The main conclusion of the Chinese and Turkish case studies in this report is that the development of fertilizer production in these countries is primarily targeting the domestic market. Other regions endowed with substantial phosphate rock reserves, such as North Africa and the Middle East, responded to the potential benefits of export-oriented production of phosphates. Initially these exports were limited to phosphate rock, but as these regions developed the required technological capability, they also moved downstream into the production of processed phosphates. Therefore, their exportable surpluses of phosphate rock decreased in favour of processed phosphate exports.

However, the increasing importance of resource-processing fertilizer producers from developing countries is evolving in parallel with further specialization of producers in advanced countries in specific segments of the industry (nitrogen products and high value added products). Individual firms have also demonstrated an increasing focus on developing further their links with the farmers. These factors provide the explanation for the survival and indeed, in some cases, further expansion of fertilizer manufacturers from advanced countries. They have implemented long-term restructuring strategies based on the technical characteristics of the production process of specific segments in the fertilizer industry that provided opportunities for capital deepening and for the introduction of energy efficient environmental technologies. This investment process was supported with product innovation in better quality fertilizers and organizational innovation with the improvement of customers' support. The introduction of environmental concerns was an integrated part of the design of new products because, apart from the enforcement of environmental regulation, these products were targeting a market with increasing concerns about the environment.

The competitiveness of developing countries in the fertilizer industry depends on a different set of factors, that is, endowments of resources, labour costs, protected markets and distribution networks and environmental regulation. It is evident from the case studies in China, Turkey and Morocco that we need to take account of all these factors for the assessment of market trends and the evolution of fertilizer production in developing countries. The role of government-owned distribution networks, for example, is extremely important in these countries because it effectively determines access to the local market. Environmental regulation is only one factor in this process and in many cases its contribution is smaller than other factors. This observation has some broader policy implications when it comes to the role of international institutions and other initiatives for the enforcement of environmental regulation. It is very difficult for these initiatives to exercise significant influence on the production processes of polluting industries in developing countries when these industries are targeting the domestic market. The distinction is very clear in our case studies. Morocco, with its export-oriented production capacity, is trying to respond to the stringent environmental regulation which is being introduced in the European Union. That is obvious because this is its main export market. In contrast, fertilizer firms in China and Turkey are much more reluctant to take any initiative in the introduction of cleaner technologies because they do not foresee any risk in the domestic market, which in fact is their main market.

Finally, that brings us to the challenges regarding the introduction of cleaner technologies in developing countries. One of the main conclusions of our fieldwork is that we could start thinking about two areas of problems and consequently policies to respond to these challenges. The first set of issues refers to existing production capacity. Usually these are old and heavily polluting plants, without efficient environmental management, producing for the domestic market (in most cases for the regional market). The introduction of cleaner technologies is limited to 'end-of-pipe' technical equipment and some improvements in energy efficiency. At the same time, better house-keeping and other organizational changes provide opportunities for significant improvement of environmental standards. The potential for more radical improvement is in the second area of problems, that is new investment in fertilizer production capacity. The case studies in Chapter 11 indicated that developing countries are building up their production capacity in the fertilizer industry. The introduction of environmental regulation and the adoption of specific requirements for cleaner technologies in investment grants or subsidies, especially when they come from international financial institutions, have influenced the decision-making process during the implementation of new investment projects in the fertilizer industry in Turkey and, to some extent, in China also. This is an important consideration for the design of a realistic policy, which could facilitate the improvement of existing production capacity and the introduction of environmentally sound technologies in the fertilizer industry.

NOTES

1. See USITC (1998, p. 32).
2. There are many regulations relevant to the fertilizer industry. Direct regulations are the following: Emission Standards of Waste Water for the Chemical Industry (code: GB13458–92) and Emission Standards of Waste Water for the Phosphate Fertilizer Industry (code: GB15581–95), which are issued by NEPA and the State Technical Supervision Bureau (see NEPA, 1992, 1995).
3. Data from the Dafeng Chemical Fertilizer plant (see HuTao, 1999).
4. For the study, we interviewed all Turkish fertilizer producers, a total of six firms. We also interviewed 11 other organizations. These were the Ministries of Environment, Industry and Trade, and Agriculture and Rural Affairs, the Scientific and Technological Research Institute of Turkey, the State Planning Organization, a university, the Association of Fertilizer Producers, the Association of Firms Selling Environment Technologies, the Environmental Foundation of Turkey, the Chamber of Environment Engineers, and the Association of Ecological Agriculture Organization. For the detailed presentation of the findings of the fieldwork in Turkey, see Çetindamar (1999).
5. The market share of European companies in compound fertilizer imports to Turkey has increased from 70 percent in 1993 to 85 percent in 1998 (own calculations, UNCTAD COMTRADE Data Base).

6. In 1997, a shortage of phosphoric acid due to the very high demand for acid in the company's export markets, particularly India, led to the company running its TSP facilities at reduced capacity.

7. For a general discussion on these trends, see Heerings (1993). Traditional phosphate producers, such as Norsk Hydro, have been engaging in joint ventures in North Africa or the Middle East. Of course the intention of these joint ventures is of a completely different nature. Unlike the aims of joint ventures by Asian countries, the output of those by traditional phosphate producers has no guaranteed markets and is marketed on world export markets. As such these joint ventures are a way of relocating the production process to regions in which phosphate production is more cost-efficient.

8. For more details and an extensive review of technical and trade press reports on this issue, see Demandt (1999).

9. Compare, for example, the existing European regulation presented in note 2 of Chapter 10.

10. A perfect example would be the Dutch group DSM which wanted to form a 50:50 joint venture with OCP in September 1987. The cooperative arrangement centred on DSM's complex at Pernis, where OCP would supply phosphate rock and DSM ammonia for the production of APs, which would have been marketed by the joint-venture company. The problem of dumping phosphogypsum with a high cadmium content delayed the implementation of the scheme. By the time a compromise was reached with the Dutch government, the Kemira proposal involving a sale to Kemira of DSM's Dutch and UK phosphate facilities, in exchange for Kemira's stake in the DSM Geleen ammonia plant, proved more attractive (field work interviews, see Demandt, 1999).

PART V

Conclusion

Rhys Jenkins

12. Environmental regulation, trade and investment in a global economy

The previous three parts of this book have provided case studies which illustrate in some detail the changes in competitiveness and industrial location that have taken place in iron and steel, leather tanning and the fertilizer industry. In this final chapter an attempt will be made to locate these findings within the broader context of the debates on the impact of environmental regulation which were raised in Part I of the book.

TRADE, INVESTMENT AND INDUSTRIAL POLLUTION

A number of different hypotheses have been advanced concerning the relationship between environmental regulation, competitiveness and industrial location and it is necessary to distinguish between them and to clarify some of the terminology used. Previous studies have not always been consistent in the way in which they refer to the phenomena that are set out here.

In general terms there are two sets of linkages: those running from environmental regulation to trade, investment and competitiveness, and those which run in the opposite direction, from globalization to environmental regulation. These were referred to in Chapter 1 as *competitiveness* issues and *governance* issues respectively. This book has been primarily concerned with the first of these, although it has touched on the second. Within each area, there are a number of specific hypotheses that have been put forward.

There are several ways in which it has been suggested that environmental regulation may affect competitiveness and industrial location. First of all there is the *industrial flight hypothesis*[1] that firms relocate their operations from highly regulated economies through investment in less strictly regulated jurisdictions. The emphasis here tends to be on the 'push' factor of stricter environmental regulation in the North leading firms to transfer production to less regulated areas. The focus is on foreign investment by firms from the developed countries which relocate to the South.

A rather broader approach revolves around the *loss of competitiveness hypothesis*. As was seen in Chapter 2, there is a considerable literature which discusses the possibility that highly polluting industries will become less competitive in more regulated economies as regulation is increased and/or trade is liberalized. This loss of competitiveness hypothesis does not necessarily involve any relocation of production by firms from the North but does affect the global distribution of industry as a result of differences in costs between firms located in different jurisdictions. In other words, firms which face high environmental compliance costs may lose market share to those located in less regulated jurisdictions.

Whereas the last hypothesis refers to inter-industry shifts in location, the *'source-and-hide' hypothesis* refers to intra-industry shifts (Bergstø *et al.*, 1998). As international production is increasingly organized in *commodity (or value) chains* (Gereffi, 1994b) new opportunities arise for firms to externalize their pollution by using less regulated suppliers. In other words, those parts of the commodity chain which generate most pollution can be located in developing countries where environmental regulation is less stringent.[2]

All the hypotheses referred to so far are essentially pessimistic in that they assume that there is a conflict between stricter environmental regulation and competitiveness. As was seen earlier, the *Porter hypothesis* claims that, on the contrary, environmental regulation can, and often does, lead to economic benefits and hence to increased competitiveness. Were this found to be generally the case, then the concerns raised above would be quite unfounded.

The *pollution haven hypothesis* is often conflated with the industrial flight hypothesis, but strictly speaking it refers to the view that host countries adopt lax environmental regulations in order to attract foreign investment. It is analogous to the tax havens which apply low tax rates (and often less stringent banking regulations than are found onshore) in order to attract financial capital. It implies a deliberate strategy on the part of host governments to 'purposely undervalue the environment in order to attract new investment' (Dean, 1992). A number of studies adopt, implicitly if not explicitly, a similar definition (see Jensen, 1996). Although still dealing with the impact of environmental regulation on trade and investment, this hypothesis focuses on government policy as opposed to firms' responses.

Turning now to governance issues, there are two alternative hypotheses concerning the impact of globalization on environmental standards. The stronger version is the *'race-to-the-bottom' hypothesis* which claims that competition will lead to a reduction in environmental standards (Wilson, 1996). Governments which attempt to maintain high standards will see their efforts undermined by the existence of less stringent regulations elsewhere and this will lead to an overall lowering of environmental standards internationally.

A less extreme version of this is the *'stuck-in-the-mud' hypothesis* that competition, while not necessarily leading to a reduction in environmental standards, does discourage governments from raising standards (Zarsky,

1997). This is also sometimes referred to as the 'chilling' effect of globalization on environmental regulation (Mabey and McNally, 1999).

Although often discussed together, it should be noted that these hypotheses relate to different actors/levels. The pollution haven, the 'race to the bottom' and the 'stuck-in-the-mud' hypotheses are all about the behaviour of governments. However, the first is mainly about the impacts of government policy on international investment, while the last two relate to the impact of globalization on government policy. They potentially complement each other in that the adoption of a pollution haven strategy to attract investment by some countries could trigger a race-to-the-bottom as other countries seek to maintain their attractiveness as investment sites.

The industrial flight and 'source-and-hide' hypotheses are both about firm strategies. The first relates to investment decisions and the second to sourcing decisions. Both have implications for the distribution of industrial activity. They are clearly linked to the other hypotheses in that decisions are influenced by differences in environmental regulation in different countries. So too is the loss of competitiveness hypothesis, although this refers to changes at the industry level. All six hypotheses relate to the links between environmental regulation, competitiveness and the location of production.

The empirical literature on the impact of environmental regulation on competitiveness was reviewed in Chapter 2. There it was found that many of the studies reflected considerable scepticism as to the validity of the various hypotheses. It was suggested then that this was due, in part, to the high level of aggregation in most studies. It was also noted that there was a tendency to isolate environmental regulation and not consider how it interacts with other factors.

This led us to adopt an industry case study approach in the central parts of this book, which would make it possible to examine the impact of environmental regulation in the context of the competitive dynamic of different industries. This chapter looks at the debates once more in the light of the evidence from our three case studies.

GLOBALIZATION AND THE LOCATION OF INDUSTRIAL PRODUCTION

The Distribution of Production in Three Industries

Along with the general trend of globalization, iron and steel, leather and fertilizers have seen the significance of international trade increase in recent years. In the steel industry the share of production traded internationally almost doubled from 23.2 percent in 1975 to 43.3 percent in 1997 (see above,

Chapter 4). An even more dramatic change occurred in the tanning industry, where the volume of light leather exported increased as a share of world production from 25.6 percent in 1979–81 to 61.5 percent in 1994–6 (calculated from FAO, 1998, tables VI and VII). In the case of phosphate fertilizer, despite the decline in world consumption between the mid-1980s and the mid-1990s, trade in processed phosphates increased by over 70 percent (Demandt, 1999, table 8).

Increased trade in iron and steel, leather and fertilizers has been accompanied by significant changes in the location of production and, in particular, an increase in the share accounted for by developing countries (see Table 12.1).

Table 12.1   Share of developing countries in world production of three industries (%)

	1979	1997
Steel	14.2	36.8
Leather[a]		
Heavy	34.1	56.2
Light	40.5	58.9
Fertilizer	20.2	45.2[b]

Notes:
[a] Averages for 1979–81 and 1994–6.
[b] 1998.

Sources: IISI, FAO.

The share of world iron and steel production located in developing countries has more than doubled since the late 1970s. In tanning the share of production located in the South increased from 26 percent for heavy leather and 35 percent for light leather in 1969–71 to 56 percent for both types of leather by the mid-1990s (see Table 7.1). Fertilizer production in developing countries has also more than doubled its share of global production since the end of the 1970s.

Factors Contributing to Changes in Distribution of Industrial Activity

The case studies have turned up no evidence of industrial flight, in the narrow sense in which it was defined above, of firms relocating production from more regulated countries in the North to take advantage of less stringent regulations in the South. Except for fertilizers, these are not sectors where TNCs or FDI are very significant. In the case of the steel industry, there has been some investment in joint ventures overseas, but these have not been motivated by a desire to relocate production from the North but rather to get a foothold in rapidly growing markets in the South. In leather there has been a certain amount of foreign investment by German capital in Poland and the Czech Republic and by Italian capital in Brazil, but again this has not been a generalized phenomenon.

In the fertilizer industry two European firms, Norsk Hydro and Kemira, have adopted global strategies and made important investments in developing countries, including a number of joint ventures. There is no evidence that these have been motivated by a desire to take advantage of less stringent environmental regulations in host countries. Again, as in steel, a desire to participate in rapidly growing markets has been an important factor in some instances, while in other cases, as for example in North Africa and the Middle East, the main factor has been access to raw materials.

Indeed, demand has played a part in the changing pattern of industrial location in all three industries. There is evidence in the three cases that the share of world consumption in the South has increased significantly. In tanning this has been caused by the relocation of the footwear industry to developing countries. Between 1979–81 and 1994–6 the share of world leather shoe production located in developing countries more than doubled from 35 percent to 71 percent (FAO, 1998, table VIII). This represented an increased demand for leather of almost 3,000 million square feet (ibid., table IX).

It has been observed that the steel-intensity of GDP tends to increase as countries become more industrialized. Thus it is not surprising to find that steel consumption has increased rapidly in a number of less developed countries in recent years. On the other hand, at higher levels of per capita income, the growth in demand for steel tends to level off. Finally, in the fertilizer industry, the intensification of agriculture in the South has led to a rapid growth in demand for artificial fertilizers, as the case studies of Turkey and China illustrated. At the same time environmental concerns over the excessive use of agricultural chemicals and the growth in organic agriculture in the North tend to reduce the growth of demand. Thus growth in the world fertilizer market tends to be increasingly concentrated in developing countries.

The fact that demand patterns are changing does not, however, rule out the possibility that other factors have also played a role in the changing pattern of industrial production in the three industries. In particular, it is important to examine the changes which have taken place in international competitiveness within these industries. In all three, the share of developing countries in world exports has increased significantly since the late 1970s (see Table 12.2).

Although this lags behind their share of world production, it does indicate that they have been gaining competitiveness, and that changes in the location of production are reflecting more than just shifts in demand patterns.

Table 12.2   Share of developing countries in world exports of three industries (%)

	1979	1997
Steel	7.8	24.2
Light leather[a]	44.5	57.9
Fertilizer	11.7	19.2[b]

Notes:
[a] Averages for 1979–81 and 1994–6.
[b] 1998 based on value of exports.

Sources: IISI, FAO.

There is also evidence from the case studies of shifts in the location of production within each industry which is not picked up by looking at aggregate figures. The study of tanning, which explicitly adopts a commodity chain approach, brings this out most clearly. The most polluting part of the tanning chain is the production of wet-blue. Unfortunately data on leather production and trade do not distinguish between different stages of production but only separates out different types of leather (light/heavy). Thus it is impossible to provide detailed evidence at the global level of the shifts which are taking place within the commodity chain.

The case studies however illustrate that such changes are indeed taking place. In particular it was found that tanners in Germany and Italy had entered into sourcing arrangements with wet-blue producers in Eastern Europe and Brazil. This enables the European manufacturers to avoid the most polluting stages of production and to maintain the high value added processes at home. Both in Italy and Germany this strategy is seen as a way of coping with local environmental regulations. The other side of the coin, as illustrated by the case study of Brazil, is that the tanning industry in some countries in the South has become increasingly oriented towards more polluting parts of the production process. Thus not only is the share of pollution-intensive industries in manufacturing increasing, as was indicated above, but within those industries the significance of the most polluting stages of production may also be increasing.

While the clearest evidence of this trend comes from the tanning industry, there is also some suggestion that a similar trend may have occurred in the iron and steel industry. The most polluting stages of the integrated steel making process are the coke ovens and the sinter plant. Production of both coke and sinter have been falling in the North but have tended to increase in the South since the late 1970s. In the European Union imports of coke oven products increased by more than 150 percent between 1988 and 1998 (Eurostat).

In the case of the fertilizer industry there have also been changes in the location of different parts of the commodity chain. Historically, the raw material producing countries tended to export phosphate rock, and down-stream processing occurred in the North. Over the past two decades however exports of phosphate rock have been declining and exports of phosphoric acid have increased, particularly to Western Europe and to India. In the case of Europe most of the local phosphoric acid plants were closed down for economic and environmental reasons (see Chapter 10). Thus the outsourcing of phosphoric acid has been an important factor in the phosphate fertilizer industry.

The processes in which the South has tended to specialize in these industries have not only been relatively pollution-intensive, but have also tended to have low value added. In the case of the leather industry wet-blue accounts for a relatively small share of the value added of finished leather despite being responsible for most of the pollution. In the iron and steel industry, value added per tonne of steel produced is much higher in Japan, the US, Germany and the UK than in developing countries (Figure 4.3). An implication of this is that geographical shifts in the share of value added towards developing countries will lag behind increases in their share of physical output.

ENVIRONMENTAL REGULATION AND COMPETITIVENESS

Factors affecting Competitiveness

The key determinants of competitiveness differ from industry to industry, and an understanding of these is essential in order to evaluate the impact of environmental regulation.

Iron and steel

Competition in bulk steel is primarily based on price. Although raw materials are not as significant a part of total costs as in tanning, access to low-cost iron ore, coke and energy can be a source of competitive advantage in the industry. Steel making is a capital-intensive activity subject to significant scale economies and consequently competitiveness depends both on a significant volume of production and on access to capital. Moreover continuous technological improvement in the industry also means that the vintage of plant is an important determinant of firm competitiveness.

Because iron and steel has long been regarded a strategic industry, there has often been extensive government involvement in the sector, including of course state ownership, although this has become less important as a result of the privatizations of recent years. However, national government policies, including trade policies, subsidies and procurement policies, continue to be an important element influencing the competitive position of firms.

The steel industry is characterized by cyclical variations in demand and has also experienced international overcapacity in recent years. As a result profit rates overall have been low which has meant that cost reductions have been important for firms which wish to remain competitive. Substantial rationalization has taken place in the EU iron and steel industry since the 1980s, involving mergers, plant closures, joint ventures and niche market diversification.

Leather tanning

The tanning industry produces primarily for the footwear industry but also supplies a range of other leather product industries such as upholstery, fashion goods and clothing. Tanners compete on both quality and price. As far as quality is concerned, the key factors are the quality of the raw materials which the tanner uses, and technology, particularly tacit knowledge regarding production processes and chemical inputs. These are important at the top end of the market.

For the bulk of the leather market, price competition is a major consideration. The cost of raw materials accounts for a significant share of the finished product, usually over half in Europe (Knutsen, 1999). Tanning is also a relatively labour-intensive industry so labour costs are an important contributory factor in price competitiveness.

Many countries have placed export restrictions on exports of salted hides and this tends to reduce the cost to local producers in those countries *vis-à-vis* producers elsewhere. Thus access to competitive hides of either good quality or low price is an important competitive advantage for some tanners. Some countries, including Poland and the Czech Republic removed such export restrictions as part of their economic liberalization in recent years, and this has tended to reduce the cost advantage enjoyed by local tanners.

Tanning is a low profit activity within the leather commodity chain. Environmental costs therefore, although not necessarily high relative to the value of sales, can be quite significant in relation to profit and value added at the tanning stage. This is particularly true for those firms which compete in the most price sensitive segments of the market.

Fertilizers

Price competition is also important in the fertilizer industry. Major sources of competitive advantage here are access to raw materials, particularly phosphate rock in the case of phosphates and natural gas in the case of nitrogenous fertilizers. Thus some of the most successful EU producers in the industry such as Kemira and Norsk Hydro base their competitive position on their raw materials. In the case of phosphate fertilizers, the high cost of transporting phosphate rock also gives a cost advantage to firms whose fertilizer production is close to rock deposits.

Like steel, and in contrast to tanning, the industry is relatively capital intensive and large scale so that access to capital is an important factor. Some of the major producers form part of large chemical groups while others, although specializing in fertilizers, are relatively large firms in their own right.

A further important element in the competitiveness of fertilizer manufacturers is their distribution networks. As application techniques are becoming an increasingly important element in the productivity of fertilizers from the point of view of farmers, user–producer links have become an important strategic factor for firms.

Developments in the agricultural sector are crucial to the demand for fertilizers. Although world demand continues to be strong, there is a shift in demand towards developing countries. In the EU demand is very much affected by the Common Agricultural Policy. This, together with the environmental requirements imposed on agriculture, for example through the Nitrate Directive and the Drinking Water Directive, is likely to mean a downward trend in fertilizer consumption within the EU.

The Impact of Environmental Regulation

The impact of environmental regulation on competitiveness differs from industry to industry and within industries between different segments.

Iron and steel

As was seen above, price competition is an important factor in the iron and steel industry. It is also estimated that environmental investments account for around 10 percent of total investment and of operating costs in the industry in the EU. It might seem likely therefore that environmental regulation would be a significant factor in competitiveness.

However, other factors appear to be far more important in the case of the steel industry. Differences in the cost of steel between different producers and countries are substantial, varying by as much as $100 a ton. These may derive from access to low cost sources of iron ore, as in Brazil, or to large scale production in modern, efficient plants, as in South Korea. Modern plants also tend to be more energy efficient and therefore less polluting than older vintage plants. Pollution control is often built in to newly constructed plants wherever they are located so that although local regulation may be less stringent than within the EU, this is not necessarily reflected in substantial cost savings where new plants are being opened. However, there is a particular problem for older plants, as for example in Central and Eastern Europe. Retrofitting to reduce pollution is expensive and, because of less modern technology, operating costs tend to be higher.

Although steel producers fear the impact of future environmental regulation, particularly carbon taxes, on their competitiveness, they have not so far been a major factor overall. There are some areas of steel production however where there continue to be significant emissions, particularly from coke ovens and sinter plants. New DRI technologies are being developed which obviate the need for these processes in steel production but so far these have not been extensively adopted in Europe. These technologies depend crucially on access to cheap energy and have been developed in Mexico (based on natural gas) and South Africa (based on coal).

Leather tanning

To a much greater extent than the steel industry, tanning would appear to be vulnerable to competition from countries where production is not subject to the same stringent regulations that exist in Europe. This is particularly true of those segments of the industry where competition is largely based on price.

Estimates of pollution abatement costs in Europe put them at around 5 percent of total production costs. While this may seem not to be excessively high, profit margins in the industry are only 2-3 percent, suggesting that the cost of environmental regulation does significantly reduce profitability. Other factors which contribute to low profitability have been the decline in demand as a result of relocation of the footwear industry to developing countries and greater use of synthetic substitutes, and increased competition from overseas manufacturers who have access to cheap raw materials as a result of local policies to increase domestic value added.

These problems have been particularly acute in Northern Europe, which has also tended to be the area with the strictest environmental regulations within the EU. The experience of the German tanning industry, where tighter environmental regulation in the mid-1980s came at a time when the industry was already weakened by these other factors since the mid-1960s provides a good illustration. As a result the industry was poorly placed to deal with increased environmental costs since profits were low and its competitive position already eroded.

In the top end of the market however competition is mainly on quality and therefore firms that produce this type of leather are much less exposed to price competition. Value added in the tanning and finishing process is also greater than in the price competitive section of the market. It is thus much more feasible for firms to absorb or pass on the costs of environmental improvements, and they are less subject to competition from less regulated producers who may not have the technological capacity to produce a similar quality of product.

Fertilizers

The fertilizer case study illustrates how there may be considerable differences between segments of the same industry. In nitrogenous fertilizers, pollution abatement costs are relatively low so the overall impact of NO_X regulations on firm competitiveness is not very significant. The key factor affecting the competitive position of the EU in this sector is increasing imports based on cheap natural gas from Central and Eastern Europe and the former Soviet Union.

The situation is quite different in the phosphate fertilizer industry, where there are still technological and economic difficulties in removing cadmium from phosphate rock and phosphoric acid and in disposing of phosphogypsum. As a result of the stringent regulations on phosphogypsum, there has been a significant reduction in production capacity of phosphoric acid and a fall in output in the EU since 1980. This has been associated with increased imports of phosphate fertilizers from integrated plants near deposits in the US, Africa and the Middle East.

Technological Change

The view that environmental regulation can lead to increased competitiveness is based very much on the argument that it will lead to technological changes which are not only environmentally beneficial but also reduce costs or lead to an improved product. This is central to the 'win-win' scenario propounded by Porter and others (see above, Chapter 2).

A recent review of the literature on technological change and the environment concluded that there was general agreement that environmental regulation is likely to stimulate innovation and technology adoption, which will facilitate environmental compliance. It was also agreed that external pressures can sometimes stimulate innovation that leaves the firm better off, and that where domestic regulation correctly anticipates worldwide trends, first-mover advantages may arise. However, there was considerable disagreement over the extent to which 'innovation offsets' exist in practice. There is also controversy over whether or not, when they do exist, they are sufficiently large, relative to R&D and management costs, to give rise to true 'win-win' situations (Jaffe *et al.*, 2000, table 1).

Innovation offsets can arise in a number of ways. The most significant are where resources are used more efficiently and/or waste is reduced, byproducts are recycled or converted into a form which can be sold, thus generating additional revenues, or new technologies reduce production costs. In general, end-of-pipe measures to reduce pollution are unlikely to generate innovation offsets, since they do not change the production process. As a result they are likely to increase total costs.

To what extent have any of these occurred in the three industries studied? In the steel industry two major technological changes have had significant environmental implications in recent years. The first of these is the growth of electric arc furnaces, which are particularly significant in many new producing countries. Although these are dependent on the existence of scrap, where this is available, it is a less polluting route to steel production than the integrated route (see Chapter 4). The second is continuous casting, which considerably reduces the amount of energy required in production. Although the introduction of both of these processes has reduced environmental damage caused by the steel industry, in neither case was the technology a response to environmental regulation. The environmental benefits were rather incidental to the economic advantages which motivated the introduction of these technologies.[3]

Most of the other steps which have been taken in the steel industry to reduce pollution have involved end-of-pipe treatment. These include electrostatic precipitation to treat flue gas and wastewater treatment. The rising cost of landfill in many countries has also led firms to increase recycling and to seek ways of reusing or disposing of their waste. Where landfill is not a problem however there is less interest in such measures since they also require new investments. It is not surprising therefore that steel companies tend to regard environmental improvements as involving additional costs and not to perceive them in 'win-win' terms.

In the leather tanning industry suppliers of machinery and chemicals are the main innovators, rather than the tanners themselves. Moreover technological change in the industry has been incremental and there have been no significant reductions in the costs of production. Indeed, as Part III shows, the industry is currently bumping against a technological ceiling.

The main technological responses to environmental regulation have been to utilize less-polluting chemicals and end-of-pipe measures, particularly wastewater treatment. Not surprisingly, therefore, the leather manufacturers in Germany and Italy are clear that the cost of complying with environmental regulations are not compensated through innovation offsets (see Chapter 8). The new chemicals that are used do not produce such good leather as the traditional ones and 'ecological leather' is both more expensive and of lower quality than that produced by traditional methods.

Production technology in the fertilizer industry has remained essentially unchanged since the late 1960s with most subsequent innovation being focused on reducing energy use and intermediate inputs. Increased energy efficiency does of course have beneficial environmental impacts through reductions in emissions such as NO_x and CO_2; however, the main motivation behind energy saving is economic rather than environmental.

Measures specifically designed to reduce environmental damage by the fertilizer industry are mainly end-of-pipe technologies, including gas scrubbers and dust collectors, and reuse and recycling of process waters (Bartzokas and Yarime, 1997, p. 42). Other examples of additional investments required to deal with effluents are specialized equipment to reduce nitric oxide emissions in the production of nitric acid, and units designed to remove fluoride compounds in phosphoric acid plants. Reuse and recycling measures usually involve concentration of process streams prior to recycling and also involve additional costs.

As was indicated in Part IV, a major environmental problem in the phosphate fertilizer industry is cadmium. The use of magmatic phosphate rock with a low cadmium content is one solution but world reserves are very limited so that this would lead to increased input costs, while measures to reduce the cadmium content by calcination are also very costly (Bartzokas and Yarime, 1997, p. 44). As in the iron and steel industry, therefore, environmental improvements in the fertilizer industry have either been an incidental benefit from technological changes introduced primarily for cost reasons or have involved additional investments or production costs.

In summary, therefore, none of the three industries studied here provides any significant examples of innovation offsets, which would suggest that environmental regulation led to increased competitiveness.

CORPORATE STRATEGIES

Given that all three industries are technologically mature and that significant segments are characterized by price competition, it is particularly interesting to discover the strategies which have been used by firms in the industry to maintain their competitive position in the face of more stringent environmental regulation and intensified international competition.

One strategy is to concentrate on the less price sensitive segments of the market, usually by moving into production of high quality products and/or those which incorporate more value added. This has clearly been an important strategy in tanning, where firms, particularly in Northern Europe, have focused their production on the quality market, and there has been a growing emphasis on upholstery leather. By emphasizing quality these firms seek to insulate themselves against competition from lower cost overseas sources. This is not easy to achieve and price remains an important consideration even among high quality producers. Those firms which have successfully adopted this type of strategy have been able to do so, despite the fact that there is little demand in Europe for environmentally friendly leather so that there is no product offset to be gained.

It is possible to detect a similar strategy in the steel industry, where EU firms are concentrating more on high value added steel, rather than on primary steel. This is not so much driven by environmental regulation, as in the case of tanning, but is a means of trying to avoid direct competition with firms which have lower costs of production often, as indicated above, for non-environmental reasons. Nevertheless, a similar outcome is likely since the most polluting processes in steel production are at the early phases of production.

A second strategy is to out-source the most polluting stages of the production process and to concentrate on producing the end product. The tendency for the tanning industry to import wet-blue is an example of this, since it is this part that is the most pollution-intensive stage of the production process. By concentrating on finishing and using imported wet-blue, some firms have been able to retain a position in the European market despite increasing environmental costs. The case study illustrated particularly clearly the effects of increasing demand for wet-blue in the case of Brazil, where environmental regulation was much less strictly enforced than within the EU, and a similar pattern was evident in Poland and the Czech Republic.

The tanning industry provides the clearest example of a competitive strategy of outsourcing amongst the three case studies. However, as was indicated above, some changes in the other two industries can be interpreted in a similar light. Coke ovens are one of the most polluting processes in the steel industry and there has been a tendency in recent years to make increasing use of imported coke within the EU while local production has declined. Germany, for instance, has relied increasingly on imports of Polish coke. Similarly, in the phosphate fertilizer industry European regulations of cadmium content has led to the outsourcing of phosphoric acid and the closure of European plants.

Another important source of competitive advantage can derive from close producer–user relations. This was found to be particularly important in the fertilizer industry, where some firms, faced with competition from the former Soviet Union and Eastern Europe and from North Africa, pursued a strategy of securing their own local market within Europe. A close relationship with local farmers is seen as a key part of this regional strategy.

There are also some tanning firms, especially those producing for the top end of the market, who have developed close relationships with customers.

Several of the Scandinavian tanners studied by Gjerdåker (1999) emphasized the importance of developing loyal and long-lasting relationships with their clients as an important part of their competitive strategy.

Although traditionally the steel industry has not been thought of as a customer focused industry, there is some indication that this is beginning to change and that some companies are trying to improve their profitability by paying more attention to customer service. This seems to be becoming more significant as a result of changes taking place in major downstream industries such as automobiles which have become highly globalized and have increased their demand for uniformity of standards worldwide and reliability of supply.[4]

All these strategies which have enabled firms to maintain their competitiveness in highly polluting industries have usually involved focusing production within the EU on higher value added products or processes. In some cases, most clearly tanning, these processes or products tend to be less environmentally damaging. In others, specialization in high value added products, often incorporating a strong element of service, makes them less subject to price competition and therefore it is easier to pass on higher environmental costs.

CORPORATE STRATEGIES TOWARDS ENVIRONMENTAL REGULATION

Corporate strategies are not only about adapting to external conditions, but also involve trying to shape those external conditions. There is therefore a feedback from competition to environmental regulation which is what the literature on the 'race-to-the bottom' and 'stuck-in-the-mud' is about.

The case studies in this volume have not directly examined the ways in which the three industries have influenced environmental regulation, either within the EU or in the developing and transition economies, since the main focus of the study has been the impacts of regulation on competitiveness and location. However, there is sufficient anecdotal evidence to indicate that firms do not simply take environmental regulations as a given.

In Europe energy-intensive industries lobbied strongly against the introduction of a carbon tax, arguing that it would undermine the competitiveness of European industry. Simulations of the impact of a carbon or energy tax on different sectors show that the iron and steel industry is one of, if not the most adversely affected (Ekins and Speck, 1998, tables 3.5. and 3.6). It is not surprising therefore that the industry has been vocal in its opposition to any form of carbon tax. The failure to introduce the tax in Europe is cited in support of the regulatory chill hypothesis discussed earlier in this chapter.

Because of its size and strategic importance, the iron and steel industry is in a stronger position to influence environmental regulation than many other sectors. In Brazil the steel industry association, IBS, is the only industry group which is represented on the Federal Environment Committee. This obviously gives it considerable influence over the evolution of government environmental policy.

The tanning industry probably suffers from the fact that it is a relatively small industry and is fragmented between a large number of small firms. In Germany in the 1980s the industry was unable to convince the authorities of the problems which new environmental regulations would cause. This has been attributed to the small size of the industry. In contrast in Italy where the industry is nationally more significant, and also highly concentrated in a few major towns, pressure was brought to bear on the government, and this led to a revision of the Merli Law on wastewater discharges in 1979 (see Chapter 8 above).

The fragmentary evidence from the iron and steel and leather industries suggests that where an industry is significant and therefore has some political clout, as in the case of European steel and Italian leather, it will use its influence to delay or water down environmental regulations that are likely to increase costs. On the other hand, where the industry is insignificant, governments are able to introduce tighter controls despite the negative impact on a particular sector. Since the argument is often put in terms of the impact of regulation on the competitive position of the industry, it seems plausible that there is a 'chilling' effect on environmental standards, although none of the case studies was characterized by reduced environmental standards as the race-to-the-bottom hypothesis implies.

ENVIRONMENTAL IMPLICATIONS OF INDUSTRIAL RELOCATION

Independently of whether environmental factors are a prime cause of the growth of pollution-intensive industries in developing and transition economies, the fact that they are growing significantly in these areas has major implications for the local environment.

Environmental Regulation in Host Countries

Weak environmental regulation is a major problem in all the developing and transition economies in which research was carried out. The case studies of industries in countries outside the EU revealed that environmental regulations were, as expected, considerably less stringent than within Europe. Often this was not so obvious in terms of environmental norms because the key differences were at the level of inspection, monitoring and enforcement.

In Central and Eastern Europe there is a considerable gap between compliance levels and those found in the EU (Table 6.14). The steel industry continues to have some technologically obsolete plants with very high pollution levels, although these are now declining in significance because of closures and new investment. In the leather tanning industry in the Czech Republic and Poland it was found that tanners are often able to avoid inspections by claiming that they do not perform polluting processes, and many smaller tanners in Poland are not inspected and dump their waste secretly (Gjerdåker and Odegard, 1999, pp. 21-4).

In Latin America, Brazil and Mexico also lag behind EU standards. In Brazil there are differences between the various states, with some in the South having more effective regulation, but in much of the country regulators are under-resourced and inspection and enforcement are limited. In Mexico, although the water discharge standards for the tanning industry were not significantly less stringent than those in the North, there was little enforcement and a lack of disposal sites for solid waste.

In Turkey the environmental agency is new, politically weak and underfunded, and there are problems of enforcement, with firms able to use their political influence or financial resources to avoid compliance. Moreover, in the fertilizer industry, although Turkey has similar regulations and standards to those of the EU for wastewater and air emissions, there are no special regulations to cover solid waste, primarily phosphogypsum, which, as was seen above, was one of the major environmental problem areas for the industry (see Chapter 11). Environmental protection was also found to be extremely weak in Morocco where there are no specific Moroccan environmental norms and regulation is embryonic.

In China although there are numerous environmental laws, regulations and standards, again enforcement was found to be a key problem. Most of the firms in the fertilizer industry showed an inadequate environmental performance and this was attributable primarily to the weak enforcement of regulations. The case study of leather in India highlighted the problems of environmental regulation in that country too. Water and air pollution levels exceed the norms set by the pollution control board, suggesting that inspection and enforcement are not effective.

Although environmental regulations outside the EU were generally not as stringent as inside, the studies showed that this did not mean that firms overseas always chose the lowest possible environmental standards they could get away with. Although lax regulation meant that many firms did not meet local norms, there were also examples of firms which exceeded such norms and had a proactive environmental policy. In the steel industry, for instance,

POSCO in South Korea and USIMINAS in Brazil were amongst the best environmental performers, ahead of some producers in the EU.

Environmental Impacts in Host Countries

The combination of rapid growth of production by pollution-intensive industries and inadequate enforcement of environmental standards has led to substantial environmental stress in the countries where research for the case studies was carried out.

Poland and the Czech Republic are partial exceptions to this generalization. In common with other countries from the former Soviet block, they underwent major restructuring in the 1990s and a significant decline in industrial production. As a result there was a general reduction in industrial pollution in the two countries simply as a result of industrial contraction. As the case study of iron and steel shows, this meant the closure of older plants and these tended to be the most polluting. Thus it is quite possible that the drop in pollution was even greater than the decline in industrial production would indicate.

On the other hand, some of the structural changes associated with closer integration with the world economy which were identified in the case studies tended to increase the level of pollution locally. Thus the location of wet-blue production in Poland and the Czech Republic to supply the German leather industry and increased German imports of Polish coke both increased demand for products produced by particularly polluting processes.

China and South Korea have both experienced exceptionally rapid industrial growth in recent years. In China, the evidence from the chemical industry suggests that most firms do not have any facilities to treat wastewater or atmospheric emissions and that this is a particularly acute problem amongst small and medium enterprises. In South Korea, too, there was a clear difference between the environmental performance of the largest steel producer, POSCO, and the other smaller companies studied. In both countries the sheer speed of industrial growth means that controlling pollution presents a major challenge.

In India, despite lower growth than in the East Asian economies, industrial pollution is also on the increase. The leather industry case study illustrates the impact that this has had on rivers and groundwater and hence on crop yields in neighbouring areas. Where attempts have been made to regulate the industry more strictly, firms have responded by shifting the most polluting processes to more remote areas in the interior of the country. This illustrates the difficulties of tackling industrial pollution in a country the size of India.

In the two Latin American countries in which case studies were carried out, Brazil and Mexico, the economic context in recent years has been dominated by trade liberalization and privatization. In Brazil the tanning case study shows that this has had a negative environmental impact because of the increased emphasis on exports of wet-blue. In the iron and steel industry, however, the privatization of the major state firms has been accompanied by a significant increase in the level of environmental investments, and there does not appear to have been a major structural shift towards more polluting segments of the industry.

Mexico has undergone an even more dramatic liberalization than Brazil, particularly since 1994 as a result of the creation of NAFTA. There is some evidence that in the tanning industry this has led to reductions in pollution as a result of access to more advanced chemicals. Some Mexican tanners have also used wet-blue imported from Brazil; while reducing environmental stress in Mexico, this tends to intensify the problem in Brazil. Even though Mexico has not specialized increasingly in pollution-intensive industries as a result of its increased integration with the US, rapid industrial growth, particularly in the north of the country, has contributed to environmental stress (Barkin, 1999).

The other two countries discussed in the case studies, Turkey and Morocco, also provide evidence of the considerable environmental impacts of industrial development. Even though there have been some attempts at regulation, these have not prevented serious environmental problems, particularly in terms of disposal of phosphogypsum.

Potential for Environmental Improvement

Despite the problems associated with the growth of pollution-intensive industries in developing and transition economies, the case studies show that some advances have been made, and there are examples of good practice amongst the firms which were studied.

In the steel industry, Usiminas in Brazil and POSCO in South Korea have been environmental leaders within their local industry and have introduced environmental measures and management systems which are comparable to those found in the North, and are better than those of some European steel producers. There are clear opportunities in the steel industry, where new investments are being made, to introduce equipment which incorporates the latest environmental technologies. Because retrofitting is relatively costly and may not reduce emissions to the same level as can be achieved in modern plants, the industry can achieve lower emissions per tonne of steel in countries where production is growing rapidly.

A second important factor identified in the steel case study is the commitment of top management to improving environmental performance. This was clearly an important factor at Usiminas, where the CEO emphasized the importance of environmental issues and the firm became the first in Brazil to obtain ISO 14.001 certification. In Korea, POSCO created an environment and technology team in 1983 and has also recently been certified for ISO 14.001.

Although tanning is a very different industry from steel, as it is made up of much smaller firms and has not generally adopted environmental management systems, there are also some positive experiences which illustrate what can be achieved in the right circumstances. In India, the United Nations Industrial Development Organisation (UNIDO) has been involved in upgrading technology to reduce pollution in the leather industry. In Mexico too, the UNIDO Clean Technology Centre has provided technical support to clean up the activities of some of the Leon tanneries. This shows that where there is a will, and support is forthcoming, there are technological solutions which can lead to substantial reductions in pollution levels.

POLITICAL DEBATES AND IMPLICATIONS FOR POLICY

The discussion of the relationship between environmental regulation, competitiveness and the location of industry has given rise to heated debate. This book has tried to throw some light on these debates through detailed case studies of specific pollution-intensive industries. In this section we summarize our conclusions in relation to these debates and draw out the policy implications of the study.

First of all, our case studies lead us to reject the view that environmental regulation does not affect competitiveness and the global distribution of industrial activity. They suggest that in certain industries, for certain parts of the value chain, environmental regulation, in combination with other factors, has led to significant shifts. However, outcomes were found to be highly context specific, both in terms of the industries and countries involved. It is not surprising therefore that general studies of environment-competitiveness linkages have often failed to find any specific impacts.

The case studies also show that in these industries environmental regulation does not lead to 'win–win' situations *à la* Porter. There are cases where new technologies have led to both economic benefits and environmental improvements, as for example in the case of continuous casting of steel, but, as this example illustrates, these are technologies which are adopted for economic reasons which have incidental environmental benefits. None of the case studies found significant examples of either product or process innovation offsets arising from changes motivated by environmental regulation, which are at the heart of the Porter hypothesis. There is only limited evidence, in the case of the steel industry specifically, of European firms which have been able to achieve first-mover advantage in the field of environmental technology.

A third debate concerns the impact of globalization or increased international competition on the ability of governments to protect the environment. The arguments over whether or not there is a 'race-to-the-bottom' or a 'regulatory chill' which affects environmental policy was not a focus of the research on which this book was based. Nevertheless, the case studies did provide some evidence on these issues. This suggests that where producers are strong and well organized, they can successfully deploy competitiveness arguments against government efforts to raise environmental standards.

The findings of the study have a number of implications for the policy debates on trade and environment. As far as trade policy is concerned, one of the findings of the research is that it is often firms and industries that are under considerable competitive pressures for other reasons which find it most difficult to deal with stricter environmental regulation. There is therefore a real danger that, as many developing countries fear, measures against alleged 'eco-dumping' would become an additional weapon in the North's protectionist arsenal. In other words, firms who find themselves under competitive pressure will take advantage of environmental clauses to remove potential competitors from the market. The use of protectionist measures on environmental grounds should therefore be resisted.

An alternative approach is to use eco-labelling as a means of identifying products produced under environmentally sound conditions. This is of limited applicability to the industries which were studied because they produce intermediate goods which are rather removed from the final producer. Even in the case of leather, which at least can be associated with clearly identifiable final products and would therefore appear to have the greatest potential for eco-labelling, it has not been developed on a significant scale. A certain scepticism concerning the scope for eco-labelling is therefore indicated.

Turning to environmental policies, arguments about competitiveness should not be used to block improvements in environmental standards in the North. The case studies show that successful firms are able to develop corporate strategies in response to such increased standards. The most desirable outcome is for firms to upgrade successfully, moving out of the most price competitive markets into those where high environmental standards can be combined with competitiveness. There is evidence of this happening even within an industry such as leather tanning where the basic conditions of technological maturity and relatively labour-intensive production are not particularly conducive to such a strategy.

It should also be remembered that the purpose of environmental regulation is to prevent excessive environmental damage. Thus reduced competitiveness in a particular industry leading to a reduction in the output of that industry is not necessarily a bad thing. It may indeed be desirable to reduce the output of an industry which causes considerable environmental damage, since this can raise overall welfare when negative external effects are taken into account. This conclusion is reinforced when it is recognized that reduction in output in one industry as a result of environmental regulation leading to reduced competitiveness may, in a general equilibrium context, lead to increased output from other industries which cause less environmental damage. There is a danger that by focusing on the effects of regulation on competitiveness in particular industries, the negative impacts at the macro level will be exaggerated.

The study showed that there is a clear problem in the South resulting from the growth of pollution-intensive industries (partly in response to growth in demand and partly to changes in international competitiveness). This is taking place in a context where environmental regulation is weak and lags behind the growth of the problem. As a result, the environmental damage caused by these industries is likely to be even greater than in the North.

However, these industries provide important sources of employment, income and foreign exchange so that preventing their growth is not a desirable (or feasible) solution. Efforts therefore need to be concentrated on strengthening environmental regulation and encouraging the transfer of cleaner technologies at reasonable prices and without preconditions. Measures could include financial support and technical assistance to regulators in the South, credit for cleaner technology and so on.

NOTES

1. This has also been referred to as the *exodus hypothesis* (Knutsen, 1994).
2. For a concrete example of the application of this aproach to two industries, see Knutsen (2000).
3. As Johnstone (1997, p. 22) points out, this is not an uncommon pattern: 'Since technological change is only partially driven by efforts to save on environmental factors, many of the resulting environmental benefits (and costs) arise almost incidentally out of efforts to save on the use of other factors of production.'
4. An example is the collaboration between British Steel (now Corus) and Toyota.

References

Abicouro (1998), *Síntese do Estudo da Competitividade dos Curtumes Europeus e Brasileiros/Argentinos*, Novo Hamburgo: Abicouro.

Abicouro/Aicsul (1997), *Boletim Estatístico do Couro 1997*, Novo Hamburgo: Abicouro.

Acevedo de Oliveira, M.A. and Tourinho Furtado, M.A. (1996), 'Estudo da Productividade no Sector Siderúrgico Mundial: Uma Comparação Possível', *51 Congreso Anual da ABM*, 5-9 August, Porto Alegre, pp. 835-851.

Adams, J. (1997), 'Environmental Policy and Competitiveness in a Globalized Economy: Conceptual Issues and a Review of the Empirical Evidence', in OECD, *Globalization and the Environment: Preliminary Perspectives*, Paris: OECD, pp. 53-99.

Agrolinz Melamin GmbH (1998), *Annual Report 1997*, Linz: Agrolinz Melamin GmbH.

Alanen, L. (1996), *The Impact of Environmental Cost Internalization on Sectoral Competitiveness: A New Conceptual Framework*, Discussion Paper no. 119, Geneva: UNCTAD.

Alcamo, J. (1992), 'A Geographic Overview of Environmental Problem Areas in Central and Eastern Europe', in J. Alcamo (ed.), *Coping with Crisis in Eastern Europe's Environment*, Carnforth: Parthenon, pp. 27-47.

Almeida e Silva, R. de (1995), 'A Gestão Ambiental na CST', in IBS, *Encontro Regional, Meio Ambiente na Industria Siderúrgia 5* (IBS/ILAFA), 2-16 STI-1/1-15.

Alperowicz, N. (1999), 'Norsk Hydro Shutters its Last Phosphoric Acid Plant', *Chemical Week*, **161** (3).

Amann, E. and F. Nixson (1999), 'Globalisation and the Brazilian Steel Industry: 1988-97', *Journal of Development Studies*, **35** (6), 59-88.

Ambler, M. and J. Marrow (1998), *Priorities for Environmental Expenditures in Industry: Eastern Europe and the Former Soviet Union*, Washington, DC: IBRD/World Bank.

Ambroz, P. (1997), 'The Czech Steel Industry', *Czech Business and Trade* (Ministry of Industry), **8**, 35-36.

Administration for Environment, Nature, Land and Water Management (AMINAL) (1996), *Flanders: An Introduction to Environmental Policy*, Brussels: AMINAL.

Amsden, A.H. (1989), *Asia's Next Giant: South Korea and Late Industrialisation*, Oxford: Oxford University Press.

Anderson, T., C. Folke and S. Nyström (1995), *Trading with the Environment: Ecology, Economics, Institutions and Policy*, London: Earthscan.

Antweiler, W., B. Copeland and S. Taylor (1998), *Is Free Trade Good for the Environment?*, University of British Colombia, Department of Economics, Discussion Paper no. 98-11.

Appl, Max (1993), 'Modern Ammonia Technology: Where Have We Got To, Where Are We Going?', *Nitrogen*, **202**, 44-53.

Appl, Max (1997), *The Haber–Bosch Heritage: The Ammonia Production Technology*, Paper presented at the 50th Anniversary of the International Fertilizer Association Technical Conference, Seville, Spain, 25–26 September.

Archer, J.R. and M.J. Marks (1997), *Control of Nutrient Losses to Water from Agriculture in Europe*, Fertiliser Society, Proceedings no. 405.

Associação Portuguesa des Indústrias de Cortumes (APIC) (1997), Leather statistics 1988–1996, obtained from APIC, Av. Fernao Magalhaes 460-4, 4300 Porto, and Bairro Mota 7, 2380 Alcanena.

Association of Fertilizer Producers (AFP) (1998), *Gübre Ýstatistikleri* (Fertilizer Statistics), Ankara: AFP.

Atkinson, R. (1996), 'International Differences in Environmental Compliance Costs and United States Manufacturing Competitiveness', *International Environment Affairs*, **8** (2), 107–134.

Auty, R. (1991) 'Creating Comparative Advantage: South Korean Steel and Petrochemicals', *Tijdschrift voor Economische en Sociale Geografie*, **82** (1), 15–29.

Auty, R. (1994), *Economic Development and Industrial Policy: Korea, Brazil, Mexico, India and China*, London: Mansell.

Bain, T. (1992), *Banking the Furnace: Restructuring of the Steel Industry in Eight Countries*, Kalamazoo, MI: W.E. Upjohn Institute.

Baldock, D. (1996), 'Environmental Impacts of Agri-environmental Measures', in OECD, *Subsidies and Environment: Exploring and Environment*, Paris: OECD, pp. 123–138.

Ballance, R. (1988), 'Trade Performance as an Indicator of Comparative Advantage', in D. Greenaway (ed.), *Economic Development and International Trade*, London: Macmillan, pp. 6–24.

Ballance, R.H., G. Robyn and H. Forstner (1993), *The World's Leather and Leather Products Industry*, Liverpool: UNIDO and Shoe Trades Publishing House.

Barkin, D. (1999), *The Greening of Business in Mexico*, Discussion Paper 110, Geneva: UNRISD.

Barton, J. (1998), 'The North–South Dimension of the Environmental and Cleaner Technology Industries', *CEPAL Review*, **64**, 129–150.

Barton, J. (1999), 'Restructuring and Environmental Management in the EU Iron and Steel Sector', *European Environment*, August.

Bartzokas, A. and Y. Masaru (1999), *Environmental Regulation and Corporate Strategies in the European Fertiliser Industry*, Background Report no. 21, Maastricht: UNU/INTECH.

Bartzokas, A. and M. Yarime (1997), *Technology Trends in Pollution-intensive Industries: A Review of Sectoral Trends*, Discussion Paper no. 9706, Maastricht: UNU/INTECH.

Bartzokas, A., I. Demandt and Y. Ruijters (1997), *Environmental Legislation on Pollution Control in the European Union*, Maastricht: UNU/INTECH, mimeo.

BASF (1993), *Environmental Protection: Conception, Planning, Action, 11th edn*, Ludwigshafen: BASF.

BASF (1998), *Annual Report 1997*, Ludwigshafen: BASF.

Bates, R., S. Gupta and B. Fiodor (1998), 'Economywide Policies and the Environment: a Case Study of Poland', in W. Cruz, M. Munasinghe and J. Warford (eds), *The Greening of Economic Policy Reform, vol. 2: Case Studies*, Washington, DC: World Bank, pp. 101–130

Beghin, J. and M. Potier (1997), 'Effects of Trade Liberalisation on the Environment in the Manufacturing Sector', *World Economy*, June, 435–456.

Benchekroun, A. (1992), 'Identifying and Managing the Environmental Issues Facing the Phosphate Fertilizer Production Sector: the Viewpoint of the World Phosphate Institute', presented at 'Phosphates and the Environment', Tampa, Florida.

Bennett, G. (ed.) (1991), *Air Pollution Control in the European Community: Implementation of the EC Directives in the Twelve Member States*, London: Graham and Trotman.

Bergstø, B., S. Endresen and H. Knutsen (1998), '"Source and Hide Pollution": Industrial Organisation, Location and the Environment. Sourcing as a Firm Strategy', in H. Knutsen (ed.), *Internationalisation of Capital and the Opportunity to Pollute*, FIL Working Paper no. 14, Oslo: University of Oslo.

Berman, E. and L. Bui (1998), *Environmental Regulation and Productivity: Evidence from Oil Refineries*, Working paper no. 6776, Cambridge, MA: National Bureau of Economic Research.

Besserer, D. (1996), 'Experiences of German Tanneries with Waste-water Treatment According to Statutory Regulations', extract, *Das Leder*, 11–1996.

Birdsall, N. and D. Wheeler (1993), 'Trade Policy and Industrial Pollution in Latin America: Where Are the Pollution Havens?', *Journal of Environment and Development*, **2** (1), 137–149.

Blazejczak, J. (1993), 'Environmental Policies and Foreign Investment: the Case of Germany', in OECD, *Environmental Policies and Industrial Competitiveness*, Paris: OECD.

British Chamber of Commerce, Poland (1997a), 'Polish Steel Industry', *Contact*, **4**, 25.

British Chamber of Commerce, Poland (1997b), 'Meeting with Anna Zawiejska, Director, Environment Department, Katowice Voivodship', *Contact*, **6**, 25–28.

British Iron and Steel Producers Association (1996), *Annual Report*, London: BISPA.

Bumb, B.L. (1995), *Global Fertiliser Perspective, 1980-2000: The Challenges in Structural Transformation*, Muscle Shoals, AL: International Fertilizer Development Center, 95-6535.

Business Central Europe (1996a), 'Bankruptcy' (March), 30.

Business Central Europe (1996b), 'Unavoidable Truth' (November), 27–28.

Business Central Europe (1997), 'The Past - or the Future' (November), 41–49.

Business Central Europe (1998), 'Sticking to Steel' (February), 29–30.

Caddy, J. (1997), 'Harmonization and Asymmetry: Environmental Policy Co-ordination Between the European Union and Central Europe', *Journal of European Public Policy*, **4** (3), 318–336.

Cairncross, F. (1995), *Green Inc.*, London: Earthscan.

Campos Soares, R. (1990), 'Gerenciamento Ambiental: A Visão e Experiencia da Usiminas', in *Anais I: Simposio Nacional de Gerenciamento Ambiental na Indústria*, São Paulo: ABIQUIM, pp. 1-21.

Cao, X. (1998), 'A Study on Chemical Fertilizer Market in China', *Chemical Industry*, **25** (4), 3-7.

Carruth, R.A. (1989), *Industrial Policy Coordination in International Organizations*, Frankfurt: Peter Lang.

Central Leather Research Institute (1998), *India's Foreign Trade in Leather and Allied Products*, Chennai: Economic Research Division.

Central Pollution Control Board (1996), *Annual Report 1995-96*, Delhi: CPCB.

Çetindamar, Delik (1999), *The Impact of Environmental Regulations on the Turkish Fertiliser Industry*, Background Report no. 16, Maastricht: UNU/INTECH.

Chandramouli, D. (n.d.), 'Global Demand for Indian Leather', in *The Leather Industry*, Madras: Kothari's Deskbook Series, pp. 206-216.

Chang, R.-W. (1997) 'Environmental Management System in Korea', in International Iron and Steel Institute (ed.), *ENCOSTEEL: Steel for Sustainable Development*, Brussels: IISI, pp. 31-40.

Clapp, J. (1998), 'Foreign Direct Investment in Hazardous Industries in Developing Countries: Rethinking the Debate', *Environmental Politics*, 7 (4), 92-113.

Cockerill Sambre (1996), *Group Information Publicity*, Brussels: Cockerill Sambre.

Companhia Siderúrgica Nacional (CSN) (1997a), 'A CSN e o Meio Ambiente', *Metais e Materiais*, July, 38-39.

Companhia Siderúrgica Nacional (CSN) (1997b), *General Information*, Rio de Janeiro: CSN.

Companhia Siderúrgica de Tubarão (CST) (1997), *General Information*, Serra: ES, CST.

Companhia Siderúrgica de Tubarão (CST) (n.d.), *CST's Environmental Profile*, Serra: ES, CST.

Copeland, B. and S. Taylor (1994), 'North–South Trade and the Environment', *Quarterly Journal of Economics*, **109** (3), 755-87.

Cordeiro, J. and J. Sarkis (1997), 'Environmental Proactivism and Firm Performance: Evidence from Security Analyst Forecasts', *Business Strategy and the Environment*, **6**, 110-114.

Cosipa (1997), *A Gestão do Meio Ambiente na Cosipa: Retrospectiva e Perspectivas (Sumario Executivo)*, Cubatão: Cosipa.

Crandall, R.W. (1996), 'From Competitiveness to Competition: the Threat of Minimills to Large National Steel Companies', *Resources Policy*, **22** (1/2), 107-118.

Daly, H. and J. Cobb (1989), *For the Common Good*, London: Green Print.

Dasgupta, S., A. Mody, S. Roy and D. Wheeler (1995), *Environmental Regulation and Development: A Cross-country Empirical Analysis*, Policy Research Working Paper 1448, Washington, DC: World Bank.

Dasgupta, S., B. Laplante and N. Mamingi (1999), 'Pollution and Capital Markets in Developing Countries', in P. Frederiksson (ed.), *Trade, Global Policy and the Environment*, Washington, DC: World Bank, pp. 141-159.

Davies, S. and B. Lyons (1996), *Industrial Organisation in the European Union*, Oxford: Oxford University Press.

Davister, A. (1996), 'Studies and Research on Processes for the Elimination of Cadmium from Phosphoric Acid', in OECD (ed.), *Fertilizers as a Source of Cadmium*, Paris: OECD.

D'Costa, A. (1994), 'State, Steel and Strength: Structural Competitiveness and Development in South Korea', *Journal of Development Studies*, **31** (1), 44-81.

Dean, J. (1992), 'Trade and the Environment: a Survey of the Literature', in P. Low (ed.), *International Trade and the Environment*, Discussion Paper no. 159, Washington, DC: World Bank.

Demandt, I. (1999), *The World Phosphate Fertilizer Industry*, Background Report no. 10, Maastricht: UNU/INTECH.

Diário da República (1990), Discharge limits, *No. 55 7-3-1990*, Lisbon: Nacional-Casa da Moeda, SA (INCM).

Diário da República (1992), Discharge limits, *Series-B No. 141-22-6-1992*, Lisbon: Nacional-Casa da Moeda, SA.

Ding, Z. (1995a), 'Current Situation and Development Trends of Large Size Chemical Fertilizer Industry (Part I)', *Chemical Industry*, **22** (3), 3-57.

Ding, Z. (1995b), 'Current Situation and Development Trends of Large Size Chemical Fertilizer Industry (Part II)', *Chemical Industry*, **22** (4), 7-13.

DSM (1999a), *Annual Report 1998*, Heerlen: DSM.

DSM (1999b), *Responsible Care Progress Report 1998: Safety, Health and Environmental Management at DSM*, Heerlen: DSM.

Economic Commission for Europe (ECE) (1998), *Role of Economic Instruments in Integrating Environmental Policy with Sectoral Policies*, Paris: ECE.

Eder, N. (1995), *Poisoned Prosperity: Development, Modernization, and the Environment in South Korea*, New York: Amonk.

Edmonson, N. (1995), 'Phosphate Trade Patterns in the New World Order', *Mining Engineering*, **47**, 1129–1135.

Edwards, D. (1998), *The Link Between Company Environmental and Financial Performance*, London: Earthscan.

Ekins, P. (1997), 'The Kuznets Curve for the Environment and Economic Growth: Examining the Evidence', *Environment and Planning A*, **29**, 805–830.

Ekins, P. and S. Speck (1998), 'The Impacts of Environmental Policy on Competitiveness: Theory and Evidence', in T. Barker and J. Köhler (eds), *International Competitiveness and Environmental Policy*, Cheltenham, UK and Northampton, MA: Edward Elgar, pp. 33–70.

Eskeland, G. and A. Harrison (1997), *Moving to Greener Pastures? Multinationals and the Pollution-haven Hypothesis*, Policy Research Working Paper 1744, Washington, DC: World Bank.

Esty, D. (1994), *Greening the GATT: Trade, Environment and the Future*, Washington, DC: Institute for International Economics.

European Commission (EC) (1992), *Towards Sustainability: A European Community Programme of Policy and Action in Relation to the Environment and Sustainable Development*, Brussels: Commission of the European Communities.

European Commission (EC) (1993), *Growth, Competitiveness, Employment: The Challenges and Ways Forward into the 21st Century*, Luxembourg: Office for Official Publications of the European Communities.

European Commission (EC) (1995), *Techno-economic Study in the Reduction Measures, Based on Best Available Technologies, of Water Discharges and Waste Generation from the Primary and Secondary Iron and Steel Industry*, Luxembourg: European Commission.

European Commission (EC) (1996), *Co-ordinated 'Steel-Environment' Programme*, Luxembourg: European Commission.

European Commission (EC) (1997a), *Report from the Commission on the Implementation of Decision no. 3855/91/ECSC of 27 November 1991 Establishing Community Rules for Aid to the Steel Industry (Steel Aid Code) in 1996*, Brussels: EC.

European Commission (EC) (1997b), *Panorama of EU Industry 97, vol. 1*, Luxembourg: Office for Official Publications of the European Communities.

European Confederation of Iron and Steel Industries (Eurofer) (1996), *Annual Report*, Brussels: Eurofer.

European Fertilizer Manufacturers Association (EFMA) (1994), *The Fertilizer Industry of the European Union*, Brussels: EFMA.

European Fertilizer Manufacturers Association (EFMA) (1995a), *Best Available Techniques for Pollution Prevention and Control in the European Fertilizer Industry*, Booklet no. 1 of 8: *Production of Ammonia*, Brussels: EFMA.

European Fertilizer Manufacturers Association (EFMA) (1995b), *Best Available Techniques for Pollution Prevention and Control in the European Fertilizer Industry*, Booklet no. 2 of 8: *Production of Nitric Acid*, Brussels: EFMA.

European Fertilizer Manufacturers Association (EFMA) (1995c), *Best Available*

Techniques for Pollution Prevention and Control in the European Fertilizer Industry, Booklet no. 3 of 8: *Production of Sulphuric Acid*, Brussels: EFMA.

European Fertilizer Manufacturers Association (EFMA) (1995d), *Best Available Techniques for Pollution Prevention and Control in the European Fertilizer Industry*, Booklet no. 4 of 8: *Production of Phosphoric Acid*, Brussels: EFMA.

European Fertilizer Manufacturers Association (EFMA) (1995e), *Best Available Techniques for Pollution Prevention and Control in the European Fertilizer Industry*, Booklet no. 5 of 8: *Production of Urea and Urea Ammonium Nitrate*, Brussels: EFMA.

European Fertilizer Manufacturers Association (EFMA) (1995f), *Best Available Techniques for Pollution Prevention and Control in the European Fertilizer Industry*, Booklet no. 6 of 8: *Production of Ammonium Nitrate and Calcium Ammonium Nitrate*, Brussels: EFMA.

European Fertilizer Manufacturers Association (EFMA) (1995g), *Best Available Techniques for Pollution Prevention and Control in the European Fertilizer Industry*, Booklet no. 7 of 8: *Production of NPK Fertilizers by the Nitrophosphate Route*, Brussels: EFMA.

European Fertilizer Manufacturers Association (EFMA) (1995h), *Best Available Techniques for Pollution Prevention and Control in the European Fertilizer Industry*, Booklet no. 8 of 8: *Production of NPK Fertilizers by the Mixed Acid Route*, Brussels: EFMA.

European Fertilizer Manufacturers Association (EFMA) (1997a), *Code of Best Agricultural Practice: Nitrogen*, Brussels: EFMA.

European Fertilizer Manufacturers Association (EFMA) (1997b), *The Fertilizer Industry of the European Union: The Issues of Today, the Outlook for Tomorrow*, Brussels: EFMA.

European Fertilizer Manufacturers Association (EFMA) (1998a), *10th Anniversary*, Brussels: EFMA.

European Fertilizer Manufacturers Association (EFMA) (1998b), *Annual Review 1997/98*, Brussels: EFMA.

European Fertilizer Manufacturers Association (EFMA) (1998c), *Forecast of Food, Farming and Fertilizer Use to 2008*, Brussels: EFMA.

European Fertilizer Manufacturers Association (EFMA) (1998d), *Market Overview 1997/98*, Brussels: EFMA.

European Round Table (ERT) (1997), *Climate Change - ERT Report on Positive Action*, Brussels: ERT.

Eurostat (1997), *External and Intra-European Union Trade: Statistical Yearbook 1958-1996*, Luxembourg: EC.

Eurostat (2000), *External and Intra-European Union Trade: Statistical Yearbook 1958-1999*, Luxembourg: EC.

Eyüpoðlu, F. (1992), *Türkiyede Kullanýlan Ticaret Gübrelerinin Fiziksel ve Kimyasal Özellikleri*, 'Physical and Chemical Characteristics of Fertilizers Used in Turkey', Ankara: Ministry of Agriculture.

Fagin, A. and P. Jehlicka (1998), 'Sustainable Development in the Czech Republic: a Doomed Process?', *Environmental Politics*, **7** (1), 113–128.

Food and Agricultural Organization (FAO) (1996a), *Yearbook of Fertiliser 1996*, Rome: FAO Publication.

Food and Agricultural Organization (FAO) (1994), *World Statistical Compendium for Raw Hides and Skins, Leather and Leather Footwear 1974-1992*, Rome: FAO.

Food and Agricultural Organization (FAO) (1996b), *World Statistical Compendium for*

Raw Hides and Skins, Leather and Leather Footwear 1977-1995, Rome: FAO.

Food and Agricultural Organization (FAO) (1998), *World Statistical Compendium for Raw Hides and Skins, Leather and Leather Footwear 1979-1997*, FAO: Rome.

FAO-STAT: On-line Agricultural Machinery, Fertilizer and Pesticides Trade Data database (http://apps.fao.org/page/form?collection=Fertilizers&Domain).

Ferrantino, M. (1995), *International Trade, Environmental Quality and Public Policy*, Working Paper, Washington, DC: US International Trade Commission, Office of Economics.

Ferrantino, M. and L. Linkins (1999), 'The Effect of Global Trade Liberalization on Toxic Emissions in Industry', *Weltwirtschaftliches Archiv*, **135** (1), 129-155.

Fertiliser Manufacturers Association (FMA) (1997), *Fertiliser Review 1997*, Peterborough: FMA.

Fertiliser Week (1999), 'Hydro to Import P_2O_5 - Dutch Plant Closes', *Fertiliser Week*, **12** (35).

France, G.D. and D.C. Thompson (1993), *An Overview of Efficient Manufacturing Processes*, Fertiliser Society, proceedings of the International Fertiliser Society, no. 337.

Francis, A. (1989), 'The Concept of Competitiveness', in A. Francis and P. Tharakan (eds), *The Competitiveness of European Industry*, London: Routledge.

Gerdau Group (1996), *Relatório Annual*, Porto Alegre: Gerdan Group.

Gereffi, G. (1994a), 'The Organization of Buyer-driven Global Commodity Chains: How US Retailers Shape Overseas Production Networks', in G. Gereffi and M. Korzeniewicz, *Commodity Chains and Global Capitalism*, London: Praeger.

Gereffi, G. (1994b), 'Capitalism, Development and Global Commodity Chains', in L. Sklair (ed.), *Capitalism and Development*, London: Routledge, pp. 211-231.

Gereffi, G. (1996), 'The Elusive Last Lap in the Quest for Developed-country Status', in J. Mittelman (ed.), *Globalization: Critical Reflections*, London: Lynne Rienner, pp. 53-81.

Gereffi, G., M. Korzeniewicz and R.P. Korzeniewicz (1994), 'Introduction', in G. Gereffi and M. Korzeniewicz (eds), *Commodity Chains and Global Capitalism*, London: Praeger.

Ghoshesh, Arafat, Saleh Bashir, and Lana Dabbas (1996), 'Managing the Cadmium Content of Phosphate Rock: a Contribution to Environmental Impact Mitigation', in Organisation for Economic Co-operation and Development (OECD) (ed.), *Fertilizers as a Source of Cadmium*, Paris: OECD.

Gjerdåker, A. (1998), *Miljøreguleringer og konkurranseevne i garveri-industrien. Et eksempel fra Santa Croce sull'Arno, Italia.* (Environmental Regulations and Competitiveness: the Case of Santa Croce, Italy), M.Phil. thesis in Human Geography, Department of Sociology and Human Geography, University of Oslo, Dissertation and thesis no. 2/98, Oslo: Centre for Development and the Environment, University of Oslo.

Gjerdåker, A. (1999), *Leather Tanning in Scandinavia*, FIL Working Paper no. 18, Oslo: University of Oslo.

Gjerdåker, A. and J.T. Odegard (1999), 'The Tanning Industry in Poland and the Czech Republic', in J. Hesselberg (ed.), *International Competitiveness: The Tanning Industry in Poland, the Czech Republic, Brazil and Mexico*, FIL Working Paper no. 15, Oslo: University of Oslo.

Gladwin, T. (1987), 'Environment, Development and Multinational Enterprise', in C. Pearson (ed.), *Multinational Corporations, Environment, and the Third World: Business Matters*, Durham, NC: Duke University Press, pp. 3-31.

Gore, A. (1992), *Earth in the Balance: Forging a New Common Purpose*, London, Earthscan.

Grandzinski, Michael, Mireille Vanoverstraeten, Dirk Schröder and Richard Finch (1998), *Using Maps and Local Calculation Methods for Spatially Variable Fertiliser Recommendations*, proceedings of the International Fertilizer Society, no. 422.

Gray, W. and M. Deily (1996), 'Compliance and Enforcement: Air Pollution Regulation in the US Steel Industry', *Journal of Environmental Economics and Management*, **31** (1), 96–111.

Gray, W. and R. Shadbegian (1993), *Environmental Regulation and Manufacturing Productivity at the Plant Level*, Discussion Paper, Washington, DC: Department of Commerce, Center for Economic Studies.

Gray, W. and R. Shadbegian (1995), *Pollution Abatement Costs, Regulation and Plant-level Productivity*, Working Paper no. 4994, Cambridge, MA: National Bureau of Economic Research.

Greenaway, D. and C. Milner (1993), *Trade and Industrial Policy in Developing Countries*, London: Macmillan.

Gregory, D.I. (1992), 'Global Structure of the Phosphate Industry', presented at 'Phosphates and the Environment', Tampa, Florida.

Grossman, G. and A. Krueger (1991), *Environmental Impacts of a North American Free Trade Agreement*, Working Paper no. 3914, Cambridge, MA: National Bureau of Economic Research.

Guimarães, M. (1996), 'O Controle Ambiental: Relaçionamento Governo, Comunidade, Indústria e Universidade', in IBS, *Encontro Regional, Meio Ambiente na Industria Siderúrgia 5* (IBS/ILAFA), STI-5/1.

Hagin, Josef and Anat Lowengart-Aycicegi (1999), *Fertigation: State of the Art*, proceedings of the International Fertilizer Society, no. 429.

Haid, A. and H. Wessels (1996), *Entwicklung und Aussichten der Deutschen Leder- und Shuhindustrie*, Berlin: Deutsches Institut für Wirtschafts Forschung. Gutachten.

Haigh, N. and C. Lanigan (1995), 'Impact of the European Union on UK Environmental Policy Making', in T. Gray (ed.), *UK Environmental Policy in the 1990s*, Basingstoke: Macmillan and New York: St Martin's Press, pp. 18–37.

Hammer, J. and S. Shetty (1995), *East Asia's Environment: Principles and Priorities for Action*, World Bank Discussion Paper no. 287, Washington, DC: World Bank.

Hart, S. and G. Ahuja (1996), 'Does it Pay to be Green? An Empirical Examination of the Relationship between Emission Reduction and Firm Performance', *Business Strategy and the Environment*, **5**, 30–37.

Heerings, H. (1993), 'The Role of Environmental Policies in Influencing Patterns of Investments of Transnational Corporations: Case Study of the Phosphate Fertiliser Industry', in OECD, *Environmental Policies and Industrial Competitiveness*, Paris: OECD, pp. 113–119.

Hesselberg, J. (1994), 'Industrial Pollution: a Shift from North to South?', in I.L. Backer, H. Chr. Bugge and A. Hellum (eds), *Environment and Development in Developing Countries: National and International Law*, Miljorettslige Studien nr. 9, Oslo: Oslo University, pp. 199–223.

Hesselberg, J. (1997), 'Fieldwork in Tanneries in Germany, Italy and Portugal', Paper, Human Geography, Oslo: Department of Sociology and Human Geography, University of Oslo.

Hesselberg, J. (2000), *Industriforurensing i India - En Bhopal-katastrofe i sakte bevegelse?* in Frøystad, K., E. Mageli and A.E. Ruud (eds), *Næbilder av India*, Oslo: Cappelen Akademisk Forlag, pp. 215–239.

Hettige H., P. Martin, M. Singh and D. Wheeler (1995), *The Industrial Pollution Projection System*, Policy Research Working Paper 1431, Washington, DC: World Bank.

Hewett, J. (ed.) (1995), *European Environmental Almanac*, London: Earthscan.

Hirai, N. (1974), 'Two Approaches to Prevention of Air Pollution by Sulfur Oxides', in *Symposium on Environmental Control in the Steel Industry, Tokyo, February 18-21, 1974*, Brussels: International Iron and Steel Institute, E105, 0-10.

Hirschhorn, J.S. (1981), 'Future Steel Technology and the Environment', *Materials and Society*, **5** (1), 75-80.

Hitchens, D., J. Birnie and A. McGowan (1998), 'Investigating the Relationship Between Company Competitiveness and Environmental Regulation in European Food Processing: Results of a Matched Firm Comparison', *Environment and Planning A*, **30**, 1585-1602.

Hogan, W.T. (1994), *Steel in the 21st Century*, New York: Lexington Books.

Hong, S.-B. (1996), *The Korean Steel Industry and Sustainable Development*, Pohang: POSCO, unpublished.

Hong, Y.-S. (1995), 'Technology Transfer: the Korean experience', *Republic of Korea Economic Bulletin*, January, 9-30.

House of Lords (1985), *Report of the Select Committee of the House of Lords on Overseas Trade*, London: Her Majesty's Stationery Office.

Howell, T.R., W.A. Noellert, J.G. Kreier and A.W. Wolff (1988), *Steel and the State: Government Intervention and Steel's Structural Crisis*, Boulder, CO: Westview Press.

Hudson, R. (1994), 'Restructuring Production in the West European Steel Industry', *Tijdschrift voor Economische en Sociale Geografie*, **85** (2), 99-113.

HuTao, Tom (1998), *Agriculture is One of the Most Polluted Industries in China*, World Bank/NPEA processed report.

HuTao, Tom (1999a), *Environmental Regulation, Globalisation of Production and Technological Change in the Fertiliser Industry: a Case Study of China*, UNU/INTECH Background Report no. 24, Maastricht.

HuTao, Tom (1999b), *Environmental Impacts of China's Agriculture Policy: An Overview*, paper presented at the Biannual Workshop of the Economy and Environmental Program for SE Asia (EEPSEA), Singapore.

ICI (1999), *Annual Report 1998*, London: ICI.

IMPEL (1996), *The Impel Network*, Brussels: EC.

Instituto Brasileiro Siderurgia (IBS) (1993), *Gestão Ambiental no Setor Siderúrgico Brasileiro*, Rio de Janeiro: IBS.

Instituto Brasileiro Siderurgia (IBS) (1995), *Environmental Management in the Brazilian Steel Industry*, Rio de Janeiro: IBS.

Instituto Brasileiro Siderurgia (IBS) (various), *Yearbook/Anuario Estatístico da Indústria Siderúrgica Brasileira*, Rio de Janeiro: IBS.

Instituto Brasileiro Siderurgia (IBS), Comissão de Assuntos Ambientais (1990), 'Gerençiamento Ambiental na Indústria', *Revista Engenharia Ambiental*, **3** (9), 23 29.

Instituto Brasileiro Siderurgia (IBS) and Booz-Allen & Hamilton (1996), *A Siderúrgia Brasileira: Competitividade*, Rio de Janeiro: IBS.

International Fertilizer Development Center (IFDC) (1998), *Environmental Challenges of Fertilizer Production: An Examination of Progress and Pitfalls*, Mussel Shoals, AL: International Fertiliser Development Center, SP-25.

International Fertilizer Industry Association (IFA) (1998a), *Processed Phosphates*

Statistics 1997, A/F/98/92, Paris: IFA.

International Fertilizer Industry Association (IFA) (1998b), *Survey of Processed Phosphates Capacities 1998*, A/98/81, Paris: IFA.

International Fertilizer Industry Association (IFA) (1998c), *Sustainable Agricultural Systems for the Twenty-first Century: The Role of Mineral Fertilisers*, Paris: IFA.

International Fertilizer Industry Association (IFA) (1999), *Fertiliser Indicators*, Paris: IFA.

International Fertilizer Industry Association (IFA), United Nations Environment Programme (UNEP) (1998), *Mineral Fertiliser Use and the Environment*, Paris: IFA.

International Fertilizer Industry Association (IFA), United Nations Environment Programme (UNEP) and United Nations Industrial Development Organization (UNIDO) (1998), *Mineral Fertilizer Production and the Environment: Part 1. The Fertilizer Industry's Manufacturing Processes and Environmental Issues*, Paris: UNEP.

International Iron and Steel Association (IIASA), Task Force on the Environment in Eastern Europe (1992), 'The Environment in Eastern Europe: Common Problems and Corrective Actions in the Region' in J. Alcano (ed.), *Coping with Crisis in Eastern Europe's Environment*, Carnforth: Parthenon, 17–27.

International Iron and Steel Institute (IISI) (1993), *Preparing the Future: Towards a Better Environment*, Brussels: IISI.

International Iron and Steel Institute (IISI) (1994), *IISI Survey of Ferruginous Iron and Steelmaking By-products*, Brussels: IISI.

International Iron and Steel Institute (IISI) (1998), *Energy Use in the Steel Industry*, Brussels: IISI.

International Iron and Steel Institute (IISI) (n.d.a), *Life Cycle Assessment*, Brussels: IISI.

International Iron and Steel Institute (IISI) (n.d.b), *United Nations' Framework Convention on Climate Change: Policy Statement*, Brussels: IISI.

International Iron and Steel Institute (IISI) (various), *Steel Statistical Yearbook*, Brussels: IISI.

International Iron and Steel Institute (IISI) and United Nations Environment Programme (UNEP) (1997), *Steel Industry and the Environment: Technical and Management Issues*, Brussels: IISI.

International Management Development (IMD) and World Economic Forum (WEF) (1996), *The World Competitiveness Yearbook 1996*, Geneva: International Management Development/World Economic Forum.

Irwin, A. and P. Hooper (1992), 'Clean Technology, Successful Innovation and the Greening of Industry: a Case Study Analysis', *Business Strategy and the Environment*, **1** (2), 1–11.

Jaffe, A., S. Peterson, P. Portney and R. Stavins (1993), *Environmental Regulations and the Competitiveness of US Industry*, Cambridge, MA: Economics Resource Group, Report Prepared for Economics and Statistics Administration, US Department of Commerce.

Jaffe, A., S. Peterson, P. Portney and R. Stavins (1995), 'Environmental Regulation and the Competitiveness of US Manufacturing: What Does the Evidence Tell Us?', *Journal of Economic Literature*, **33** (March), 132–163.

Jaffe, A., R. Newell and R. Stavins (2000), *Technological Change and the Environment*, Working Paper 7970, Cambridge, MA: National Bureau of Economic Research.

Jaggi, B. and M. Freedman (1992), 'An Examination of the Impact of Pollution Performance on Economic and Market Performance: Pulp and Paper Firms', *Journal of Business Finance and Accounting*, **19** (5), 697–713.

Jänicke, M., M. Binder and H. Mönch (1997), '"Dirty Industries": Patterns of Change in Industrial Countries', *Environmental and Resource Economics*, **9**, 467–491.

Jayadevappa, R. and S. Chhatre (2000), 'International Trade and Environmental Quality: a Survey', *Ecological Economics*, **32**, 175–194.

Jenkins, R. (1984), 'Divisions Over the International Division of Labour', *Capital and Class*, **22**, 28–57.

Jenkins, R. (1998), *Environmental Regulation and International Competitiveness: A Review of Literature and Some European Evidence*, UNU/INTECH Discussion Paper no. 9801, Maastricht: United Nations University, Institute for New Technologies.

Jensen, V. (1996), 'The Pollution Haven Hypothesis: Some Perspectives on Theory and Empirics', in S. Hansen, J. Hesselberg and H. Hveem (eds), *International Trade Regulation, National Development Strategies and the Environment: Towards Sustainable Development?*, Occasional Paper no. 2, Oslo: University of Oslo, Centre for Development and the Environment, pp. 317–332.

Jha, V. (2000), 'The Role of Foreign Direct Investment: The Case of India', in H. Ward and D. Brack (eds), *Trade, Investment and the Environment*, London: Earthscan and Royal Institute of International Affairs, pp. 211–229.

Jha, V. and A. Teixeira (1994), *Are Environmentally Sound Technologies the Emperor's New Clothes?*, Discussion Paper no. 89, Geneva: UNCTAD.

Jingru Guo (1992), 'An Analysis of National Fertilizer Production and Technological policy', *Research of Agriculture and Animal Husbandry Information*, **5**, 25–32.

Johnstone, N. (1997), 'Globalization, Technology and Environment', in OECD, *Globalization and the Environment: Preliminary Perspectives,* Paris: OECD pp. 227–267.

Juhn, S.-I. (1998), 'Challenge of a Latecomer: the Case of the Korean Steel Industry with Special reference to POSCO', in E. Abe and Y. Suzuki (eds), *Changing Patterns of International Rivalry: Some Lessons from the Steel Industry,* Tokyo: University of Tokyo Press, pp. 269–294.

Kalt, J. (1988), 'The Impact of Domestic Environmental Regulatory Policies on US International Competitiveness', in M. Spence and H. Hazard (eds), *International Competitiveness*, Cambridge, MA: Ballinger Publishing, pp. 221–261.

Kang, J.-S. (1994), 'Dynamic Comparative Advantage and Sources of International Competitiveness in the Korean Steel Industry', unpublished Ph.D., Canberra: Australian National University.

Kazgan, G. (1992), 'Current Trends and Prospects in Turkish Agriculture', *METU Studies in Development*, **19** (3), 337–360.

Kazmierczyk, P. (ed.) (1997), *The Environmental Technology Market in Central and Eastern Europe,* Szentendre: Regional Environmental Center for Central and Eastern Europe.

Keat, P. (2000), 'Penalizing the Reformers: Polish Steel and European Integration', *Communist and Post-Communist Studies*, **33** (2), 201–222.

Kiiski, H. (1998), 'Flexibility and Environmental Performance of Kemira's Mixed Acid NPK Process', paper presented at the IFA Technical Conference, Marrakech, Morocco, 28 September–1 October.

Kim, S.-Y. (1997), 'International Joint Venturing in the Steel Industry: a Theoretical Perspective', *Korean Economic Review*, **13** (1), 143–166.

Kjellberg, F. and G.K. Prasad (1997), 'Industrial Expansion and the Environment in a Developing Country: the Paradoxes of Pollution Control in a South Indian State', paper delivered at the 17th IPSA World Congress, 17–21 August, Seoul.

Kloz, M., E. Guess, J. Bečvář and P. Bendová (1998), 'Internalization of Environmental Costs in the Energy and Industrial Sectors: Role of Economic Instruments in the Czech Republic', in O. Godard (ed.), *Role of Economic Instruments in Integrating Environmental Policy with Sectoral Policies*, Paris: ECE, pp. 69–79.

Knodgen, G. (1988), 'Does Environmental Regulation Cause Industrial Flight?', in R.P. Misra (ed.), *International Division of Labour and Regional Development*, New Delhi: Concept Publishing House, pp. 95–118.

Knutsen H.M. and K. Wiik (1999), *Tanning and the Environment in Mexico: The Case of León*, FIL Working Paper no. 15, Oslo: University of Oslo.

Knutsen, H. (1994), 'International Location of Polluting Industries: Review of the Literature', in J. Hesselberg and H. Knutsen, *Location of Pollution-intensive Industry in a North/South Perspective: Review of Literature*, FIL Working Paper no. 1, Oslo: University of Oslo, pp. 7–49.

Knutsen, H. (1996a), 'Polluting Industries: "Industrial Flight" or "Locational Shift"', in S. Hansen, J. Hesselberg and H. Hveem (eds), *International Trade, Regulation, National Development Strategies and the Environment: Towards Sustainable Development*, Oslo: University of Oslo, Centre for Development and the Environment, pp. 301–316.

Knutsen, H. (1996b), *Changes in the International Location of Polluting Industries: A Case Study of the Dyestuff Industry in India*, D.Phil. thesis, Oslo: Department of Human Geography, University of Oslo.

Knutsen, H. (1997), 'Environmental Regulation, Globalisation of Production and Technological Change: Methodology for the Second Phase of the Research Programme', paper presented at the Maastricht workshop, April 1997, Joint research programme: School of Development Studies, University of East Anglia; Intech – UN University in Maastricht; and the Department of Sociology and Human Geography University of Oslo.

Knutsen, H. (1998a), 'Restructuring, Stricter Environmental Requirements and Competitiveness in the German, Italian and Portuguese Tanning Industry', *Norwegian Journal of Geography*, **52** (4), 167–180.

Knutsen, H. (1998b), 'Globalisation and International Division of Labour: Two Concepts – One Debate?', *Norwegian Journal of Geography*, **52**, (3) 151–163.

Knutsen, H. (1999), *Leather Tanning, Environmental Regulations and Competitiveness in Europe: A Comparative Study of Germany, Italy and Portugal*, FIL Working Paper no. 17, Oslo: University of Oslo.

Knutsen, H. (2000), 'Environmental Practice in the Commodity Chain: the Dyestuff and Tanning Industries Compared', *Review of International Political Economy*, **7** (2), 254–288.

Kolk, A. and E. van der Weij (1998), 'Financing Environmental Policy in East Central Europe', *Environmental Politics*, **7** (1), 53–68.

Kolstad, C. and Y. Xing (1994), *Do Lax Environmental Regulations Attract Foreign Investment?*, Working Paper, Department of Economics and Institute for Environmental Studies, Urbana, IL: University of Illinois.

Kongshaug, G. (1998), 'Energy Consumption and Greenhouse Gas Emissions in Fertiliser Production', paper presented at the IFA Technical Conference, Marrakech, Morocco, 28 September–1 October.

Krüger Consult (1995), *Techno-economic Aspects of Measures to Reduce Water*

Pollution in Small and Medium Sized Enterprises on the Basis of an Industry and Market Driven Approach, prepared for European Commission, Directorate General XI.C5. Environment, Nuclear Safety and Civil Protection. Contract no. B4-3040/93/001170.

Krugman, P. (1994), 'Competitiveness: a Dangerous Obsession', *Foreign Affairs*, March/April, 28–44.

Krugman, P. (1996), 'Making Sense of the Competitiveness Debate', *Oxford Review of Economic Policy*, **12** (3), 17–25.

Kuesters, J. and T. Jenssen (1998), 'Selecting the Right Fertilizer from an Environmental Life Cycle Perspective', paper presented at the IFA Technical Conference, Marrakech, Morocco, 28 September–1 October.

Kumar, S.C. (1997), *Indian Leather Industry: Growth, Productivity and Export Performance*, New Delhi: Aph Publishing Corporation.

Kwon, O.Y. (1997), 'Korean Economic Development and Prospects', *Asian-Pacific Economic Literature*, **11** (2), 15–39.

Lanoie, P., B. Laplante and M. Roy (1998), 'Can Capital Markets Create Incentives for Pollution Control', *Ecological Economics*, **26**, July–Sept.

Lee, B.-W. (1995), 'Environmental Issues and Implications for the Steel Industry', *Journal of Environmental Policy and Administration*, **4** (2), 29–44.

Lee, H. and D. Roland-Holst (1994), 'International Trade and the Transfer of Environment Cost and Benefits', in J. Francois and K. Reinert (eds), *Applied Trade Policy Modelling*, Cambridge: Cambridge University Press.

Lee, J.-E. (n.d.), *Energy Optimization in the Steel Industry: The Case of POSCO*, unpublished manuscript.

Lee, J.-M. (1995), 'Comparative Advantage in Manufacturing as a Determinant of Industrialization: the Korean case', *Republic of Korea Economic Bulletin*, November, 10–38.

Leonard, J. (1984), *Are Environmental Regulations Driving US Industry Overseas?*, Washington, DC: Conservation Foundation.

Leonard, J. (1988), *Pollution and the Struggle for the World Product*, Cambridge: Cambridge University Press.

Levenstein, C. and S. Eller (1985), 'Exporting Hazardous Industries: "For Example" is Not Proof', in J. Ivens (ed.), *The Export of Hazards: Transnational Corporations and Environmental Control Issues*, London: Routledge & Kegan Paul, pp. 51–59.

Leveque, F. (1993), 'How Can Environmental Policymakers Tackle Industrial Diversity?', in OECD, *Environmental Policies and Industrial Competitiveness*, Paris: OECD.

Levinson, A. (1996), 'Environmental Regulations and Industry Location: International and Domestic Evidence', in J. Bhagwati and R. Hudec (eds), *Fair Trade and Harmonization: Prerequisites for Free Trade*, vol. I, Cambridge, MA: MIT Press, pp. 429–457.

Levy, D. (1995), 'The Environmental Practices and Performance of Transnational Corporations', *Transnational Corporations*, **4** (1), 44–67.

Lin, I.J. and S. Michael (1997), 'A Challenge for the Phosphate Industry: Cd Removal', *Phosphorus & Potassium*, **208**, 27–32.

Lin, Justin Yifu and Fan Zhang (1998), *The Effects of China's Rural Policies on the Sustainability of Agriculture in China*, EEPSEA workshop.

Lin, L. (1997), 'The Prospect of China's Phosphate Industry', *Chemical Industry*, **24** (6), 3–6.

Louis, P.L. (1997), 'Fertilizers and Raw Materials Supply and Supply/Demand

Balances', presented at 65th IFA Annual Conference, Beijing.

Low, P. (1992), 'Trade Measures and Environmental Quality: the Implications for Mexico's Exports', in P. Low (ed.), *International Trade and the Environment*, Discussion Paper 159, Washington, DC: World Bank, pp. 105–119.

Low, P. and Yeats, A. (1992), 'Do "Dirty" Industries Migrate?', in P. Low (ed.), *International Trade and the Environment*, Discussion Paper 159, Washington, DC: World Bank.

Lubbe, A. (1993), 'Transforming Poland's Industry', H. Kierzkowski, M. Okolski and S. Wellisz (eds), *Stabilization and Structural Adjustment in Poland*, London: Routledge, pp. 188–205.

Lucas, R., D. Wheeler and H. Hettige (1992), 'Economic Development, Environmental Regulation and the International Migration of Toxic Industrial Pollution: 1960-88', in P. Low (ed.), *International Trade and the Environment*, Discussion Paper 159, Washington, DC: World Bank, pp. 67–86.

Mabey, N. and R. McNally (1999), *Foreign Direct Investment and the Environment: From Pollution Havens to Sustainable Development*, London: Worldwide Fund for Nature UK.

Maciel, J.C. (1993), 'O Custo da Poluição', *Anais, Simposio sobre Controle Ambiental na Siderúrgia 6*, Rio de Janeiro.

Mal-Soo, C. (1987), 'Development of the Steel Industry in Korea', Seminar Paper, 12th International Development Exchange Program Policy Forum, Seoul: Korea Development Institute.

Mani, M. and D. Wheeler (1999), 'In Search of Pollution Havens? Dirty Industry in the World Economy, 1960-1995', in P. Frederiksson (ed.), *Trade, Global Policy and the Environment*, Washington, DC: World Bank, pp. 115–128.

Manser, R. (1994), 'Going West: Market Reform and the Environment in Eastern Europe – the First Three Years', *Ecologist*, 24 (1), 27–32.

Masuyama, S. (1996), 'Industrial Development Strategies in East Asia', *Nomura Research Institute (NRI) Quarterly*, 5 (3), 68–83.

Medeiros, J.X. (1995), 'Aspectos Econômico-Ecológicos da Produção e Utilização do Carvão Vegetal na Siderúrgia Brasileira', in P.H. May (org.), *Economia Ecológica: Aplicações no Brasil*, Rio de Janeiro: Editora Campus, pp. 83–114.

Mensink, J.S. and V.P.A. de Lange (1996), *Environmental Quick Scan: Leather Products*, Rotterdam: CREM (Consultancy and Research for Environmental Management) for CBI.

Metallurgical Chamber of Industry and Commerce (1996), *The Polish Steel Industry 1996*, Katowice.

Metallurgical Chamber of Industry and Commerce (1997), *The Polish Steel Industry 1997*, Katowice.

Mikoczy, Z., A. Schütz, U. Strömberg and L. Hagmar (1996), 'Cancer Incidence and Specific Occupational Exposures in the Swedish Leather Tanning Industry: a Cohort Based Case-control Study', *Occupational and Environmental Medicine*, 53, 463–467.

Miljøministeriet [Denmark] (1992), 'Brancheveijledning for forurenede garverigrunde', *Veijledning fra Miljøstyrelsen*, no. 5, Copenhagen: Luna-Tryk Aps.

Millard, F. (1998), 'Environmental Policy in Poland,' *Environmental Politics*, 7 (1), 143–161.

Ministry of Chemical Industry [China] (1998), *The Statistical Bulletin of Chemical Industry 1997*, China's Chemical Industry Press.

Ministry of Environment (MOE) [Korea] (1996), *The Development of Korean*

Environmental Policy, 1996, Seoul: MOE.

Ministry of Housing, Spatial Planning and Environment [The Netherlands] (1997*)*, *Dutch Notes on BAT for Production of Primary Iron and Steel*, The Hague.

Moody's Investors Service (1995), *Moody's In-depth Analysis: Integrated Steel*, June.

Moody's Investors Service (1996), *Moody's In-depth Analysis: POSCO*, January.

Morandi, A. (1997), *Na Mão da Historia: A CST na Siderúrgia Mundial*, Vitoria: EDUFES.

Morris, R.J. (1993), 'A Business Perspective on Trade and the Environment', in D. Zaelke, P. Orbuch and R.F. Housman (eds), *Trade and the Environment: Law, Economics and Policy*, Washington, DC: Island Press, pp. 121–132.

Murphy, J. and A. Gouldson (n.d.), *Environmental Policy and Industrial Competitiveness: Searching for Synergy*, mimeo.

Nakajima, K. (1995), 'Recent Trends of Steel Science and Technology for Environmental Strategy', *Journal of Materials Processing Technology*, **59**, 221–232.

National Environmental Protection Agency (NEPA) [China] (1994), *Action Plan for China's Environmental Protection*, China's Environmental Science Press.

Nokta (1997), 'Çevre Cezalarý Neden Caydýrmýyor? (Why Don't Environment Penalties Work?)', *Nokta*, 16–22 February, 53–55.

Nordisk Ministerråd [Denmark] (1993), 'Möjligheter att minska miljöbelastningen från garverier', *Nordiske Seminar-og Arbeidsrapporter 1993: 517*, Copenhagen.

Nordström, H. and S. Vaughan (1999), *Trade and Environment*, Special Studies 4, Geneva: World Trade Organization.

Norsk Hydro (1999), *Annual Report 1998*, Oslo: Norsk Hydro.

Norges offentlige utredninger (NOU) (1995), 'Virkemidler i miljøpolitikken', *Norges offentlige utredninger, no. 4.*

National Environmental Protection Agency (NPEA) and State Technical Supervision Bureau (1992), *Water Emission Standards for Synthesis Ammonia Industry (GB13458-92)* China: NEPA.

National Environmental Protection Agency (NPEA) and State Technical Supervision Bureau (1995a), *Emission Standards of Air Pollutants (GB16297-1996)* China: NEPA.

National Environmental Protection Agency (NPEA) and State Technical Supervision Bureau (1995b), *Water Emission Standards for Phosphate Fertiliser Industry (GB15580-95)* China: NEPA.

Odegard, J.T. (1998), 'Economic Liberalization and the Environment: a Case Study of the Leather Industry in Brazil', paper for delivery at the 1998 meeting of the Latin American Studies Association, Chicago, Illinois, 24–26 Sept.

Odegard, J.T. (1999), 'Economic Liberalization and the Environment: a Case Study of the Leather Industry in Brazil', FIL Working Paper no. 15, Oslo: University of Oslo.

OECD (1985), *The Macro-economic Impact of Environmental Expenditure*, Paris: OECD.

OECD (1993), *Environmental Policies and Industrial Competitiveness*, Paris: OECD.

OECD (1995), 'Fertilizers as a Source of Cadmium', presented at OECD Cadmium Workshop, Saltsjöbaden, Sweden.

OECD (1996a), *The Global Environmental Goods and Services Industry*, Paris: OECD.

OECD (1996b), *Integrating Environment and Economy: Progress in the 1990s*, Paris: OECD.

OECD (1996c), *Subsidies and Environment: Exploring and Environment*, Paris:

OECD.

OECD (1996d), *Agricultural Policies, Markets and Trade in OECD Countries: Monitoring and Evaluation 1996*, Paris: OECD.

OECD (1997), *Economic Globalization and the Environment*, Paris: OECD.

OECD (1998), *Economic Surveys 1998: Poland*, Paris: OECD.

Ohn, K.-U. and H.-S. Shin (1997), 'The Changing Structure of Korean Exports and Imports', *KIET Economic Review*, **2** (5), 3–10.

OMV Aktiengesellschaft (1997), *Environmental Performance Report 1996*, Vienna: OMV Aktiengesellschaft.

OMV Aktiengesellschaft (1998), *Annual Report 1997*, Vienna: OMV Aktiengesellschaft.

Oosterhuis F.H., F.M. Brouwer and H.J. Wijnants (2000), *A Possible EU Wide Charge on Cadmium in Phosphate Fertilizers: Economic and Environmental Implications*, Report E-00/02: Institute for Environmental Studies, Vrije Universiteit, The Netherlands.

Palmer, K., W. Oates and P. Portney (1995), 'Tightening Environmental Standards: the Benefit-Cost or the No-Cost Paradigm?', *Journal of Economic Perspectives*, **9** (4), 119–132.

Pandya, C.G. (1998), *The Tanning Sector in India: A Study*, consultancy report for the Department of Human Geography, University of Oslo.

Panorama (1997), *Panorama of EU Industry*, Brussels: European Union.

Panorama of EU Industry (1996) 'European Competitiveness: the importance of management practices', Luxembourg: EC.

Park, S. and W. Labys (1998), *Industrial Development and Environmental Degradation: A Source Book on the Origins of Global Pollution*, Cheltenham, UK and Northampton, MA: Edward Elgar.

Pearson, C. (ed.) (1987), *Multinational Corporations, Environment, and the Third World: Business Matters*, Durham, NC: Duke University Press.

People's Republic of China, State Statistical Bureau (1998), *China's Statistical Yearbook 1998*, China's Statistical Press.

Persson, K. (1998), *Physical Qualities of Fertilizers and Variable Rate Spreading: Interactions*, proceedings of the International Fertilizer Society, no. 424.

Phosphorus & Potassium, various issues.

Pickman, H. (1998), 'The Effect of Environmental Regulation on Environmental Innovation', *Business Strategy and the Environment*, **7**, 223–233.

Pollack, S. (1995), *Improving Environmental Performance*, London: Routledge.

Porter, G. and J. Brown (1991), *Global Environmental Politics*, Boulder, CO: Westview Press.

Porter, M. (1990), *The Competitive Advantage of Nations*, New York: Free Press.

Porter, M. (1991), 'America's Green Strategy', *Scientific American*, April.

Porter, M. and C. van der Linde (1995), 'Toward a New Conception of the Environment–Competitiveness Relationship', *Journal of Economic Perspectives*, **9** (4), 97–118.

Porter, M. and C. van der Linde (1996), 'Green and Competitive: Ending the Stalemate' in R. Welford and R. Starkey (eds), *The Earthscan Reader in Business and the Environment*, London: Earthscan.

Portney, P. (1981), 'The Macroeconomic Impacts of Federal Environmental Regulation', in H. Peskin, P. Portney and A. Kneese (eds), *Environmental Regulation and the US Economy*, Baltimore, MD: Johns Hopkins University Press.

POSCO (1995), *Environment and POSCO*, September, unpublished.

POSCO (1996), *POSCO's Environment Management*, March, unpublished.

POSCO (1997), *Environmental Progress Report*, Pohang: POSCO.

POSRI (POSCO Research Institute) (1996), *Smart Steel: A Story of POSCO. Leadership and Vision in the Age of Globalization*, Seoul: POSRI.

Policy Research Center for Environment and Economy (PRCEE) (1997), *Development Policy for Promoting Cleaner Production in China*, World Bank/National Environmental Protection Agency reports.

Qin, P. (1996), 'Promoting Cleaner Production and Sustainable Development of Nitrogen Fertilizer Industry', *Chemical Industry*, **23** (4), 3–6.

Rainbow, A. (1999), *Speciality Mineral and Organo-mineral Fertilizers: Products and Markets*, proceedings of the International Fertilizer Society, no. 432.

Rauscher, M. (1997), *International Trade, Factor Movements, and the Environment*, Oxford: Clarendon Press.

Regional Environmental Center for Central and Eastern Europe (1996), *Approximation of European Union Environmental Legislation*, Bulgaria.

Reinhardt, F.L. (2000), *Down to Earth: Applying Business Principles to Environmental Management*, Boston, MA: Harvard Business School Press.

Repetto, R. (1995), *Jobs, Competitiveness and Environmental Regulation: What Are the Real Issues?*, Washington, DC: World Resources Institute.

Repetto, R., D. Rothman, P. Faeth and D. Austin (1996), *Has Environmental Protection Really Reduced Productivity Growth?*, Washington, DC: World Resources Institute.

Reppelin-Hill, V. (1999), 'Trade and Environment: an Empirical Analysis of the Technology Effect in the Steel Industry', *Journal of Environmental Economics and Management*, **38** (3), 283–301.

Robison, D. (1988), 'Industrial Pollution Abatement: the Impact on Balance of Trade', *Canadian Journal of Economics*, **21** (1), 187–199.

Rodriguez-Abitia, A. (1997), *A Comparative Analysis of CT Potential in the Tanning Industry: The Case of Sweden and Mexico*, thesis for M.Sc. in Environmental Management and Policy, Lund University, Sweden.

Rodrik, D. (1997), *Has Globalization Gone Too Far?*, Washington, DC: Institute of International Economics.

Rosenberg, N. (1976), *Perspectives on Technology*, Cambridge: Cambridge University Press.

Rothman, D. (1998), 'Environmental Kuznets Curves: Real Progress or Passing the Buck? A Case for Consumption-based Approaches', *Ecological Economics*, **25**, 177–194.

Rugman, A. and A. Verbeke (1998), 'Corporate Strategies and Environmental Regulations: an Organizing Framework', *Strategic Management*, **19**, 363–375.

Russo, M. and P. Fouts (1994), *The Green Carrot: Do Markets Reward Corporate Environmentalism?*, University of Oregon, Department of Management, mimeo.

Rydin, S. (1997), *Evaluation of Job Creation by LIFE Projects in Tanneries. Final Report*, prepared by Department of Trade and Industry Environment Service (contract B4-3040/97/000018/MAR/B2), London: DTI.

Sabah (1995), *TÜGSAÞ'tan GAP Ýçin Dev Proje* ('A Mega Project from TÜGSAÞ for SAP'), Sabah.

Sachs, J. (1998), 'International Economics: Unlocking the Mysteries of Globalization', *Foreign Policy*, Spring.

Schmidheiny, S. (1992), *Changing Course*, Cambridge, MA: MIT Press.

Schmitz, H. (1995), 'Small Shoemakers and Fordist Giants: a Tale of a Supercluster',

World Development, **23** (1), 9–28.

Schultz, J. (1992), 'An Examination of the Environmental Issues Facing the Phosphate Fertilizer Production Sector: Indicated Cost of Environmental Compliance', presented at 'Phosphate Fertilizers and the Environment', Tampa, Florida.

Schultz, J.J. and G.T. Harris (1997), 'An Examination of the Dynamics of the Fertilizer Industry: Structure, Economics, and Technology', presented at 'Environmental Challenges of Fertilizer Production: an Examination of Progress and Pitfalls', Atlanta, Georgia.

Schultz, J.J. and Gene T. Harris (1998), 'An Examination of the Dynamics of the Fertilizer Industry: Structure, Economics, and Technology', in J.J. Schultz and E.N. (Beth) Roth (eds), *Environmental Challenges of Fertilizer Production: An Examination of Progress and Pitfalls*, Mussel Shoals, AL: International Fertilizer Development Center.

Sendzimir Steelworks (1996), *Annual Report 1996*, Krakow: Sendzimir.

Shaikh, A. (1979), 'Foreign Trade and the Law of Value', Parts 1 and 2, *Science and Society*, **43** (3) and **44** (1).

Shaviv, Avi (1999), *Preparation Methods and Release Mechanisms of Controlled Release Fertilisers: Agronomic Efficiency and Environmental Significance*, proceedings of the International Fertiliser Society, no. 431.

Shikimura, T. and A. Miyawaki (1974), 'The Creation of Native Forests: the Path from Anti-pollution to Environmental Creation', in *Symposium on Environmental Control in the Steel Industry, Tokyo, 18–21 February*, Brussels: International Iron and Steel Institute, E100, 0-13.

Shrivastava, P. (1995), 'Environmental Technologies and Competitive Advantage', *Strategic Management Journal*, **16**, 183–200.

Shrivastava, P. and S. Hart (1994), 'Greening Organizations – 2000', *International Journal of Public Administration*, **17** (3/4), 607–635.

Soerbotten, A. (1998), 'Hydro Agri International in the Middle East', paper presented at the 1998 IFA Production and International Trade Committee Meeting, Amman, Jordan, 18–19 October.

Song, B.-N. (1997), *The Rise of the Korean Economy*, Oxford: Oxford University Press.

Sorsa, P. (1994), *Competitiveness and Environmental Standards: Some Exploratory Results*, Policy Research Working Paper 1249, Washington, DC: World Bank.

Sprenger, R.-U. (1997), 'Globalization, Employment and Environment', in OECD, *Globalization and the Environment: Preliminary Perspectives*, Paris: OECD, pp. 315–366.

Sprenger, R.-U. (1998), 'Environmental Policy and International Competitiveness: the Case of Germany', in T. Barker and J. Köhler (eds), *International Competitiveness and Environmental Policy*, Cheltenham, UK and Northampton, MA: Edward Elgar, pp. 197–240.

Stanners, D. and P. Bordeau (eds) (1991), *Europe's Environment: The Dobris Assessment*, Copenhagen: European Environment Agency.

State Planning Organization [Turkey] (SPO) (1996), *Special Commission Report on Fertilizers, Seventh Five Year Development Plan (1996–2000)*, Ankara.

Statisches Bundesamt (1995), *Country Profile – Poland 1994*, Brussels: Eurostat.

Stern, D. (1998), 'Progress on the Environmental Kuznets Curve?', *Environment and Development Economics*, **3**, 173–196.

Stevens, C. (1993), 'Synthesis Report: Environmental Policies and Industrial Competitiveness', in OECD, *Environmental Policies and Industrial*

Competitiveness, Paris, OECD.

Storper, M. and R. Walker (1989), *The Capitalist Imperative: Territory, Technology and Industrial Growth*, New York: Basil Blackwell.

Swamy, D.S. (1994), *The Political Economy of Industrialisation: From Self-reliance to Globalisation*, Delhi: Sage.

Taeger, T. (1996), 'Progress in Leather Chemistry: What Kind of Milestones Are to Be Expected? An Excursion Four Years Before the Millennium', *Journal of American Leather Chemists Association*, The 1996 John Arthur Wilson memorial lecture, **91**, 211–225.

Thorstensen, T.C. (1997), *Fundamentals of Pollution Control for the Leather Industry*, special commemorative printing, 23rd Annual American Leather Chemists Association Meeting, 22–26 June, Pconono Manor, Pennsylvania, Arlington, VA: Shoe Trades Publishing.

Thyagarajan, G., A.V. Srininvasan and A. Amudeswari (eds) (1994), *Indian Leather 2010*, Madras: Central Leather Research Institute.

Tobey, J. (1990), 'The Effects of Domestic Environmental Policies on Patterns of World Trade: an Empirical Test', *Kyklos*, **43** (2), 191–209.

Toda, H. (1995), 'The Emerging Asian Steel Industry in the 21st Century', in International Iron and Steel Industry (ed.), *The Steel Industry in the Year 2005*, Brussels: IISI, pp. 61–72.

Törmälä, Timo (1998), 'Kemira Agro: Activities in Asia', paper presented at the IFA Regional Conference for Asia and the Pacific, Hong Kong, China, 7–10 December.

Trenkel, Martin (1997), *Improving Fertilizer Use Efficiency: Controlled-release and Stabilized Fertilizers in Agriculture*, Paris: International Fertilizer Industry Association.

Turkish Manufacturing Survey (TUMAS) (1987), *Türkiye Kimya Sanayi Envanteri* ('Turkish Chemical Industry Inventory'), Ankara: State Planning Organisation, vol. 2.

Ulph, A. (1997), 'Environmental Policy and International Trade', in C. Carraro and D. Siniscalco (eds), *New Directions in the Theory of the Environment*, Cambridge: Cambridge University Press, pp. 147–192.

United Nations (UN) (1992), *World Investment Report 1992: Transnational Corporations as Engines of Growth*, New York: United Nations, Transnational Corporations and Management Division, Department of Economic and Social Development.

United Nations Centre on Transnational Corporations (UNCTC) (1982), *Transnational Corporations in the Fertiliser Industry*, ST/CTC/25, New York: United Nations Centre on Transnational Corporations.

United Nations Conference on Trade and Development (UNCTAD) (1994), *Sustainable Deveiopment: Trade and Environment: The Impact of Environment-related Policies on Export Competitiveness and Market Access*, Geneva: UNCTAD, TD/B/41 (1)/4.

UNCTAD (1999), *World Investment Report, 1999: Foreign Direct Investment and the Challenge of Development*, New York and Geneva: United Nations.

United Nations Environment Programme (UNEP) (1994), *Tanneries and the Environment: a Technical Guide*, New York: UNEP IE/PAC (United Nations Environment Programme, Industry and Environment, Programme/Activity center).

United Nations Industrial Development Organization (UNIDO) (1995), *Environmental Policies and Industrial Competitiveness: Are They Compatible?*, ID/WG.542/27(SPEC.), paper prepared for Global Forum on Industry, New Delhi,

India.

United Nations Industrial Development Organisation (UNIDO) (1997), *Industrial Development - Global Report 1997*, New York: Oxford University Press.

United Nations Industrial Development Organisation (UNIDO) (1997), *Yearbook of Industrial Statistics*, New York: United Nations.

United Nations Industrial Development Organisation (UNIDO) (1998), *Yearbook of Industrial Statistics*, New York: United Nations.

United Nations Industrial Development Organisation (UNIDO) (1999), *Yearbook of Industrial Statistics*, New York: United Nations.

United Nations Industrial Development Organisation (UNIDO) (various), *Industrial Development Global Report*, Oxford: Oxford University Press.

United Nations Industrial Development Organization (UNIDO) and International Fertilizer Development Center (IFDC) (eds) (1998), *Fertilizer Manual*, Dordrecht, The Netherlands: Kluwer Academic Publishers.

United States. General Accounting Office (US GAO) (1991), *US-Mexico Trade: Some US Wood Furniture Firms Relocated from Los Angeles Area to Mexico*, Washington, DC: US General Accounting Office.

United States. International Trade Commission (USITC) (1998), *Industry and Trade Summary: Fertilizers*, Washington, DC: USITC, Publication no. 3082.

United States. President's Commission (1985), *The Report of the President's Commission on Industrial Competitiveness*, vol. II: *Global Competition: The New Reality*, Washington, DC: US Government Printing Office.

Usiminas (1996), *Gerenciamento Ambiental*, Belo Horizonte: Usiminas.

Van Beers, C. and J. van den Bergh (1997), 'An Empirical Multi-country Analysis of the Impact of Environmental Regulations on Foreign Trade Flows', *Kyklos*, **50** (1), 29–46.

Varadarajan, D.B. and S. Krishnamoorthy (1993), *Environmental Implications and Leather Tanneries*, New Delhi: Ashish Publishing House.

Various Authors (1996), 'The Challenge of Going Green,' in R. Welford and R. Starkey (eds), *The Earthscan Reader in Business and the Environment*, London: Earthscan.

Verband der Deutschen Lederindustrie (VDL) (1997), *Statistische Übersichten über die Entwicklung der Deutschen Lederindustrie*, Frankfurt/Main: VDL.

von Moltke, K. (1993), 'A European Perspective on Trade and the Environment', in D. Zaelke, P. Orbuch and R.F. Housman (eds), *Trade and the Environment: Law, Economics and Policy*, Washington, DC: Island Press, pp. 93–108.

Walley, N. and B. Whitehead (1996), 'It's Not Easy Being Green', in R. Welford and R. Starkey (eds), *The Earthscan Reader in Business and the Environment*, London: Earthscan.

Wang, H. (1998), 'Basic Situation and Strategy of Small Size Nitrogen Chemical Industry', *Chemical Fertiliser Design*, **36** (1), 5–7.

West, P. and P. Senez (1992), *Environmental Assessment of the NAFTA: The Mexican Environmental Regulation Position*, report prepared for the Province of British Columbia, Ministry of Economic Development, Small Business and Trade.

Wheeler, D. and A. Mody (1996), 'International Investment Location Decisions: the Case of US Firms', *Journal of International Economics*, **33**, 57–76.

Wiik, K. (1999), *Competitive Strategies and Environmental Practice in the Tanning Industry in León, Mexico*, M.Phil. thesis in Human Geography, Department of Sociology and Human Geography, University of Oslo (in Norwegian).

Wilson, J. (1996), 'Capital Mobility and Environmental Standards: Is There a

Theoretical Basis for the Race to the Bottom?', in J. Bhagwati and R. Hudec (eds), *Fair Trade and Harmonization: Prerequisites for Free Trade*, vol. I, Cambridge, MA: MIT Press, pp. 393–427.

Wollring, J., S. Reusch, and C. Karlsson (1998), *Variable Nitrogen Application Based on Crop Sensing*, proceedings of the International Fertilizer Society, no. 423.

Wolf, G. (2000), 'Avoiding Cr (V1) in Leather Manufacture', *World Leather*, May, 39–40.

World Bank (1992), *World Development Report, 1992*, Oxford: Oxford University Press.

World Bank (1997a), *At China's Table: Food Security Options*, Washington, DC: World Bank.

World Bank (1997b), *China's Environment in 21st Century*, Washington, DC: World Bank.

World Economic Forum (2000), *Pilot Environmental Sustainability Index*, Davos: WEF in collaboration with Yale Centre for Environmental Law and Policy, Yale University and Centre for International Earth Science Information Network, Columbia University.

World Trade Organization (WTO) (1997), *Annual Report 1997*, vol. II, Geneva: World Trade Organization.

World Trade Organization (WTO) (2000), *International Trade Statistics 2000*, Geneva: World Trade Organization.

Wubben, E. (1999), 'What's In It for Us? Or; The Impact of Environmental Legislation on Competitiveness', *Business Strategy and the Environment*, **8**, 95–107.

Xu, X. (1999), 'Do Stringent Environmental Regulations Reduce the International Competitiveness of Environmentally Sensitive Goods? A Global Perspective', *World Development*, **27** (7).

Xu, X. and L. Song (2000), 'Regional Co-operation and the Environment: Do "Dirty" Industries Migrate?', *Weltwirtschaftliches Archiv*, **136** (1), 137–157.

Yeats, A. (1985), 'On the Appropriate Interpretation of the Revealed Comparative Advantage Index: Implications of a Methodology Based on Industry Sector Analysis', *Weltwirtschaftliches Archiv*, **121**, 61–73.

You, J.-I. (1995), 'The Korean Model of Development and its Environmental Implications', in V. Bhaskar and A. Glyn (eds), *The North, the South and the Environment*, London: Earthscan, pp. 158–183.

Yum, K.-J. (n.d.), *Water Quality Management in Korea*, Korea Environment Institute, unpublished.

Yýldýrým, A.E. (1997), 'Gübre'de Neden Yatýrým Yapýlmýyor? (Why There Is No Investment in the Fertilizer Industry?)', *Dünya*, 21 October.

Zarsky, L. (1997), 'Stuck in the Mud? Nation States, Globalization and Environment', in OECD, *Globalization and the Environment: Preliminary Perspectives*, Paris: OECD, pp. 27–51.

Zegers, P. (1997), *Steel Research: Achievements under the ECSC and Future Perspectives*, Brussels: European Coal and Steel Community.

Zylicz, T. (1993), 'Problems of the Environment', in H. Kierzkowski, M. Okolski and S. Wellisz (eds), *Stabilization and Structural Adjustment in Poland*, London: Routledge, pp. 243–255.

Index